Ius Gentium: Comparative Perspectives on Law and Justice

Volume 136

Ius Gentium is a book series which discusses the central questions of law and justice from a comparative perspective. The books in this series collect the contrasting and overlapping perspectives of lawyers, judges, philosophers and scholars of law from the world's many different jurisdictions for the purposes of comparison, harmonisation, and the progressive development of law and legal institutions. Each volume makes a new comparative study of an important area of law. This book series continues the work of the well-known journal of the same name and provides the basis for a better understanding of all areas of legal science.

The *Ius Gentium* series provides a valuable resource for lawyers, judges, legislators, scholars, and both graduate students and researchers in globalisation, comparative law, legal theory and legal practice. The series has a special focus on the development of international legal standards and transnational legal cooperation.

Roberto Mastroianni · Claudia Massa
Editors

Disinformation in New and Old Media in the XXI Century

Shaping the New Boundaries of Free Speech?

Springer

Editors
Roberto Mastroianni
University of Naples Federico II
Naples, Italy

Claudia Massa
University of Naples Federico II
Naples, Italy

ISSN 1534-6781 ISSN 2214-9902 (electronic)
Ius Gentium: Comparative Perspectives on Law and Justice
ISBN 978-3-032-18829-8 ISBN 978-3-032-18830-4 (eBook)
https://doi.org/10.1007/978-3-032-18830-4

This Springer imprint is published by the registered company Springer Nature Switzerland AG
The registered company address is: Gewerbestrasse 11, 6330 Cham, Switzerland

Contents

Contributors

Björnstjern Baade Department of Law, Freie Universität, Berlin, Germany

Claudio Di Turi Department of Business and Legal Sciences, University of Calabria, Rende, Italy

Francesca Finelli Luxembourg School of Business, Luxembourg, Luxembourg

Barbara Guastaferro Department of Political Sciences, University of Naples Federico II, Naples, Italy

Rebecca J. Hamilton American University Washington College of Law, Washington, DC, USA

András Koltay Ludovika—University of Public Service, Budapest, Hungary; Pázmány Péter Catholic University, Budapest, Hungary

Sarah Madsen American University Washington College of Law, Washington, DC, USA

Claudia Massa Department of Law, University of Naples Federico II, Naples, Italy

Roberto Mastroianni Former Judge at the General Court of the European Union, Department of Law, University of Naples Federico II, Naples, Italy

Fernanda G. Nicola American University Washington College of Law, Washington, DC, USA

Oreste Pollicino Bocconi University, Milan, Italy

Andrei Richter Journalism Department, Comenius University, Bratislava, Slovakia

Siniša Rodin Court of Justice of the European Union, Luxembourg, Luxembourg

Russell L. Weaver Louis D. Brandeis School of Law, University of Louisville, Louisville, KY, USA

Abbreviations

AG	Advocate General/Advocates General
art./arts	Article/Articles
CFREU	Charter of Fundamental Rights of the European Union
CJEU	Court of Justice of the European Union
ECHR	European Convention on Human Rights
ECJ/Court	Court of Justice
ECtHR	European Court of Human Rights
EU	European Union
ff.	Following
GC	General Court
ICJ	International Court of Justice
n.	Number/Numbers
OJ	Official Journal
ord.	Order
para./paras	Paragraph/Paragraphs
TEU	Treaty on European Union
TFEU	Treaty on the Functioning of the European Union
USA/US	United States of America

Introduction

Roberto Mastroianni

Abstract Freedom of expression, together with media independence and pluralism, constitutes a cornerstone of democratic societies and enables the effective exercise of other fundamental rights, especially the right to vote. By allowing the dissemination of information and competing viewpoints, freedom of expression supports public debate, accountability and informed decision-making. International and European Union instruments consistently affirm that media pluralism is essential to freedom of expression and that States bear ultimate responsibility for guaranteeing it through law and institutions. In recent years, the media landscape has undergone dramatic transformations, shifting from "old media" (in particular, newspapers and radio and TV broadcasting) to "new media" (digital platforms, social media and artificial intelligence); yet one issue remains unchanged: disinformation. The present volume addresses disinformation in two particularly sensitive contexts: elections and war. Recent global elections and the prolonged Russia-Ukraine conflict illustrate how disinformation and propaganda can distort public opinion, erode trust in democratic institutions and justify restrictive measures. Against this background, the volume assesses the current "state of health" of freedom of expression.

1. Freedom of expression—and its corollaries freedom, independence and pluralism of the media—is the cornerstone for the functioning of modern democracies and the exercise of other fundamental rights, such as the right to vote. It enables the dissemination of information and ideas, and the juxtaposition of different views; it is one of the best ways of finding out and forming a view on the opinions of political leaders; it facilitates accountability, and the generation of public discourse. It is thus pivotal to resolving political conflict through dialogue and enabling decision-making

R. Mastroianni (✉)
Former Judge at the General Court of the European Union, Department of Law, University of Naples Federico II, Naples, Italy
e-mail: roberto.mastroianni@unina.it

R. Mastroianni and C. Massa (eds.), *Disinformation in New and Old Media in the XXI Century*, Ius Gentium: Comparative Perspectives on Law and Justice 136,
https://doi.org/10.1007/978-3-032-18830-4_1

through a process of rationalization.[1] For this reason, it is particularly important that information and diverse opinions can be diffused in pre-election periods.[2]

It is widely recognized that a close relationship exists between democracy and freedom of information, since free media and a plurality of voices in society and in the media are *indispensable preconditions* of, and *essential safeguards* for a healthy democracy. The ECtHR has stressed on many occasions that the fundamental role of freedom of expression in a democratic society, in particular where it serves to impart information and ideas to the public, «cannot be successfully accomplished unless it is grounded in the principle of pluralism, of which the State is the ultimate guarantor».[3]

As recently stated in the *United Nations Global Principles for Information Integrity*,[4] «[i]nformation integrity is achievable only with an independent, free and pluralistic media. A free press underpins the rule of law and serves as a cornerstone of democratic societies, enabling an in formed civic discourse, holding power to account and protecting human rights».

2. This volume deals with disinformation[5] in times of elections and in times of war. It starts with the—rather obvious—evidence that in recent years, the media landscape

[1] European Law Institute (2024, pp. 25–37).

[2] ECtHR, *Bowman v the United Kingdom*, 24839/94, 19 February 1998, para 42; *Teslenko and Others v Russia*, 49588/12, 5 April 2022, para 119.

[3] ECtHR, *Informationsverein Lentia and Others v Austria*, 13914/88, 15041/89; 15717/89; 15779/89; 17207/90, 24 November 1993, para 38; *Centro Europa 7 S.R.L. and Di Stefano v. Italy*, 38433/09, 7 June 2012, para 129. Significantly, in the recent judgment *Associazione Politica Nazionale Lista Marco Pannella et Radicali Italiani v. Italy*, 20002/13, 31 August 2021, at para 82, the ECtHR underscored that «*Une situation dans laquelle une fraction économique ou politique de la société peut obtenir une position de domination sur les médias audiovisuels et exercer ainsi une pression sur les diffuseurs pour finalement restreindre leur liberté éditoriale porte atteinte au rôle fondamental qu'est dans une société démocratique celui de la liberté d'expression consacrée par l'article 10 de la Convention, en particulier lorsqu'il s'agit de communiquer des informations et des idées d'intérêt général, que le public a de plus le droit de recevoir*».

[4] UN Global Principles For Information Integrity. Recommendations for Multi-stakeholder Action. The UN Global Principles for Information Integrity stem from a proposal outlined in the UN Secretary-General's (2021) "Our Common Agenda" report, further developed in the (2023) "Information Integrity on Digital Platforms" policy brief. According to the above mentioned Principles, integrity of the information ecosystem occurs «where freedom of expression is fully enjoyed and where accurate, reliable information, free from discrimination and hate, is available to all in an open, inclusive, safe and secure information environment».

[5] It is not necessary at this stage to dwell on the complex question of defining "disinformation" as distinguished from "misinformation", "fake news" or other similar concepts (see on this aspects, Koltay [2025, p. 133 ff]). In any event, we assume as correct the definition adopted by the EU Code of Practice on Disinformation, established in 2018 and amended in 2022, that refers to disinformation as «verifiably false or misleading information which, cumulatively, (a) Is created, presented and disseminated for economic gain or to intentionally deceive the public; and (b) May cause public harm, intended as threats to democratic political and policymaking processes as well as public goods such as the protection of EU citizens' health, the environment or security». It is important to note that on 13 February 2025, the Commission and the European Board for Digital Services endorsed the official integration of the voluntary Cose of Practice on Disinformation into the framework of the Digital Services Act (DSA).

has undergone dramatic transformations, shifting from "old media" (in particular, newspapers and radio and TV broadcasting) to "new media" (digital platforms, social media and artificial intelligence). Like with the old media, disinformation channeled via social media is believed to potentially have an impact on the outcome of the elections as well as in the perception of the general public in situations of armed conflicts. Artificial intelligence, in particular, can be used to generate realistic disinformation, automate censorship, and influence public opinion at scale during electoral periods or international conflicts. Nevertheless, in this volume we assume that the fundamental role that new media have today is not a good argument to exclude traditional media from the spotlight: it is common knowledge, and confirmed by recent surveys,[6] that the latter are still the main source of information, at least for the portion of population more incline to exercise their voting rights.

Although it is difficult to draw a clear dividing line between the two (an "old media" may diffuse content on "new" distribution means, for example), it is also true that traditional mass media present same characteristics that distinguish them from digital platforms. In the case of media using radio frequencies (radio and TV broadcasting), it follows from the circumstance that (limited) *public goods* are at stake that access to the relevant market is based on a decision of the competent authorities (license, authorisation, etc.). This entails that in many jurisdictions the activity of such media is framed in—and determined by—a specific set of public law rules, including the prohibition of forms of speech like calls for violence, hate speech, propaganda of war and so on, and gives the authorities in charge of monitoring their programs specific powers to eventually intervene (and adopt sanction) in case of violations. In same jurisdictions, specific rules apply in election periods to prohibit the dissemination of false information.

Much more difficult is to intervene in the case of social media platforms: since broadcasting frequencies are not involved, the diffusion of information on such media does not require a formal, legal link with the government, and this brings to the delicate questions of the liability of internet hosting providers for the information they convey. None the less, efforts to regulate social media platforms are taking place on both sides of the Atlantic. For the EU, it is certainly the case of the Digital Services Act,[7] where actual or foresseable *effects on electoral processes* are expressly mentioned as part of the risk assessments that very large online platforms ("VLOPs") need to identify,[8] and more recently of the Regulation on the transparency

---

[6] The EU Media & News Survey 2023 (available via: https://europa.eu/eurobarometer/surveys/detail/3153) shows that for 71% of respondents, TV was one of their most used media to access news. TV is followed by online press and/or news platforms (42%). Radio and social media platforms (both 37%) are on shared third position followed by the written press (21%).

[7] Regulation (EU) 2022/2065 of the European Parliament and of the Council of 19 October 2022 on a Single Market For Digital Services and amending Directive 2000/31/EC (Digital Services Act), OJ L 277, 27.10.2022, p. 1-102.

[8] See Section 5 of Regulation (EU) 2022/2065, dedicated to «Additional obligations for providers of very large online platforms and of very large online search engines to manage systemic risks», and in particular art. 34. On 17 December 2024 the Commission, in relation to the above mentioned Romanian presidential elections of 24 November, opened formal proceedings against TikTok in

and targeting of political advertising.[9] The debate is also very lively today in the USA, as witnessed by some important cases brought to the attention of the Supreme Court and recently decided.[10] These concerned the disputes over laws in Florida and Texas aiming to restrict social medias companies from moderating content.

3. As anticipated, this volume deals with the new challenges to the dissemination of information via both traditional and "new" media in two specific situations: elections and war. The starting point is that both situations emerge in legal theory and practice as specific, if not "exceptional", from the point of the acceptance of justifications to free speech restrictions or limitations. This (admittedly not new in principle) phenomenon has become more relevant nowadays due to the dramatic increase of the number and of the nature of the media involved, as well as of the rapidity of the diffusion of information, and merits to be discussed in the light of significant events of the recent years.

First, 2024 has marked a year of general elections in numerous regions globally, involving seventy-six countries. These include, within Europe, the elections for the European Parliament as well as parliamentary and presidential elections in several EU Member States such as Portugal, Belgium, Austria, and, on the fringes of the Union, the UK. On the other side of the Atlantic, it is sufficient to refer to the Presidential elections in the USA in November. 2025 presents a more limited but still significant number of electoral events, including national, presidential ad regional ones.[11] For many of these processes, a strong discussion has emerged before and after the elections as to the real or potential impact of disinformation on the electoral results[12] and, according to some analysis, false claims have eroded trust in elections and, in the USA, provoked a wave of anti-voter laws.[13]

Second, 2025 is unfortunately the forth year of the Russia-Ukraine military conflict, a terrible event whose impact cannot be confined, and for many reasons, to the territory of the two States concerned. This war brings about the question of the impact of propaganda of war on the outbreak and development of the armed conflict, an issue already emerged in other past conflicts (the role of hate speech and disinformation in the mass media for the outbreak of the genocide in Rwanda may be a similar example[14]).

---

order to assess whether the platform has complied with its obligation to properly assess and mitigate systemic risks linked to election integrity.

[9] Regulation (EU) 2024/900 of the European Parliament and of the Council of 13 March 2024 on the transparency and targeting of political advertising, PE/90/2023/REV/1, OJ L. See in this volume Massa, How to regulate online political advertising to ensure democratic electoral processes? Effectiveness, differences and influences of the EU and US measures.

[10] US Supreme Court, 7 January 2024, 603 U.S., *Moody v. NetChoice and NetChoice v. Paxton.*

[11] Limiting our view to the Member States of the EU, see 2025 elections in the EU available via: https://en.wikipedia.org/wiki/2025_elections_in_the_European_Union.

[12] For an analysis concerning the European Parliament elections see Casero-Ripollés et al. (2025).

[13] For the debate in the US, see for example Brennan Centre for Justice (2024) where it is held that «misinformation interferes with voters' ability to understand and participate in political processes and it has been weaponized by lawmakers to justify new voter suppression legislation».

[14] Lower and Hauschildt, (2014 pp. 1–7) and Wilson (2015).

Third, as a direct consequence of the first two elements, we have witnessed, and are still witnessing, in different jurisdictions, *an increase of court cases* at the highest level concerning both disinformation in times of elections and propaganda of war. It is interesting to note, first of all, that this kind of issues have become a matter for litigation, so increasing the role of courts to guarantee the respect of the fundamental rights at stake. It may be useful to cite some examples of this important trend. As to reactions to alleged *disinformation in times of elections*, probably the most striking decision is the Romania's constitutional court judgment of 6 December 2024, where the Court annulled the result of the first round of voting in the presidential election.[15] According to the Court, the elections results merited to be annulled because they were influenced (*inter alia*) by the spread of false information via social networks (expecially, Tik-Tok). With regard to *propaganda of war*, as we will see more in details in different chapters of this volume, the restrictive measures adopted by the EU in the context of the Russian/Ukrainian war has caused the first judgments by the European courts on the impact of propaganda of war on freedom of information. In particular, with two judgment delivered in 2023[16] and 2025[17] the GC of the EU acknowledged the risks emanating from propaganda and disinformation campaigns conducted by media outlets—established in the EU but controlled by Russian public entities—as posing a serious threat to the public order and security of the EU, thus justifying the use of sanctions ("restrictive measures") prohibiting the broadcasting of such content.

These recent events confirm serious concerns about the influence that disinformation and propaganda can have on public opinion and, consequently, on the choices that governments can make when involved in political conflicts. In the first scenario, during a national or supranational political process, citizens are invited to directly express their preferences through the election of representatives in legislative assemblies or presidential offices, or through referenda. In the second, citizens are called to provide (or deny) the public support that each party in a conflict seeks to secure in order to "accept" the loss of human lives and the economic efforts or sacrifices that wars, unfortunately, require.

The *fil rouge* or common thread that binds these two situations is clear: the danger that distorted or manipulated information significantly impacts the formation of public opinion. This can lead to public decisions that risk being based on false or seriously distorted news. In essence, this poses a threat to the very existence of democracy, even in contexts where democratic procedures required by fundamental constitutional rules are formally observed.

4. This volume examines these various issues from the point of view of the legal rules, *de lege lata* and *de lege ferenda*, taking into account, when feasible, whether

[15] See Curtea Constituțională A României, 6 December 2024, n. 32, as summarized by a press release of the same Court (https://www.ccr.ro/en/press-release-6-dec/). For some critical remarks, see Kuti (2024).

[16] GC, case T-122/23, 22 July 2023, *RT France vs. Council*. See Szep and Wessel (2023).

[17] GC, case T-307/22, 26 March 2025, *A2B Connect and a. vs. Council* (currently under appeal). See Bogdanova (2025).

such risks warrant a *preventive reaction* and what types of public responses are admitted under basic "constitutional" rules of international and European law. Our analysis incorporates both an international and a comparative constitutional approach by looking into the current debates about disinformation in the USA and in the EU. The obvious starting point is that, at least in the main instruments of international and European law, freedom of information forms the bedrock of a democratic system. This «constitutes the essential foundation of a democratic society and one of the basic conditions for its progress and for each individual's self-fulfillment».[18] On the other side of the Atlantic, the US Supreme Court constantly insists on the same conclusion: in *New York Times v. Sullivan*, Justice Brennan underlined that: «[t]he maintenance of the opportunity for free political discussion [...] is a fundamental principle of our constitutional system».[19]

This encompasses an individual right *to diffuse* information but also a general right of the public *to receive* information: as Lord Bingham of the United Kingdom House of Lords famously puts it in *Regina v. Shayler*: «[m]odern democratic government means government of the people by the people for the people. But there can be no government by the people if they are ignorant of the issues to be resolved, the arguments for and against different solutions and the facts underlying those arguments».[20]

It is also undisputed that freedom of expression is *not* an absolute right, and all the international or regional human rights treaties, as well as domestic Constitutions, justify to a certain degree governments' interference and restrictions, if they are deemed necessary to safeguard other fundamental rights or values, being them individual (privacy, honour, intellectual property) or collective (democracy, public order, public security, peace). In any legal system, courts are empowered with a delicate balancing exercise that may lead to different results in different jurisdictions, in particular as far as the proportionality text is concerned.

For instance, in the ECtHR jurisprudence concerning Article 10 of the ECHR, there are circumstances where lesser protection is afforded to the right of every person to freely disseminate information. These include cases where the speech involves a call for violence or hate, or is intended to disrupt the smooth functioning of political processes. There may even be cases where the diffusion of certain expressions (promoting and justificating terrorism, war crimes and incitement to hate) is deemed intolerable for a democratic society.[21]

As frequently emphasized in different jurisdictions,[22] it would be wrong to extend equal protection to all speech: the marketplace of ideas itself can be distorted by speech. In essence, is the deliberate diffusion of false information protected in any

[18] ECtHR, *Sunday Times vs UK*, 6538/74, 26 April 1979, para. 13.

[19] U.S. Supreme Court, 7 January 1964, 376 U.S. 254, *New York Times v. Sullivan.*

[20] United Kingdom House of Lords, 21 March 2002, UKHL 11, *Regina v. Shayler*, para. 21.

[21] See, for example, ECtHR, *Erbakan v. Turkey*, 59405/00, 6 July 2006, para. 56.

[22] For example, High Court of Justice, King's Bench Division, 12 January 2024, AC-2023-LON-1868, *Phillips v. The Secretary of State for Foreign, Commonwealth and Development Affairs*, para 46.

situation, or can this protection be limited in case of violations of other fundamental constitutional values? Are elections "free", as requested by the ECtHR protocol,[23] if they are conditioned by the dissemination of false information, in particular where the media markets suffer a situation of lack of pluralism so that only some voices can actually be heard? The answer to this question should be given having in mind that, as firmly stated by the ECtHR in *Bowman v. The United Kingdom*, «[f]ree elections and freedom of expression, and particularly the freedom of political debate, form the foundation of any democracy. The two rights are inter-related and operate to reinforce each other. It is particularly important in the period preceding an election that opinions and information of all kinds are permitted to circulate freely».[24]

As to the second situation covered by this volume, can a State or a supra-national entity such as the EU restrict or ban the dissemination of information that provokes turbolence in international relations or even corresponds to propaganda in favour of an armed conflict? This question has become highly relevant in the European continent before and after the outbreak of the Ukrainian war and, as anticipated, is currently subject to scrutiny before the European Courts, as further evidence of the importance that EU law is acquiring also in areas of law so close to the core of national sovereignty.

5. This volume addresses the protections to and limits of free speech under international and European law. It is considered whether States are subject to a "positive obligation" to combat interferences on the democratic processes, for example by investigating hostile State interference in their democratic elections.[25]

Starting from the two scenarios mentioned above, the chapters selected for the present volume concern the current "state of health" of freedom of expression in both old and new media. The way in which we selected the chapters for this volume stems from assessing the different ways through which judges, legal scholars and lawyers would deal with the dangers exposed before, starting with three questions.

First, are governmental repressive, corrective or even preventive actions against "false" information in the two scenarios discussed here the right solution? Could any prohibition of disinformation rather lead, paradoxically, to the opposing result of producing a "chilling effect", in itself harmful to the free circulation of ideas, including those who "shock or disturb"?

Second, is propaganda of war a specific situation that merits to be distinguished from any other form of disinformation?

Third, is it still valid, also in case of diffusion of disinformation in times of elections and in times of war, that the best antidote to disinformation and hate speech

[23] See Article 3 of Protocol No. 1 to the ECHR—Right to free elections: «The High Contracting Parties undertake to hold free elections at reasonable intervals by secret ballot, under conditions which will ensure the free expression of the opinion of the people in the choice of the legislature». On the relationship between freedom of expression as an essential part of democracy and the right to vote in the specific context of European Union law, see Mastroianni (2022).

[24] ECtHR, *Bowman v. The United Kingdom*, 24839/94, 19 February 1998, para. 42.

[25] This issue was addressed in the judgment of the ECtHR of 22 July 2025 in case *Brashaw and others vs. UK*, 15653/2. The Court answered in the affirmative (see para 130 to 140)

is more speech? Is this conclusion still correct in case of absence of pluralism in the media, when the main sources of information are controlled by one or few media companies?

All three questions are addressed by the various chapters in this volume in different ways. Finding the right balance between, on one hand, the imperatives of free speech and, on the other hand, the protection of basic liberal constitutional values such as the correct functioning of democratic societies or the preservation of peace and of national security, represents the challenging task that we are facing in these turbulent times. Overall, with this volume we wish to highlight that disinformation significantly impacts the formation of public opinion, thereby prompting public decisions that risk being based on false or seriously distorted news.

Finally, as to the structure of the volume, it is divided into two parts and includes an Introduction and a Conclusion written by the Editors. The two parts are entitled respectively:

I. *Disinformation and propaganda in times of elections;*
II. *Disinformation and propaganda in times of war.*

Each part is divided into seven chapters, containing evaluations, first, on the measures to combat disinformation and propaganda from both a *de lege lata* and a *de lege ferenda* perspectives, and second, on how to strike a balance between the need to protect democratic values and protect economic freedoms.

Since our edited volume is based on a comparative approach and looks into the current debate on disinformation in the EU and the USA, we have carefully selected the participants in this project, by inviting distinguished academics from both sides of the ocean. The various contributions where already orally discussed at the international conference "*Disinformation in new and old media in the XXI Century. Shaping the new boundaries of free speech?*" held at the University of Naples Federico II on the 11th of March 2024, and are updated by the authors until February 2026.

References

Bogdanova I (2025) EU Sanctions against disinformation and war propaganda: a threat to freedom of expression? (T-307/22, A2B Connect and Others v Council). EU Law Live. https://eulawlive.com/analysis-eu-sanctions-against-disinformation-and-war-propaganda-a-threat-to-freedom-of-expression-t-307-22-a2b-connect-and-others-v-council/. Accessed 30 Apr 2025

Brennan Centre for Justice (2024) Election misinformation. https://www.brennancenter.org/election-misinformation. Accessed 30 Apr 2025

Casero-Ripollés A, Alonso-Muñoz L, Moret-Soler D (2025) Spreading false content in political campaigns: Disinformation in the 2024 European Parliament Elections. Protecting democracy from fake news: The EU's role in countering disinformation, media and communication, vol. 13

European Law Institute (2024) Charter of Fundamental Constitutional Principles of a European Democracy. Vienna, 2024

Koltay A (2025) Freedom of information and the regulation of disinformation in the European Union. In: Krotoszynski RJ, Koltay A, Garden C (eds) Disinformation, misinformation, and democracy: legal approaches in comparative context. Cambridge University Press, pp 133 ff
Kuti C (2024) On means and ends, the annulment of the Romanian presidential elections. Verfassungsblog. https://verfassungsblog.de/on-means-and-ends/. Accessed 30 Apr 2025
Lower M, Hauschildt T (2014) The media as a tool of war: propaganda in the Rwandan genocide. Human Rights Conflict Resolut 2(1):1–7
Massa C (2026) How to regulate online political advertising to ensure democratic electoral processes? Effectiveness, differences and influences of the EU and US measures. In: Mastroianni R, Massa C (eds) Disinformation in new and old media in the XXI century. Springer Nature Switzerland, Cham
Mastroianni R (2022) Freedom and pluralism of the media: an European value waiting to be discovered? MediaLaws, p 100 ff
Szep V, Wessel R (2023) Balancing restrictive measures and media freedom: RT France v Council. Common Market Law Rev 60:1383–1396
UN Global Principles For Information Integrity. Recommendations for multi-stakeholder action. https://www.un.org/en/information-integrity/global-principles. Accessed 30 Apr 2025
UN Secretary-General (2021) "Our Common Agenda" report. https://sdg.iisd.org/news/secretary-general-unveils-vision-for-future-oriented-un/. Accessed 30 Apr 2025
UN Secretary-General (2023) "Information Integrity on Digital Platforms" policy brief. https://sdg.iisd.org/commentary/policy-briefs/towards-a-code-of-conduct-to-ensure-inclusive-information-ecosystem/. Accessed 30 Apr 2025
Wilson RA (2015) Inciting genocide with words. Mich J Int'l L 36:277

Part I
Disinformation and Propaganda in Times of Elections

Should Social Media Disinformation be Subject to Regulation and Control?

Russell L. Weaver

Abstract There has been much controversy regarding disinformation on the internet, especially on social media platforms. However, it is important to put the current debate into perspective. Disinformation has been with us throughout the ages. It existed in ancient Rome, as well as in most of Europe throughout the Middle Ages. Today, even outside of the social media context, disinformation is rampant. Many politicians lie. Donald Trump, for example, may be the all-time champion of lying, and Joe Biden is hardly a paragon of virtue when it comes to telling the truth. In addition, rather than pursue neutrality and objectivity, many media outlets try to shape the truth to their preferred advocacy positions. This is true for Fox News in the U.S., as well as for National Public Radio. So, there is a dilemma. The U.S. does not generally allow the government to prohibit disinformation unless the speech is illegal or falls into an unprotected category of speech (e.g., child pornography). Thus, we would generally not allow the government to regulate the speech of politicians or the media (again, absent proof that the speech is unprotected or illegal). So, it seems odd that are numerous calls to regulate social media. The great advantage of social media platforms is that they allow ordinary people to communicate (really, for the first time in history) on a mass scale. As a society, are we so afraid of what ordinary people might say that we feel compelled to regulate and control their speech?

Professor Weaver wishes to thank his research assistant, Mackenzie Williams, for her help on this article.

R. L. Weaver (✉)
Louis D. Brandeis School of Law, University of Louisville, Louisville, KY, USA
e-mail: Russell.weaver@louisville.edu

R. Mastroianni and C. Massa (eds.), *Disinformation in New and Old Media in the XXI Century*, Ius Gentium: Comparative Perspectives on Law and Justice 136,
https://doi.org/10.1007/978-3-032-18830-4_2

1 Introduction

There has been much controversy regarding misinformation and disinformation on the internet, especially on social media platforms, and much discussion regarding whether it should be regulated or controlled.[1] Congress has held hearings on the issue,[2] and the Biden Administration even proposed the creation of a "Disinformation Governance Board."[3] Some commentators have argued that governments should censor or regulate social media disinformation,[4] or that social media platforms should be required to be more aggressive about censoring social media content.[5]

Disinformation, referred to by some as "fake news" or sometimes as "misinformation," is problematic because it has the potential to undermine the democratic process.[6] It does so by introducing inaccurate information into the public debate, and thereby deluding or misleading the public.[7] Indeed, as one commentator asked "how can the people be well informed in a world where misinformation is intentionally circulated?"[8] For those who believe in the Marketplace of Ideas theory,[9] brought into U.S. jurisprudence by Justice Holmes,[10] disinformation hardly advances the search for "truth."[11] And disinformation can have real world consequences: "coordinated disinformation campaigns threaten to exacerbate public health emergencies, stoke ethnic and racial divisions and even undermine democracy itself."[12]

In the U.S. system, legitimate questions can be raised regarding the extent to which government should be allowed to restrict or regulate speech. In the U.S. Declaration of Independence, Thomas Jefferson implicitly rejected monarchy and the concept of hereditary succession in favor of a democratically elected government: "Governments are instituted among Men, deriving their just powers from the consent of the governed."[13] In democratic societies, freedom of expression and freedom of the press are essential components.[14] Indeed, the Court has stated that, "Speech concerning

---

[1] Chang (2023, p. 4); Sun (2023, p. 367); Weaver (2025, pp. 316–320, 394–398).

[2] Mak (2019); Parks and Bond (2021).

[3] Seganga (2022).

[4] Sun (2023, pp. 389–416); Chang (2023, p. 22).

[5] Ibid.

[6] Chen (2020, p. 379); Sanders et al. (2019, p. 206); Schuyler (2019, p. 213).

[7] Ibid.

[8] Schuyler (2019, p. 212).

[9] Weaver and Hancock (2023, pp. 10–12).

[10] United States Supreme Court, 1919, 250 U.S. 616, *Abrams v. United States* p.630 (Holmes, J., dissenting).

[11] Wu (2020, pp. 169, 170).

[12] Myers and Sullivan (2022).

[13] National Archives (2024).

[14] Baker (1978, p. 990); Bork (1971, p. 20); Emerson (1963, p. 878); Meiklejohn (1961, p. 256); Weaver and Hancock (2023).

public affairs is more than self-expression; it is the essence of self-government."[15] It "was fashioned to assure unfettered interchange of ideas for the bringing about of political and social changes desired by the people"[16] so that "changes may be obtained by lawful means."[17] If the power to govern derives from the consent of the governed, then it places ultimate authority in the hands of the people themselves, and the people should be allowed to express their opinions and ideas.[18]

This article explores the problem of disinformation and inquires whether there are remedies that can or should be imposed in a democratic society. It begins by examining the scope of the problem and then explores possible remedies.

2 The Scope of Disinformation

Although some suggest that disinformation is a problem of the internet era and is particularly attributable to the rise of social media,[19] the reality is that "disinformation" has existed since virtually the beginning of time. In ancient Rome, Octavian purportedly engaged in a campaign of disinformation against Marc Anthony.[20] In the 1400s, fictitious stories were circulated depicting Jews as drinking the blood of Christian children.[21] In 1782, Benjamin Franklin purportedly created a counterfeit issue of his newspaper which included false stories about "Indians mercilessly scalping the family members of colonists."[22]

---

[15] Supreme Court of the United States, 1983, 461 U.S. 138, *Connick v. Myers*, p. 145 (quoting Supreme Court of the United States, 1964, 379 U.S. 64, *Garrison v. Louisiana*, pp. 74–75); Supreme Court of the United States, 1992, 505 U.S. 377, *R.A.V. v. City of St. Paul*, p. 423 (Blackmun, J., concurring) («core political speech occupies the highest, most protected position»).

[16] Supreme Court of the United States, 1957, 354 U.S. 476, *Roth v. United States*, p. 484 («The protection given speech and press was fashioned to assure unfettered interchange of ideas for the bringing about of political and social changes desired by the people»).

[17] Supreme Court of the United States, 1964, 376 U.S. 254, *New York Times, Co. v. Sullivan*, p. 269 (quoting Supreme Court of the United States, 1931, 283 U.S. 359, *Stromberg v. California*); Supreme Court of the United States, 2010, 558 U.S. 310, *Citizens United v. Federal Election* p. 339 («Speech is an essential mechanism of democracy, for it is the means to hold officials accountable to the people. The right of citizens to inquire, to hear, to speak, and to use information to reach consensus is a pre-condition to enlightened self-government and a necessary means to protect it. The First Amendment 'has its fullest and most urgent application' to speech uttered during a campaign for political office. It is inherent in the nature of the political process that voters must be free to obtain information from diverse sources in order to determine how to cast their votes»); Supreme Court of the United States, 2003, 538 U.S. 343, *Virginia v. Black*, p. 365 («Political speech, of course, is 'at the core of what the First Amendment is designed to protect.'»).

[18] Supreme Court of the United States, 2022, 595 U.S. 468, *Houston Community College System v. Wilson*, p. 480 (quoting Madison J (1794) 4 Annals of Cong. 899).

[19] Roose (2018) («digging up large-scale misinformation on Facebook was as easy as finding baby photos or birthday greetings»).

[20] Titcomb and Carson (2018).

[21] Sanders et al. (2019–2020, p. 205).

[22] Watson (2018, p. 95).

Undoubtedly, the internet has exacerbated the problem of disinformation. For most of human history, ordinary people lacked the ability to mass communicate.[23] Information passed between people by word of mouth, or by handwritten methods.[24] Not until the fifteenth century, when Johannes Gutenberg invented the printing press,[25] did it become possible to easily create multiple copies of documents.[26] Although the printing press did not increase the speed at which information moved, it allowed information to spread more broadly, and led to a flowering of knowledge, information and ideas, as well as the Protestant Revolution and dramatic changes in governmental theory.[27]

But the printing press, like the more advanced technologies that came later (e.g., radio, television, satellite and cable) was under the control of "gatekeepers" (wealthy individuals or corporations) that controlled how they could be used.[28] The Gutenberg printing press was relatively expensive to obtain, requiring not only the purchase of a printing press, but also the purchase of lead type, ink and other essential components, meaning that only a few individuals could afford to own or operate it.[29] Subsequent technologies, including radio,[30] television[31] and satellite communications,[32] all came with their own gatekeepers.[33] All required substantial technological investments, and some (e.g., broadcast communications like radio and television also required an operating license) limited who could own and operate them. Those who controlled communications technologies had the power to decide who could use them, as well as the messages that were communicated,[34] and some freely exercised that authority.[35] Ordinary people were at the mercy of the gatekeepers in terms of their ability to use those technologies.[36]

The internet transformed communication because it was the first technology that allowed ordinary individuals to communicate on a mass scale,[37] and allowed them

---

23 Weaver (2025, p. 322).

24 *Ivi,* pp. 3–13. Of course, over the centuries, there were attempts to move information more quickly than people could move. *Ivi,* p. 3, 59–74. Information could move faster than people could move through the use of carrier pigeons. However, although pigeons could discreetly communicate a particular piece of information relatively quickly, they were not suited to mass communication in the sense of the modern radio, television or internet.

25 *Ivi,* p. 15.

26 Ibid.

27 *Ivi,* pp. 18–25.

28 *Ivi,* pp. 39–58.

29 *Ivi,* pp. 50–51.

30 Crowley and Heyer (eds) (2007, p. 204).

31 *Ivi,* p. 243.

32 Schwartz (2007, p. 313).

33 Weaver (2025, pp. 75–97).

34 *Ivi,* pp. 3–35.

35 Swanberg (1961, pp. 100, 119–127).

36 Weaver (2025, pp. 75–97).

37 *Ivi,* pp. 103–105.

to avoid the traditional media which had historically served as the principal gatekeeper and filter of communication and information.[38] This broadening of communicative capacity has had a profound impact on modern societies, enabling mass communication on a scale never seen before, and resulting in profound societal changes.[39]

However, the great strength of the internet – the enabling of mass communication by ordinary individuals – has also proven to be its greatest weakness.[40] As the internet has enabled virtually everyone to mass communicate, it has simultaneously led to a flood of disinformation. In addition, "bots" (essentially, automated programs that perform automated tasks to masquerade as humans[41]) have become increasingly commonplace on the internet in what one commentator described as a "'Cambrian explosion' of robotics technologies"[42] with millions and millions of bot accounts and bot messages.[43] At one point, "YouTube had as much traffic from bots masquerading as people as it did from real human visitors."[44] And of course, bots can easily spread disinformation.

It must be recognized, however, that disinformation goes well beyond the internet and social media. For example, it is not at all uncommon for politicians and governmental officials to lie to the public. Following Edward Snowden's revelation that the U.S. government was running a massive cybersurveillance operation, then National Security Agency (NSA) Director James Clapper was asked about the program.[45] In response to a direct question regarding whether the NSA was collecting "any type of data at all on millions or hundreds of millions of Americans," he flatly stated, "No, sir. Not wittingly."[46] Clapper later admitted that he had lied and tried to explain it away by stating that it was the "most truthful" or "least untruthful" thing that he could say at the time.[47] About the same time, then President Barrack Obama assured the U.S. public that the NSA's cybersurveillance program was not focused on ordinary U.S. citizens, but rather only on individuals who pose a terrorist threat to the United States and on communications of "foreign intelligence value"[48] and foreign

---

[38] *Ivi*, p. 111.

[39] *Ivi*, pp. 111–115.

[40] *Ivi*, pp. 315–316.

[41] Longe et al. (2009).

[42] Weaver (2025, p. 323) (citing Manjoo F (2017) How Twitter Is Being Gamed to Feed Misinformation. In: The New York Times. https://www.nytimes.com/2017/05/31/technology/how-twitter-is-being-gamed-to-feed-misinformation.html)).

[43] Fox (2020, pp. 114–166); Newberg (2017); Nicas (2019).

[44] Keller (2018).

[45] The Editorial Board (2014) («[Snowdens'] leaks revealed that James Clapper Jr., the director of national intelligence, lied to Congress when testifying in March that the N.S.A. was not collecting data on millions of Americans. (There has been no discussion of punishment for that lie.)»); Rosenthal (2013); Savage and Shane (2013) (suggesting that Snowden decided to go public because Director Clapper had lied to the American public regarding the NSA data collection program).

[46] Savage and Shane (2013).

[47] Rosenthal (2013).

[48] Shane (2013a, b).

intelligence targets.[49] That turned out to be a lie as well. The U.S. government was in fact collecting large amounts of data about virtually everyone.[50] And these lies are significant. If the U.S. people are going to challenge governmental activities like the cybersurveillance operation, they must first know that it exists.

Clapper and Obama are hardly the only politicians who have lied to the American public. Former President Donald Trump may be the all-time champion of disinformation and has been widely denounced as a compulsive "liar."[51] "The Big Lie," Trump's claim that the 2020 presidential election was stolen, is the example that comes most readily to mind.[52] But presidential lying goes well beyond Trump. Former President Joe Biden was hardly a paragon of virtue when it came to telling the truth. For example, following the disasterous withdrawal of U.S. troops from Afghanistan, when the media asked President Biden why he did not keep more U.S. troops in the country to help with the withdrawal, Biden flatly stated that his senior military advisors had advised against it.[53] Both Gen. Mark Milley, chairman of the Joint Chiefs of Staff, and Gen. Kenneth McKenzie Jr., head of U.S. Central Command, subsequently disputed Biden's claims in sworn testimony.[54] Secretary of Defense Lloyd Austin flatly agreed with Milley and McKenzie, stating that Biden's military advisers "were in lock step in recommending that the U.S. leave 3,000 to 4,500 troops in Afghanistan."[55] So, either Biden lied, the three officials all perjured themselves under oath, or Biden simply did not remember correctly given his mental acuity problems.

There are plenty of other examples of political disinformation. The Wall Street Journal labeled California Congressman (now U.S. Senator) Adam Schiff as "disinformation man."[56] According to the report, Intelligence Committee Chairman Devin Nunes tried in 2018 to inform the public about the FBI's alleged abuse of the FISA warrant process in regard to its investigation into Trump's alleged collusion with Russia.[57] Congressman Schiff, who had full access to all of the intelligence information, made a variety of false statements designed to undercut the Nunes report.[58] Schiff's statements caused the media to denounce the Nunes report as a "joke."[59]

---

[49] Ibid.

[50] Shane (2013a, b); Stanglin (2013).

[51] Cohen (2019) (suggesting that White House Counsel Donald McGahn, «wants a contemporaneous record of the truth to protect himself and—God knows—the Republic against Trump's lies.»); Friedland (2022) (referring to the «lies and fantasies of Donald Trump»); Liasson (2021).

[52] Smith (2022); Hakim and Berzon (2022).

[53] Stephens (2021).

[54] Ibid.

[55] Ibid.

[56] The Editorial Board (2023).

[57] Ibid.

[58] Ibid.

[59] Ibid.

The validity of the Nunes report was later confirmed by Justice Department Inspector General Michael Horowitz.[60] In other words, Schiff lied.

But, if we are concerned about disinformation, and its impact on the ability of the American people to make educated decisions, we also need to be concerned about the media. Media bias has the potential to mislead and manipulate the public with limited or deceptive information and emotionally charged pleas. When discussions of media bias occur, commentators often focus on Fox News, contending that it has a right-wing bias and that it skews the news in favor of that bias.[61] And, indeed, there is evidence indicating that Fox News deliberately disseminated disinformation regarding the outcome of the 2020 election.[62] But do other media outlets, such as National Public Radio (NPR), On the Media (OTM), and the Public Broadcasting System (PBS), have less bias?[63] The simple answer is "no."[64] All three have exhibited considerable bias in their reporting.[65]

So, if we are legitimately concerned about the possibility of disinformation undermining the democratic process, should we also be concerned about lying politicians and media bias as well as the internet and social media?

3 But Are There Appropriate Remedies for Disinformation?

While it is relatively easy to identify the scope of disinformation, it is much more difficult to come up with an appropriate solution. A solution that is consistent with the premises and values of free and democratic societies. The reality is that the possible remedies may be worse than the problem.

3.1 Disinformation Board

One possible way to control fake news is to establish systems designed to regulate and control disinformation.[66] For example, during the Biden Administration, the

---

[60] Ibid.

[61] James (2011).

[62] Ibid.

[63] Ibid («'The bias of the mainstream media is towards sensationalism, conflict and laziness,' said [Comedian Jon] Stewart as he spelled out what, at least to his mind, differentiated other major news outlets from Fox News, an operation Stewart has repeatedly targeted in his comedy as on an ideological mission.").

[64] Weaver (2025, pp. 92–93, 254, 344–345, 494).

[65] Ibid.

[66] Goodyear (2021, p. 194) (suggesting that courts apply a lower standard of review, and that certain public health initiatives be subject to fake news regulation); Schuyler (2019, p. 240) (suggesting that fake news should be controlled through a notice-and-correction-or-exclusion procedure).

Department of Homeland Security (DHS), proposed to create a "Disinformation Governance Board" to respond to disinformation.[67] In theory, the Board was designed to create a set of standardized practices that could be used by federal agencies to respond to violent threats against the nation.[68] However, the effort was halted when it was met with a firestorm of public criticism.[69]

It is not surprising that the proposal was met with such hostility. A disinformation board would be inconsistent with the U.S. free speech tradition, which generally denies government the ability to regulate the content or viewpoint of speech[70] (except for limited categories of speech).[71] Even if society could agree that we should have a "disinformation board," it would face questions regarding the scope of the board's authority and jurisdiction. Should the board only police disinformation on the internet? Should it also intervene and check false statements by public officials like Clapper, Trump, Obama, and Biden? Should it also police media bias? Presumably, any of these proposals would be met with a similar firestorm of criticism.

Once it is decided whether there should be a disinformation board, and who it should police, other questions will arise. For example, should the board be given the power to require takedowns or to issue injunctions against the dissemination of disinformation? From a legal perspective, such efforts would be treated as "prior restraints" on speech and therefore would be presumptively unconstitutional unless they involved fraud, perjury or some other valid basis for suppression.[72] Moreover, as with the Biden Administration proposal, presumably such a board would be met with public hostility. Would the American people trust the government to determine what speech is false, and engage in regulation and prohibition?

It could be argued that, since there is so much disinformation on the internet, particularly on social media, a disinformation board should only focus on disinformation on social media platforms. But it seems somewhat inappropriate to allow politicians and the media to freely express their views, including the dissemination of disinformation or biased perspectives by the media, but to squash the views of ordinary people on social media. As previously noted, for most of human history, ordinary people were unable to mass communicate except with the permission of those who owned the means of communication.[73] Only with the advent of the internet and social media have ordinary people been able to communicate on a broad scale.[74] It would be ironic if a new disinformation board allowed those who have always been able to express their opinions (e.g., wealthy individuals who control the media and the means of communication and politicians) to be exempt from regulation, but limited, regulated and censored the views of ordinary people.

[67] Shivaram (2022).

[68] Seganga (2022).

[69] Shivaram (2022).

[70] Weaver and Hancock (2023, p. 70).

[71] Ibid.

[72] Supreme Court of the United States, 1931, 283 U.S. 697, *Near v. Minnesota*, pp. 71–73.

[73] Weaver (2025, pp. 39–58).

[74] *Ivi*, pp. 103–105.

Another issue is how the board would go about determining what constitutes disinformation. Many might fear whether the government would exercise such power impartially, or whether it would use the power to suppress views with which it disagreed. As a result, the definition of "truth" could change with each change of presidential administration. For example, suppose that during the Obama Administration, the Disinformation Board had decided that climate change was a "fact," and that climate change denial was fake news. Could the Disinformation Board have criminally prosecuted those who argued that climate change was a hoax? Would the Board have been free to redefine the truth regarding climate change when Donald Trump came to power? In other words, could the Board have changed its definition of the "truth," dismissed all charges against climate change deniers, and criminally prosecuted those who were arguing that climate change is a real phenomenon? Would we, as a society, feel comfortable giving the government the power to define truth, to determine which facts are true or false, and punish anyone who articulates a contrary view? Given that the last three administrations have lied to the American people at various times, would we be comfortable giving them the power to censor disinformation?

Indeed, the entire process of seeking out and purging disinformation is fraught with peril and has the potential for political interference and political bias. For example, there was considerable controversy regarding Hunter Biden's laptop. The story broke during the middle of a political campaign and allegedly involved a laptop, owned by Joe Biden's son, Hunter Biden, which purportedly showed potential corruption on the part of Joe Biden.[75] The Biden Administration managed to get fifty-one former foreign security experts to issue a letter branding the story as "Russian propaganda" and disinformation.[76] Relying on the letter, most reputable news organizations dismissed the allegations and refused to report the story even though there were allegations of corruption by the Bidens and even though an election was imminent.[77] For example, NPR, in a segment issued just a couple of weeks before the presidential election, dismissed the laptop story as "questionable,"[78] and suggested that the allegations were part of a conspiracy theory pushed by then President Trump and his allies.[79] The Public Broadcasting Service (PBS) similarly dismissed the allegations, suggesting that Trump's allies were pushing "Russian disinformation."[80] *The New York Times* suggested that Trump was colluding with the Russians and dismissed the

[75] Simon (2022).

[76] Ibid («And then there was this cohort of paid pundits—50 former national security officials, many of them appearing frequently in mainstream media outlets—who came together for a statement saying that this surfacing of the laptop bore all the hallmarks of a Russian misinformation campaign») (quoting David Folkenflik).

[77] Ibid.

[78] Folkenflik (2020).

[79] Ibid («The story fits snugly into a narrative from President Trump and his allies that Hunter Biden's zealous pursuit of business ties abroad also compromised the former vice president»).

[80] Woodruff (2020).

story, stating that "Giuliani's dirty tricks are the scandal, not Hunter Biden's hard drive."[81] Twitter squelched the story.[82]

Today, the same news organizations that denounced the Hunter Biden laptop story recognize that it was true and not "disinformation," "fake news," or "Russian propaganda." A *New York Times* article, citing reporting by a staff member at Politico, stated that "the most explosive emails from Hunter Biden's purported laptop were entirely genuine" and were not simply Russian-planted disinformation.[83] Even National Public Radio has recognized that there was some validity to the allegations regarding the laptop: "much of the mainstream media dismissed a story about Hunter Biden's business dealings. Now emails supporting the story have been authenticated,"[84] and the *Boston Globe* questioned the decision to suppress the story.[85] If the government had tried to suppress the story, it would have been regarded as imposing an unconstitutional "prior restraint" on speech.

The bottom line is that it is not clear that anyone (especially the government or social media platforms) should set themselves up as the arbiter of "truth." Censorship of the Hunter Biden laptop story by media organizations and social media platforms resulted in the withholding of important information from the public during a presidential election. Moreover, the media's flip-flop on the story gives the public good reason to distrust the media, and the government's regulation of it, because narratives are being manipulated.

3.2 *Criminalizing Disinformation*

It is also doubtful whether either the federal government, or state and local governments, would have the power to criminalize the publication of disinformation. Under the U.S. First Amendment, the U.S. Supreme Court has made clear that the government may not criminalize the publication of libel.[86] Moreover, in general, the government is prohibited from imposing content-based or viewpoint-based restrictions on speech. While there are limited exceptions to this rule for a few categories of speech

---

[81] Goldberg (2020).

[82] Simon (2022) («First, let's acknowledge social media's role. A number of platforms tamped down on sharing of the Post's story. In the case of Twitter, not only did they try to block sharing of it, they suspended The New York Post's actual Twitter account for sharing its own article. That was a wild overreach, and even Twitter had to acknowledge that.») (quoting David Folkenflik).

[83] Stephens (2021).

[84] Simon (2022).

[85] Bray (2023) («Another discovery: There's no evidence of any 'deep state' conspiracy behind Twitter's decision to suppress the New York Post's October 2020 story about the contents of a laptop belonging to President Biden's son Hunter. Twitter executives screwed up that decision all by themselves. They chose to believe a false allegation that the data had been stolen by hackers.»).

[86] Supreme Court of the United States, 1964, 379 U.S. 64, *Garrison v. Louisiana*.

such as child pornography,[87] obscenity[88] fighting words,[89] and true threats,[90] there is no exception for false speech. *United States v. Alvarez*[91] involved an individual's false assertion that he won the Congressional Medal of Honor. While *Alvarez* recognized that individuals can be prosecuted for false speech in limited and defined circumstances (e.g., perjury in a judicial proceeding or making false statements to a governmental official or agency),[92] he could not be convicted simply for making a false statement to the effect that he had won the medal.

Alvarez is consistent with the Court's general free speech jurisprudence. If the legitimacy of our governmental system depends on the consent of the governed, it is inconsistent with our foundational premises to give government the power to control, limit and suppress the range of ideas that the people can hear or consider. James Madison made this very point when he denounced a congressional resolution, criticizing "self-created societies" that some believed had "misrepresent[ed] the conduct of the Government."[93] Madison's view was that, in a Republic, "the censorial power is in the people over the Government, and not in the Government over the people."[94] Likewise, as the U.S. Supreme Court recognized in *Ashcroft v. American Civil Liberties Union*,[95] as "a general matter, the First Amendment means that government has no power to restrict expression because of its message, its ideas, its subject matter, or its content."[96]

Of course, the modern aversion to governmental control of speech has deep roots. Following Johannes Gutenberg's invention of the printing press in the fifteenth century, monarchs feared that widespread use of the press might undermine their power, and therefore they sought to control and limit its use.[97] For example, the English government used the decision in *de Libellis Famosis*,[98] to criminally prosecute those who criticized the Crown or religious officials of high station, and it did so in an effort to prosecute, intimidate and silence governmental critics.[99] Moreover, under English law, truth was an aggravating factor that lead to a more severe punishment.[100] Similar restrictions were imposed in the American colonies where the British

---

[87] Supreme Court of the United States, 1982, 458 U.S. 747, *Ferber v. New York*.

[88] Supreme Court of the United States, 1973, 413 U.S. 15, *Miller v. California*.

[89] Supreme Court of the United States, 1942, 315 U.S. 568, *Chaplinsky v. New Hampshire*.

[90] Supreme Court of the United States, *Virginia v. Black*, cit.

[91] Supreme Court of the United States, 2012, 567 U.S. 709, *United States v. Alvarez*.

[92] Ibid.

[93] Supreme Court of the United States, *Houston Community College System v. Wilson*, cit. p.480 (quoting 4 Annals of Cong. 899 (1794)).

[94] *Ivi*, p.481 (quoting 4 Annals of Cong., at 934).

[95] Supreme Court of the United States, 2002, 535 U.S. 564, *Ashcroft v. ACLU*, p.573.

[96] Supreme Court of the United States, *United States v. Alvarez*, cit. p.716; Supreme Court of the United States, 2011, 564 U.S. 786, *Brown v. Entertainment Merchants Ass'n*, pp. 790–791.

[97] Weaver and Hancock (2023).

[98] Star Chamber, 1606, 77 Eng. Rep. 250, *The Case De Libellis Famosis*.

[99] Mayton (1984, p. 1291).

[100] Ibid.

prosecuted "criticism directed against the government or public officials" because it was considered to be "a threat against public order and a criminal offense."[101]

3.3 Regulation by Social Media Platforms

Social media platforms (as private entities) are generally regarded as private, are exempt from the First Amendment which is a restriction on government, and therefore have the power to censor speech on their platforms.[102] Indeed, in the U.S., Section 230 of the Communications Decency Act explicitly authorizes social media platforms to regulate and censor information posted on their platforms,[103] and social media platforms have frequently exercised that authority.[104]

Even if one could argue that social media platforms could or should ban "disinformation," it is not clear that they have the capacity to make good decisions regarding what constitutes "disinformation." For example, Facebook's moderators are "overwhelmed" by the total volume of work.[105] Purportedly, Facebook receives more than 6.5 million reports a week regarding allegations of fake or improper accounts,[106] and Facebook's moderators are sometimes forced to make decisions regarding the permissibility of content in as little as 10 seconds.[107] The time pressures inevitably result in bad decisions. For a while, Facebook banned all claims that Covid-19 was man-made,[108] but it eventually decided to allow such claims.[109] In addition, Facebook purportedly banned references to certain Bible passages, as well as links to Biblehub.com.[110] After investigating, Facebook confirmed that links to Biblehub.com had been banned, eventually admitted that it had acted in error, and rectified the problem.[111] Facebook even went so far as to ban academics who were doing research on ad transparency and the spread of misinformation on Facebook.[112]

Moreover, there is a very real risk that governmental officials will try to unduly influence the censorship decisions of social media platforms for their own political purposes. For years, congressional committees have called the heads of social media

---

101 Ibid.

102 Weaver (2022, p. 619).

103 47 U.S.C. § 230 (1934). In: Cornell Law School, Legal Information Institute. https://www.law.cornell.edu/uscode/text/47/230.

104 Weaver (2022, pp. 620–622).

105 Hern and Solon (2018).

106 Ibid.

107 Ibid.

108 Barrabi (2021).

109 Ibid.

110 Marnin (2021).

111 Ibid.

112 Vincent (2021).

platforms before them, and pressured those companies to engage in censorship.[113] Whether such pressure is enough to transform the actions of social media companies into state actors is unclear, but there is much more governmental involvement in social media platform censorship, including pressure from the White House. The Biden Administration called for Twitter to silence speakers who dissented from the official government line on the origins of Covid, the Hunter Biden laptop, and things like the safety of vaccines.[114] Moreover, during the Biden Administration, there was evidence of constant communication between the FBI and Twitter officials responsible for content moderation.[115] In *Missouri v. Biden*,[116] a federal district court found strong evidence that governmental officials had tried to coerce, pressure and threaten social media companies regarding their censorship of content.

Although Twitter sometimes refused the FBI's requests for censorship, the company was paid $3,415,323 to cover the cost of working with the feds.[117] While it is not unethical for Twitter to be compensated for its efforts, the sheer size of the payment suggests a level of government influence over content decisions.[118] Moreover, there is plenty of evidence showing that the federal government worked the refs (social media executives) like an aggressive football coach, hectoring and goading the company's executives into exercising ever-stricter control over what users are permitted to say.[119] This was true for not only the FBI, but also the White House.[120] Since the US government has the power to make things very unpleasant for companies that resist, the temptation to comply likely proved irresistible.[121]

The Twitter files reveal that the Biden Administration interfered with the former Twitter (now X) in an effort to encourage Twitter to suppress content.[122] For example, "the Twitter Files" suggest that the FBI warned Twitter "to expect a flood of fake news out of Russia just in time for the election."[123] Indeed, there were approximately 150 emails between Yoel Roth, Twitter's chief in charge of weeding out inappropriate content, and FBI officials over a two year period.[124] Roth admitted that these emails played a role in his decision to quash the Hunter Biden story.[125] The FBI even went so far as to give Twitter officials temporary security clearances, so they could

---

[113] Mak (2019); Parks and Bond (2021).

[114] Bray (2023).

[115] Ibid.

[116] U.S. District Court for the Western District of Louisiana, 2023, 680 F.Supp.3d 630, *Missouri v. Biden.*

[117] Brown (2022).

[118] U.S. District Court for the Western District of Louisiana (2023).

[119] Ibid.

[120] Younes and Kheriaty (2023) («Newly released documents show that the White House played a major role in censoring Americans on social media.»).

[121] Bray (2023).

[122] Ibid.

[123] Ibid.

[124] Ibid.

[125] Ibid.

receive classified briefings prior to the 2020 election.[126] In addition, the FBI notified Twitter regarding tweets that it regarded as "suspicious," and suggested that the tweets should be suppressed.[127] If governmental pressure is involved, social media platform censorship may be politically rather than objectively based. Interestingly, when the Biden Administration's actions were challenged on First Amendment grounds in *Murthy v. Missouri*,[128] the U.S. Supreme Court refused to entertain the case.

3.4 Flagging Disinformation

One potential solution to the problem of disinformation is to "flag" it as constituting "disinformation," and then perhaps direct the viewer to sources that contain accurate information. This approach would be less objectionable than outright suppression of information because the information would still be distributed, but would be met with counter-speech that attempts to set the record straight.

In some respects, efforts to flag or question disinformation might prove to be an effective remedy. For example, in the case of "fake news" on the internet, the reader could be referred to more accurate information. The remedy could also work for false statements by politicians. For example, when President Biden lied about the recommendations from his military advisers regarding the Afghanistan withdrawal,[129] the Biden comments (to the extent that they are reported online) could be linked to verbatim transcripts of the contrary testimony by his military advisers.[130] Flagging might also be used to combat media bias. For example, when then Judge Kavanaugh was nominated to the U.S. Supreme Court, NPR engaged in extremely biased reporting regarding and posted its reporting online.[131] The NPR post could be flagged with a reference to the *New York Times* analysis of the allegations, or to the *Washington Post* article questioning the allegations.[132]

However, there is always the risk that the flag will involve disinformation and point the reader to inaccurate information. In the case of the Hunter Biden laptop story, the media got it wrong. So, an attempt to link the laptop story to articles questioning its validity, would itself constitute disinformation. Likewise, if the Nunes intelligence report were linked to the Schiff denunciation of that report, the responsive speech might again involve the promotion of disinformation.[133]

---

[126] Ibid.

[127] Ibid.

[128] Supreme Court of the United States, 2024, 603 U.S. 43, *Murthy v. Missouri.*

[129] Stephens (2021).

[130] Ibid.

[131] Weaver (2025, pp. 88–91).

[132] *Ivi*, p. 376.

[133] Raj (2022).

In any event, it is not clear that fact checking or warnings have much impact on what people believe.[134] One study showed that such labels have some impact on believability.[135] For example, following the 2020 presidential election, 30% of the electorate believed that President Biden had prevailed because of fraud.[136] Three years later, after dozens of fact-checking organizations had weighed in on the issue, the numbers had not changed much with 30% of the people still believing that Biden had prevailed because of fraud.[137] As a result, although fact-checking operations blossomed during the pandemic and after the 2020 election, they seem to be in decline now.[138] X (formerly Twitter), which attached labels to Trumps posts, no longer does since it got rid of its fact checkers.[139] X now uses "Community Notes," which allows individual users to question the accuracy of information.[140]

The trend towards declining fact-checking is evident, not only in the U.S., but elsewhere.[141] The number of new fact-checking sites being created has declined, and some existing organizations have "gone quiet."[142] Part of the problem is that fact-checking organizations are not always viewed as "neutral" or "unbiased."[143] Because society has become so polarized, some choose to ignore fact-checking labels as unreliable.[144] As one commentator asked, "Who fact-checks the fact-checkers?"[145] Similar concerns were raised regarding a fact checking organization in India because one of the organizers is regarded as opinionated and abrasive.[146] Moreover, users may gravitate to other sources.[147]

There are also concerns regarding whether fact-checking labels are (or will be) accurate. Essentially, someone (the social media platform or an independent group) sets themselves up as the "arbiter of truth," and there is no assurance that they will get it right. In addition, there is always the possibility that the fact-checking label will itself involve disinformation and point the reader to inaccurate information. In the case of the Hunter Biden laptop story, the media got it wrong. So, any attempt to link the laptop story to articles questioning its validity, would itself constitute disinformation. Likewise, if the Nunes intelligence report were linked to the Schiff denunciation of that report, the responsive speech might again promote disinformation.

---

[134] Hsu and Thompson (2023).

[135] Nyhan (2017).

[136] Ibid.

[137] Ibid.

[138] Ibid («The number of fact-checking operations at news organizations and elsewhere has stagnated, and perhaps even fallen.»).

[139] Rutenberg and Conger (2024).

[140] Hsu and Thompson (2023).

[141] Ibid.

[142] Ibid.

[143] Ibid.

[144] Ibid.

[145] Ibid (Quoting Yasmin Green, chief executive of Jigsaw).

[146] Raj (2022).

[147] Ibid.

3.5 Community Notes

X did introduce a new system which it called "Community Notes" which allows anyone to post "corrections" on posts.[148] Users can respond by indicating whether the notes were "helpful."[149] Some question whether such notes have much impact: a study found that "the presence of a Community Note did not keep false information from spreading widely. Users who created misleading posts saw no change in their engagement for subsequent posts, suggesting that they paid no penalty for sharing falsehoods."[150] Moreover, since most posts received a "surge of attention" immediately after they are posted, Community Notes may come too late to counteract the disinformation.[151] Facebook created a similar system.

4 Conclusion

Disinformation is nothing new and is present in modern U.S. society. The problem of disinformation is undoubtedly heightened by the internet, and the fact that the internet enables virtually everyone to engage in widespread communication. However, the evidence clearly shows that our politicians have not been shy about spreading disinformation. Moreover, there is the problem of media bias which presents the public with limited and incomplete information regarding issues of public importance. The more difficult problem is how to deal with the problem of disinformation. The concept of a "disinformation board" seems to be inconsistent with the American tradition. In addition, it is doubtful whether government officials or social media platforms themselves can be trusted to weed our disinformation. Not only may governmental officials lack the competency to determine what is disinformation, there is ample evidence of governmental attempts to manipulate and control the censorial decisions of social media companies. In the final analysis, even though we realize that disinformation can distort the democratic process, the Court made clear in decisions like *New York Times, Inc. v. Sullivan,*[152] and *Near v. Minnesota,*[153] that information should not be withheld from the public even though it may contain an element of untruth. In the case of Hunter Biden's laptop, the American people were denied accurate information, during an election, because it was regarded as misinformation. Not only the media, but also social media platforms sought to suppress the Hunter Biden story.

---

[148] Hsu and Thompson (2023).

[149] Ibid.

[150] Ibid.

[151] Ibid.

[152] Supreme Court of the United States, *New York Times Co. v. Sullivan*, cit. p. 269.

[153] Supreme Court of the United States, *Near v. State of Minnesota*, cit.

References

47 U.S.C. § 230 (1934) In: Cornell Law School, Legal Information Institute. https://www.law.cornell.edu/uscode/text/47/230.
Baker CE (1978) Scope of the First Amendment Freedom of Speech. U.C.L.A. L Rev 25:964
Barrabi T (2021) Facebook ends ban on posts claiming COVID-19 is man-made: Facebook had previously insisted the claim had been 'debunked'. In: Fox Business. https://www.foxbusiness.com/technology/facebook-ends-ban-posts-claiming-covid-19-man-made [https://perma.cc/9RWH-CHBB]
Bork RH (1971) Neutral principles and some first amendment problems. Ind LJ 47(1):1
Bray H (2023) We ignore musks "Twitter files" at our peril. In: The Boston Globe. https://www.bostonglobe.com/2023/01/19/business/we-ignore-musks-twitter-filesour-peril/.
Brown EN (2022) The FBI paid Twitter $3.4 Million for processing requests. In: reason. https://reason.com/2022/12/19/the-fbi-paid-twitter-3-4-million-for-processing-requests/ [https://perma.cc/KAM2-BREW]
Chang CCK (2023) Revisiting disinformation laws in the age of social media. Ariz L J Emerg Technol 6(4)
Chen AK (2020) Free speech, rational deliberation and some truth about lies. Wm Mary L Rev 62(2):357
Cohen R (2019) Robert Mueller in the age of the unicorn. In: The New York Times. https://www.nytimes.com/2019/04/19/opinion/mueller-trump-russia-report.html.
Crowley D, Heyer P (eds) (2007) Communication in history: technology, culture, society, 5th edn. Boston
Emerson TI (1963) Toward a general theory of the first amendment. Yale LJ 72:877
Folkenflik D (2020) Analysis: questionable 'N.Y. Post' scoop driven by Ex-Hannity Producer and Giuliani. In: National Public Radio. https://www.npr.org/2020/10/17/924506867/analysis-questionable-n-y-post-scoop-driven-by-ex-hannity-producer-giuliani[https://perma.cc/3LEC-WEWY]
Fox A (2020) Automated political speech: regulating social media bots in the political sphere. First Amendment L Rev 18:114
Friedland T (2022) America dodged an arrow. In: The New York Times. https://www.nytimes.com/2022/11/09/opinion/midterms-election-america-arrow.html
Goldberg M (2020) Is the trump campaign colluding with Russia again? In: The New York Times. https://www.nytimes.com/2020/10/19/opinion/trump-campaign-rudy-giuliani.html
Goodyear MP (2021) Priam's Folly: United Stats v. Alvarez and the Fake News Trojan Horse. Stanford L Rev 73:194
Hakim D, Berzon A (2022) A big lie in a new package. In: The New York Times. https://www.nytimes.com/2022/05/29/us/politics/2000-mules-trump-conspiracy-theory.html
Hern A, Solon O (2018) Facebook closed 583m fake accounts in first three months of 2018: Firm's first quarterly moderation report also shows scale of spam, hate speech and violence. In: The Guardian. https://www.theguardian.com/technology/2018/may/15/facebook-closed-583m-fake-accounts-in-first-three-months-of-2018 [https://perma.cc/6W66-QLU7]
Hsu T, Thompson SA (2023) Fact checkers take stock of their efforts: 'It's Not Getting Better'. In: The New York Times. https://www.nytimes.com/2023/09/29/business/media/fact-checkers-misinformation.html
James F (2011) Jon Stewart 'Defends' Mainstream Media Against Fox News, Sort Of. In: National Public Radio, It's All About Politics. https://www.npr.org/sections/itsallpolitics/2011/06/20/137298761/jon-stewart-defends-mainstream-media-against-fox-news-sort-of [https://perma.cc/C2UC-JB4Z]
Keller MH (2018) The Flourishing Business of Fake YouTube Views. In: The New York Times. https://www.nytimes.com/interactive/2018/08/11/technology/youtube-fake-view-sellers.html#:~:text=Drawing%20on%20dozens%20of%20interviews,is%20not%20offering%20real%20viewership

Liasson M (2021) Democrats and some republicans fear how Trump's election lies may affect democracy. In: National Public Radio, All Things Considered. https://www.npr.org/2021/11/05/1052968081/democrats-and-some-republicans-fear-how-trumps-election-lies-may-affect-democrac [https://perma.cc/5LF6-RJ49]
Longe OB, Robert AB, Onwudebelu U (2009) Checking Internet masquerading using multiple CAPTCHA challenge-response systems. Paper presented at the 2nd International Conference on Adaptive Science & Technology (ICAST), Accra, Ghana, 14 Jan 2009
Mak T (2019) Congress may soon impose new regulations on Facebook. In: NPR. https://www.npr.org/2019/01/15/685656036/congress-may-soon-impose-new-regulations-on-facebook [https://perma.cc/D6UT-A55A]
Marnin J (2021) Fact check: is Facebook banning bible passages? In: Newsweek. https://www.newsweek.com/fact-check-facebook-banning-bible-passages-1565190
Mayton WT (1984) Seditious libel and the lost guarantee of a freedom of expression. Colum L Rev 84(1):91
Meiklejohn A (1961) The first amendment as an absolute. Sup Ct Rev 1961:245
Myers SL, Sullivan E (2022) Disinformation has become another untouchable problem in Washington. In: The New York Times. https://www.nytimes.com/2022/07/06/business/disinformation-board-dc.html
National Archives (2024) Declaration of Independence: a transcription. https://www.archives.gov/founding-docs/declaration-transcript
Newberg M (2017) As many as 48 million Twitter accounts aren't people, says study. In: CNBC. https://www.cnbc.com/2017/03/10/nearly-48-million-twitter-accounts-could-be-bots-says-study.html [https://perma.cc/MLP8-Q99J]
Nicas J (2019) Does Facebook really know how many fake accounts it has? In: N.Y. Times. https://www.nytimes.com/2019/01/30/technology/facebook-fake-accounts.html
Nyhan B (2017) Why the fact-checking at facebook needs to be checked. In: The New York Times, The Upshot. https://www.nytimes.com/2017/10/23/upshot/why-the-fact-checking-at-facebook-needs-to-be-checked.html.
Parks M, Bond S (2021) 5 Takeaways from Big Tech's misinformation hearing. In: NPR. https://www.npr.org/2021/03/25/981203566/5-takeaways-from-big-techs-misinformation-hearing [https://perma.cc/9RGD-NKAY]
Raj S (2022) In India, Debunking Fake News and running into the authorities. In: The New York Times. https://www.nytimes.com/2022/09/22/world/asia/india-debunking-fake-news.html
Roose K (2018) Facebook had a good election, but it can't let up on vigilance. In: The New York Times, The Shift. https://www.nytimes.com/2018/11/07/business/facebook-midterms-misinformation.html
Rosenthal A (2013) Clapper and carney get slippery on surveillance. In: The New York Times, Taking Note. https://archive.nytimes.com/takingnote.blogs.nytimes.com/2013/10/24/clapper-and-carney-get-slippery-on-surveillance/
Rutenberg J, Conger K (2024) Elon Musk is spreading election misinformation, but X's fact checkers are long gone. In: The New York Times. https://www.nytimes.com/2024/01/25/us/politics/elon-musk-election-misinformation-x-twitter.html
Sanders AK, Jones RL, Liu X (2019) Stemming the tide of fake news: a global study of decisions to regulate. J Int Med Ent Law 8:203
Savage C, Shane S (2013) N.S.A. leaker denies giving secrets to China. In: The New York Times. https://www.nytimes.com/2013/06/18/world/asia/nsa-leaker-denies-giving-classified-data-to-china.html
Schuyler AJ (2019) Regulating facts: a procedural framework for identifying, excluding and deterring the intentional or knowing proliferation of fake news online. U. Ill. J.L.T.P. 2019(1):211
Schwartz R (2007) The social shape of electronics. From communication in history: technology, culture, society, 5th edn. Pearson Allyn & Bacon, Boston

Seganga N (2022) What is DHS' Disinformation Governance Board and why is everyone so mad about it? In: CBS News. https://www.cbsnews.com/news/what-is-dhs-disinformation-governance-board-and-why-is-everyone-so-mad-about-it/ [https://perma.cc/9GPV-KHAE]

Shane S (2013a) Documents Detail Restrictions on N.S.A. Surveillance. In: The New York Times. https://www.nytimes.com/2013/06/21/us/politics/documents-detail-nsa-surveillance-rules.html

Shane S (2013b) No Morsel too minuscule for all-consuming NSA: from Spying on Leader of U.N. to tracking Drug Deals, on Ethos of 'Why Not?' In: The New York Times. https://www.nytimes.com/2013/11/03/world/no-morsel-too-minuscule-for-all-consuming-nsa.html

Shivaram D (2022) DHS pauses a board created to combat disinformation amid a campaign to discredit it. In: National Public Radio, Politics. https://www.npr.org/2022/05/18/1099848240/dhs-disinformation-group-pause[https://perma.cc/53QH-2QX6]

Simon S (2022) More details emerge in federal investigation into Hunter Biden. In: National Public Radio, Weekend Edition Saturday. https://www.npr.org/2022/04/09/1091859822/more-details-emerge-in-federal-investigation-into-hunter-biden[https://perma.cc/W3UH-FWDP]

Smith T (2022) Why is the "Big Lie" proving so hard to dispel? In: National Public Radio, All Things Considered. https://www.npr.org/2022/01/04/1070337968/why-is-the-big-lie-proving-so-hard-to-dispel [https://perma.cc/SNA9-H25Q]

Stanglin D (2013) Report: snowden says NSA can tap e-mail, Facebook chats. In: USA Today. https://www.usatoday.com/story/news/nation/2013/07/31/edward-snowden-guardian-nsa-facebook-tap-email-documents/2602519/ [https://perma.cc/93RE-4HBQ]

Star Chamber, 1606, 77 Eng. Rep. 250, *The Case De Libellis Famosis.*

Stephens B (2021) an ethically Challenged Presidency. In: The New York Times. https://www.nytimes.com/2021/10/05/opinion/biden-ethics-son.html

Sun H (2023) Regulating algorithmic disinformation. Colum J L Arts 46:367

Supreme Court of the United States, 1931, 283 U.S. 697, *Near v. Minnesota*

Supreme Court of the United States, 1942, 315 U.S. 568, *Chaplinsky v. New Hampshire*

Supreme Court of the United States, 1957, 354 U.S. 476, *Roth v. United States*

Supreme Court of the United States, 1964, 376 U.S. 254, *New York Times Co. v. Sullivan*

Supreme Court of the United States, 1964, 379 U.S. 64, *Garrison v. Louisiana*

Supreme Court of the United States, 1973, 413 U.S. 15, *Miller v. California*

Supreme Court of the United States, 1982, 458 U.S. 747, *Ferber v. New York*

Supreme Court of the United States, 1983, 461 U.S. 138, *Connick v. Myers*

Supreme Court of the United States, 1992, 505 U.S. 377, *R.A.V. v. City of St. Paul*

Supreme Court of the United States, 2002, 535 U.S. 564, *Ashcroft v. ACLU*

Supreme Court of the United States, 2003, 538 U.S. 343, *Virginia v. Black*

Supreme Court of the United States, 2010, 558 U.S. 310, *Citizens United v. Federal Election*

Supreme Court of the United States, 2011, 564 U.S. 786, *Brown v. Entertainment Merchants Ass'n*

Supreme Court of the United States, 2012, 567 U.S. 709, *United States v. Alvarez*

Supreme Court of the United States, 2022, 595 U.S. 468, *Houston Community College System v. Wilson*

Supreme Court of the United States, 2024, 603 U.S. 43, *Murthy v. Missouri*

Swanberg WA (1961) Citizen hearst: a biography of William Randolph Hearst. New York

The Editorial Board (2014) Edward Snowden, Whistle-Blower. In: The New York Times https://www.nytimes.com/2014/01/02/opinion/edward-snowden-whistle-blower.html

The Editorial Board (2023) Adam Schiff, disinformation man. In: The Wall Street Journal. https://www.wsj.com/articles/adam-schiff-disinformation-man-house-intelligence-committee-russia-devin-nunes-memo-twitter-files-matt-taibbi-11674166043

Titcomb J, Carson J (2018) Fake News: what exactly is it—and how can you spot it? In: The Telegraph

United States Supreme Court, 1919, 250 U.S. 616, *Abrams v. United States*

U.S. District Court for the Western District of Louisiana, 2023, 680 F.Supp.3d 630, *Missouri v. Biden*

Vincent J (2021) Facebook bans academics who researched ad transparency and misinformation on Facebook: the researchers say their work is being silenced. In: The Verge. https://www.theverge.com/2021/8/4/22609020/facebook-bans-academic-researchers-ad-transparency-misinformation-nyu-ad-observatory-plug-in[https://perma.cc/G2JF-34QS]
Watson CA (2018) Information literacy in a fake/false news world: an overview of the characteristics of fakes news and its historical developments. Int J Inf Literacy 46(2):93
Weaver RL (2022) Social media, Section 230, and free expression. Mercer L Rev 73(2):615–619
Weaver R (2025) Disinformation. From Gutenberg to the Internet: free speech, advancing technology & the implications for democracy, 3rd edn. Carolina Academic Press, Durham (in press)
Weaver R, Hancock C (2023) The first amendment: cases, materials and problems, 7th edn. Durham
Woodruff J (2020) Are trump allies sharing Russian disinformation about biden? In: PBS NewsHour. https://www.pbs.org/video/warning-signs-1602880956/.
Wu T (2020) Disinformation in the marketplace of ideas. Seton Hall L Rev 51(1):169–170
Younes J, Kheriaty A (2023) The white house covid censorship machine. In: The Wall Street Journal. https://www.wsj.com/articles/white-house-covid-censorship-machine-social-media-facebook-meta-executive-rob-flaherty-free-speech-google-11673203704

How Seriously Should Be Taken Disinformation? Constitutional and Policy Dilemmas in a Comparative Perspective

Oreste Pollicino

Abstract The spread of disinformation, particularly false and fabricated content in times of elections and war, as also amplified by the expansion of artificial intelligence systems, has captured the attention of policy-makers on a global scale. However, constitutional democracies tend to disagree about the strategies to address disinformation, moving from mostly protecting that type of content as free speech, such as in the USA, to approaching this issue as a risk for democracy as in the EU. If, on the one hand, freedom of expression can be considered the living core of a democratic society, on the other hand, concerns for democracy, particularly, in times of elections, pushes towards a more restrictive approach, thus leading the conversation towards a constitutional deadlock. Furthermore, no matter the approach taken by constitutional democracies, the different views on the constitutional relevance of disinformation are deeply influenced by online platforms which become essential tiles of a mosaic picturing the potential strategies and the limit of public enforcement. Within this framework, the author argues that the Union is advancing a different strategy to address online disinformation. By considering the need to strike a balance between the need to protect democratic values and protect economic freedoms in the internal market, the author examines the constitutional challenges of the European way to address disinformation which, as underlined by the Digital Services Act and the Strengthened Code of Practice on Disinformation, is not based on a top-down, vertical and rights-based approach but to a bottom-up, horizontal and risk-based framework.

O. Pollicino (✉)
Bocconi University, Milan, Italy
e-mail: oreste.pollicino@unibocconi.it

R. Mastroianni and C. Massa (eds.), *Disinformation in New and Old Media in the XXI Century*, Ius Gentium: Comparative Perspectives on Law and Justice 136,
https://doi.org/10.1007/978-3-032-18830-4_3

1 Freedom of Expression and Information as a Prerequisite for Democracy

Historically, the concept of freedom of expression has been recognised within the legal culture of Western democracies since the end of the eighteenth century. Art. 11 of the Declaration of the Rights of Man and of the Citizen adopted on 26 August 1789 expressly states that «The free communication of ideas and of opinions is one of the most precious rights of man» and accordingly that «Any citizen may therefore speak, write and publish freely, except what is tantamount to the abuse of this liberty in the cases determined by Law». Similarly, the First Amendment of the Constitution of the United States of America, which was adopted in 1791 and is still a cornerstone of US constitutional jurisprudence on free speech, provides that Congress (and indeed any other government institution at federal or state level) «shall make no law... abridging the freedom of speech, or of the press; or the right of the people peaceably to assemble, and to petition the Government for a redress of grievances».

Later, in the wake of European totalitarian regimes that severely violated rights associated with (amongst other things) freedom of expression, the new instruments of international human rights law put in place during the second half of the twentieth century resolutely reasserted the core role of freedom of expression as an indispensable right of every person. Accordingly, art. 19 of the Universal Declaration of Human Rights of 1948, provides that «Everyone has the right to freedom of opinion and expression; this right includes freedom to hold opinions without interference and to seek, receive and impart information and ideas through any media and regardless of frontiers». Later, this provision was subsequently reiterated by art. 19 of the International Covenant on Civil and Political Rights of 1966.[1]

In Italy, the case law and constitutional doctrine from the post-WW2 era placed particular importance on the essential role played by freedom of expression, which was crystallised within art. 21 of the newly adopted Constitution, within a democratic framework. This freedom was a core focus of the writings of renowned commentators of the time—including for instance, amongst others, the fundamental studies in this area by Paolo Barile.[2] It was recognised by the Italian Constitutional Court during the 1960s and 1970s as a «precondition... for the way of being and the development of the life of the country in all of its cultural, political and social aspects»,[3] and also as a genuine «cornerstone of the democratic order»,[4] so much so as to constitute «the

---

[1] «1. Everyone shall have the right to hold opinions without interference. 2. Everyone shall have the right to freedom of expression; this right shall include freedom to seek, receive and impart information and ideas of all kinds, regardless of frontiers, either orally, in writing or in print, in the form of art, or through any other media of his choice. 3. The exercise of the rights provided for in paragraph 2 of this article carries with it special duties and responsibilities. It may therefore be subject to certain restrictions, but these shall only be such as are provided by law and are necessary: (a) For respect of the rights or reputations of others; (b) For the protection of national security or of public order (ordre public), or of public health or morals».

[2] Barile (1975).

[3] Italian Constitutional Court, 4 February 1965, n. 9, para. 3 *in diritto*.

[4] Italian Constitutional Court, 17 April 1969, n. 84, para. 5 *in diritto*.

highest perhaps» of all the «primary and fundamental rights»[5] provided for under the Constitution. At the same time, the European Court of Human Rights pursued a similar approach in acknowledging the importance of freedom of expression under art. 10 of the ECHR, while however stressing the primary importance of freedom of the press and journalism within the democratic context.[6]

It has been apparent since the outset how freedom of expression is characterised primarily by an individual dimension. It corresponds to the fundamental right of all individuals to express their own positions and ideas through any medium of their choosing: speech, writing, the press, art, music, satire and even online. Indeed, art. 21 of the Italian Constitution clarifies specifically that the right to speak one's mind freely must be exercised through «speech, writing or any other broadcast medium»: as the clause is worded openly, it clearly leaves scope for using new digital technology to express ideas.[7]

Moreover, it is an essential instrument through which people can express their personality and intellectual background and values, thereby participating fully in the social community. That said, freedom of expression and of information also has a fundamental collective dimension as it is for all intents and purposes a precondition for the proper operation of democratic debate, and hence of democracy itself. In its famous key judgment in *Handyside v. United Kingdom*, the ECtHR cast light on that dual dimension to freedom of expression, holding that it is essential not only for the personal development of all human beings but also for achieving social progress as a whole.[8]

On the other hand, as has been observed by Michel Rosenfeld[9] in relation to the USA, free speech has been regarded as an essential precondition for the quest for truth, and thus as being fundamentally important for the advancement of society as a whole. As such, it has exerted a particularly significant influence on the decisions of the US Supreme Court. Indeed, this interpretation of freedom of expression can account for the success of the metaphor of the "free marketplace of ideas", which has been so central within US constitutional case law since the start of the twentieth century. Within this perspective, the specific aim of policies that aim to ensure the utmost priority for that free marketplace of ideas is to enable society, in the aggregate, to arrive at the truth.[10] However, it must be stressed that this approach under US

---

[5] Italian Constitutional Court, 5 July 1971, n. 168, para. 3 *in diritto*.

[6] ECtHR, *Sunday Times v. United Kingdom*, 6538/74, 26 April 1979, para. 65: «Freedom of expression constitutes one of the essential foundations of a democratic society […] These principles are of particular importance as far as the press is concerned».

[7] On this topic, see Bassini (2019).

[8] ECtHR, *Handyside v. United Kingdom*, 5493/72, 7 December 1976, para. 49: «Freedom of expression constitutes one of the essential foundations of such a [democratic] society, one of the basic conditions for its progress and for the development of every man». Accordingly, see, *ex multis*, ECtHR, *Bouton v. France*, 22636/19, 13 October 2022.

[9] Rosenfeld (2003, pp. 1523–1568), specifically pp. 1529–1535.

[10] The reference is clearly to Justice Holmes' famous dissenting opinion in *Abrams v. United States*, 250 US 616 (1919), p. 630: «But when men have realized that time has upset many fighting faiths, they may come to believe even more than they believe the very foundations of their own conduct

constitutional law underscores another substantial difference between US free speech case law and the European paradigm on freedom of expression and information.

The relationship between free speech and democracy in the terms described above can be construed from a "collective" perspective: the inevitability of the victory of the "best" point of view, recognised as a direct consequence of the free marketplace of ideas, is desirable precisely in view of its aim to benefit society as a whole. On the other hand, this approach seemingly disregards the issue as to whether individuals have an interest in receiving those particularly persuasive forms of expression. Besides, an approach of this type also appears to be in keeping with the traditional suspicion within First Amendment case law of any governmental limits on phenomena such as hate speech, based on the assumption that there is no individual right not to be exposed to these types of "polluting" expression.[11] Moreover, considered also in formal terms, the First Amendment does not make any reference to a "passive" dimension to free speech, namely to the rights of individuals when exposed to the speech of others.

On the other hand, under the European system both art. 10 of the ECHR and art. 11 of the CFREU expressly provide—in keeping with art. 19 of the Universal Declaration of Human Rights and art. 19 of the International Covenant on Civil and Political Rights—that freedom of expression includes the right to "receive" information and ideas: in other words, there is an express recognition of the passive dimension to freedom of expression and information.

In the light of these considerations, we need to consider what the relationship between freedom of expression, democracy and technology will look like in future. Specifically, if, as has been demonstrated, freedom of expression (and in Europe the

---

that the ultimate good desired is better reached by free trade in ideas—that the best test of truth is the power of the thought to get itself accepted in the competition of the market, and that truth is the only ground upon which their wishes safely can be carried out. That, at any rate, is the theory of our Constitution [...] I think that we should be eternally vigilant against attempts to check the expression of opinions that we loathe and believe to be fraught with death, unless they so imminently threaten immediate interference with the lawful and pressing purposes of the law that an immediate check is required to save the country». The metaphor was later taken up, in the digital contest in *Reno v. ACLU*, 521 US 844 (1997), p. 885.

[11] In this sense, see, *ex multis*, US Supreme Court, *Snyder v. Phelps*, 562 US 443, 2011, pp. 459–460, in which the Supreme Court emphasized that only in very limited cases-specifically, in cases of "captive audiences"-the right of individuals not to be exposed to unwanted modes of expression is to be protected. The case, specifically, concerned an action for compensation for non-pecuniary damages suffered by the plaintiff as a result of the organization by a fundamentalist Christian congregation of a demonstration of a homophobic nature on the occasion of the funeral of his 20-year-old son, who died during a military action in Iraq. In that judgment, the Court also points out that the doctrine of captive audience is to be interpreted in a generally restrictive sense, such that in the case at hand it concluded that the demonstration had been held at a sufficient distance from the place of the funeral that it did not permit recourse to that doctrine: «As a general matter, we have applied the captive audience doctrine only sparingly to protect unwilling listeners from protected speech [...] Here, Westboro stayed well away from the memorial service. Snyder could see no more than the tops of the signs when driving to the funeral. And there is no indication that the picketing in any way interfered with the funeral service itself. We decline to expand the captive audience doctrine to the circumstances presented here».

related freedom of information) is closely interlinked with a society's progress and democratic development, there is a compelling need to consider how the dissemination of digital platforms and the advance of artificial intelligence (hereinafter: "AI") technologies have had (or will have) an impact on that aspect of this freedom.

In this regard, is evident that disinformation is a perfect laboratory to assess how constitutional democracies are facing the dilemma between, on the one hand and, protecting the need to protect freedom of speech and, on the other hand, avoiding the pollution of the digital public sphere through the explosive cocktail disinformation-AI.

2 Disinformation: Theoretical Basis and Technological Reloading

Disinformation is not a product of the digital age. False news has always circulated across society, as demonstrated by the case of the "Great Moon Hoax" in 1835. However, the circulation of false and inaccurate content on the Internet, and particularly on social media, has amplified the phenomenon, as is usually the case in cyberspace. The Pizzagate example is only one case that underlines how disinformation in the digital age has raised new critical constitutional questions.[12] Growing concern about potential risks for democratic discourse and processes has emerged in recent years,[13] particularly in the wake of the Brexit referendum and the US presidential election, both in 2016.[14] Democratic concerns about disinformation have soared back to the political forefront in the context of the Cambridge Analytica scandal and the COVID-19 pandemic.[15] And recent conflicts, particularly in Ukraine, have underlined how disinformation is far beyond only a concern for individual freedoms or national borders.[16]

Disinformation is primarily connected with the right to freedom of expression, thus raising questions about the tolerance of false content in a democratic society,[17] and consequently what degree of limits on freedom of speech can be constitutionally justified in this case.[18] Primarily, the question is not whether regulating disinformation influences freedom of expression but the reasons for considering that as a challenge for freedom of expression.[19]

---

[12] Sunstein (2017).

[13] Martens et al. (2018).

[14] Bayer et al. (2019, p. 15).

[15] Joint Communication to the European Parliament, the European Council, the Council, the European Economic and Social Committee and the Committee of the Regions, Tackling COVID-19 disinformation—Getting the facts right, JOIN(2020) 8 final.

[16] Susi et al. (eds) (2022, p. 4).

[17] Pitruzzella and Pollicino (2020).

[18] Pollicino (2020).

[19] Sunstein (2020, p. 388).

There is no doubt that the Internet has significantly contributed to information pluralism,[20] promoting exchange of information and opinions to unprecedented levels.[21] Nevertheless, great quantities of information may pose problems as to their substantive quality, trustworthiness and the reliability of sources, mitigating the benefits of a purely quantitative pluralistic information ecosystem, at the expense of a truly qualitative one. Although the rise of information pluralism is generally to be welcomed, the governance of the digital environment raises concerns in terms of the 'quality' of the information sources.

In this sense, the "marketplace of ideas" has been exposed to a process of transformation in the digital age. Later we will discuss why this metaphor, and metaphors in comparative constitutional law in general, should be taken seriously, as demonstrated by the metaphor encapsulated in the dissenting opinion of Justice Holmes in *Abrams v. United States*.[22] According to Justice Holmes, although men try to support their positions by criticising opposing ideas, they must not be persuaded that their opinions are certain. Only the free exchange of ideas can confirm the accuracy of each position, creating a "free marketplace of ideas". This metaphor leads to constitutional implications in terms of defining the boundaries between freedom of expression and falsehood. By adopting this liberal view, even falsehood has the possibility to contribute to the competition of ideas, and there should be no interferences by public powers in this space. There is no need to regulate disinformation, since any approach aiming to tackle disinformation would affect the free competition of ideas that leads to the balance.

However, this view does not consider the possible failures of the marketplace of ideas. The digital environment has underlined how the marketplace of ideas is not free but is shaped by public and private influences. In the eyes of the US Supreme Court, the Internet—the new free marketplace of ideas—offers new coordinates and spaces for the exercise of freedom of speech, where it is necessary to look through lenses and categories different from those that apply to traditional media. Hence, in *Reno v. ACLU*,[23] the use of the metaphor of the free marketplace of ideas has been one of the main causes of the constitutional issues raised by the consolidation of new private actors such as online platforms.

The concept of disinformation is not only influenced by public actors, but also by other actors governing online speech. One inevitable element of the discussion is the key role of private parties, particularly online platforms, within the current news and information ecosystem. The process of content moderation contributes to setting standards for tackling disinformation, increasing the power of online platforms to make decisions on constitutional conflicting interests. The constant development of technology, embedding algorithmic systems and the risk of abuse of deep fakes, may

---

[20] ECtHR, *Ahmet Yıldırım v. Turkey*, 3111/10, 18 December 2012, para 54.

[21] ECJ, case C-160/15, *GS Media v. Sanoma Media Netherlands*, para. 45.

[22] US Supreme Court, *Abrams v. United States*, 250, U.S. 616 (1919).

[23] US Supreme Court, *Reno v. American Civil Liberties Union*, 521 U.S. 844 (1997).

be a threat to democracy and national security,[24] causing fears for users' privacy and autonomy, which are at the heart of the individual right to dignity.[25] Fundamental rights and liberties have traditionally been devised *vis-à-vis* state powers and authorities; therefore, the traditional paradigm of fundamental rights proves hard to uphold against private parties.

As public actors increasingly rely on online platforms to perform monitoring and enforcement activities, sometimes delegating de facto public functions, such as removing or blocking content, to these platforms, the role and actions of these platforms raise constitutional questions. In the aftermath of the COVID-19 pandemic, this process of delegation has accelerated consistently. The need to ensure social distancing, as a tool to break the chain of infections, led individuals and institutions to turn to digital technologies for public services such as education, work and healthcare. Against this backdrop, online intermediaries and private digital firms acquired an increasingly central role, since the infrastructures and services offered by them covered a necessary instrumental function to ensure the continuance of everyday life.[26] Moreover, public policy and governmental practices soon began to rely heavily on cooperation with these private actors, as well as on the exploitation of the technical apparatuses designed by online platforms, thus complementing the role of courts in the digital age.[27]

Besides, the marketplace of ideas metaphor does not consider the existence of alternative constitutional models for looking at the relationship between freedom of expression and falsehood. Against the backdrop of increasing fear for the relationship between disinformation and democratic discourse, and its subsequent impact on deliberative democracy, governments around the world have attempted to address this challenge by adopting different approaches.[28] Laws, codes of practice, task forces and social media community standards are only some of the norms that have been shaped the fight against disinformation. The Digital Services Act is, as we will see, a paradigmatic example of the approaches to online disinformation.[29] Likewise, the new Strengthened European Code of Practice on Disinformation is an example of how strategies to address disinformation are no longer left only to hard law and self-regulation.[30] However, some states have made no regulatory responses to disinformation, while others criminalised the spread of rumours and false content even before the challenges raised by online disinformation.

---

[24] Chesney and Citron (2018, p. 1753). For instance, California Assembly Bill No. 730, approved on 3 October 2019, establishes the illegality of circulation of doctored videos, images or audio of politicians during a 60-day pre-electoral period.

[25] Federal Constitutional Court, Population Census Decision, 1 BvR 209/83, 15 December 1983, BVerfGE 65, 1.

[26] Rahman (2018, p. 1621).

[27] Balkin (2009, p. 427).

[28] Robinson (2019); De Gregorio and Perotti (2019).

[29] Regulation (EU) 2022/2065 of the European Parliament and of the Council of 19 October 2022 on a Single Market for Digital Services and amending Directive 2000/31/EC (Digital Services Act), PE/30/2022/REV/1, OJ L 277, 27.10.2022, pp. 1–102.

[30] Strengthened Code of Practice on Disinformation (2022).

The central issue relates to the opportunity to impose restrictions on content designed to circulate online, and to introduce mechanisms for limiting this content. This raises questions on the 'constitutional feasibility' of a design aimed at repressing the phenomena of disinformation, moving from the recognition of their detrimental effects for users within a multitude of situations and contexts.

The response to disinformation entails dealing with the degree of protection of free speech. The decision to intervene to filter falsehoods online requires questioning whether, and to what extent, it is acceptable to enforce limitations on freedom of expression regarding falsehoods. This is a multifaceted question, since each legal system adopts a different paradigm of protection, even where they share a common liberal matrix, such as in the case of Europe and the US; in other words, it is a matter of understanding the limits of freedom of speech and the balancing of this right with legitimate interests or the safeguarding of other constitutional rights. Therefore, the principle of the rule of law cannot be neglected when defining the boundaries for addressing the fight against disinformation online.

The relevance of the right to freedom of expression, and the crucial role of falsehood, were underlined in the seventeenth century by Milton,[31] and in the nineteenth century by Mill,[32] supporting a liberal view considering that even falsehoods could contribute towards reaching the truth, especially avoiding the risk of knowledge's dogmatisation.[33] Milton, in his *Aeropagitica*, lashed out against censure of the press, citing the concept of truth and comparing knowledge to water, and the truth to a gushing foundation. What must be avoided, in this paradigm, is whatever can block the free flow of ideas that leads to progress towards truth. For Milton, censure could thus affect that process of approaching the truth, by impeding or restricting the emergence of new ideas. According to Milton, the truth prevails in a free and open context of ideas. Therefore, those ideas cannot be subject to limitations ahead of time that can "compete" in the battle against dogmas. But Milton's experience is emblematic: despite this strenuous opposition, he accepted the role of censor, based on the law he had so strongly challenged. This passage marks the connection between trust in the search for truth and the possibility of enforcing sanctions when, after appropriate investigations, it is possible to distinguish truth from falsehood, denying protection for the latter. Freedom of expression is thus enhanced by a conception based on the notion of truth; free and open flow is the key concept of this paradigm, which has not, however, become a true model of freedom of speech.

These liberal ideas protecting individuals against the interferences of public actors are still the core of the right to freedom of expression, as underlined in the twentieth century by Justice Holmes in his dissenting opinion in the aforementioned US Supreme Court decision *Abrams v. United States*.[34] Constitutional democracies tend to tolerate the political exchange of views as a precondition of pluralism, or, to use a

---

[31] Milton (1644).

[32] Mill (1859).

[33] *Ibid.*

[34] US Supreme Court, *Abrams v. United States*, cit.

neo-liberal metaphor, of the free marketplace of ideas. Although the spread of disinformation can produce serious consequences in the offline world, disinformation has still been considered an opportunity for promoting the exchange of ideas. This liberal view of free speech has also extended to Japan. As underlined by Mizutani, post-war Japanese constitutional jurisprudence has mainly been influenced by US constitutional jurisprudence.[35]

Even if, as underlined by Abbamonte and Gori, freedom of expression is a critical value of the EU, freedom of expression is limited in order to protect other constitutional values.[36] It is not by chance that the ECHR and the CFREU both contain clauses for the abuse of rights, as a means to avoid granting absolute protection to one right and leading to the destruction of other fundamental rights, undermining de facto their constitutional relevance.[37]

It is interesting to look at *United States v. Alvarez* as an example of how strategies against disinformation are shaped by the constitutional protection of free speech, and the concept of falsehood.[38] The case, which made it to the Supreme Court, was triggered by a false statement by the petitioner of having received a Medal of Honor, and his subsequently being charged under the Stolen Valor Act, a law that punishes whoever falsely claims the possession of medals or other military decorations. The Supreme Court was called on to judge the conformity of the charges with the First Amendment. The case provided the occasion for the Supreme Court to revisit its arguments regarding the limits on freedom of expression admissible under the Constitution. For the Supreme Court, simple falsity is not sufficient to exclude the use of certain expressions from protection under the First Amendment. This characterisation, finding that falsity is never relevant per se, is also found, for example, in the context of defamation, a crime that punishes the use of false statements only if they are supported by the mental categories of intent or negligence, coinciding with the awareness of the falsity or the negligent omission of measures sufficient to reveal the falsity of the information. Precisely with regard to this example, the Supreme Court stresses that the existence of requirements beyond that of mere falsity serves to guarantee greater freedom of speech, not to restrict it. The charge against Alvarez was thus declared unconstitutional by the Supreme Court, including due to the absence of a causal connection between the limitation of freedom of speech and the interest of the state in protecting the integrity of the military honour system. The Supreme Court concluded that, «[t]he remedy for speech that is false is speech that is true».

These different approaches are increasingly subject to comparison, with the advent of a means of communication—the Internet—that has allowed the connection of users and their ideas, opinions and expressions of thought, in various parts of the world. Discussions that involve activists on the Web, and from non-governmental organisations, often invoke the idea of self-regulation[39]—which tends to be recessive, in light

---

[35] See the special report on Japan by Mizutani E.

[36] See the special report on the EU by Abbamonte G, Gori P.

[37] Art. 54 CFREU; art. 17 ECHR.

[38] See the special report on the US by Jacobs L.

[39] Johnson and Post (1996, p. 1371).

of the unquestioned ability of public authorities to interfere with the functioning of Internet[40]—or the idea of supranational charters of rights.[41]

Therefore, with respect to disinformation, the essential questions on its limitability first encompass whether, and to what extent, falsehoods may be granted protection under freedom of expression; and, second, whether dissemination of a falsehood with an intent to harm identified targets, or society at large, may be restricted or subject to sanctions.

The primary challenge for any kind of intervention on disinformation, whether *ex post* or *ex ante*, is that of defining its scope in a sufficiently clear yet neutral manner. Vague or overly broad definitions display the risk of overenforcement, thus causing a chilling effect on free speech, as well as deepening legal uncertainty; or, on the other hand, of making the law hardly enforceable in practice, and therefore ineffective. This is why words and definitions matter.

3 Disinformation, Misinformation and Fake News: Definitions

In order to understand the effective scope of the impact of AI and developments in digital technology, one preliminary aspect of particular importance concerns the very terminology used to refer to disinformation.[42] Indeed, although the term "fake news" has increasingly crept into everyday language, usage of that expression has increasingly attracted criticism in recent years not only within an academic setting but also, above all, from a policy making perspective.

This position was expressed in particular by the High Level Group on Fake News and Online Disinformation (HLEG) established by the European Commission. In its Final Report[43] published in 2018 it rejected the term "fake news" essentially for two reasons: first of all, the notion of fake news risks being too narrowly framed, as it excludes a variety of different types of disinformation[44]; secondly, over time, the way in which the term is used in the media and in everyday language has caused its meaning to become distorted, above all in the light its exploitation by certain

[40] Goldsmith and Wu (2006).

[41] Segura-Serrano (2006, p. 191).

[42] In this sense, see Dunn and Durante (2023, pp. 58–61).

[43] De Cock Buning et al. (2018).

[44] *Ivi.*, p. 10. For example, disinformation consists not only of completely false news, but also of forms of mixing together elements of information that are more or less true; in addition, certain instances of disinformation may take forms other than those traditionally associated with the concept of "news," in fact including such cases as the creation of fake accounts or networks of followers, as well as the fabrication or manipulation of videos, the use of targeted advertisements, trolling activities (especially when organized and coordinated), and the dissemination of memes. On this point, see also Dupuis and Williams (2019, pp. 1412–1418). On the meme phenomenon, see Marino (2015, pp. 43–66).

politicians and their supporters with the aim of discrediting or rejecting unfavourable news, information and opinions.[45]

In view of the above, it makes more sense to speak in terms of "disinformation" which, according to the HLEG, includes all forms of free expression that assert false, inaccurate, or misleading information (in many cases having been created with spurious intent) that is presented and spread with the specific purpose of securing economic, political or ideological gain and/or causing public harm, including interference with electoral and democratic processes.[46] In line with this approach, also the European Democracy Action Plan adopted in 2020 defines the concept of "disinformation" as "false or misleading content that is spread with an intention to deceive or secure economic or political gain and which may cause public harm".[47]

However, it must be pointed out that the concept of disinformation, construed in these terms, covers not so much conduct that the law regards as being inherently unlawful (such as for instance defamation or slander) but rather all cases in which the production and spreading of false content is not in itself unlawful but nonetheless causes potential harm to democratic principles and values. It is moreover precisely these cases that represent the greatest challenge for national and European lawmakers as they require the public interest in the proper functioning of the democratic state to be offset against the need not to interfere disproportionately with the freedom of individual citizens to behave in a manner that the law considers, in itself, to be lawful.

However, a distinction can be drawn between disinformation and the related yet clearly different notion of "misinformation" based on the whether or not there was any intention to create and spread false content, coupled with an intention to cause harm or to secure a gain. Classification as "information disorder"[48] is conditional upon a subjective element as it implies specifically the absence of any intention to disseminate false information, and hence involves the dissemination of material that is considered to be genuine.[49] It is important to note that, in most cases, online disinformation tends to be shared and spread further by people different from those who created it. This means that the very same content can amount to *disinformation* if one considers the people who created and spread it with the aim of causing harm or drawing benefit from it, despite being aware of the fact that it was false. On the

[45] De Cock Buning et al. (2018, p. 10).

[46] *Ibid.*: «We define it as false, inaccurate, or misleading information designed, presented and promoted to intentionally cause public harm or for profit. The risk of harm includes threats to democratic political processes and values, which can specifically target a variety of sectors, such as health, science, education, finance and more. It is driven by the production and promotion of disinformation for economic gains or for political or ideological goals, but can be exacerbated by how different audiences and communities receive, engage, and amplify disinformation».

[47] Communication from the Commission to the European Parliament, the Council, the European Economic and Social Committee and the Committee of the Regions on the European democracy action plan, COM/2020/790 final.

[48] Wardle and Derashkan (2017).

[49] A historical example of misinformation, described in Jack (2017) was the one, long before the advent of the Internet, in which the Chicago Daily Tribune, relying on the opinions of its political analysts and election polls of the previous days, had erroneously reported in its morning edition that Dewey had defeated Truman in the 1948 U.S. presidential election.

other hand, it may be classified as *misinformation* it one considers those people who, after receiving the information, helped to spread it in the mistaken conviction that it was true. This is in fact typical of the internet as an ecosystem, where disinformation is liable to spread like wildfire and can easily "go viral".[50]

Bad faith information is yet another phenomenon, albeit one less significant for our present purposes. It involves the spreading of information that, whilst being true (or in any case based on genuine facts) is however communicated and spread with the specific aim of causing harm.

These three phenomena—disinformation, misinformation and bad faith information—represent potentially significant dangers, albeit of different intensity, to the healthy functioning of a democratic society as they can all interfere with decision making processes. Disinformation in particular directly aims to manipulate or distort reality with a view to shifting public opinion or reinforcing particular positions that are favourable to the "disinformer". And it is precisely for this reason that it has attracted the attention of European and national lawmakers, which have defined it as a synthesis between the objective element of "falseness" and the subjective element of "fault", defined in terms of an awareness of the falseness coupled with the spreading of those falsehoods for selfish purposes.

Moreover, it must be stressed that the very concept of disinformation can embrace a range of different scenarios with varying degrees of severity.[51] As a result, there is a clear need for nuanced and calibrated strategies, above all in view of the requirement, at the same time, to guarantee full protection for freedom of expression and information. Moreover, the HLEG has noted that, as it is itself a multifaceted phenomenon, disinformation has to be dealt with according to a "multi-dimensional" approach incorporating not only legal sanctions but also, and above all, initiatives aimed at promoting transparency, developing citizens' media and information literacy, emancipating and empowering users and journalists, and promoting a pluralist media ecosystem characterised by diversity and sustainability.[52]

4 The Digital Free Marketplace of Ideas

«The Internet is a new free marketplace of ideas»: this is the preferred metaphor of those who, within scholarly and public debate, take the view that the issue of fake news need not be addressed (and confronted) by public authorities (and public law). As underlined by Jacobs, the constitutional protection of free speech aims to facilitate representative democracy and promote individual autonomy. These values lead to the

[50] Wardle (2020): «When disinformation is shared it often turns into misinformation. Misinformation also describes false content, but the person sharing doesn't realize that it is false or misleading. Often a piece of disinformation is picked up by someone who doesn't realize it's false and that person shares it with their networks, believing that they are helping».

[51] Wardle (2017).

[52] De Cock Buning (2018, p. 10).

distinction between government regulations of speech, and speech regulations that are content-neutral.

Consequently, according to the marketplace of ideas paradigm, if it is true that, under the First Amendment, there is «no such thing as a false idea» in the material world,[53] this is even truer in the digital word, thanks to the enhanced opportunity to express thoughts. In other words, public authorities should not have any role in dealing with the ever-growing phenomena of disinformation on the Internet, because users are (optimistically) supposed to have all the tools they need in order to select the most convincing ideas and true news, disregarding news that is unconvincing or fake.

This position underlines an expression of complete trust in the capacity for self-correction of the market for information. However, the real challenge is how such a process of verification should be conducted, according to the champions of the free market of ideas metaphor, since by definition scarcity of resources is an analogue and not a digital limit, with the result that there is no need to protect pluralism of information on the Internet, and that legal rules (and especially public law) should take a step back in the name of the alleged self-corrective capacity of the information market. Just as the economic market knows no test of product "validity" but allows demand to drive supply, relying on the market to distinguish between viable and shoddy products, the best way of dealing with the phenomenon of disinformation in the information market is to secure the widest possible dissemination of all news, including news from contradictory and unreliable sources.

However, this thesis is unconvincing, as demonstrated by the constitutional tensions underlined by recent events such as the COVID-19 pandemic and the conflict in Ukraine. The limits of the free marketplace of ideas in the digital age relate primarily to at least three reasons: the scarcity of users' attention, the differing levels of protection of free speech across legal systems, and the limits of a neo-liberal metaphor.

Firstly, while it may be the case that the problem of scarcity of technical resources does not affect the Internet, our attention and time continue to be scarce "products". In fact, while the amount of available information is growing, the 24 h comprising a day cannot be extended. Against this background, when faced with this information overload, the temptation for users will be to search for news, information and ideas that enhance their previous thoughts and preferences, leading to the process of group polarisation.

The need to regulate pluralism becomes more pressing in markets characterised by scarcity of resources: it is here that those who occupy a dominant or oligopolistic position can influence or distort the functioning of the market. When the character of scarcity of a resource is lost, the scenario changes. Therefore, the issue of pluralism, today, does not appear to raise the same criticalities as it did in the past. In the information system, the advent of Internet allows small and large operators to emerge in a market framework that tends to be fragmented and varied. Even with the advent of Internet, the condition of scarcity persists, that no longer regards frequency resources

[53] US Supreme Court, *Gertz v. Welch*, 418 U.S. 323 (1974).

but, rather, an even more precious resource: the attention of the user. The result seems to be that, quite paradoxically, despite (or perhaps precisely due to) the unlimited amount of information on the Internet, there is a less pluralistic exchange of different opinions than in traditional media, where the scarcity of sources is still an issue.

Secondly, it is reasonable to ask whether the marketplace of ideas metaphor is well suited to the scope (and limits) of protection of free speech on a global scale. For instance, the protection for freedom of expression in Europe is more limited than in the US. Regarding this issue, it is sufficient to compare the wording of the First Amendment of the US Constitution with art. 10 ECHR. Besides, it is not simply a question of differences in scope, but also of a difference in focus. While the First Amendment mainly addresses the active dimension of the right to freely express one's own thoughts, art. 10 ECHR emphasises the passive dimension of the right to be pluralistically informed (as does art. 11 CFREU). In this respect, it could be argued that fake news is not constitutionally covered by the European vision of free speech. Or, to put it differently, the European courts would find it very difficult to accept the view of the US Supreme Court, according to which, as alluded to previously, «Under the First Amendment there is no such thing as a false idea. However pernicious an opinion may seem, we depend for its correction not on the conscience of judges and juries but on the competition of other ideas».[54]

Thirdly, metaphorical language fits in very well with legal reasoning, but it should be handled properly (and with care).[55] The word "metaphor" implies knowledge transfer across domains (from the Greek *meta pherein*, to "carry over"), thus leading to the source domain and the target domain. The "free market of ideas" metaphor carries over, from the source domain of economic activity to the target domain of speech, a systematic set of entailments that supersedes the limitations of the older free-speech model. In order to fully understand it, it is important not to forget the features of the source "market" domain when Judge Holmes used the metaphor in 1919, and when the US Supreme Court subsequently adapted it to the Internet in 1997. Holmes wrote during a period of *laissez-faire* capitalism, in which both the liberal state and market competition were at their zeniths. If Judge Holmes was sceptical about any external verification of the truth, and removal of news proven to be false, the concept of a free market provided a meaningful alternative model for the notion that truth, just like economic well-being, could result from competition between (true and false) ideas and information. Similarly, when the US Supreme Court of 1997 borrowed the metaphor, referring to the Internet as the "new market place of ideas", the economic market of the Web (during its period of genesis) was absolutely free, and was not in any way affected by dominant positions, never mind monopolies or oligopolies.

However, if these considerations would provide solid grounds to protect even false expressions, it is necessary to observe that even democratic states do not ensure the same degree of protection to the right to freedom of expression. Within this context, the metaphor of the free marketplace of ideas and the proposed test for the truth

[54] *Ibid.*

[55] Morelli and Pollicino (2020, p. 616).

(competition in the absence of any public control) made perfect sense. By contrast, today the same metaphor seems to have been completely decontextualised, given that the economic market, as the source domain from which the metaphor has been taken, is far from free. Against this background, if disinformation is arguably the most significant and pervasive source of failure in the marketplace of ideas, one can surely not exclude the possibility of intervention by public authorities, because, in contrast to the US Supreme Court's definition of the Internet as the "new free marketplace of ideas", the source domain of the relevant digital market is anything but a free market, being characterised by economic concentration and the strength of (a few) private operators. Nobody is advocating for a "public tribunal of the true", or for enhancement of the liability regime of new (and old) social platforms. The only point that should be quite clearly made is that metaphors in digital law should (also) be managed with care. Otherwise, the concrete risk is of being lost in legal metaphors.

If these considerations would be enough to explain the constraints for democratic states when deciding to address falsehoods, the role of the digital environment as a channel for disseminating false content makes the entire picture even more intricate. The digital environment amplifies the challenges raised by disinformation, not only for the architectural characteristics of the Internet—a channel allowing people to communicate on a global scale with fewer barriers to entry to the market of ideas—but also for the role of online platforms, including social media. Indeed, today, addressing disinformation involves not just traditional media outlets, but also transnational actors such as social media, whose business and incentive models challenge traditional media regulation approaches. As observed by Balkin, in the information society, freedom of expression is like a triangle[56]: the regulation of speech no longer involves just the states and the speakers, but also multiple players outside the control of the state, such as social media companies. Unlike traditional media outlets, social media companies usually perform content moderation activities, implementing automated systems which can decide, in a heartbeat, whether to maintain or delete the vast amount of global online content.

5 The Role of Online Platforms

Disinformation would not have become such an issue if online platforms had not risen to become gatekeepers of the information society.[57] In particular, social media no longer limit their activities to hosting content, but actively monitor consent for business (and opaque) purposes. As observed by Gillespie, content moderation is not an ancillary activity, but quite the opposite: it is essential for platforms, in order to ensure a safe environment where users can freely share their content.[58] As a result, the

[56] Balkin (2018a, b).

[57] Klonick (2018, p. 1598); Laidlaw (2012, p. 263); Zittrain (2006, p. 253).

[58] Gillespie (2018).

interests of platforms are not just focused on facilitating the spread of opinions and ideas across the globe, but also on establishing a digital environment where users feel free to share information and data that can feed commercial networks and channels and, especially, attract profits from advertising. In other words, the activity of content moderation serves the function of attracting revenues by ensuring a healthy online community, protecting platforms' corporate image, and showing their commitment to ethical values.

The recent moves by Elon Musk, in the aftermath of his Twitter acquisition, have underlined the relevance of content moderation, not only for the business model of social media, but also for ensuring online trust and addressing the spread of harmful content, including disinformation and misinformation. This situation also underlines how the protection of free speech online is primarily driven by logic that is far from the traditional constitutional narratives coming from national authorities or courts. Notwithstanding several social media providers exploiting rhetorical statements advocating to represent a global community by enhancing free speech transnationally, online platforms increasingly focus their attention on content moderation. This responsibility comes from the need to avoid losing users' trust while also answering regulatory pressures. Therefore, on the one hand, social media providers commit to protecting free speech, while, on the other, moderating content regulating their communities for business purposes.

Furthermore, online platforms rely on automated technologies to cope with the amount of content loaded by users, the non-automated management of which would require enormous costs in terms of human, technological and financial resources. The increasing involvement of platforms in the organisation of content and the profiling of users' preferences, by using AI technologies, has transformed the role of online platforms as hosting providers. If, on the one hand, content moderation constitutes an important resource for social media, on the other hand, the use of technologies (for example, machine learning) for moderating content on a global scale challenges the protection of freedom of expression in a digital environment that extends far beyond domestic boundaries.[59] The information uploaded by users is processed by automated systems that define (or at least suggest to human moderators) content that must be removed within seconds, according to non-transparent standards, and without providing the user with access to any remedy against a specific decision.

In the case of disinformation, and even during the COVID-19 pandemic, social media, such as Meta and Twitter, have proposed voluntary measures and policies to monitor and conduct fact-checking activities to address disinformation, and have been at the forefront in removing or signalling alleged false content.[60] This voluntary fight against disinformation has also led to the adoption, in the US, of an executive order, as a reaction to Twitter's discretion in placing fact-checking labels on presidential tweets relating to mail-in ballots and election fraud.[61] However, the pandemic

[59] Balkin (2018a, b, p. 1149).

[60] Peters (2020).

[61] Executive Order on Preventing Online Censorship, 28 May 2020, https://www.whitehouse.gov/presidential-actions/executive-order-preventing-online-censorship/.

has underlined how the implementation of AI in content moderation can contribute to spreading disinformation without human oversight. The decisions of Google and Facebook to limit the process of human moderation has affected the entire process of content moderation, with the result that different accounts and content have been suspended or removed even where there was no reason to remove them.[62] This situation not only affected users' rights, but also led to the spread of disinformation at a time when reliance on good health information was critical.[63]

This legal uncertainty encourages online platforms to monitor and remove even lawful content, to limit any risk of being sanctioned for hosting unlawful third-party content. This situation, called collateral censorship,[64] occurs when private actors are entrusted with removing unlawful content when they become aware of its presence. Indeed, this obligation encourages online intermediaries to censor even content whose illicit nature is not clear, to avoid any economic sanctions. Such a system of liability indirectly entrusts online intermediaries with autonomously deciding whether to maintain and remove content, based on their risk of being held liable. Since online platforms are privately run, these actors will try to avoid the risks of being sanctioned for non-compliance. In other words, online intermediaries, as business actors, will likely focus on minimising this economic risk rather than adopting a human rights-based approach.

Therefore, the primary question is how to ensure that freedom of expression in the digital age is not driven by unaccountable logic and business interests. This is relevant when considering that the spread of online disinformation has not only raised questions for the protection of the right to freedom of expression, but also for public interests and democratic values.

6 Disinformation, Public Interests and Democratic Values

Undeniably, technology has improved opportunities to search, receive and impart information and ideas beyond the individual sphere. Nevertheless, serious concerns have been cast as to the effects that such information flow generates on public debates and democratic values.[65] Institutions such as the European Commission have recognised that disinformation is capable of undermining trust in institutions, and in the media—both traditional and digital outlets—and may harm democracy by affecting citizens' ability to make informed decisions.[66] In fact, according to the HLEG report, «special attention should be paid to the threat represented by disinformation aimed

[62] Dwoskin and Tiku (2020).

[63] Keller and Gillett (2020).

[64] Wu (2013, p. 293); Kreimer (2006, p. 11).

[65] Tucker (2017, p. 46).

[66] Communication from the Commission to the European Parliament, the Council, the European Economic and Social Committee and the Committee of the Regions, Tackling online disinformation: a European Approach', COM/2018/236 final, p. 1.

at undermining the integrity of elections»,[67] as accurate information is necessary to ensure full enjoyment of the right to vote. The element of information in connection with the public sphere illustrates a number of relations that are typically recognised and protected in liberal constitutional orders.

The interplay between freedom of expression, the right to receive information and informed participation in a democracy is an example of the interdependency and "triangular" nature of the relationship between democracy, the rule of law and fundamental rights.[68] The freedom of speech paradigm is wider than the notion of democracy solely understood in the frame of electoral and public deliberation processes, as it broadly embraces the notion of "democratic culture".[69] Nevertheless, the role of information, and the ability to freely express and receive it, remains undeniably essential during that time frame when citizens are called on to express their political views through the election of representatives. Factual information and knowledge are necessary to ensure the genuine ability of a citizen to take informed decisions, as well as to participate in public debates.[70] Accordingly, freedom of speech is not an end in itself, but is instrumental to the self-government and determination of a people.[71] In other words, disinformation not only touches upon the individual sphere, but also the collective dimension of democracy.

The consolidation of the digital marketplace of ideas has led politicians, political organisations and parties to communicate with citizens and exchange information in an unprecedented way. As free participation in the public sphere during electoral periods presupposes awareness of public policies, and their effects and alternatives,[72] the lack of freedom of information, or being subject to information that is systematically deceitful, may cause a distortion of the opinion-forming process, which might ultimately be reflected in the election ballot. Along these lines, if disinformation practices were to attain such a degree of intensity as to alter or misrepresent public discourse, the exercise of citizens' voting rights would be at risk in that this could, ultimately, lead to electoral results distorted by a perverted public discourse.[73] Elections call on the electorate to express political choices which then affect the polity. It follows that factual information and related public debates are necessary to ensure that the vote authentically expresses the electorate's views; and the heart of the problem lies in investigating the development of political ideas into the digital sphere, to understand whether and how disinformation practices may affect the informative process prior to electoral consultations.

In recent years, the massive spread of populist narratives online has raised questions for constitutional democracies. New (digital) populist narratives, manipulating

---

[67] *Ivi*, p. 12.

[68] Carrera et al. (2013).

[69] Balkin (2004).

[70] Bayer et al. (2019).

[71] Meiklejohn (1961, p. 245).

[72] Confirmed in a number of decisions of the ECtHR: see *LCB v. United Kingdom*, 23413/94, 9 June 1998, paras 38–39; *Roche v. United Kingdom*, 32555/96, 19 October 2005, paras 165–66.

[73] Bayer et al. (2019).

information for political purposes, have populated digital spaces. By exploiting the opportunities of online platforms, populist voices have become a relevant part of both the public debate online and the political situation.[74] The success of these movements is the result of the exploitation of the technological factor by populist movements; that, is of the phenomenon of digital populism,[75] in its multiple definitions of a political communication style, a political strategy framed within certain types of organisation, and an ideology.[76] The cases of the Brexit referendum and of the US elections, both in 2016, have provided examples of how populist movements have relied on digital technologies, and primarily online platforms, as instruments to spread their narratives.[77]

This situation not only applies to the online environment, but also to other constitutional norms and safeguards. According to Fournier, populists cannot bring to reality their electoral programme in the anti-law principle part.[78] The digital populist narrative is coherent with this approach. Populist movements also use social media as a tool to challenge traditional media, by dismantling dissent and making the possibility to disagree difficult. This framework is also connected with the spread of disinformation. Social media have proven to be one of the primary fields where political parties promote their extremist theses, which often overcome the threshold of truthfulness.

It is worth underlining that, when relying on digital technologies, populist groups and leaders are exercising constitutional rights and liberties, and so are acting within the constitutional framework. Still, they exploit it for their purposes, shielding themselves behind democratic safeguards such as freedom of expression, to share opinions which inevitably undermine the same values that allow them to perform their activities. In other words, they exploit constitutional values to run their unconstitutional projects.[79] Besides, when they use social media, they also exercise other pluralist values like freedom of assembly and association, which allow everyone to participate in social and political life, including those minorities which populism aims to fight as a threat to the people's unity.

The digital environment has been the perfect place for the spread of populist narratives. The influence of the digital environment goes beyond even national populism, also extending to the field of international politics. The Cambridge Analytica scandal is a clear example of how even states can interfere in foreign presidential elections, by exploiting social media services to polarise and influence communities across the globe. Therefore, populism seems to be one of the prices democracies need to pay in order to tolerate pluralism. The case of digital populism provides a paradigmatic example of the complexity, for constitutional democracies, of protecting constitutional principles and, primarily, the rule of law, particularly to address the use of disinformation.

---

[74] Engesser et al. (2016, p. 1109).

[75] Bartlett et al. (2011).

[76] Rovira Kaltwasser et al. (2012).

[77] Flew and Iosifidis (2020, p. 7).

[78] Fournier (2019, p. 362).

[79] Blokker (2019, p. 519).

This issue has even extended to the COVID-19 pandemic, which has constituted an opportunity for populist movements to challenge the elite and spread false news. US President Donald Trump referred to the coronavirus as a "hoax",[80] while Brazilian President Jair Bolsonaro described the virus a "fantasy", and preventive measures as "hysterical".[81] The spread of disinformation online has not stopped in times of pandemic. The health crisis is also an information crisis. Social media have been the site of numerous rumours and deep-seated accusations about the origin of the virus and other false information. Conspiracy theories around 5G, or false information about COVID-19 treatments, are only two examples of the health disinformation affecting public discourse in times of pandemic. This tendency is, most notably, well represented by two examples: the fight against the so-called "infodemic".[82] i.e. the mass dissemination of misinformation and disinformation concerning the novel disease, the medical guidelines that followed and, subsequently, the risk–benefit ratio of anti-COVID-19 vaccines.

7 Policies to Combat Disinformation in Europe

7.1 The First Steps in European Efforts to Combat Disinformation

In recent years, initiatives have been adopted in Europe to combat disinformation, understood in the terms described above, on an increasingly significant scale. This has involved the adoption at EU level of increasingly stringent measures aimed at reducing the impact of disinformation on internal democratic principles and processes. The EU's strategies could be said to have evolved in at least three different phases.

The first phase in the EU policy to combat disinformation started in 2015 following the outbreak of the Russia-Ukraine conflict and the occupation of Crimea. During this phase, the EU's specific objective was to promote a more effective communication strategy within the Member States and in its neighbours directly to the east, as well as a more vigorous response to attempts by third countries to exploit disinformation.[83] In particular, the Union envisaged the creation of a dedicated task force, the East Stratcom Task Force, with the specific aim of achieving these goals and combatting the impact of pro-Russian propaganda above all through strategic communication.

The second phase on the other hand saw a steady increase in the focus on digital disinformation, with the aim of reducing online disinformation, acting also in partnership with the various platforms. This second phase was launched specifically in April

[80] Egan (2020).
[81] Paraguassu (2020); Phillips (2020).
[82] Radu (2020).
[83] On this topic, see, among the others, Bjola and Pamment (2016, pp. 131–142).

2018—around one year before the 2019 European Parliament elections—with the publication of the Commission Communication entitled "Tackling online disinformation: a European Approach". Within the framework of the indications contained in the HLEG report mentioned above,[84] the Communication specified that EU action should be based specifically on the pursuit of the following four objectives[85]:

- improving transparency regarding the origin of information and the way it is produced, sponsored, disseminated and targeted;
- promoting diversity of information, through amongst other things support to high quality journalism, the encouragement of media literacy and the rebalancing of the relation between information creators and distributors;
- increasing the credibility of information with the help also of trusted flaggers that provide indications concerning the trustworthiness of a given source;
- the adoption of inclusive solutions resulting in greater stakeholder involvement (public authorities, online platforms, advertisers, trusted flaggers, journalists and media groups etc.).

The Commission's concerns about the impact of disinformation on decision making by voters were already apparent within the Commission's 2018 Communication. It was accordingly permeated by an awareness of the need for specific action by national authorities in order to «identify best practices for the identification, mitigation and management of risks to the electoral process from cyberattacks and disinformation».[86]

The pursuit of these objectives subsequently led, again in 2018, to the adoption of a Code of Practice on Disinformation.[87] This was a soft law instrument under which platforms undertook—on an exclusively voluntary basis—to adhere to a series of commitments and standards in order to ensure better quality information.[88] In addition, again in the same year, the Commission draw up an Action Plan against Disinformation in concert with the High Representative of the Union for Foreign Affairs and Security Policy.[89] It specified, amongst other things, that the coordinated Union response should be based on improving the capabilities of institutions to detect, analyse and expose disinformation; strengthening coordinated and joint responses to disinformation; mobilising the private sector to tackle disinformation; and supporting initiatives to raise awareness and improve societal resilience.[90]

---

[84] De Cock Buning et al. (2018).

[85] Communication COM/2018/236, cit., p. 7.

[86] *Ivi*, pp. 12–13.

[87] Code of Practice on Disinformation, 20 September 2018, https://ec.europa.eu/newsroom/dae/redirection/document/87534.

[88] On the 2018 Code of Practice on Disinformation, see, among the others, Monti (2020, pp. 214–225).

[89] Joint communication to the European Parliament, the European Council, the Council, the European Economic and Social Committee and the Committee of the Regions, Action Plan against Disinformation, JOIN/2018/36 final.

[90] *Ivi*, p. 6.

The strategy adopted during this second phase pursued a self-regulatory approach in this area, which was thus in some sense close to the US model and the metaphor, typical of that model, of the "free marketplace of ideas"; however, it soon proved to be unsatisfactory. Specifically, the substantial failure of the Code of Practice was cast into sharp relief, above all in the wake of the outbreak of the pandemic in 2020[91] and the Russian invasion of Ukraine in 2022. Moreover, almost in parallel with the adoption of these strategies, some nation states had chosen to pursue (or, as we shall see below in relation to Italy, attempted to pursue) much more far-reaching options.

The trailblazer in this area is without doubt the German Network Enforcement Act (*Netzwerkdurchsetzungsgesetz*, NetzDG),[92] the stated aim of which is to combat the spread of illegal content online, including numerous instances of hate speech and disinformation.[93] The NetzDG imposes a variety of obligations on operators of social networks and video-sharing platforms with the aim, first and foremost, of achieving greater transparency as regards their policies and practices on the moderation of unlawful content, and secondly of putting in place "notice-and-take-down" mechanisms. These involve, in practice, the adoption of procedures that enable users to notify providers concerning the presence of any unlawful content on the platforms operated by them. If a report is made, the provider is obliged to respond and, if the content does indeed violate any provision of the German Criminal Code, to remove it within a short period of time. Providers are liable to massive fines if they systematically fail to comply with these obligations.[94]

---

[91] Commission Staff Working Document, Assessment of Practice on Disinformation. Achievements and areas for further improvement, 10 settembre 2020, SWD(2020)180, https://ec.europa.eu/newsroom/dae/document.cfm?doc_id=69212, p. 19: «[T]his overall assessment highlights that [...] the Code should be further improved in several areas by providing commonly-shared definitions, clearer procedures, more precise commitments as well as transparent key performance indicators and appropriate monitoring, all taking into account applicable regulatory frameworks. Further efforts should also be made to broaden the participation to other relevant stakeholders, in particular from the advertising sector».

[92] *Gesetz zur Verbesserung der Rechtsdurchsetzung in sozialen Netzwerken*. On this law, see, among the others, Claussen (2018, pp. 110–136); Wischmeyer (2020, pp. 28–56); Fiano (2021, pp. 155–165); Hong (2022, pp. 76–96).

[93] Actually, the law does not introduce a specific definition of disinformation (nor of hate speech), but merely makes a reference to a number of criminal offenses already identified in the federal criminal code. Thus, there is a lack of legislative recognition of an independent legal identity for the phenomenon of disinformation.

[94] This discipline has been the subject of much criticism, coming not only from platform operators themselves, but also from activists and academics who have pointed out the inherent risks of such legislation in terms of protecting freedom of expression. Indeed, the imposition of obligations to moderate illicit content could push digital platforms to enact forms of "collateral censorship" that are potentially harmful to the rights of Internet users themselves. See, among others, Tworek and Leerssen (2019); Canaan (2022, pp. 101–133). On the concept of "collateral censorship," see Balkin (1999, p. 2298).

On the other hand, in 2018 France enacted various legislative measures in order to combat the "manipulation of information",[95] with a particular focus on its impact on elections. These initiatives were moreover launched in the wake of the fake news that blighted the 2017 presidential election campaign, even though it did not have any significant effect on the outcome.[96] The specific legislation applicable during elections imposes first of all a number of additional transparency requirements, including an obligation to publish the source and amount of any payments received by platforms. Secondly, it provides for a special procedure before the courts as well as an administrative procedure before the *Authorité de régulation de la communication audiovisuelle et numérique* (ARCOM) aimed at stopping the spread of disinformation via public online communication services and also impeding the broadcast on radio and television of "false information" originating from third countries.[97]

Repeated attempts were also made in Italy to regulate these matters in 2017 and 2018: however, these efforts were largely unsuccessful. In particular, two draft bills concerning online disinformation, known as the Gambaro Bill[98] and the Zanda-Filippin Bill[99] (the latter inspired by the German NetzDG) were tabled in the Senate in 2017, although were never discussed on the floor of Parliament. On the other hand, the experiment launched at the start of 2018 by the Interior Minister and the Chief of the *Polizia di Stato* concerning the creation of an "emergency button" that could enable citizens to report online fake news directly to the police attracted extremely harsh criticism[100] and was almost immediately withdrawn. Finally, in response to these unsuccessful attempts to enact legislation and administrative rules, the Communications Regulatory Authority (*Autorità per le Garanzie nelle Comunicazioni*, AGCOM) embarked upon a different (and in some respects more effective) approach with the aim of promoting fruitful cooperation between institutions and the operators of digital platforms rather than persisting with the unsuccessful attempts to adopt hard law strategies.

---

[95] Loi organique n. 2018-1201 du 22 décembre 2018 relative à la lutte contre la manipulation de l'information and Loi n. 2018-1202 du 22 décembre 2018 relative à la lutte contre la manipulation de l'information.

[96] Feertchak (2017); Sénécat (2018).

[97] Moreover, the new French legislation was the subject of some preliminary questions of constitutionality: one of the most relevant problems concerned, in particular, the identification of what can actually be considered "false." In this regard, the Conseil Constitutionnel, through an interpretive rejection ruling, affirmed, as a condition for the constitutional validity of the law, the need for the falsity of information to be able to be demonstrated objectively, as well as the need for the *action judiciaire en référée* not to invest mere opinions, parodies, partial inaccuracies or exaggerations; in addition, the misleading nature of the misinformation content and the impact on electoral procedures must be manifest. See Conseil Constitutionnel, 2018-773 DC, 20 December 2018, para. 21.

[98] A.S. n. 2688/2017, "Disposizioni per prevenire la manipolazione dell'informazione online, garantire la trasparenza sul web e incentivare l'alfabetizzazione mediatica".

[99] A.S. n. 3001/2017, "Norme generali in materia di social network e per il contrasto della diffusione su internet di contenuti illeciti e delle fake news".

[100] On the "emergency button" the UN Special Rapporteur on the right to freedom of opinion and expression also commented negatively. See Kaye (2018).

7.2 The Dawn of a Third Phase?

In view of the need to avoid the failures of past strategies (including in particular the 2018 Code of Practice) whilst also ensuring a harmonised, unitary approach at supranational level, a "third phase" in the fight against disinformation in Europe appears to have started recently. It has been characterised specifically by the adoption of more far-reaching and impactful legislation at EU level.

In addition, the first and most significant development within this context has concerned the Code of Practice on Disinformation and its relationship with the new Digital Services Act (hereinafter "DSA"). Indeed, after the Code was found to be ineffective in 2018, the Commission started to work along two parallel tracks: first of all thoroughly overhauling the Code,[101] and secondly transforming it from an instrument of self-regulation into an instrument of co-regulation.

As far as the second aspect is concerned, art. 34 and 35 DSA impose an obligation on providers of very large online platforms and of very large online search engines to put in place mechanisms for the assessment and mitigation of systemic risks involving, amongst other things, "any actual or foreseeable negative effects on civic discourse and electoral processes". This clause clearly engages directly with the problem of disinformation. At the same time, art. 45 DSA provides for the possibility of drawing up codes of conduct, generally at the instigation of the Commission, providing amongst other things for the taking of specific risk mitigation measures, as well as a regular reporting framework on any measures taken and their outcomes.[102] As mentioned, whereas these codes enable the Union to put in place adequate common standards, and hence to achieve targets more effectively, they also ensure greater certainty for providers as regards the risk mitigation measures that need to be implemented.

This explains the pre-eminent role that the new 2022 code has played in that, having particular regard to the rules laid down by the DSA on codes of conduct, it was adopted specifically with the core aim of operating not only as an interpretative instrument but also as a common standard for combatting disinformation in accordance with arts 34 and 35.[103] Therefore, it is clearly apparent from the Strengthened Code of Practice adopted in 2022 that the Union has shifted from a strictly self-regulatory strategy towards a co-regulatory strategy. Adherence to the commitments provided for under the Code (which are much broader than those contained in its predecessor from 2018) is now backed up by the new DSA and as such—whilst not being mandatory—is at least strongly advocated.

---

[101] See, in this sense, Communication COM/2020/790, cit.; Communication from the Commission to the European Parliament, the Council, the European Economic and Social Committee and the Committee of the Regions, European Commission Guidance on Strengthening the Code of Practice on Disinformation, COM/2021/262 final.

[102] Art. 45(2) Regulation (EU) 2022/2065 (DSA).

[103] See, among the others, Monti (2022, pp. 317–321).

However, the novel aspects of the new phase of the European approach to disinformation are not limited solely to a move beyond the primacy of *self-regulation* towards a more top-down intervention.

The shift from a self-regulation to co-regulation which has been described with regard the new (hard law based) developments in the governance of information online.

More precisely, in recent years, the fundamental question concerning online information and the impact that it has on internal democratic values and processes has led to the adoption of additional legislative measures aimed at promoting a digital ecosystem that is commensurate with the EU's "constitutional" requirements. A particularly important development came with the approval during the first few months of 2024, and thus shortly before elections to the European Parliament, of two regulations intended of better regulate the dissemination of online journalism and online political advertising respectively. These were specifically Regulation (EU) 2024/900 "on the transparency and targeting of political advertising"[104] and Regulation (EU) 2024/1083 on media freedom—the latter commonly referred to also as the European Media Freedom Act (hereinafter "EMFA").[105]

The ultimate aim of Regulation (EU) 2024/900 was to introduce uniform EU rules to govern the dissemination and distribution of political advertising, also and above all in the light of the fragmentary nature of previously applicable national legislation.[106] The preamble to the new Regulation once again shows that it aspires to strike a balance among inherently constitutional and democratic values. It does so first and foremost by ensuring a high degree of transparency as regards the distribution of political advertising, whilst ensuring that "the provision of political advertising is in full respect of fundamental rights",[107] as well as requirements related to the promotion of the digital market, and above all the need to protect the interests of providers of political advertising services—in particular «micro, small and medium-sized undertakings, which often do not have the resources to absorb or pass on the high compliance costs connected to the preparation, placement, promotion, publication, delivery or dissemination of political advertising in more than one Member State».[108]

As its title in any case suggests, Regulation (EU) 2024/900 is focused specifically on "targeting techniques", which are defined as «techniques that are used either to address a political advertisement only to a specific person or group of persons or to exclude them, usually with tailored content, on the basis of the processing of personal data».[109] It is clear that this new legislation operates at the intersection between data

---

[104] Regulation (EU) 2024/900 of the European Parliament and of the Council of 13 March 2024 on the transparency and targeting of political advertising, PE/90/2023/REV/1, OJ L.

[105] Regulation (EU) 2024/1083 of the European Parliament and of the Council of 11 April 2024 establishing a common framework for media services in the internal market and amending Directive 2010/13/EU (European Media Freedom Act), PE/4/2024/REV/1, OJ L. See, Pollicino and Paolucci (2024).

[106] Regulation (EU) 2024/900, cit., recital 9.

[107] *Ivi*, recital 5.

[108] *Ivi*, recital 10.

[109] *Ivi*, art. 3(11).

governance and online information governance, amending the rules governing the recourse to user profiling techniques for the purpose of distributing content as well as the very structure of the online digital ecosystem. The Regulation stresses how the usage of these types of automated decision-making systems is associated with a risk of significant collateral effects in terms of the protection of fundamental rights and individual self-determination, in particular where «special categories of data» within the meaning of art. 9(1) GDPR are involved[110]:

«Such processing of personal data has specific and detrimental effects on individuals' fundamental rights and freedoms, such as to be treated fairly and equally, not to be manipulated, to receive objective information, to form their opinion, to make political decisions and exercise their voting rights. Furthermore, it negatively impacts the democratic process as it leads to fragmentation of the public debate about important societal issues, selective outreach and, ultimately, the manipulation of the electorate. It also increases the risk of the spreading of information manipulation and foreign interference».[111]

It therefore comes as no surprise that the Regulation subjects the usage of these techniques to significant restrictions. It requires, amongst other things, that the only valid legal basis for data processing for targeting purposes is express consent by the data subject. Moreover, it expressly prohibits these techniques morphing into forms of profiling that use special categories of data pursuant to art. 9(1) GDPR.[112] Lawmakers were clearly concerned about the possibility of undue interference in the very "cognitive freedom"[113] of internet users, which could have significant ramifications not only for individual rights but also, in the aggregate, for democratic and political decision-making processes.

Also the second legislative instrument mentioned, the EMFA, is fully consistent with the European strategy of promoting online debate rooted in pluralism, greater transparency and better quality information transmitted through digital infrastructures. At this juncture, it seems fitting that automation and the use of automated decision-making systems plays a particularly important role also within the EMFA, in particular as regards the need to establish sufficient guarantees to protect users in the face of undue interference in their personal freedom when searching for information.

Accordingly, the EMFA has provided for the creation of a specific "right to customise the media offering", i.e. the right:

---

[110] Art. 9(1) Regulation (EU) 2016/679 of the European Parliament and of the Council of 27 April 2016 on the protection of natural persons with regard to the processing of personal data and on the free movement of such data, and repealing Directive 95/46/EC (General Data Protection Regulation), OJ L 119, 4.5.2016, pp. 1–88: «Processing of personal data revealing racial or ethnic origin, political opinions, religious or philosophical beliefs, or trade union membership, and the processing of genetic data, biometric data for the purpose of uniquely identifying a natural person, data concerning health or data concerning a natural person's sex life or sexual orientation shall be prohibited».

[111] Regulation (EU) 2024/900, cit., recital 74.

[112] *Ivi*, art. 18(1).

[113] See, on this topic, Pollicino (2021, pp. 9–17).

«to easily change the configuration, including default settings, of any device or user interface controlling or managing access to and the use of media services providing programmes in order to customise the media offering in accordance with their interests or preferences in compliance with Union law».[114]

The legal framework established by the two new Regulations adopted in 2024 appears once again to confirm the aspiration to move the Union into a new legislative phase, which has been defined as "digital constitutionalism". This approach seeks to imbue the law with democratic and constitutional principles and values, including the right to obtain pluralist, high-quality information, the right to self-determination in decision making and the right to free elections within the ambit of a new algorithmic society. Indeed, here too efforts have been made to strike a correct balance between, on the one hand, the interest in the full development of new technologies—which moreover have the potential to act as extraordinary powerful instruments for advancing democratic debate—and, on the other hand, the need to contain the risks associated with the emergence of algorithms and private digital actors as new players on the global stage.

Another particularly significant aspect concerns the active promotion of the values of information pluralism as well as the attempt to guarantee an overall improvement in the quality of media communication. This objective is pursued specifically by the new EMFA.[115]

As previously indicated in the report on the proposal,[116] the main aim of the new Regulation is to support the fundamental role played by independent media within civil society, insofar as the media contribute to shaping public opinion, providing citizens with a variety of options and reliable information. With this outcome in mind, the stated aim of the Regulation is to guarantee media pluralism and independence, as well as pluralist and independent journalism. For instance, art. 4 introduces important rights and guarantees, which can be exercised by media service providers against the Member States. Art. 5 sets out some safeguards in order to protect the independence of public media service providers. On the other hand, art. 6 imposes a number of transparency obligations on media service providers in general (concerning above all the identity of owners and financing bodies), as well as specifically on media service that provide news and current affairs content (to take appropriate steps to guarantee the independence of individual editorial decisions).

Moreover, the EMFA recognises the importance of digital media within the contemporary world, as well as the impact that online platforms' business models have in terms of their contribution to increasing polarisation and online disinformation. It is also mindful of the risk to media independence caused by third country financing and/or control.[117] As such, the EMFA lays down interesting rules to govern

[114] Regulation (EU) 2024/1083, cit., art. 20(1).

[115] On this point, see Pollicino and Paolucci (2024).

[116] Proposal for a Regulation of the European Parliament and of the Council establishing a common framework for media services in the internal market (European Media Freedom Act) and amending Directive 2010/13/EU, COM/2022/457 final.

[117] Regulation (EU) 2024/1083, recital 3 and 4.

relations between media service providers and providers of VLOPs, which seek to supplement the DSA with specific reference to the journalism sector.

In particular, providers of very large online platforms must incorporate a function that enables media service providers: to identify themselves as such; to declare that they are editorially independent from Member States and third countries; to declare that they are subject to regulatory requirements for the exercise of editorial responsibility in one or more Member States or that they adhere to a co-regulatory or self-regulatory mechanism that is «widely recognised and accepted in the relevant media sector in one or more Member States"; and to "declare that they do not provide content generated by AI systems without subjecting it to human review or editorial control».[118] Once this declaration has been made and the media service provider has been recognised as having "professional" status, it will be treated differently as regards moderating activity on the platform. This involves, for instance, the prior notification of any decision to suspend the provision of intermediation services.

On the other hand, the EMFA also provides for the option of launching "structured dialogue" among the parties involved, the European Board for Media Services and civil society. The objective of this dialogue is to ensure an exchange of experiences and to develop best practices in the application of that moderation mechanism and the promotion of media pluralism on online platforms. The need to society from harmful content is specifically mentioned, including «disinformation and foreign information manipulation and interference».[119]

The resulting legislation thus essentially seems to incentivise forms of cooperation among online platforms, European authorities and media service providers. The specific underlying aim is to protect the spread of independent, pluralist and correct information, to combat fake or polluting content originating also (although not exclusively) from foreign countries and finally to enhance network users' self-determination in relation to information (and decision making).

Finally, a third aspect of particular significance concerns the acknowledgement at European level of the close interlinkage between disinformation and AI, as well as the impact that this interlinkage has on the proper operation of internal democratic processes. This acknowledgement reflects the renewed awareness of the paradigm shift that recent developments relating to AI—and in particular progress in machine learning, generative AI, LLMs etc.—have brought about on the global technological and social scene.

In general, it is clear that the EU's new approach seeks to engage on multiple fronts with the various aspects of disinformation. This involves a focus in particular on how disinformation interacts with the development and dissemination of AI on the one hand, and with the consequences for the media (and by extension, for democratic processes) on the other hand. Moreover, this multi-front approach appears to be characterised by a strong tendency on the part of the EU to move beyond the purely diplomatic, communicative strategy of phase one, and the self-regulatory approach

[118] *Ivi*, art. 17.

[119] *Ivi*, art. 19(1).

of phase two, towards a co-regulatory form of disinformation governance, or indeed in some cases full-blown hard law.

References

Balkin JM (1999) Free speech and hostile environments. Columbia Law Rev 99(8):2295–2320

Balkin JM (2004) Digital speech and democratic culture: A theory of freedom of expression for the information society. New York Univ Law Rev 79(1)

Balkin JM (2009) The future of free expression in a digital age. Pepperdine Law Rev 36(2)

Balkin JM (2018a) Free speech is a triangle. Columbia Law Rev 118

Balkin JM (2018b) Free speech in the algorithmic society: Big data, private governance, and new school speech regulation. UC Davis Law Rev 1149

Barile P (1975) Libertà di manifestazione del pensiero. Giuffrè, Milan

Bartlett J et al (2011) The new face of digital populism

Bassini M (2019) Internet e libertà di espressione. Prospettive costituzionali e sovranazionali, Aracne, Canterano

Bayer J et al (2019) Disinformation and propaganda—impact on the functioning of the Rule of Law in the EU and its member states. Study for the LIBE Committee, European Parliament

Bjola C, Pamment J (2016) Digital containment: revisiting containment strategy in the digital age. Glob Aff 2(2):131–142

Blokker P (2019) Populist counter-constitutionalism, conservatism, and legal fundamentalism. Eur Constit Law Rev 15(3):519

Canaan I (2022) NetzDG and the German precedent for authoritarian creep and authoritarian learning. Columbia J Eur Law 28:101–133

Carrera S et al (2013) The Triangular Relationship between Fundamental Rights, Democracy and the Rule of Law in the EU: Towards an EU Copenhagen Mechanism. Centre for European Policy Studies. https://www.ceps.eu/ceps-publications/triangular-relationship-between-fundamental-rights-democracy-and-rule-law-eu-towards-eu/.

Chesney R, Citron DK (2018) Deep fakes: A looming challenge for privacy, democracy, and national security. Calif Law Rev 107

Claussen V (2018) Fighting hate speech and fake news. The Network Enforcement Act (NetzDG) in Germany in the context of European legislation. Rivista di diritto dei Med 3:110–136

de Cock Buning M et al (2018) A multi-dimensional approach to disinformation: Report of the independent High level Group on fake news and online disinformation, Luxembourg

De Gregorio G, Perotti E (2019) Tackling disinformation around the world. https://www.wan-ifra.org/reports/2019/05/03/public-affairs-media-policy-briefing-tackling-disinformation-around-the-world

Dunn P, Durante M (2023) Disinformazione e Internet. In: Giacomini G, Taddio L (eds) La politica nel mondo digitale, Milano—Udine, Mimesis, pp 58–61

Dupuis MJ, Williams A (2019) The spread of disinformation on the web: an examination of memes on social networking. IEEE SmartWorld, Ubiquitous Intelligence & Computing, Advanced & Trusted Computing, Scalable Computing & Communications, Cloud & Big Data Computing, Internet of People and Smart City Innovation, pp 1412–1418

Dwoskin E, Tiku N (2020) Facebook sent home thousands of human moderators due to the coronavirus. Now the Algorithms are in Charge'. The Washington Post. https://www.washingtonpost.com/technology/2020/03/23/facebook-moderators-coronavirus/

Egan L (2020) Trump calls coronavirus democrats "New Hoax". https://www.nbcnews.com/politics/donald-trump/trump-calls-coronavirus-democrats-new-hoax-n1145721

Engesser S et al (2016) Populism and social media: How politicians spread a fragmented ideology. Inf Commun Soc 20(8):1109

Feertchak A (2017) Les cinq "fake news" qui ont pollué la campagne présidentielle. https://www.lefigaro.fr/elections/presidentielles/2017/04/22/35003-20170422ARTFIG00048-les-cinq-fake-news-qui-ont-pollue-la-campagne-presidentielle.php
Fiano N (2021) Il linguaggio dell'odio in Germania: Tra Wehrhafte Demokratie e Netzwerkdurchsetzungsgesetz. In: D'Amico M, Siccardi C (eds) La costituzione non odia: Conoscere, prevenire e contrastare l'hate speech online, Torino, Giappichelli, pp 155–165
Flew T, Iosifidis P (2020) Populism, globalisation and social media. The International Communication Gazette 82(1). OUP, Oxford, p 7
Fournier T (2019) From rhetoric to action, a constitutional analysis of populism. German Law J 20(3):362
Gillespie T (2018) Custodians of the internet: Platforms, content moderation, and the hidden decisions that shape social media
Goldsmith J, Wu T (2006) Who controls the internet?
Hong M (2022) Regulating hate speech and disinfomration online while protecting freedom of speech as an equal and positive right—comparing Germany, Europe and the United States. J Med Law 14:76–96
Jack C (2017) Lexicon of lies: Terms for problematic information. https://datasociety.net/pubs/oh/DataAndSociety_LexiconofLies.pdf
Johnson DR, Post D (1996) Law and borders: The rise of law in cyberspace. Stanford Law Rev 48(5)
Kaye D (2018) Mandate of the Special Rapporteur on the promotion and protection of the right to freedom of expression. www.ohchr.org/sites/default/files/Documents/Issues/Opinion/Legislation/OL-ITA-1-2018.pdf
Keller TR, Gillett R (2020) Why is it so hard to stop COVID-19 misinformation spreading on social media?. The Conversation. https://theconversation.com/why-is-it-so-hard-to-stop-covid-19-misinformation-spreading-on-social-media-134396
Klonick K (2018) The new governors: The people, rules, and processes governing online speech. Harv Law Rev 131:1598
Kreimer SF (2006) Censorship by proxy: The first amendment, internet intermediaries, and the problem of the weakest link. Univ Pennsylvania Law Rev 155:11
Laidlaw EB (2012) A framework for identifying internet information gatekeepers. Int Rev Law Comput Technol 24(3):263
Marino G (2015) Semiotics of spreadability. Punctum 1:43–66
Martens B et al (2018) The Digital Transformation of News Media and the Rise of Disinformation and Fake News. JRC Digital Economy Working Paper no. 2, https://ec.europa.eu/jrc/sites/jrcsh/files/jrc111529.pdf
Meiklejohn A (1961) The first amendment is an absolute. Supreme Court Review, p 245
Mill JS (1859) On liberty
Milton J (1644) Aeropagitica
Monti M (2020) The EU code of practice on disinformation and the risk of the privatisation of censorship. In: Giusti S, Piras E (eds) Democracy and fake news: information manipulation and post-truth politics, London, Routledge, pp 214–225
Monti M (2022) Lo strengthened Code of Practice on Disinformation: un'altra pietra della nuova fortezza digitale europea? Rivista di diritto dei Med 2:317–321
Morelli A, Pollicino O (2020) Metaphors and judicial enforcement of fundamental rights. Am J Comp Law 68(3):616
Paraguassu L (2020) Brazil's Bolsonaro Says Coronavirus is Not All the Media Makes It Out to Be. https://www.reuters.com/article/us-brazil-bolsonaro-idUSKBN20X24P
Peters J (2020) Twitter introducing new labels for tweets with misleading COVID-19 information. The Verge, https://www.theverge.com/2020/5/11/21254733/twitter-covid-19-misleading-information-label-warnings-misinformation

Phillips T (2020) Brazil's Jair Bolsonaro Says Coronavirus Crisis is a Media Trick. https://www.theguardian.com/world/2020/mar/23/brazils-jair-bolsonaro-says-coronavirus-crisis-is-a-media-trick
Pitruzzella G, Pollicino O (2020) Disinformation and hate speech. A European constitutional perspective
Pollicino O (2020) The European approach to disinformation: Comparing supranational and national measures. In: Comandé G, Graziadei M (eds) Annuario di diritto comparato 2020, Edizioni editoriali scientifiche
Pollicino O (2021) Costituzionalismo, privacy e neurodiritti. Rivista di diritto dei Med 2:9–17
Pollicino O, Paolucci F (2024) Unveiling the Digital Side of Journalism: Exploring the European Media Freedom Act's opportunities and challenges. La Revue des Juristes de Sciences Po, 1
Radu R (2020) Fighting the "Infodemic": Legal responses to COVID-19 disinformation. Soc Med Soc 6(3) https://journals.sagepub.com https://doi.org/10.1177/2056305120948190
Rahman KS (2018) The new utilities: Private power, social infrastructure, and the revival of the public utility concept. Cardozo Law Rev 39
Robinson O (2019) A report on antidisinformation initiative. https://comprop.oii.ox.ac.uk/wp-content/uploads/sites/93/2019/08/A-Report-of-Anti-Disinformation-Initiatives
Rosenfeld M (2003) Hate speech in constitutional jurisprudence: Comparative analysis. Cardozo Law Rev 24(4):1523–1568
Rovira Kaltwasser C et al (2012) Populism: An overview of the concept and the state of the art. In: Rovira Kaltwasser C et al (eds) The Oxford Handbook of Populism
Segura-Serrano A (2006) Internet Regulation and the Role of International Law. Max Planck Yearbook of United Nations Law 10
Sénécat (2018) A Fake news et élections: De Trump à l'Italie, le risque de tout mélanger. https://www.lemonde.fr/les-decodeurs/article/2018/02/16/fake-news-en-periode-electorale-le-risque-de-tout-melanger_5258138_4355770.html
Sunstein CR (2017) #Republic: Divided democracy in the age of social media
Sunstein CR (2020) Falsehoods and the first amendment. Harvard J Law Technol 33(2)
Susi M et al (eds) (2022) Governing information flows during war: A comparative study of content governance and media policy responses after Russia's attack on Ukraine. GDHRNet Working Paper. https://www.ssoar.info/ssoar/bitstream/handle/document/78580/ssoar-2022-susi_et_al-Governing_Information_Flows_During_War.pdf?sequence=5&isAllowed=y&lnkname=ssoar-2022-susi_et_al-Governing_Information_Flows_During_War.pdf
Tucker JA (2017) From liberation to turmoil: Social media and democracy. J Democr 28(4):46
Tworek H, Leerssen P (2019) An analysis of Germany's NetzDG Law», www.ivir.nl/publicaties/download/NetzDG_Tworek_Leerssen_April_2019.pdf
Wardle C (2017) Fake news. It's complicated, First Draft. https://medium.com/1st-draft/fake-news-its-complicated-d0f773766c79
Wardle C (2020) Understanding information disorder. https://firstdraftnews.org/long-form-article/understanding-information-disorder
Wardle C, Derashkan H (2017) Information disorder: TOWARD an interdisciplinary framework for research and policy making. Report n. DGI(2017)09of the Council of Europe. https://rm.coe.int/information-disorder-toward-an-interdisciplinary-framework-for-researc/168076277c
Wischmeyer T (2020) What is illegal offline is also illegal online: The German Network Enforcement Act 2017. In: Petkova B, Ojanen T (eds) Fundamental Rights Protection Online: The Future Regulation of Intermediaries, Cheltenham, Edward Elgar, pp 28–56
Wu FT (2013) Collateral censorship and the limits of intermediary immunity. Notre Dame Law Review 87:293
Zittrain JA (2006) History of online gatekeeping. Harvard J Law Technol 19(2):253

A Critique of European Attempts to Regulate Online Disinformation

András Koltay

Abstract To put it simply, information is useful, disinformation is harmful, however, just as it is completely impossible to force people to get informed, so it is almost futile to resist to disinformation solely by legal means. The goals and economic interests of the other two actors involved in (dis)information, the 'channels' (for example, large online platforms, social media and popular search engines) and the (dis)informers—even if unintentionally—may boost that of each others'. What can legislators do, without disproportionate restrictions on freedom of expression, what can the audience do, breaking through various filter bubbles or echo chambers, and what can media companies do, without decreasing user experience and their own share price, to ensure that the veracity of communications be easily and quickly recognised, the acceptance and spreading of disinformation be reduced, and the information be factual? But, sometimes the remedy is worse than the disease. This chapter highlights some issues and problems that illustrate the threats to freedom of expression posed by attempts to address the problem in the European Union, and tries to make some cautious suggestions for regulations on disinformation that do not unjustifiably or disproportionately restrict individual freedom of expression.

I would like to thank the participants of the conference Disinformation in the new and old media in the 21st century: Shaping the new boundaries of free speech?, organised by Università Degli Studi di Napoli Federico II (Naples) on 11 March 2024 for their support and comments. Thanks are also due to Enrique Armijo, Mark Cole, Julia Hörnle, Michael Losavio, Gideon Parchomovsky, Anthony Sebok, and Russell Weaver, participants of the Free Speech/Media Law Discussion Forum at the Ludovika – University of Public Service (Budapest) on 13 June 2024, for their valuable comments and suggestions.

A. Koltay (✉)
Ludovika – University of Public Service, Budapest, Hungary
e-mail: koltay.andras@uni-nke.hu

Pázmány Péter Catholic University, Budapest, Hungary

R. Mastroianni and C. Massa (eds.), *Disinformation in New and Old Media in the XXI Century*, Ius Gentium: Comparative Perspectives on Law and Justice 136,
https://doi.org/10.1007/978-3-032-18830-4_4

1 Introduction

The problem of online disinformation is well known and has been discussed across various academic disciplines. The internet, and social media in particular, provide ample opportunity for the spread of untrue information.[1] However, neither the desire to invent "facts" as one sees fit is new, nor is the appearance of untrue facts in the media.[2] What are new, in the era of social media, are the volume of false information and the speed with which it spreads, and this makes it almost impossible to take effective legal measures against such content. Moreover, the potential for deliberate disinformation is not due to a fault in the operation of the social media platforms, which could be addressed with appropriate intervention, but is instead an almost inevitable consequence of the very nature of such platforms.[3]

The mass collection of data and information about users by social media platforms has enabled their in-depth profiling, which can be used to determine, via algorithms, the content presented to individuals, and to target advertisements at them. With the help of the data collected, the designers of platforms try to make their users feel a psychological urge to return to the service as often as possible. The architecture of the platforms and the nature of the communication that takes place on them are thus conducive to the spread of sensational, fast and short-lived content. A leak in 2021 by a former Facebook employee, Frances Haugen, revealed that users spend more time on the platform and interact more intensely with it when they encounter disinformation, and this in turn increases the revenue of the platforms, which therefore have no interest in cracking down on false news.[4] The phenomenon and effects of online filtering bubbles and mass disinformation are also interlinked: opinion groups are more vulnerable to disinformation, and the typically emotive approach these groups take to public issues makes them immune to falsehoods being debunked.[5]

There are grounds to fear that the even greater challenges are yet to come. The use of deepfake technology already makes it impossible for the average person to recognise fake videos.[6] The need for legal and regulatory action to address this is therefore self-evident. At the same time, legislators, governments and policymakers must also ensure that freedom of expression remains constitutionally protected. These fundamentally opposing interests create a tension that is difficult to resolve. Previously, it was generally believed that the best antidote to untruthful or offensive speech was counterspeech,[7] that more speech is always better than less,[8] and that these principles narrow the scope for state or government intervention. However, in the age of online

---

[1] Levi (2018).

[2] Bernal (2018a, pp. 516–519).

[3] Ibidem, pp. 522–527 and Bernal (2018b, pp. 241–245).

[4] Facebook files. A Wall Street Journal investigation (2021). For more on the leaks, see Perrigo (2021).

[5] Napoli (2019, pp. 60–86).

[6] See, for example, Darer Littman (2020).

[7] *United States v Alvarez* 567 US 709 (2012) 726.

[8] Chemerinsky (1998).

communication, these ideas are being sidelined, and regulators are seeking new ways to deal with disinformation that is immune to rational debate and which, because it is so massive in scale, can hardly be countered by more speech. These new paths nevertheless inevitably lead to restrictions on users' freedom of expression. This chapter does not seek to provide a comprehensive overview of European action against disinformation[9] but instead highlights some issues and problems that illustrate the threats to freedom of expression posed by attempts to address the problem, and tries to make some cautious suggestions for regulations on disinformation that do not unjustifiably or disproportionately restrict individual freedom of expression.

2 Appropriate Restrictions on Freedom of Expression Are Important Tools in the Fight Against Disinformation

The first and most secure line of defence against disinformation—from the point of view of the doctrine of freedom of expression—are the restrictions on speech that allow untrue statements to be countered in legal proceedings. According to the general European approach, freedom of expression can only be restricted by applying an appropriate legal standard, where it is necessary and proportionate to the danger caused by the speech.[10] Speech on public affairs is subject to special protection, which may be limited by the need to protect the rights of others or by a public interest of some sort (public safety, public health, ensuring the integrity of electoral processes, etc.). Within the framework of the protection of freedom of expression in Europe, according to the current doctrine, deliberate lies (intentional publication of untruthful information) cannot, in themselves and without other compelling reasons, be subject to a general prohibition.

In line with the above, the following types of speech may be restricted: untrue statements that damage the reputation of others (defamation),[11] speech inciting hatred against individual social groups,[12] denial of the Holocaust and other genocides,[13]

---

[9] I have tried to do this elsewhere, see Koltay (2025).

[10] Villiger (2023, pp. 511–515).

[11] For the case law of the ECtHR, see ECtHR, *Lingens v Austria*, 9815/82, 8 July 1986; ECtHR, *Castells v Spain*, 11798/85, 23 April 1992; ECtHR, *Thorgeir Thorgeirson v Iceland*, 47/1991/299/370, 28 May 1992; ECtHR, *Bladet Tromsø and Stensaas v Norway*, 21980/93, 20 May 1999. For a summary, see Oster (2017, pp. 73–89).

[12] For the relevant EU legislation see Council Framework Decision 2008/913/JHA of 28 November 2008 on combating certain forms and expression of racism and xenophobia by means of criminal law, arts 1(a) and 1(b); Directive 2010/13/EU on the coordination of certain provisions laid down by law, regulation or administrative action in Member States concerning the provision of audiovisual media services (AVMS Directive), art. 6. For an overview of national legislation, see Blasphemy, insult and hatred: Finding answers in a democratic society (2010).

[13] See Council Framework Decision 2008/913/JHA, arts 1(c) and 1(d). For examples of national laws, see the French "Gayssot Act" (Loi n° 90-615 du 13 juillet 1990 tendant à réprimer tout acte raciste, antisémite ou xénophobe, amending the Law on the Freedom of the Press of 1881, by adding

false statements made during election campaigns,[14] misleading commercial communications,[15] (in particular tobacco advertising[16]) and scaremongering.[17] It is evident that these prohibitions cover a wide range but not all forms of disinformation, nor are all these restrictions present in the legal system of all EU Member States. It clearly follows from this that many cases, disinformation are actually speech protected by freedom of expression – a contradiction that has dogged both national and EU-level efforts against disinformation throughout the EU, casting a shadow over every attempt to limit it. This does not mean that the protected content has the right to reach an audience or to have its volume amplified by a particular service (for example, through social media), but rather that its restriction by the state is not allowed.

A key question is whether it is possible or necessary to think about introducing new speech prohibitions in Europe in the face of the phenomenon of online disinformation. Extending the scope of prohibitions would not be inherently incompatible with the European doctrine of freedom of expression. Cass Sunstein, for example, argues that intentional lies, if they cause at least moderate harm, may be constitutionally prohibited, while even negligent or mistaken misrepresentations can be restricted, if the harm incurred by them is serious.[18] Sunstein sees this as a possibility, even in the light of the US First Amendment and the related case law of the Supreme Court. According to the traditional European understanding of freedom of expression, the boundaries between free and prohibited speech can only be defined by national parliaments (and possibly, although exceptionally, by EU bodies), or by courts and constitutional courts. Such restrictions are subject to strict constitutional guarantees that ensure strong protection of free speech, especially in public debates.

In any legal proceedings which have been brought on the basis of a specific act of speech, the issue of freedom of expression is a question to be decided by binary logic. A speech is either protected or not, and, similarly, a particular piece of content is either allowed under freedom of expression or not. In other words, if the sometimes complex question of whether a particular piece of content constitutes defamation, hate speech, etc. is answered satisfactorily, then the court will either conclude, after careful consideration, that it is unlawful (and thus sanctionable) or not (and thus

---

a new art. 24), and the German Criminal Code (Strafgesetzbuch in der Fassung der Bekanntmachung vom 13. November 1998 – BGBl. I S. 3322), 130(3) §. See also Kahn (2004) and Hennebel and Hochmann (2011).

[14] See the UK's Representation of the People Act 1983, s. 106 (False statements as to candidates); Austria's Criminal Code (Bundesgesetz vom 23. Jänner 1974 über die mit gerichtlicher Strafe bedrohten Handlungen – BGBl. Nr. 60/1974), 264. § (spreading false information in election or referendum campaign period). On the UK legislation, see Rowbottom (2012).

[15] ECtHR, *Markt Intern and Beerman v Germany*, 10572/83, 20 November 1989; ECtHR, *Barthold v Germany*, 10/1983/66/101, 25 February 1985.

[16] Directive 2003/33/EC of the European Parliament and of the Council of 26 May 2003 on the approximation of the laws, regulations and administrative provisions of the Member States relating to the advertising and sponsorship of tobacco products, OJ L 152, 20.6.2003, pp. 16–19.

[17] See, for example, the Hungarian Criminal Code (Act C of 2012), art. 337. For further details, see Koltay (2021).

[18] Sunstein (2021, pp. 12–18, pp. 128–130).

protected by freedom of expression). This traditional approach is being disrupted by online platforms, which, according to their general practice, themselves restrict content that is not legally prohibited, for their own reasons and based on their own terms and conditions. The same problem applies to action at national or EU level against disinformation protected by the freedom of expression. As a result, various laws and other legal instruments, mainly at EU level, also encourage and require online platforms to restrict content that is otherwise protected by the freedom of expression. The relevant documents concerning these regulations do not attempt to resolve this contradiction.

The United Kingdom has recently introduced a rule that specifically prohibits online communication containing disinformation, in a move unparalleled in Europe. Under the Online Safety Act 2023, a person commits a false communications offence if the person sends a message through an online platform (social media, video sharing portal, etc.) conveying information that the person knows to be false and at the time of sending it the person intended the message, or the information in it, to cause non-trivial psychological or physical harm to a likely audience, and the person has no reasonable excuse for sending the message.[19] The new provision has already been widely debated, and there are indeed a number of valid objections that can be made to it,[20] for example that it also prohibits intent to cause damage without there being actual damage. However, for the purposes of this paper, it is worth mentioning chiefly to illustrate that specific state (legislative) action against disinformation is not at all inconceivable, nor is it contrary to the European (in this case British) conception of freedom of expression.

Overall, even with the concerns raised, it is preferable that the line between forbidden and permissible speech be drawn by the legislature and the courts, constrained by strict constitutional guarantees, rather than by private organisations, such as social media platforms, operating without such guarantees. However, this can only be a first step in tackling disinformation. It is clear that legal procedures are not as fast and efficient as they need to be, and the volume and speed of online disinformation is staggering, making it impossible for the justice system to deal with it all. It is simply impossible to take every individual posting of misleading content on social media to court or to another authority. Even so, it is important that the scope of legal prohibitions is specified and that those affected have the possibility to take action, and in particular, that the platforms are obliged to remove illegal content after notification, even without a judicial or administrative decision to that effect.[21] Such a possibility, while not without concerns from a freedom of expression perspective, can be a powerful tool in the hands of complainants. However, from the perspective of freedom of expression, it is equally important to protect content that is not prohibited, even if it is untrue.

---

[19] Online Safety Act 2023 (c. 50), s. 179.

[20] See Coe (2023, pp. 230–232).

[21] Regulation (EU) 2022/2065 of the European Parliament and of the Council of 19 October 2022 on a Single Market For Digital Services and amending Directive 2000/31/EC (Digital Services Act), art. 6(1).

3 Online Platforms Are the Main Decision-Makers on Disinformation, Which Is Not Very Good News for Freedom of Expression

Under the current legislation, it is not really the courts or other authorities, but the platforms themselves that are the key decision-makers in relation to disinformation—or any other illegal or otherwise "dangerous" or "harmful" user content. This situation is the inevitable consequence of the technology itself, and it is understandable that the laws addressing disinformation also use the platforms themselves as an extended arm of the public authorities.

The European Union's Digital Services Act (DSA), which implements the detailed regulation of online platforms, preserves the key principles of the European regulation of online platforms and the notice and take-down procedure that had been laid down in the previous regulation.[22] Platforms cannot be required to monitor user content (Article 8), but if they receive a notification that a certain piece of content is illegal, and they find the allegations to be justified, they are obliged to remove it (Article 6(1)). The DSA also goes some way towards protecting users' freedom of expression. It requires users to be informed of the content removed by platforms, and gives them the opportunity to have recourse to dispute resolution mechanisms in their own country, as well as to refer the case to the competent authorities or courts, if the platform has infringed those provisions that seek to strengthen the position of users, in particular by providing procedural guarantees. These include guarantees ensuring greater transparency, such as the obligation to state the reasons for deleting content and for its ranking, to state the reason for suspending an account, and the right to an independent review of moderation decisions.[23] The DSA also states that any restrictions stipulated in the terms and conditions for using a site must take freedom of expression and media pluralism into account (Article 14(1)).[24] The DSA does not explicitly address disinformation, but if user content involving disinformation constitutes an infringement, then the platform must remove it after receiving notice, as it does for other infringements.

Even so, these rules are not the DSA's strongest response to the problem of disinformation. The imposition of greater social responsibility on the very large online platforms and the very large online search engines[25] to assess and manage risk seems to be potentially more effective. The providers of these services are obliged to identify and analyse the potential negative effects of their operations (in particular their algorithms and recommender systems) on, *inter alia,* freedom of expression, the exercise of fundamental rights, civil discourse, the electoral process and public safety (Article

[22] Directive 2000/31/EC of the European Parliament and of the Council of 8 June 2000 on certain legal aspects of information society services, in particular electronic commerce, in the Internal Market (Directive on electronic commerce), OJ L 178, 17.7.2000, pp. 1–16, art. 14.

[23] DSA, arts 17, 21 and 24.

[24] Quintais et al. (2023).

[25] These are platforms or search engines that are used by at least ten percent of the total EU population, currently at by least 45 million users in EU Member States (DSA, art. 33(1)).

34(1)) and to take appropriate and effective measures to mitigate these risks (Article 35). In addition, the rules of the DSA on codes of practice also make it worthwhile for companies to manage such risks, and promote the enforcement of codes of practice (including, for example, the EU Code of Practice on Disinformation adopted before the DSA, see below). They also serve as tools to combat disinformation. One of the main purposes of the DSA is to protect the freedom of expression of users, but users' speech can also contain disinformation, so it will be difficult to reconcile these conflicting interests when applying the regulation.

The first examples of what the European Commission means by risk management have already emerged. In examining the platforms' response to Russian disinformation campaigns, the Commission published a detailed study on how to identify and manage the risk under the DSA, concluding that the platforms have only done what was expected of them to a limited extent.[26] In the run-up to the European Parliament elections, the Commission issued a Communication in March 2024, providing guidance to very large online platforms and very large online search engines on what they need to do about systemic risks related to the election process.[27] The document, while not formally binding, makes a number of recommendations to the platforms concerned regarding their activities. For example, it recommends that platforms ensure access to official information on the electoral process, engage in media literacy initiatives, place fact-checking labels on disinformation and examples of foreign information manipulation and interference that have been identified by independent fact-checkers and fact-checking teams of independent media organisations, and they urge users to read content and evaluate its accuracy and source before sharing it. In addition, the Commission also recommends that platforms designate official accounts, as well as accounts providing authoritative information on the electoral process, accounts that provide official and credible information on elections, as well as user accounts controlled by Member States and third countries, or that are controlled by organisations controlled or funded by third countries. Platforms should provide tools and information to help users assess the trustworthiness of information sources, such as trust marks focused on the integrity of the source based on transparent methodologies and which were developed by independent third parties. It also refers to the platforms' recommender systems and the treatment of political advertising, which they must label in a clear, prominent and unambiguous way.

The European Commission therefore expects platforms to identify and flag disinformation and to take steps to ensure that credible information is widely disseminated. While risk assessment and management are mandatory under the DSA, the specific and detailed obligations contained in the above-mentioned study and communication cannot be derived from the text of the DSA alone. Although the European Commission does not formally impose these measures as directly enforceable legal obligations, they do seem to have the potential to be binding. Indeed, if the Commission later finds that a platform has not complied with the risk management related

---

[26] Digital Services Act—application of the Risk Management Framework to Russian disinformation campaigns (2023).

[27] Communication to the Commission (2024).

obligations defined under the DSA and relies on its own previous documents to identify these obligations, it will give them quasi-legal force and may use them as a basis for finding that platforms have acted in breach of the DSA, including by imposing fines.

In addition to the legal rules, platforms can also make their own provisions binding on their users, although these must be compatible with DSA. However, the Regulation does not determine the details of speech prohibitions set by platforms, which are left to the platforms themselves to determine, subject to the general obligations set out in the Regulation. This form of regulation can be called private regulation, which becomes legal (meaning enforceable against the users) through a contract between the platform and the user.[28]

In some cases, the EU and national governments themselves have encouraged private regulation by platforms. In relation to hate speech, the EU took the initiative as early as 2016 and called for tougher action on hate speech by platforms. The result is the Code of Practice on countering illegal hate speech online, which was signed by Facebook, Microsoft, Twitter and YouTube.[29] The Code represents the EU's attempt to force platforms to take effective action against hate speech, regardless of whether the content is illegal. In the Code, the platforms committed themselves to implementing an effective process, to the proper examination of notifications and to deciding on content, not only in accordance with their own rules and policies but also in the light of national legislation transposing Council Framework Decision 2008/913/JHA. According to the Code, the platforms shall «review the majority of valid notifications for removal of illegal hate speech in less than 24 h and remove or disable access to such content, if necessary».

The expectation of social media companies taking action against content that is not illegal but still "dangerous" or "harmful" is one of the doubtful points of cooperation between platforms and public policy makers. While states are reluctant to tighten the framework for freedom of expression, they expect platforms to take action against content that is protected by law, but which is nonetheless considered dangerous or harmful. While a platform does this by its own choice, without state coercion, to protect its users, this choice is also protected by law (although one might wonder whether speech restrictions stipulated in the terms and conditions should not also be subject to some form of external control[30]). However, when the EU or the states responsible for defining the limits of free speech encourage platforms to limit speech in this way, such restrictions on free speech raise concerns.

A gentler solution than removal of (potentially) infringing content is when the platform flags content that is of concern to the platform for some reason. This flagging (labelling) can take the form of information provided about the specific user content, such as the result of a fact-check or a warning about possible sensitivities related to viewing or reading it.[31] For example, some of President Donald Trump's posts had

[28] See Koltay (2020–2021, 2022).

[29] Countering illegal hate speech online, #NoPlace4Hate (2018).

[30] Gowder (2023, pp. 167–200).

[31] Morrow et al. (2022).

been tagged by Twitter before he was thrown out of the platform, drawing attention to the fact that the platform believed they contained falsehoods.[32] Besides Twitter, Facebook also uses this approach. The use of contracted or internal fact-checkers is itself a source of further controversy (see below). Labelling after fact-checking makes platforms somewhat "press-like", in that they explicitly react to and enter into quasi-debate with their users, inserting their own opinions into their users' content.

Disinformation is also subject to specific co-regulation within the EU. In 2018, online platforms, leading technology companies and advertising industry players agreed, under pressure from the European Commission, on a code of practice to tackle the spread of online disinformation. The Code of Practice on Disinformation (2018)[33] was designed to set out commitments in a number of areas, ranging from transparency in political advertising to the demonetisation of disinformation spreaders. The Code may appear to be formally voluntary, and to be a self-regulatory instrument, but it is in fact a co-regulatory solution that was clearly imposed on the industry players by the European Commission. Its primary objectives are to deprive the disseminators of disinformation of advertising revenue from that activity, to facilitate the easy identification of publishers of political advertising, to protect the integrity of the platform's services (by taking steps against fake accounts and bots) and to support researchers and fact-checkers working on the subject. In fact, the Code further strengthens and even forces the application of private regulation by platforms, putting decisions on specific content firmly in the hands of the platform operators.[34]

After a few years, it became clear that the Code needed to be revised. In 2021, the European Commission published a Communication,[35] which anticipated the content of the updated Code of Practice. As a result, in 2022, 34 parties signed up to the Strengthened Code of Practice on Disinformation.[36] The updated and strengthened Code aims to deliver on the objectives of the Commission's guidance, by setting out a broader range of commitments and measures to combat online disinformation.[37] While the Code has not yet been officially endorsed by the Commission (as it is formally a self-regulatory instrument), the Commission has set out its expectations in a communication, and has indicated that it considers that, overall, the Code meets these expectations. Since this guidance sets out the Commission's expectations in imperative terms («the Code must», «the signatories must», etc.), it is not an exaggeration to say that the fulfilment of the commitments is seen as an obligation for the platforms, which, if fulfilled, could avoid the imposition of stricter legal regulation. Consequently, it is appropriate to consider the Code not as a self-regulatory instrument but instead as a co-regulatory mechanism, which was not created and is

---

[32] Conger and Isaac (2020).

[33] EU Code of Practice on Disinformation (2018). https://ec.europa.eu/newsroom/dae/redirection/document/87534.

[34] Monti (2016, pp. 220–221).

[35] Communication from the Commission (2021).

[36] 2022 Strengthened Code of Practice on Disinformation (2022). https://digital-strategy.ec.europa.eu/hu/library/2022-strengthened-code-practice-disinformation.

[37] Communication from the Commission (2021), cit.

not followed by industry players of their own free will, but which was developed by a public body (the EU Commission) working in cooperation with industry players.

The Strengthened Code of Practice on Disinformation includes 44 commitments and 128 concrete measures in the areas of demonetisation (reducing financial incentives for the disseminators of disinformation), the transparency of political advertising (provisions to allow users to identify political ads better through better labelling), ensuring the integrity of services (steps against manipulative behaviour such as spam or disinformation), and the protection of the integrity of services (measures to curb manipulative actions such as fake accounts, bot-driven amplification, impersonation and malicious deep spoofing, etc.), empowering users through media literacy initiatives, ensuring greater transparency for platforms' recommendation systems, supporting research into disinformation, and strengthening the fact-checking community.

Such cooperation between the EU and the platforms raises a number of concerns. The lack of honesty and transparency in the cooperation is palpable. The Code was imposed by the European Commission, but is disguised as a self-regulatory instrument. Despite its formally voluntary nature, it is in fact considered by the European Commission to be a binding rule,[38] and platforms are regularly held to account,[39] indicating the Commission's concerns about the proper implementation of their obligations.[40] This is perhaps the least of the problems. The larger issue is that it does not make a substantive statement on the problem of freedom of expression, so platforms may, in order to comply with EU law, take action against content for which the protection of freedom of expression would be justified. The mass nature of moderation activity makes what platforms remove, what content is tagged, what is sent for fact-checking, and so on, completely opaque.

4 Protecting Freedom of Expression Sometimes Takes an Elitist Approach—At the Expense of Citizen Speech

While the EU focuses on the risk assessment of platforms, political advertising and organised disinformation campaigns, some of the measures to be applied also cover communication by ordinary citizens. It is a matter of concern if the speech of the members of society is disproportionately restricted by legal or other means, even if they approach public debate with bad intentions, but especially if they are unaware of the falsehood or potential for harm of the news they are spreading. It was, after all, once hoped that the internet would become a free space for citizens to express their views, constrained only by sufficiently narrow legal rules.

[38] Krukowska (2023).

[39] https://disinfocode.eu/reports-archive/?years=2024.

[40] Digital Services Act—application of the Risk Management Framework, cit.

Ian Cram argues that the ECtHR's jurisprudence privileges traditional (institutional) media over, for example, citizen journalists, imposing standards of "responsible journalism" on the latter.[41] It follows from this that the obligations of the media and other speakers are, where conceptually possible, the same. Cram finds this approach to be elitist, linked to a notion of media freedom that is democratically contradictory, which seeks to create an "enlightened public opinion" at all costs, even if it means going against members of "the people" (in other words, against individual speakers, who may be unruly, perhaps foul-mouthed, and lack the resources of the institutional media to uncover reality or form informed opinions, and who may be wrong or even lie).[42]

The privileged position of the traditional media is effectively recognised in the European Media Freedom Act,[43] adopted in the first half of 2024, which is entirely aimed at protecting the freedom of traditional media, without mentioning citizen journalists.[44] The Regulation also aims to give traditional media more protection against very large online platforms. In addition to the obligations defined in the DSA, it requires that:

> Where a provider of a very large online platform intends to take a decision to suspend the provision of its online intermediation services in relation to content provided by a media service provider … or a decision to restrict the visibility of such content, on the grounds that such content is incompatible with its terms and conditions, prior to such a decision to suspend or restrict visibility taking effect, it shall … communicate to the media service provider concerned a statement of reasons … and give the media service provider the opportunity to reply. (Article 18(4))

The rest of the article also contains other provisions on adequate information, complaint handling and the settlement of disputes (Articles 18(5) to 18(7)).

A similar approach is taken in the UK's Online Safety Act 2023, which also aims to protect traditional media from unnecessary or disproportionate interference by platforms, and explicitly protects news publishers. If a platform wishes to take action against media outlets, it must notify them and give adequate reasons for its action, as required by law. The decision to take action against journalistic content must take the aspects of freedom of expression into account, and a separate notification is required concerning the decision taken and the reasons for it (Sections 18 and 19). Only recognised news publishers and their staff are allowed to publish journalistic content (Section 19(10)), and recognition is subject to authorisation by the media authority or compliance with conditions set by law (Sections 56(1) and 56(2)). These conditions exclude the possibility for non-professional media, in other words citizen

[41] Cram (2022, pp. 30–37).

[42] Ibidem, p. 30.

[43] Regulation (EU) 2024/1083 of the European Parliament and of the Council of 11 April 2024 establishing a common framework for media services in the internal market and amending Directive 2010/13/EU (European Media Freedom Act), PE/4/2024/REV/1, OJ L, 2024/1083, 17.4.2024.

[44] Seipp et al. (2023).

journalists, to benefit from the extra protection. In addition, the traditional media cannot be held liable for the "false communications offence"[45] mentioned above.[46]

The above provisions illustrate the distinction that is drawn between the traditional media and other speakers. On the one hand, there are legitimate reasons for this distinction (the protection of institutionalised media, in line with the traditional understanding of media freedom), but, on the other hand, it leaves other speakers more vulnerable—not all of whom are online trolls or secret service agents engaged in manipulation. It would also be important to make a clear distinction between disinformation originating from governments and dis- or misinformation that comes from ordinary members of society, whether deliberate or in good faith, but in this respect the currently available EU documents are not entirely consistent. It would be worth separating disinformation from government sources or interests from those acts of citizen speech that contain untruths and, obviously, providing stronger protection for the latter. Presumably, given the sophisticated systems available to the platforms, this would technically be possible. If we adhere to the traditional understanding of freedom of expression then members of society should not be disproportionately restricted in their speech, even if they approach public debate with malicious intent, as long as they do not commit any offence in doing so, and certainly not if they are unaware of the falsity or potentially harmful nature of the news they are spreading (the good faith transmission of government disinformation may also fall into this category).

5 Somewhat Surprisingly, Steps Should Be Taken to Promote Diversity of Content on the Internet—And Media Regulation Could Inspire the Fight Against Disinformation

According to the filter bubble or echo chamber theory, people tend to prefer forums that are consistent with their views, where they receive positive feedback and can avoid people who disagree with them.[47] Social media, video-sharing sites and search engines amplify this phenomenon, delivering to each user personalised news and information from like-minded friends and their preferred media. This personalised "newspaper", targeted and specifically compiled for each reader, is the *Daily Me* predicted by Nicholas Negroponte already in the 1990s.[48] The selection of content for this "newspaper" is based on an assessment of the data collected on each user: the more time someone spends on a platform (or the more the platform is able to capture their other online activity), the more accurately they can be targeted with content and

[45] Online Safety Act 2023, s. 179.

[46] Online Safety Act 2023, s. 180(1). For further details, see Coe (n 20) p. 236.

[47] Pariser (2011).

[48] Negroponte (1995).

ads that match their interests. According to Sunstein, this makes liberal people more liberal and conservatives more conservative, while they do not meet or argue with each other's opinions.[49] Traditional media, by comparison, create their own content, without the reader/viewer having a say, so if the media act responsibly, everyone inevitably encounters multiple viewpoints, with the benefit of a more nuanced view and the strengthening of critical thinking.[50]

Internet communication widens the divide between people with different views, which, in turn, weakens social cohesion and tends to increase extremism (polarisation).[51] Social media are eroding the connective tissue of society, making it difficult for people with different opinions to engage in dialogue, while creating closed, online "enclaves" and amplifying the impact of extremist opinions.[52] Although the internet promised to strengthen dialogue between those previously excluded from the media and thus from democratic decision-making, today, in a world of infinite and easily accessible information, the lack of a common "information sphere" or "digital *agora*" used by social groups is threatening democracy and this common ground is being replaced by ideologically segregated and conflicting communities of opinion.[53] Some researchers have sought to refute Sunstein's theory, arguing that the typical internet user is "omnivorous" and calling for a more critical portrayal of the former media landscape.[54] According to these more optimistic voices, many sources of news are available on the internet, no single platform is able to entirely enclose its users in an enclave, and users tend to seek information from multiple, independent sources.[55]

The Digital Services Act rightly seeks to expand the possibilities for users to control the recommender systems (prioritising activities) of the platforms. The recommender systems of platforms must be transparent to users, and must be able to explain to users «why certain information is suggested to the recipient of the service» (Article 27(2)). Where possible, platform providers must also make available «a functionality that allows the recipient of the service to select and to modify at any time their preferred option» (Article 27(3)). Based on the regulation, the very large online platforms and the very large online search engines must provide the possibility for their users to opt out of the profiling-based operation of their recommender systems. Users can choose to have the content offered to them by the recommender systems—which are key to them accessing content—not be based on their profile on the platform, meaning the data collected about them (Article 38). This provision allows the users to break out of the filter bubble, which is partly created by the users themselves, that could potentially, among other things, facilitate the spread

[49] Sunstein (2017, Chap. 1).

[50] Ibidem, pp. 140–148.

[51] Ibidem, Chap. 3.

[52] Heller (2016).

[53] Polonski (2016).

[54] Wu (2016, pp. 214–215), Barberá (2020), Zuiderveen Borgesius et al. (2016), and Moeller and Helberger (2018).

[55] Dutton et al. (2017).

of disinformation. Of course, it is questionable how many users will take advantage of this option.

Platforms are becoming increasingly media-like, but their regulation is only partially in line with this phenomenon. Platforms edit user content (through moderation leading to removal or shadow banning), select content that is presented to individual users (through recommender systems), occasionally tag content to draw attention to concerns about the content, and employ fact-checkers to help with this. The above-mentioned European Commission guidelines also point them in this direction,[56] meaning that their activities in this area have also partly become a legal obligation. It is not entirely unimaginable that the regulation of platforms will be brought closer to that of traditional media.

Some of the tools familiar from traditional media regulation can be used indirectly to combat disinformation. One such tool could be the right of reply. The Audiovisual Media Services Directive prescribes that EU Member States should introduce national regulations with regard to television broadcasting that ensure adequate legal remedies for persons whose personality rights have been infringed through false statements (Article 28). Such regulations are applied throughout Europe, and typically impose obligations not only on audiovisual media but also on the radio and the print and online press.[57] Ensuring the right of reply is also mentioned as a possible tool in the EU High Level Expert Group's report on combating disinformation.[58] The regulation in its current form cannot be applied to platforms, as they themselves publish the communication on which the reply is based, and therefore they cannot be obliged to provide the reply. A substantially modified version of the right of reply could help users of the platforms to be better informed. Platforms could provide an opportunity for a party who has been attacked in a post to add their own position to that post, or to show others a different position in a subsequent post.

Another weapon in the war on disinformation could be some kind of transposition of the requirement for impartial news reporting to platforms. Under this rule, news and information programmes of the traditional media are required to report on public affairs in an unbiased way. The rule can apply to both television and radio broadcasters, and is enforced in many European countries.[59] For example, the British media and communications authority Ofcom took action against a television channel broadcasting Russian propaganda, based on this rule.[60] Of course, legislation can in no way require social media platforms to operate with the same impartiality as a

---

[56] Communication to the Commission (2024), cit.

[57] Ho Youm (2008), Richter (2018–2019, pp. 14–19), and Koltay (2013).

[58] Final report of the High Level Expert Group on fake news and online disinformation (2018, pp. 15–16).

[59] See, for example, the German (Medienstaatsvertrag of 14/28 April 2020, art. 59) and the British media legislation (Communications Act 2003, ss 319(2)(c) and 319(2)(d), 319(8) and 320, and Broadcasting Code, s. 5).

[60] Notice of a decision under s 3(3) of the Broadcasting Act 1990 and s 3(3) of the Broadcasting Act 1996 in respect of licences TLCS 000881, TLCS 001686 and DTPS 000072 held by ANO TV Novosti. Ofcom. https://www.ofcom.org.uk/__data/assets/pdf_file/0014/234023/revocation-notice-ano-tv-novosti.pdf.

television or radio news programme, particularly because platforms do not produce content that is relevant in this context, and no platform can monitor all the content created by its users in this respect. Requiring a platform to try to present content in a completely impartial way would mean that, despite the characteristics mentioned above, it would have the same obligations as a television or radio editor. However, it is technically feasible for a platform to show different views on a controversial public issue successively, with different content and from different sources. Requiring platforms to do so would not be the same as the obligation of balanced coverage, but it could help users to be exposed to a diversity of content and to be informed about public issues from a diversity of sources.[61] In fact, social media platforms are already acting in certain cases in accordance with the principle derived from the right of reply and balanced coverage, for example when it comes to the practice of tagging individual posts.[62] The current practice could be extended, however, and social media could be obliged to make available, alongside a post on a controversial issue, other posts that present divergent views on that issue.[63]

The accessibility of news produced by traditional media through Facebook may be drastically reduced following certain decisions by Mark Zuckerberg, the CEO of Meta,[64] which the platform announces from time to time.[65] As a result, access to public affairs content is naturally falling, while we still expect the traditional media to be the main source of reliable, verified information. As such, a third instrument could be to impose a must-carry obligation on platforms for public affairs content, or more specifically for content produced by the traditional media dealing with public affairs, along the lines of the public interest obligations imposed on media service providers. Some media service providers are obliged by national regulations to provide news programmes and to report on important local or national events (depending on their reception area). Such a rule could also require platforms to deliver a certain amount of political or public affairs content (with a view to ensuring the diversity and balanced nature of such information) to their users, whether the users explicitly request it or not.

However, user preferences should still prevail in this case; in other words, the user could, if they so wish, opt out from viewing content of public interest if they are not interested in public affairs. Even so, imposing such or similar public interest obligations would prevent the settings of platform recommender systems from overshadowing or marginalising the presentation of content on public affairs to users, and would increase the chances that such content would reach users, and this might also be beneficial for the debates on public affairs that take place on platforms. Jacob Rowbottom has also suggested that, in a similar way to the respective obligations of public media services, platforms could be required to host debates or similar events

---

[61] Rowbottom (2021, p. 246).

[62] Morrow et al. (2022).

[63] Even the US equivalent of the balanced coverage requirement, the fairness doctrine, could be applied to platforms, with appropriate adaptations. See Napoli (2021).

[64] Bell (2018).

[65] Roose and Isaac (2021).

related to electoral processes, or to ensure that candidates can communicate freely and effectively through their services.[66]

The creation of these instruments, while not without concerns—as their misuse is easily conceivable, either by the platform itself or by the users concerned—would, in an ideal scenario, contribute to wider diffusion of diverse content on social media. This diversity is of a different nature than that which media regulation seeks to promote: it does not relate to increasing the amount of content available in general but to the actual delivery of content available to individual users. Adopting these approaches would of course have a negative impact on the freedom of platforms, but, as in media regulation, convincing arguments could be made for their introduction in platform law as well. The scarcity of content and supply is gone, but user attention is finite and unlikely to increase further, and it is important that this attention is also focused on public affairs debates, while reducing the filter bubble effect where possible and drawing users' attention to the many different views on any given public affairs issue.

6 The Problems with Fact-Checkers and with the Media Are Pretty Similar

One of the tasks of fact-checkers, who are increasingly called upon to help in the fight against disinformation, is to assess whether a certain content is disinformation. This is understandable, since the EU would consider it incompatible with freedom of expression, if state bodies, courts and authorities were to decide on the veracity of otherwise legitimate assertions. However, it is also doubtful whether leaving such decisions up to private individuals is capable of facilitating informed, fair and unbiased decision-making and whether it does not itself pose a threat to freedom of expression.

The positive side of the fact-checking phenomenon is that those who are not involved in informing the public as journalists—although journalists can also be fact-checkers and the institutional media can also launch fact-checking sections—can play a role in ensuring that public discourse is based on facts, thus enabling the conduct of meaningful debate and the formation of informed opinion. However, fact-checkers themselves may also be biased, just as they can be wrong,[67] and not necessarily deliberately, out of malice, but simply because of cognitive biases arising from the limitations of human cognition.[68] Some experts argue that human cognitive mechanisms make it difficult to ensure effective fact-checking at all.[69]

The credibility of fact-checking can also be easily undermined by the fact that «fact-checkers... disagree more often than one might suppose, particularly when

[66] Rowbottom (2021, p. 247).

[67] Vinhas and Bastos (2022) and Six ways fact checkers are biased (2022).

[68] Soprano et al. (2024).

[69] See, for example, Park et al. (2021).

politicians craft language to be ambiguous».[70] According to one survey, «fact-checkers are both less likely to fact-check ideologically close entities and more likely to agree with them».[71] Others point out that political fact-checking has only reinforced what was already believed to be true knowledge and the hegemonic view of what constitutes important and reliable information. The results thus indicate that fact checking helps to reinforce the perspectives and knowledge base of political elites, rather than entailing a critical correction of them.[72] Moreover, the public cannot hold fact-checkers accountable, even less so than the traditional media (through legal regulation or self-regulation based on ethical considerations). Their activities are neither necessarily transparent, nor do they have guarantees of independence. In many cases, such as the EU-funded fact checking organisations, they operate using public money, which makes these shortcomings even more problematic.

In fact, traditionally the media is supposed to do the fact-checking, which we used to call simply journalism. However, the media's trust index is falling rapidly in the EU Member States,[73] the UK[74] and the USA.[75] It seems that the media can no longer do the job alone, and people no longer trust it. However, if people are increasingly losing trust in the traditional media, what reason is there to trust fact-checking organisations instead? While fact-checkers share similar problems with traditional media, their emergence is an interesting development and, if they can overcome their institutional problems, it is not inconceivable that they could become useful actors in the public sphere.[76] Here it is worth reiterating that those fact-checkers which work on behalf of or with the approval or support of social media platforms, and which check the veracity of users' posts on those sites, bring social media closer to traditional media in terms of the way they operate, as they have a specific editorial role. Many of them, however, have complained that social media companies (Facebook in particular) were using them as fig leaves, and that the platforms were not really interested in effective fact-checking and taking the appropriate action regarding inaccurate information.[77]

In January 2025, Meta announced that it will get rid of fact checkers on Facebook and Instagram, replacing them with user-generated "community notes". "Fact checkers have been too politically biased and have destroyed more trust than they've created," Zuckerberg said in a video announcing the new policy. "What started as a movement to be more inclusive has increasingly been used to shut down opinions and shut out people with different ideas, and it's gone too far".[78] (Presumably, the approaching second Trump presidency had also something to do with the change.)

---

[70] Lim (2018).

[71] Louis-Sidois (2022).

[72] Steensen et al. (2023).

[73] Watson (2023).

[74] Smith (2023).

[75] Brenan (2022).

[76] See Epstein (2024).

[77] Levin (2018).

[78] Meta is getting rid of fact checkers. Zuckerberg acknowledged more harmful content will appear on the platforms now (2025).

In summary, the rise of fact-checking is a sign of the media crisis. It underlines that the public sphere is being transformed, partly in correlation to this crisis, and that the new media, in many ways, share many of the problems of the traditional media. If people completely lose confidence in institutions (including the media), and their faith in the ability to get to know the objective truth is also shaken—with the result that each "tribe" of these disintegrating societies will accept only its "own truth", so everyone will have the right to "their truth", and there will be no consensus on the existence of facts that can in principle be objectively proved—then it is unlikely that such faith will be restored by fact-checkers.

7 The Communication of the Government and Platforms that Results in Restrictions on Freedom of Expression also Deserves Attention in Terms of the Fight Against Disinformation

Murthy v Missouri[79] (formerly *Missouri v Biden*) was initiated after the states of Missouri and Louisiana filed a lawsuit against the US government in the Western District of Louisiana. The parties to the lawsuit alleged that the federal government had pressured social media platforms to censor conservative views and criticism of the Biden administration, in violation of the right to free expression. The content removed was largely critical of government actions related to the COVID-19 pandemic, critical of the validity of the 2020 elections, critical of the policies of President Biden and other government officials, or was related to the Hunter Biden laptop controversy. The US government, in response, claimed that it had only made requests to the platforms through its representatives to remove posts containing misinformation.

Judge Terry A. Doughty (US District Court, Western District of Louisiana, Monroe Division), on 4 July 2023, issued a preliminary injunction prohibiting several government agencies and members of the Biden administration from contacting social media platforms to request the removal of user content, apart from content related to illegal activity.[80] On appeal, the Fifth Circuit Court of Appeals found that the government's contact with social media companies had some coercive character, in violation of the First Amendment, but narrowed the personal scope of Judge Doughty's injunction.[81] The US Supreme Court, with the dissenting opinion of three judges, suspended the Fifth Circuit's injunction and granted review of the case.[82]

Judge Doughty's argument deserves attention. According to the reasoning of the order, the critical question was whether the government had «significantly encouraged» the platforms to remove the content concerned. The question is «whether the

[79] *Murthy v Missouri* 603 US ___ (2024).

[80] *Missouri v Biden*, No. 22-cv-1213 (W.D. La., July 4, 2023).

[81] No. 23-30445 (5th Cir., October 3, 2023).

[82] *Murthy v Missouri* 601 US ___ (2023).

government's encouragement is so significant that we should attribute the private party's choice to the State».[83] «In addition to the 'significant encouragement' theory, the Government may also be held responsible for private conduct if the Government exercises coercive power over the private party in question».[84] The question is not what decision the social media platform would have made of its own volition, but whether the government influenced the private party's conduct to such an extent that the decision is essentially attributable to the government.[85] Judge Doughty wrote that the plaintiffs had outlined «a federal regime of mass censorship, and presented specific examples of how such censorship has harmed the States' quasi-sovereign interests in protecting their residents' freedom of expression».[86] «[T]he evidence produced thus far depicts an almost dystopian scenario. During the COVID-19 pandemic, a period perhaps best characterized by widespread doubt and uncertainty, the United States Government seems to have assumed a role similar to an Orwellian 'Ministry of Truth'».[87]

On the one hand, the District Court's decision can be interpreted as a victory for free speech, preventing the government censorship that has affected many Americans.[88] On the other hand, the decision has, of course, been criticised in many quarters. *The New York Times* has expressed concern that, as a result of the decision, the government's ability to counter disinformation will be significantly limited.[89] Others highlighted that to ensure substantiated content moderation in the public interest, platforms need to cooperate with government agencies that have the necessary expertise and information.[90] To label the co-operation between governmental bodies and platforms as censorship runs the risk of chilling (unduly restricting) moderation by platforms and the related scientific research.[91] A Supreme Court decision agreeing with Judge Doughty «would radically challenge the ability of platforms to conduct content moderation based on authoritative information, and likely worsen the quality of information that U.S. users are shown in social media».[92]

The Supreme Court rejected the District Court's decision in June 2024 and remanded the case for further proceedings.[93] The Court held that the moderation decisions failed to establish a causal link between the government's communications and the platform's decision.[94] Since the injunction was applicable, by definition, for future acts (the prohibition of such acts), the applicants would also have had to show

---

[83] *Missouri v Biden*, cit., p. 93.
[84] Ibidem, p. 94.
[85] Ibidem, p. 95.
[86] Ibidem, p. 124.
[87] Ibidem, p. 154.
[88] Schilke (2023).
[89] Lee Myers (2023).
[90] Macpherson (2023).
[91] Ibidem.
[92] Guarna (2023).
[93] *Murthy v Missouri*, cit.
[94] Ibidem, pp. 10–21.

that there was a significant risk of future harm to them from the government communications, which could probably be remedied by the injunction.[95] The Supreme Court did not see this as proven either.

As an interesting follow-up to the case (but without any possible legal effect), in a letter sent to House Judiciary Committee Chairman Jim Jordan in August 2024, Mark Zuckerberg admitted that the Biden administration officials repeatedly pressured Facebook to censor certain COVID-19 content.[96] Zuckerberg also expressed «regret that we were not more outspoken about it», and lamented making «some choices... [that] we wouldn't make today». In the letter he also acknowledged that the FBI warned the company about potential Russian disinformation operation regarding the Hunter Biden laptop case. Later it turned out that the story was genuine, so, as Zuckerberg wrote, «we shouldn't have demoted the story».

Regardless the decision of the Supreme Court, one problem is clear: while it is impossible to expect large internet or media companies and individual government officials or agencies not to communicate with each other behind closed doors, it is very difficult, indeed virtually impossible, to determine when such communications cross the line that should be respected in a democracy. (The problem is, of course, by no means internet- or platform-specific, and is also relevant to the relationship between the traditional media and the government.) The aim of countering disinformation is, naturally, justifiable, as is the use of expert knowledge in platform moderation decisions. However, in most cases, the government must keep its distance from the opinions of its citizens, even when they post false information or deliberate lies. Social media platforms should not be forced to engage in hidden state censorship, nor should they even be its willing enforcers. There is no really good answer to this dilemma. What can be said, however, is that the issue of covert communication between platforms and governments deserves more attention in Europe, too.

8 Conclusions

In the fight against disinformation, there is a curious timidity on the part of EU bodies and national legislators and governments. While refraining from imposing legal restrictions (new bans) on freedom of expression by traditional means that would respect constitutional rules, they essentially shift the task of restricting speech onto online platforms. I would not, of course, argue that the best and only way to combat disinformation is to expand the legal limits on freedom of expression; I would simply point out that this is also a possible tool in the fight against it.

The current approach essentially leaves the decision-making on disinformation up to the platforms, but does not exercise any meaningful control over their decisions, and this could lead to restrictions on otherwise legally and constitutionally permissible expressions. Under the doctrine of freedom of expression, the rights of

[95] Ibidem, pp. 21–27.

[96] Zuckerberg expresses regrets over COVID misinformation crackdown (2024).

the masses who finally have access to the public arena through the internet as a result of the transformation of the former media world must be protected. However, the fight against disinformation is not only detrimental to governments or intelligence services acting with ill intent but also to members of the masses themselves.

It is paradoxical, that the diversity of online content should also be a regulatory consideration, even on the Internet, which otherwise offers a wealth of content. Yet this is what we propose, drawing attention to the possibility of using some of the instruments of media regulation, albeit after thorough transformation.

The efforts of the EU, the Member States and national governments will obviously play an important role in tackling the phenomenon of disinformation. However the regulatory framework evolves in the future, it is clear that it remains primarily the responsibility of the individual—the citizen—to be well informed, to form informed opinions and to be critical of what others say. The primary task for states and governments is therefore to create an educational, social and economic environment that helps generations of capable citizens to grow up equipped to sift through the vast quantities of information available to them, and not forgetting about those who have already fallen victim to mass online disinformation as adults.

References

Blasphemy, insult and hatred: finding answers in a democratic society. Council of Europe, Strasbourg (2010). https://www.venice.coe.int/webforms/documents/?pdf=cdl-std(2010)047-e

Code of Practice on Disinformation (2018). https://ec.europa.eu/newsroom/dae/redirection/document/87534

Communication from the Commission to the European Parliament, the Council, the European Economic and Social Committee and the Committee of the Regions, 'European Commission Guidance on Strengthening the Code of Practice on Disinformation'. Brussels, 26.05.2021, final

Communication to the Commission, Approval of the content of a draft Communication from the Commission on Guidelines for providers of Very Large Online Platforms and Very Large Online Search Engines on the mitigation of systemic risks for electoral processes pursuant to the Digital Services Act (Regulation (EU) 2022/2065). Brussels, 26.3.2024, C(2024) 2121 final

Council Framework Decision 2008/913/JHA of 28 November 2008 on combating certain forms and expression of racism and xenophobia by means of criminal law

Countering illegal hate speech online, #NoPlace4Hate. European Commission (2018). http://ec.europa.eu/newsroom/just/item-detail.cfm?item_id=54300

Digital Services Act – application of the Risk Management Framework to Russian disinformation campaigns. European Union, Luxembourg (2023). https://data.europa.eu/doi/10.2759/764631

Facebook files. A Wall Street Journal Investigation. The Wall Street Journal (2021). https://www.wsj.com/articles/the-facebook-files-11631713039

Final report of the High Level Expert Group on fake news and online disinformation (2018). European Commission. https://ec.europa.eu/digital-single-market/en/news/final-report-high-level-expert-group-fake-news-and-online-disinformation

Meta is getting rid of fact checkers. Zuckerberg acknowledged more harmful content will appear on the platforms now. CNN (2025, Jan 7). https://edition.cnn.com/2025/01/07/tech/meta-censorship-moderation/index.html

Notice of a decision under s 3(3) of the Broadcasting Act 1990 and s 3(3) of the Broadcasting Act 1996 in respect of licences TLCS 000881, TLCS 001686 and DTPS 000072 held by

ANO TV Novosti. Ofcom. https://www.ofcom.org.uk/__data/assets/pdf_file/0014/234023/revocation-notice-ano-tv-novosti.pdf
Six ways fact checkers are biased. AllSides (2022, Feb 23). https://www.allsides.com/blog/6-ways-fact-checkers-are-biased
Zuckerberg expresses regrets over COVID misinformation crackdown. Washington Post (2024, Aug 24). https://www.washingtonpost.com/technology/2024/08/27/meta-zuckerberg-covid-misinformation-jordan-white-house
Barberá P (2020) Social media, echo chambers, and political polarization. In: Persily N, Tucker JA (eds) Social media and democracy: the state of the field, prospects for reform. Cambridge University Press, New York, pp 34–55
Bell E (2018, Jan 21) Why Facebook's news feed changes are bad news for democracy. The Guardian. https://www.theguardian.com/media/media-blog/2018/jan/21/why-facebook-news-feed-changes-bad-news-democracy
Bernal P (2018a) Fakebook: why Facebook makes the fake news problem inevitable. Northern Ireland Legal Quart 69(4):513–530
Bernal P (2018b) The internet, warts and all: free speech, privacy and truth. Cambridge University Press, New York, pp 241–245
Brenan M (2022, Oct 18) Americans' trust in media remains near record low. Gallup. https://news.gallup.com/poll/403166/americans-trust-media-remains-near-record-low.aspx
Chemerinsky E (1998) More speech is better. UCLA Law Rev 45:1635–1644
Coe P (2023) Tackling online false information in the United Kingdom: the Online Safety Act 2023 and its disconnection from free speech law and theory. J Media Law 15(2):213–242
Conger K, Isaac M (2020, May 28) Defying Trump, twitter doubles down on labeling tweets. The New York Times. https://www.nytimes.com/2020/05/28/technology/trump-twitter-fact-check.html
Cram I (2022) Liberal democracy, law and the citizen speaker: regulating online speech. Hart, Oxford
Darer Littman S (2020) Deepfake. Scholastic Press, New York
Dutton WH et al (2017) Social shaping of the politics of internet search and networking: moving beyond filter bubbles, echo chambers, and fake news. Quello Center Working Paper No. 2944191
Epstein MM (2024) Sustaining country-specific fact-checking remedies, the Sierra Leone experience. Stetson Bus Law Rev 3(1):53–75
Gowder P (2023) The networked Leviathan. Cambridge University Press, New York
Guarna T (2023, Aug 17) A ruling in favor of *Missouri v. Biden* would mean worse, less informed content moderation. Publicknowledge.org. https://publicknowledge.org/missouri-v-biden-could-mean-worse-content-moderation
Heller N (2016, Nov 18) The failure of Facebook democracy. The New Yorker. https://www.newyorker.com/culture/cultural-comment/the-failure-of-facebook-democracy
Hennebel L, Hochmann T (eds) (2011) Genocide denials and the law. Oxford University Press, Oxford
Ho Youm K (2008) The right of reply and freedom of the press: an international and comparative perspective. George Washington Law Rev 76(4):1017–1064
Kahn RA (2004) Holocaust denial and the law: a comparative study. Palgrave Macmillan, New York
Koltay A (2013) The right of reply in a European comparative perspective. Hung J Legal Stud – Acta Juridica Hungarica 54(1):73–89
Koltay A (2020–2021) Private censorship of internet gatekeepers. Louisville Law Rev 59(2):255–304
Koltay A (2021) On the constitutionality of the punishment of scaremongering in the Hungarian legal system. Hung Yearb Int Law Eur Law 9:23–42
Koltay A (2022) The protection of freedom of expression from social media platforms. Mercer Law Rev 73(2):523–589

Koltay A (2025) Freedom of expression and the regulation of disinformation in the European Union. In: Krotoszynski RJ, Koltay A, Garden C (eds) Disinformation, misinformation, and democracy: legal approaches in comparative context. Cambridge University Press, New York, pp 133–160
Krukowska E (2023, May 27) Twitter withdraws from EU Disinformation Code, Commissioner says. Time. https://time.com/6283183/twitter-withdraws-from-eu-disinformation-code-commissioner-says
Lee Myers S (2023, Sept 8) Appeals court rules White House overstepped 1st Amendment on social media. The New York Times. https://www.nytimes.com/2023/09/08/business/appeals-court-first-amendment-social-media.html
Levi L (2018) Real "fake news" and fake "fake news." First Amendment Law Rev 16:232–327
Levin S (2018, Dec 13) "They don't care": Facebook fact-checking in disarray as journalists push to cut ties. The Guardian. https://www.theguardian.com/technology/2018/dec/13/they-dont-care-facebook-fact-checking-in-disarray-as-journalists-push-to-cut-ties
Lim C (2018) Checking how fact-checkers check. Res Politics 5(3):1–7
Louis-Sidois C (2022) Both judge and party? An analysis of the political leaning of fact-checkers. SSRN. https://papers.ssrn.com/sol3/papers.cfm?abstract_id=4030887
Macpherson L (2023, Dec 6) A Supreme Court ruling in *Murthy v. Missouri* could help – or hinder – democracy next year. Publicknowledge.org. https://publicknowledge.org/a-supreme-court-ruling-in-murthy-v-missouri-could-help-or-hinder-democracy-next-year
Moeller J, Helberger N (2018) Beyond the filter bubble: concepts, myths, evidence and issues for future debates. Report Drafted for the Dutch Media Regulator. https://pure.uva.nl/ws/files/29285427/beyond_the_filter_bubble_concepts_myths_evidence_and_issues_for_future_debates_1_.pdf
Monti M (2016) The EU code of practice on disinformation and the risk of the privatisation of censorship. In: Giusti S, Piras E (eds) Democracy and fake news: information manipulation and post-truth politics. Routledge, Abingdon, pp 214–225
Morrow G et al (2022) The emerging science of content labeling: contextualizing social media content moderation. J Am Soc Inf Sci 73(10):1365–1386
Napoli PM (2019) Social media and the public interest: media regulation in the disinformation age. Columbia University Press, New York
Napoli PM (2021) Back from the dead (again): the specter of the fairness doctrine and its lessons for social media regulation. Policy Internet 13(3):300–314
Negroponte N (1995) Being digital. Knopf Doubleday, New York
Oster J (2017) European and international media law. Cambridge University Press, New York
Pariser E (2011) The filter bubble: what the internet is hiding from you. Penguin Books, London
Park S et al (2021) The presence of unexpected biases in online fact-checking. Harvard Kennedy School Misinformation Rev 2(1). https://misinforeview.hks.harvard.edu/wp-content/uploads/2021/01/park_unexpected_biases_online_fact_checking_20210127.pdf
Perrigo B (2021, Nov 22) Inside Frances Haugen's decision to take on Facebook. Time. https://time.com/6121931/frances-haugen-facebook-whistleblower-profile
Polonski V (2016, Aug 4) The biggest threat to democracy? Your social media feed. World Economic Forum. https://www.weforum.org/agenda/2016/08/the-biggest-threat-to-democracy-your-social-media-feed
Richter A (2018–2019) Fake news and freedom of the media. J Int Media Entertainment Law 8(2):1–34
Roose K, Isaac M (2021, Feb 10) Facebook dials down the politics for users. The New York Times. https://www.nytimes.com/2021/02/10/technology/facebook-reduces-politics-feedshtml
Rowbottom J (2012) Lies, manipulation and elections-controlling false campaign statements. Oxf J Leg Stud 32(3):507–535
Rowbottom J (2021) Transposing public service media obligations to dominant platforms. In: Moore M, Tambini D (eds) Regulating Big Tech: policy responses to digital dominance. Oxford University Press, New York, pp 235–253

Quintais JP, Appelman N, Ó Fathaigh R (2023) Using terms and conditions to apply fundamental rights to content moderation. German Law J 24(5):881–911
Schilke R (2023, Sept 8) Appeals court upholds ruling prohibiting government officials from communicating with social media companies. Washington Examiner. https://www.washingtonexaminer.com/news/2446694/appeals-court-upholds-ruling-prohibiting-government-officials-from-communicating-with-social-media-companies
Seipp T, Ó Fathaigh R, Van Drunen M (2023) Defining the "media" in Europe: pitfalls of the proposed European Media Freedom Act. J Media Law 15(1):39–51
Smith M (2023, May 25) Which media outlets do Britons trust in 2023? YouGov. https://yougov.co.uk/topics/politics/articles-reports/2023/05/25/which-media-outlets-do-britons-trust-2023
Soprano M et al (2024) Cognitive biases in fact-checking and their countermeasures: a review. Inf Process Manag 61(3). https://doi.org/10.1016/j.ipm.2024.103672
Steensen S, Kalsnes B, Westlund O (2023) The limits of live fact-checking: epistemological consequences of introducing a breaking news logic to political fact-checking. New Media Soc 26(11):6347–6365
Sunstein CR (2017) #Republic: divided democracy in the age of social media. Princeton University Press, Princeton
Sunstein CR (2021) Liars: falsehoods and free speech in an age of deception. Oxford University Press, New York
Villiger ME (2023) Handbook on the European Convention on human rights. Brill, Leiden
Vinhas O, Bastos MT (2022) Fact-checking misinformation: eight notes on consensus reality. Journal Stud 23(4):448–468
Watson A (2023, Aug 30) Share of respondents who tended to trust the written press in countries in the European Union as of February 2022. Statista. https://www.statista.com/statistics/454403/europe-trust-in-the-written-press-by-country
Wu T (2016) The attention merchants: the epic scramble to get inside our heads. Alfred A. Knopf, New York
Zuiderveen Borgesius FJ et al (2016) Should we worry about filter bubbles? Internet Policy Rev 5(1):1–16

How to Regulate Online Political Advertising to Ensure Democratic Electoral Processes? Effectiveness, Differences and Influences of the EU and US Measures

Claudia Massa

Abstract The present chapter will first assess the reasons why online political advertising constitutes a dangerous vector of disinformation, and then delve into the legislative solution adopted in the EU to address this phenomenon, namely the Regulation on transparency and targeting of political advertising ("TTPAR"), which is applicable from 10 October 2025. The relevance of this act had already emerged before the date set for its application, with the publication of a significant ruling by the Romanian Constitutional Court in December 2024, which will be analysed in order to reflect on the relationship existing between the TTPAR and, on the one hand, other international instruments such as the Code of Good Conduct in Electoral Matters adopted in the context of the Council of Europe, and, on the other hand, with the other EU tool adopted to combat disinformation, namely the Digital Services Act ("DSA"). Finally, the present chapter will offer a brief overview of the US measures adopted at both federal and state levels to somehow regulate online political advertising, in order to evaluate whether there are common trends between the EU and US legal orders and if the adopted measures are effective enough to address one of the most severe threats to democracy and the rule of law.

1 Introduction

One of the key tools of an electoral campaign is political advertising, as it allows candidates to directly convey their message to voters and influence the political debate. By running ads across various types of media, candidates can reach a wide audience, highlight important issues and also draw attention to the shortcomings of their opponents. Political advertising has evolved from primarily print-based

C. Massa (✉)
Department of Law, University of Naples Federico II, Naples, Italy
e-mail: claudia.massa@unina.it

R. Mastroianni and C. Massa (eds.), *Disinformation in New and Old Media in the XXI Century*, Ius Gentium: Comparative Perspectives on Law and Justice 136,
https://doi.org/10.1007/978-3-032-18830-4_5

(newspapers, flyers) to many formats, including radio, television and now digital advertising on social media platforms, websites, search engines and more.[1]

Political advertising, especially in the online environment, can be a means of disinformation. This risk became particularly evident during the campaigns for the 2016 US presidential election and the Brexit referendum.[2] On those occasions, the activities of the companies Cambridge Analytica and Aggregate IQ revealed the extensive use of personal data obtained from millions of Facebook users so that tailored political advertisements could be directed to them (the so-called "targeting"). Since then, a growing and widespread attention to online political advertising has been given.

The European Commission, in December 2020, presented the Democracy Action Plan, whose objectives include promoting free and fair elections and within which an initial assessment of the challenges posed by political advertising and by the new techniques used to target advertising on the basis of users' personal data was included. In this context, the Commission adopted a package of measures to protect the integrity of elections that contains the 2024 Regulation on transparency and targeting of political advertising (hereinafter: "TTPAR").[3] Its provisions are connected with those of other acts adopted within the same context of the aforementioned Action Plan but in order to pursue slightly different objectives (i.e., respectively, supporting media freedom and pluralism and combating disinformation), namely the so-called "European Media Freedom Act" (hereinafter: "EMFA")[4] and the Digital Services Act (hereinafter: "DSA").[5] With the adoption of these legal measures the EU has implemented its broader policy on disinformation inaugurated years earlier,[6] comprising the adoption of soft-law instruments such as conclusions,[7] communications,[8] resolutions and, finally, the 2018 Code of Practice on Disinformation (which later became

[1] On the characteristics of online political communication, see D'Ippolito (2020).

[2] See Confessore (2018) and Hern (2018).

[3] Regulation (EU) 2024/900 of the European Parliament and of the Council of 13 March 2024 on the transparency and targeting of political advertising, PE/90/2023/REV/1, OJ L.

[4] Regulation (EU) 2024/1083 of the European Parliament and of the Council of 11 April 2024 establishing a common framework for media services in the internal market and amending Directive 2010/13/EU (European Media Freedom Act), PE/4/2024/REV/1, OJ L. For more details on the EMFA, see in this volume Pollicino, How seriously should be taken disinformation? Constitutional and policy dilemmas in a comparative perspective, Sect. 7.2. See also Massa (2024, pp. 295–311).

[5] Regulation (EU) 2022/2065 of the European Parliament and of the Council of 19 October 2022 on a Single Market For Digital Services and amending Directive 2000/31/EC (Digital Services Act), PE/30/2022/REV/1, OJ L 277, 27.10.2022. For more details on the DSA, see in this volume Koltay, A critique of European attempts to regulate online disinformation, Sect. 3.

[6] Eskens (2024, pp. 2–6).

[7] European Council, Conclusion of the European Council Meeting of 19 and 20 March 2015.

[8] European Commission and High Representative of the Union for Foreign Affairs and Security Policy, Joint Communication to the European Parliament and the Council: Joint Framework on Countering Hybrid Threats—a European Union Response, JOIN/2016/018 final; Communication from the Commission to the European Parliament, the Council, the European Economic and Social Committee and the Committee of the Regions—Tackling Online Disinformation: A European Approach, COM/2018/236 final.

the 2022 Strengthened Code of Practice on Disinformation[9]) and an Action Plan against Disinformation, all with non-binding value.

In the US, by virtue of the different structure of the legal order, disinformation through online political advertising has been addressed with various tools adopted at both federal and state levels.

The present chapter will first assess the reasons why online political advertising constitutes a dangerous vector of disinformation (Sect. 2), and then delve into the legislative solution adopted in the EU to address this phenomenon, namely the TTPAR, which is applicable from 10 October 2025 (Sect. 3). The relevance of this act had already emerged before the date set for its application, with the publication of a ruling by the Romanian Constitutional Court in December 2024, which will be analysed in order to reflect on the relationship existing between the TTPAR and, on the one hand, other international instruments such as the Code of Good Conduct in Electoral Matters adopted in the context of the Council of Europe, and, on the other hand, with the other EU tool adopted to combat disinformation, namely the DSA (Sect. 4). Finally, the present chapter will offer a brief overview of the US measures adopted at both federal and state levels to somehow regulate online political advertising (Sect. 5), in order to evaluate whether there are common trends between the EU and US legal orders and if the adopted measures are effective enough to address one of the most severe threats to democracy and the rule of law (Sect. 6).

2 Online Political Advertising as a Vector of Disinformation

According to the European Commission, disinformation is understood as «verifiably false or misleading information that is created, presented and disseminated for economic gain or to intentionally deceive the public, and may cause public harm»,[10] whereby "public harm" includes threats to democratic political and policy-making processes as well as public goods such as the protection of EU citizens' health, the environment or security. Accordingly, the European Parliament defined disinformation as «verifiably false or misleading information that is intentionally created, presented or disseminated with a view to causing harm or producing a potentially disruptive effect on society by deceiving the public or for intentional economic gain».[11]

[9] 2022 Code of Practice on Disinformation, https://digital-strategy.ec.europa.eu/en/policies/code-practice-disinformation. For a comment on the Code, see Pollicino (2022, pp. 101–104).

[10] Communication COM/2018/236, cit., pp. 3–4.

[11] European Parliament resolution of 9 March 2022 on foreign interference in all democratic processes in the European Union, including disinformation (2020/2268(INI)), OJ C 347, 9.9.2022, para. I. For more details on the difference between disinformation and misinformation, see in this volume Baade, Possibilities and Limits of Regulating Disinformation and Propaganda in Hybrid Warfare, Sect. 2; Pollicino, How seriously should be taken disinformation? Constitutional and policy dilemmas in a comparative perspective, section 3. See also Sassi and Strepa (2025, pp. 164–165).

Political advertising can be a dangerous means of disinformation especially when the elections approach. In this period, in fact, even those who do not regularly pay attention to politics experience a media onslaught not only with the multiplication of spaces devoted to politics on "old" offline media such as newspapers, television and radio, but also increasingly with the appearance of videos, photos, posts and articles on "new" online media such as media platforms, websites, mobile applications, computer games and other digital interfaces.

Online political advertising is of greatest concern from the perspective of the spread of disinformation for three main reasons: first, the advertising may hide its political nature (for instance, a social media post could actually be a paid political message); second, it may come from sponsors outside of the Union (and this can generate an unlawful interference in democratic processes); third it may be subject to targeting or ad-delivery techniques.

From the first point of view, the problem related to the spread of disinformation arises from the difficulty in clearly demarcating between political and commercial communication.[12] The main issue is that today's key web players, the "influencers", who are most commonly engaged in commercial advertising, can express their political opinions freely in the form of videos or social media posts and earn ad revenue based on the number of views they generate. This practice is likely to deceive the public (which has no way of knowing if an influencer is getting paid for its endorsement) and can have a disruptive effect on electoral or legislative processes. Although not strictly relevant here, it must be noted that the opposite problem also exists, namely that of not being able to distinguish a commercial advertising from a political one: in fact, it increasingly occurs that instead of using their accounts to interact with voters or political competitors, politicians use their platforms to promote the interests of their supporters, thereby causing disinformation.[13]

From the second point of view, when the online political advertising comes from sponsors based outside of the Union, the issue of disinformation is intertwined with the problem of foreign interference whose objective is to «distort or falsely represent facts, artificially inflate one-sided arguments, discredit information to degrade political discourse and ultimately undermine confidence in the electoral system and therefore in the democratic process itself».[14]

From the third point of view, the problem is that today most of the political messages directed at the online public are designed by applying a segmentation of the targets to be reached.[15] Targets are homogeneous groups of citizens classified according to logics of political affiliation and other demographic and social factors, inferred through the processing of personal and other data collected on the Internet. For example, *ad hoc* online political advertising can be directed to the segment of

---

[12] De Gregorio and Goanta (2022, pp. 204–225).

[13] *Ivi*, p. 210.

[14] European Parliament resolution of 9 March 2022, cit., para. B. On the issue of foreign interference, see Morgese (2025, pp. 89–130).

[15] Brkan (2022) and Zuiderveen Borgesius et al. (2018).

voters that can be classified as "undecided", since these voters can actually determine the victory of one coalition over another, or directly to the potential electoral constituency of competing parties, even with messages that in advertising jargon could be described as "deceptive". Moreover, in order to amplify the effect of a political message, online platforms often use ad-delivery techniques, which are a wide range of optimization methods that rely on the automated processing of personal data in order to increase the circulation, reach or visibility of a political advertisement.

Thanks to these means, the spread of disinformation in the context of political campaigns is quite straightforward. Considering that online political advertising is strongly increasing (even certain linear offline forms of political advertising, such as radio and television, are also offered online as on-demand services), the disinformation phenomenon has assumed concerning dimensions, as it adversely affects the freedom of information and opinion, fundamental prerequisites for exercising the right to vote,[16] and, more generally, the development of democratic electoral processes. The latter are such if they are characterized by both freedom and secrecy, as stated in art. 3 of the Protocol to the ECHR[17] and, with specific regard to the elections of the European Parliament, in art. 39(2) of the CFREU[18] and 14(3) TEU.[19]

Hence, there is a need for transparency of political advertising, to contribute to enable voters (and individuals in general) to better understand when they are being presented with a political advertisement, on whose behalf that advertisement is being made, as well as how and why they are being targeted by a provider of advertising services, so that they can make informed choices.

Regulatory measures seem to be the most appropriate choice to combat disinformation, but they must confront several difficulties when it comes to digital platforms, social media, etc. The following sections will therefore focus on the legislative solutions found in the EU and US legal orders, on their effectiveness and practical applications.

---

[16] ECtHR, *Bowman c. Regno Unito*, 24839/94, 19 February 1998, para. 42: «[f]ree elections and freedom of expression, particularly freedom of political debate, together form the bedrock of any democratic system. The two rights are inter-related and operate to reinforce each other: for example, as the Court has observed in the past, freedom of expression is one of the "conditions" necessary to "ensure the free expression of the opinion of the people in the choice of the legislature". For this reason, it is particularly important in the period preceding an election that opinions and information of all kinds are permitted to circulate freely». See also ECtHR, *Associazione politica nazionale Lista Marco Pannella e Radicali italiani c. Italia*, 20002/13, 31 August 2021, para. 85; *Mestan c. Bulgaria*, 24108/15, 02 May 23, para. 54.

[17] Art. 3 ECHR: «Right to free elections. The High Contracting Parties undertake to hold free elections at reasonable intervals by secret ballot, under conditions which will ensure the free expression of the opinion of the people in the choice of the legislature».

[18] Art. 39(2) CFREU: «Members of the European Parliament shall be elected by direct universal suffrage in a free and secret ballot».

[19] Art. 14(3) TEU: «The members of the European Parliament shall be elected for a term of five years by direct universal suffrage in a free and secret ballot». See Mastroianni (2022, pp. 107–110).

3 The EU Regulation on Transparency and Targeting of Political Advertising ("TTPAR")

The TTPAR is the main EU tool to combat disinformation through online political advertising.[20] It aims to achieve two general purposes and four specific objectives. The general purposes are to facilitate the provision of political advertising and related services in the internal market and to help ensure more open and fair electoral processes in the EU. The four specific objectives, instead, are: to reduce legal fragmentation, remove obstacles and lower costs for cross-border services; to establish high transparency obligations for political advertising; to protect individuals regarding the processing of their personal data in the context of the dissemination of this type of advertising; and to ensure an effective supervision of the provided obligations. These four specific objectives underlie the various parts into which the regulation is divided: the first two objectives inform Chapter II on transparency and due diligence obligations for political advertising services; the third objective directs Chapter III which provides for rules on targeting and ad-delivery of online political advertising; and the fourth objective steers Chapter IV containing provisions on supervision and enforcement.

As it pursues multiple purposes simultaneously and consists of several interlinked components, the regulation rests on a dual legal basis in the EU Treaties: arts. 114[21] and 16[22] TFEU. The former was chosen because the act—as will be seen below—concerns a specific category of service providers in the internal market and aims to address the divergences in the laws of the Member States regarding the transparency of political advertising. The latter, on the other hand, was considered necessary since

[20] Holznagel (2023), Richter (2023), van Drunen et al. (2022), and Massa (2022). Prior to the TTPAR, the only existing tool dealing with disinformation through political advertising was the 2022 Strengthened Code of Practice on Disinformation (replacing the 2018 Code of Practice on Disinformation). In fact, it contains a specific section on transparency measures for political advertising that the contracting parties committed to comply with (see Part III of the Code). This co-regulatory instrument, however, only engaged the signatory parties and could certainly not have the effectiveness of an EU regulation with a general scope such as the TTPAR. For a comment on the Code and its provisions related to political advertising, see Pollicino (2022, pp. 101–104).

[21] Art. 114 TFEU: «1. Save where otherwise provided in the Treaties, the following provisions shall apply for the achievement of the objectives set out in Article 26. The European Parliament and the Council shall, acting in accordance with the ordinary legislative procedure and after consulting the Economic and Social Committee, adopt the measures for the approximation of the provisions laid down by law, regulation or administrative action in Member States which have as their object the establishment and functioning of the internal market [...]».

[22] Art. 16 TFEU: «1. Everyone has the right to the protection of personal data concerning them.

2. The European Parliament and the Council, acting in accordance with the ordinary legislative procedure, shall lay down the rules relating to the protection of individuals with regard to the processing of personal data by Union institutions, bodies, offices and agencies, and by the Member States when carrying out activities which fall within the scope of Union law, and the rules relating to the free movement of such data. Compliance with these rules shall be subject to the control of independent authorities.

The rules adopted on the basis of this Article shall be without prejudice to the specific rules laid down in Article 39 of the Treaty on European Union».

the act also lays down specific rules on the protection of individuals with regard to the processing of personal data, particularly provisions on targeting techniques regarded as capable of affecting individuals' rights when used in political advertising.[23]

Before proceeding with the analysis of the subjective and objective scope of application of the regulation, it is useful to recall the notion of "political advertising" set therein. According to art. 3(2) TTPAR, "political advertising" means «the preparation, placement, promotion, publication, delivery or dissemination, by any means, of a message, normally provided for remuneration or through in-house activities or as part of a political advertising campaign, by, for or on behalf of a political actor […], or which is liable and designed to influence the outcome of an election or referendum, voting behaviour or a legislative or regulatory process, at Union, national, regional or local level». The latter type of political advertising may be more difficult to detect: a clear and substantial link should exist between the message and its potential to influence the outcome of an election or referendum, voting behaviour or a legislative or regulatory process. In light of the preamble of the act, in order to determine the existence of such a link, account should be taken of all factors relevant at the time the message was promoted, published, delivered or disseminated, such as the identity of the sponsor of the message, the form and the content of the message, the spoken or written language used to convey the message, the context in which the message was conveyed, including the period of dissemination such as an electoral period, the objective of the message and the means by which the message was promoted, published, delivered or disseminated as well as the targeted audience.[24] In light of this, messages from influencers who receive financial or other compensation and the so-called "issue-based ads" (i.e. those advertisements on politically relevant topics that can become a powerful means to influence voters) may fall within this category of political advertising. To supplement the definition of "political advertising" contained in art. 3(2) TTPAR mentioned above, the regulation expressly clarifies that «political opinions that are expressed in a personal capacity» are not political advertising and nor are «political opinions and other editorial content […] that are subject to editorial responsibility».[25] Having a clear definition of "political advertising", it is also necessary to specify that, from a territorial perspective, the TTPAR applies to political advertising where the political advertisement is disseminated in the Union, is brought into the public domain in one or several Member States or is directed to EU citizens.[26]

Given that it is normally provided for remuneration, which may include benefits in kind,[27] political advertising constitutes a service activity under art. 57 TFEU. Therefore, from a subjective point of view, the rules contained in the TTPAR are mainly

---

[23] On the choice of the legal basis, see van Drunen et al. (2022, pp. 192–196).

[24] Regulation (EU) 2024/900, cit., recital n. 23.

[25] *Ivi*, art. 1(2) and (3). See also Communication from the Commission—Guidelines to support the implementation of Regulation (EU) 2024/900 on the transparency and targeting of political advertising, C/2025/6829, OJ C, C/2025/5514, 10.10.2025, point 2.

[26] Regulation (EU) 2024/900, cit., art. 2.

[27] See Guidelines to support the implementation of Regulation (EU) 2024/900, cit., point 2.2.1.

addressed to the general category of "providers of political advertising services" (i.e. providers involved in the preparation, placement, promotion, publication and dissemination of advertising) and to the specific category of "political advertising publishers". The latter are the part of providers of political advertising services specialised in services usually at the end of the chain, who thus publish, deliver or disseminate political advertising by broadcasting, making it available through an interface or otherwise making it accessible to the public. Moreover, there are other rules that relate to "sponsors", which are natural or legal person at whose request or on whose behalf a political advertisement is prepared, placed, promoted, published, delivered or disseminated, and to "data controllers", as defined by the GDPR[28] and the 2018/1725[29] Regulations (i.e. natural or legal person, public authority, agency or other body that, alone or jointly with others, determines the purposes and means of the processing of personal data).

From an objective point of view, the TTPAR includes two chapters (Chapters II and III) containing various provisions that set out several obligations aimed, on the one hand, at increasing the level of transparency in political advertising services and, on the other hand, at limiting the use of targeting and ad-delivery techniques.

With regard to the first group of obligations, among the main ones there is that for the sponsors to submit a declaration to the advertising service providers stating that the advertising service that they have requested constitutes a political advertising service.[30]

The advertising service providers, in turn, must retain all the information related to the political advertisement or campaign to which their service is connected, the specific services that they provided in connection with the political advertising, the amounts they invoiced for the service and the value of other benefits received in exchange for the service, the public or private origin of those amounts or benefits as well as whether they originated from inside or outside of the Union. They must also note the identity and the contact details of the sponsor or of the entity ultimately controlling the sponsor or, for legal persons, their place of establishment. Finally, they must include the election, referendum, legislative or regulatory process to which the political advertisement is linked.[31] This information must then be transmitted to the publisher of the political advertisement that will disseminate the message.[32] The latter, using labels adapted to the medium used, must ensure that every political

[28] Regulation (EU) 2016/679 of the European Parliament and of the Council of 27 April 2016 on the protection of natural persons with regard to the processing of personal data and on the free movement of such data, and repealing Directive 95/46/EC (General Data Protection Regulation), OJ L 119, 4.5.2016, pp. 1–88, art. 4, point 7.

[29] Regulation (EU) 2018/1725 of the European Parliament and of the Council of 23 October 2018 on the protection of natural persons with regard to the processing of personal data by the Union institutions, bodies, offices and agencies and on the free movement of such data, and repealing Regulation (EC) No 45/2001 and Decision No 1247/2002/EC PE/31/2018/REV/1, OJ L 295, 21.11.2018, pp. 39–98, art. 3, point 8.

[30] Regulation (EU) 2024/900, cit., art. 7(1).

[31] *Ivi*, art. 9(1) (a to f).

[32] *Ivi*, art. 10(1).

advertising message is easily identifiable as such and contains the following information: a statement that it is a political advertisement; the identity of the sponsor of the political advertisement and, where applicable, the entity ultimately controlling the sponsor; the election, referendum, legislative or regulatory process to which the political advertisement is linked; where applicable, a statement to the effect that the political advertisement has been subject to targeting or ad-delivery techniques; and a transparency notice.[33] The latter is intended to make the context of the political advertising message and its objectives clear, so it contains information including, for instance, details on the period during which the political advertisement is intended to be published, the amounts and other benefits received by the providers, on the elections or referendums and legislative or regulatory processes with which the political advertisement is linked, the links to official information about the modalities for participation in the election or referendum concerned, and where applicable, a statement to the effect that the political advertisement has been subject to targeting or ad-delivery techniques based on the use of personal data.[34] Where the information is incomplete or inaccurate and cannot be completed or corrected, the publisher shall not make the political advertisement available.[35] If a particular political advertisement does not comply with the TTPAR, natural or legal persons shall be able to notify the publishers through mechanisms put in place by the publishers themselves.[36] Finally, the publishers have a duty to make each political advertisement available in the European repository created by the European Commission,[37] to transmit to the competent authorities periodic reporting on political advertising services[38] and to respond to requests for information from national competent authorities[39] or other interested entities.[40] Even these reporting duties, in fact, are aimed at ensuring transparency.

With regard to the second group of obligations mentioned above (that is those aimed at limiting the use of targeting and ad-delivery techniques), the TTPAR first of all provides for a specific ban on the use of such methods if they involve the processing of personal data, unless the data subject has provided explicit consent and the technique does not involve profiling.[41] In this regard, it should also be noted that targeting or ad-delivery techniques that involve the processing of the personal data of a subject at least one year under the voting age established by national rules are prohibited.[42] In cases where targeting and ad-delivery techniques are instead permitted, the data controllers must adopt an internal policy clearly describing how such techniques are used, and provide additional information necessary to allow the

[33] *Ivi*, art. 11(1) and (3).

[34] *Ivi*, art. 12(1).

[35] *Ivi*, art. 12(2).

[36] *Ivi*, art. 15.

[37] *Ivi*, art. 13.

[38] *Ivi*, art. 14.

[39] *Ivi*, art.16.

[40] *Ivi*, art. 17.

[41] *Ivi*, art. 18(1).

[42] *Ivi*, art. 18(2).

individual concerned to understand both the logic underlying the technique and the main parameters used by the technique, including whether an artificial intelligence system or any additional analytical techniques have been used to target or deliver the political advertisement.[43]

In addition to fulfilling the obligations described above, the provision of political advertising services must be carried out on the basis of the principle of non-discrimination. Therefore, providers shall not restrict the provision of their services on the basis of the place of residence or establishment of the sponsor, or to a European political party or group in the European Parliament solely on the basis of its place of establishment.[44] However, according to art. 5(2) TTPAR, providers are required, in at least the three months preceding an election or referendum organised at Union level or at national, regional or local level in a Member State, to provide political advertising services only to citizens of the Union, third-country nationals permanently residing in the Union and having a right to vote in that election or referendum or legal persons established in the Union that are not controlled by third-country entities, in order to reduce the risk of foreign interference.

Finally, from the point of view of supervision and enforcement, each Member State shall designate one or more competent authorities to be responsible for the application and enforcement of the TTPAR.[45] The authority in charge of verifying compliance with the regulation is that of the Member State where the provider of political advertising has its establishment; if the provider is established in more than one Member State, it shall be deemed to be under the jurisdiction of the Member State in which it has its main establishment.[46] For providers that provide political advertising services in the Union but do not have an establishment in the Union, the TTPAR provides that they must designate a natural or legal person as their legal representative in one of the Member States where that provider offers its services. That representative will be responsible for ensuring compliance with the obligations under the regulation and for cooperating with the national competent authorities and, where relevant, the Commission.[47] All the competent authorities have cross-border cooperation duties and the possibility to carry out joint investigations.[48] Moreover, given that the TTPAR provides for a right to lodge a complaint for infringements of the regulation, the same authorities must inform the person or entity who made the notification of the follow up.[49]

In order to make the entire control and enforcement system effective, the TTPAR finally provides that Member States shall establish rules on sanctions or other measures applicable to sponsors or providers for infringements of the regulation. The sanctions shall be effective, proportionate and dissuasive, compatible with the

[43] *Ivi*, art. 19(1).
[44] *Ivi*, art. 5(1).
[45] *Ivi*, art. 22.
[46] *Ivi*, art. 23(1).
[47] *Ivi*, art. 21.
[48] *Ivi*, art. 23 from (2) to (10).
[49] *Ivi*, art. 24.

rules governing the freedom of the press and freedom of expression and the rules on the journalist profession, and they shall be based on the economic capacity of the entity subject to sanctions.[50]

In light of the analysis of the content of the TTPAR, it is now possible to identify which are the responses provided by the EU Legislator to address what were defined in the previous section of this chapter as the three main issues that make political advertising a vector of disinformation. First, in order to avoid the concealment of the political nature of advertising, the TTPAR imposes the use of digital mechanisms that enable citizens to understand unambiguously, *ictu oculi*, whether they are confronted with paid political content, to know who is behind each political communication and who is paying for it. Second, to prevent unlawful foreign interference in the democratic processes, the TTPAR establishes that, in at least the three months preceding an election or referendum organised at Union level or at national, regional or local level in a Member State, providers of political advertising services should provide their services only to citizens of the Union, third-country nationals permanently residing in the Union and having a right to vote in that election or referendum or legal persons established in the Union that are not controlled by third-country entities. Third, in order to prevent the uncontrolled exploitation of personal data aimed at achieving a manipulation of the electoral process and a reversal of its outcome, the TTPAR regulates the use of targeting or ad-delivery techniques, subjecting it to consent and transparency, so that citizens can immediately understand how and why they are reached by a given political advertising message.

4 From Theory to Practice: The TTPAR and the 32/2024 Judgment of the Romanian Constitutional Court

Although having undergone several amendments during the legislative procedure, the TTPAR was adopted with a large majority and is applicable from 10 October 2025. Even before this date, however, its relevance had already emerged in Member States' practice: the Romanian Constitutional Court (hereinafter "RCC"), in fact, cited it in the reasoning of judgment n. 32 of 6 December 2024,[51] a noteworthy (apparently the first) decision of a European Constitutional Court concerning an online disinformation episode. More specifically, with this judgment the electoral process for the election of the President of Romania of 2024 was annulled due to the violations of electoral legislation on social media and the impact of online

---

[50] *Ivi*, art. 25.

[51] Curtea Constituțională A României, 6 December 2024, n. 32, *privind anularea procesului electoral cu privire la alegerea Președintelui României din anul 2024*. For a comment on the judgment, see Monti (2025), Sassi and Sterpa (2025), and Kuti (2024).

disinformation campaigns.[52] Consequently, the RCC instructed the authorities to set a new date for the presidential elections and effectively restart the process.

The RCC based its decision on several "information notes" transmitted by the Ministry of Internal Affairs and the secret services to the Presidential Office, which were declassified and made public on 4 December 2024. These documents revealed several irregularities and unlawful acts allegedly affecting the entire electoral process: in particular, they point to voter manipulation and distortion of equal opportunities among electoral competitors, through the non-transparent use of digital technologies and artificial intelligence in the electoral campaign, as well as through the financing of the electoral campaign from undeclared sources. More specifically, one of the main irregularities emerging from the documents concerns the alleged illegitimate use of the social platform TikTok and its algorithm by the candidate Călin Georgescu, who apparently won the elections also by polarising the public opinion thanks to the promotion of a strongly populist message that attracted voters dissatisfied with traditional institutions. Moreover, it seems that on the same social platform false accounts of Russian origin in favour of that candidate were activated and a significant amount of money was invested in a non-transparent manner. In sum, apparently, all the three aspects that, as seen above, make political communication a vector of disinformation were present: the communication did not reveal its political character; it originated from non-EU sponsors; it was subjected to targeting and ad-delivery techniques.

The RCC found a violation of the national electoral legislation and reinforced its legal rationale by aligning its decision with established European rules on electoral integrity, particularly the principles outlined in the Guidelines and explanatory report of the Code of Good Conduct in Electoral Matters[53] and in the Interpretative Declaration of the same Code,[54] both adopted by the Venice Commission of the Council of Europe in the context of the European Convention on Human Rights, and in the TTPAR belonging to the EU legal order.

In relation to the Guidelines and explanatory report of the Code, the RCC quotes two paragraphs[55] to support its finding that «[e]quality of opportunity should be ensured between all candidates and all parties and should prompt the State to adopt an objective and impartial attitude towards them and to apply the same legislation

[52] There have been other cases of annulment of elections by European Constitutional Courts, but for reasons other than disinformation. For instance, the 2004 presidential elections in Ukraine were annulled by the Ukraine's Supreme Court since, according to the Court, they were marred by systemic and massive violations related to the misconduct of the central election commission. The 2016 presidential elections in Austria, instead, were annulled by the Austria's Constitutional Court after an investigation revealed irregularities in the count of the vote in several constituencies.

[53] Venice Commission, Council of Europe (2002).

[54] Venice Commission, Council of Europe (2024).

[55] Venice Commission, Council of Europe (2002, para. 18): «Equality of opportunity should be ensured between parties and candidates and should prompt the state to be impartial towards them and to apply the same law uniformly to all. In particular, the neutrality requirement applies to the electoral campaign and coverage by the media, especially the publicly owned media, as well as to public funding of parties and campaigns. [...]»; para. 21: «[...] Spending by political parties, particularly on advertising, may likewise be limited in order to guarantee equality of opportunity».

uniformly to all. Spending on electoral advertising may be limited in order to ensure equal opportunities».[56] With regard to the Interpretative Declaration of the Code, instead, the RCC recalls three of its paragraphs[57] in order to argue that the State has a positive responsibility to prevent any undue interference in the electoral process, has a duty of neutrality that also includes an obligation to build resilience among voters and to raise public awareness about the use of digital technologies in elections, and should address the challenges and risks posed by organized information disorders.[58]

It emerges that these citations of the principles of the Code by the RCC are meant to emphasise the need for the State to regulate freedom of expression in the context of political-electoral communication and online political advertising, in order to ensure a free and properly informed vote. This role of the State should be interpreted as including the possibility of annulment of elections held in violation of the aforementioned principles. Indeed, the ECtHR considered that the annulment of elections could be a consequence of electoral manipulation affecting the ultimate outcome.[59] Then, also the Venice Commission itself recently stated that the annulment of elections could also occur due to foreign interference related to online propaganda via social media.[60] Therefore, in theory the measure of the RCC is in line with the principles expressed by both the ECtHR and the Venice Commission, however it is essential to assess its proportionality. In this respect, reference must be made to the ECtHR case-law, according to which the proportionality test must take into account both the presence of an "intention" to manipulate and a "concrete effect" on the elections.[61] The Venice Commission is also very clear on this aspect, as it affirms that: «[t]he central criterion for cancelling elections […] is the question of whether

[56] Curtea Constituțională A României, cit., para 15.

[57] Venice Commission, Council of Europe (2024, para. 14): «State authorities should address the challenge posed by organised information disorder campaigns, which have the potential to undermine the integrity of electoral processes»; para. 17: «The State's duty of neutrality also includes an obligation to build resilience among voters and to raise public awareness about the use of digital technologies in elections, including through the provision of appropriate information and support»; para. 20: «The positive responsibility of the State to prevent undue interference with the principles of the European electoral heritage must not lead to undue state intervention».

[58] Curtea Constituțională A României, cit., para 10.

[59] ECtHR, *Kerimova v. Azerbaijan*, 20799/06, 30 September 2010, para. 54.

[60] Venice Commission, Council of Europe (2025), *passim*, especially para. 51: «The Venice Commission takes the view that "external influence" – not stemming from the electoral actors – can also be relevant in this context. This applies to the influence of non-governmental organisations, of the media – social media in particular –, especially those sponsored and financed from abroad, and foreign State and non-State actors: External influence, including from abroad, can have the same (or even stronger) effects as internal influence (from State officials or political parties). Therefore, the interference with the electoral process by third parties acting from outside is not less detrimental and can have the same (or even more severe) consequences as a breach of election rules by candidates, political parties and State officials».

[61] ECtHR, *Kerimova v. Azerbaijan*, cit., para. 54; *Babenko v. Ukraine*, 43476/98, 4 May 1999. Conversely, if the irregularities are minor or only of a formal nature and therefore have no effect on the outcome of the elections, annulment of the election result may infringe the right to free elections established in Article 3 of Protocol No. 1 of the ECHR (see ECtHR, *Riza and Others v. Bulgaria*, 48555/10 and 48377/10, 13 October 2015, paras 174–176).

irregularities may have affected the outcome of the vote».[62] In any case, it should be kept in mind that the cancellation of elections can be allowed only under very exceptional circumstances as *ultima ratio*.[63] In the Romanian election, according to the RCC, the proportionality test is satisfied since the evidence at hand concerning the functioning of false accounts, the promotion of political messages and the investment of financial sums originating from Russian sources clearly demonstrate intentional manipulation, and those act, put in place on TikTok, had an effect on the election outcomes, as they «distorted the free and correct nature of the vote cast by the citizens and the equal opportunities of the electoral competitors, affected the transparency and fairness of the electoral campaign, and disregarded the legal provisions relating to the funding of electoral campaigns. All these aspects have had a converging effect of disregard for the essential principles of democratic elections».[64]

While, as seen, the references in the Romanian judgment to the approaches of the Venice Commission pertain to more "constitutional" profiles regarding the role of the State in ensuring fair and free elections, the TTPAR is cited by the RCC when it deals with the more "technical" issue of the extension to the online world of the voters' freedom to form an opinion and the right to be properly informed before making a decision. More specifically, the RCC states that the voters have the right to obtain accurate information about the candidates and the electoral process from all sources, including online, and shall enjoy the protection against undue influence, through illegal and disproportionate acts or facts, on the voting behaviour. Therefore, special attention must be given to online political advertising that can turn into a vector of disinformation especially when, like in the case at hand, it comes from sponsors outside the Union (i.e. Russia). According to the RCC, in fact, «interference by State or non-State entities in carrying out propaganda or electoral disinformation campaigns must be excluded».[65]

Overall, it is possible to affirm that by referring to the aforementioned European instruments, the RCC sought to demonstrate that its decision not only adhered to national constitutional standards but also upheld Romania's obligations as a member of the Council of Europe and the European Union.

After the publication of the judgment of the RCC, given that the TTPAR was not applicable before 10 October 2025, the European Commission—in its role of monitoring compliance with the DSA—opened formal proceedings against TikTok for a suspected breach of the more general rules of the DSA (see *infra*), in relation to the platform's obligation to properly assess and mitigate systemic risks linked

---

[62] Venice Commission, Council of Europe (2025, para. 39).

[63] *Ivi*, para. 18.

[64] Curtea Constituțională A României, cit., para 5. See also paras 14, 16 and 18. It is worth noting that Mr. Georgescu requested interim measures to suspend the effect of the RCC decision to the ECtHR, but the latter rejected them finding no imminent risk of irreparable harm to an ECHR right (ECtHR, 022, 21 January 2025, https://www.echr.coe.int/w/request-for-interim-measures-refused-concerning-romania).

[65] *Ivi*, para. 13.

to election integrity in the context of the Romanian presidential elections.[66] The proceedings focus on TikTok's recommender systems (notably the risks linked to the coordinated inauthentic manipulation or automated exploitation of the service) and its policies on political advertisements and paid-for political content. Should the Commission's suspicions be proven correct, these shortcomings would constitute infringements of arts. 34(1), 34(2) and 35(1) DSA. These rules, in fact, impose on providers of very large online platforms ("VLOPs") such as TikTok an obligation to assess any systemic risks in the Union stemming from the design or functioning of their service and its related systems, including algorithmic systems, or from the use made of their services. Providers of VLOPs shall take into account, in particular, whether and how factors such as the design of their recommender systems and any other relevant algorithmic system or the systems for selecting and presenting advertisements influence any of the systemic risks. Moreover, they shall implement effective mitigation measures, tailored to the specific systemic risks identified, such as adapting their algorithmic and advertising systems.

The opening of this formal proceeding gives the opportunity to reflect on the complementary relationship existing between the rules contained in the DSA and those of the TTPAR: while the former relates more generally to the liabilities and transparency obligations of providers of intermediary services such as online platforms or search engines,[67] the latter has a narrower scope and focuses on the specific issue of transparency of online political advertising. Consequently, it is possible to assume that if the TTPAR had already been applicable, in addition to the proceedings initiated by the European Commission, TikTok could have also been subject to an investigation conducted by the competent authority (designated according to art. 22 TTPAR on the basis of the infringed obligation) for breaching the rules contained therein. Indeed, this social media may be identified as a "political advertising publisher" that is also a "VLOP" in the sense of the TTPAR, and, as such, it is subject—in addition to the DSA rules—to the obligations set out in the TTPAR.[68] Therefore, for instance, an infringement of art. 11(1) TTPAR on labelling obligations is conceivable insofar as it was found that some micro-influencers were paid to share on TikTok contents in favour of Călin Georgescu and were provided actual "scripts" to follow in their videos, but no evidence of these facts was made explicit in the online contents. On the other hand, given the complementary relationship, the RCC could (or should) have cited in its judgment also the aforementioned rules of the DSA (what is more, already applicable) and not only those of the TTPAR.

[66] European Commission (2024). https://ec.europa.eu/commission/presscorner/detail/en/ip_24_6487.

[67] For a comment on the DSA with a specific focus on disinformation issues, see Caggiano (2021).

[68] See Regulation (EU) 2024/900, cit., recital n. 46: «Political advertising publishers that are also very large online platforms and very large online search engines within the meaning of Regulation (EU) 2022/2065 should diligently identify, analyse and assess any systemic risks that their political advertising services pose in the context of their risk assessments according to Article 34 of that Regulation and put in place reasonable, proportionate and effective mitigation measures in accordance with Article 35 of that Regulation to address those risks».

5 The US Measures Regulating Online Political Advertising

In the US, by virtue of the peculiarities of the legal order, which includes a federal, state and local levels, online political advertising is regulated in different ways across the territory. It is beyond the scope of this chapter to lay out a comprehensive list of the US laws related to digital political advertising (especially of the state ones), but still a few insights into the various efforts to regulate the matter can inspire some considerations.

At the federal level, there has been a decades-long struggle to define and regulate political advertising,[69] since regulators had to thread one of the most difficult First Amendment needles, that is finding a fair balance between protected political speech and regulated political advertising.[70] The first step forward was marked by the adoption of the Federal Election Campaign Act ("FECA"),[71] passed in 1971, with amendments in 1974, which created limits on campaign contributions and independent expenditures in an attempt to thwart critical influences. Then, in 2002, the Bipartisan Campaign Reform Act ("BCRA") strengthened election law by requiring disclosure from groups that run "electioneering communications", that is «any broadcast, cable or satellite communication that refers to a clearly identified candidate for federal office and is made within 30 days of a primary and 60 days of a general election».[72] This Act, therefore, did not include the Internet as a form of "public communication". In 2004, in *Shays v. Federal Election Commission*, a US District Court found the exclusion by the Federal Election Commission ("FEC") of online political communication from "public communication" impermissible.[73] Following this decision, the FEC took action by amending the definition of "public communication" to include paid Internet advertising[74] and, later on, by establishing some disclaimer and reporting requirements. The first consist of rules surrounding the inclusion of disclaimers such as "paid for by" in the ads themselves[75]; the second speak to the circumstances under which some information such as ad expenditures must be reported to federal regulators.[76] Still at the federal level, in the wake of the 2016 US presidential election, with confirmation that foreign entities had used

69 For an in-depth reconstruction of the legal history in this field, see Fox and Ekstrand (2020, pp. 8–11).

70 First Amendment to the US Constitution: «Congress shall make no law respecting an establishment of religion, or prohibiting the free exercise thereof; or abridging the freedom of speech, or of the press; or the right of the people peaceably to assemble, and to petition the Government for a redress of grievances». Under this amendment, political speech is protected.

71 Federal Election Campaign Act of 1971, Pub. L. No. 92-225, 86 Stat. 3 (1972).

72 Bipartisan Campaign Reform Act of 2002, Pub. L. No. 107-155, sec. 201(a), (f)(3)(A).

73 US District Court, District of Columbia, *Shays v. Federal Election Commission*, 337 F.Supp.2d 28, para 79: «[T]he Court finds that […] Congress intended all other forms of 'general public political advertising' to be covered by the term 'public communication'. What constitutes 'general public political advertising' in the world of the Internet is a matter for the FEC to determine».

74 11 CFR 100.26, public communication.

75 11 CFR 110.11, communications; advertising; disclaimers.

76 Fowler et al. (2020, pp. 112–121).

online advertising to spread disinformation in order to manipulate the elections, in 2017, some Senators sponsored the so-called "Honest Ads Act".[77] The latter aimed to subject online ads to the same regulations as radio and television ads and to make publicly available the identity of the ad purchaser. The proposal failed and although it has been reintroduced in 2019, 2022 and 2023, no action has been taken so far.

In order to fill this regulatory gap, some States have enacted new legislation or amended their existing election laws to create disclosure and/or record-keeping requirements for online political advertising.[78] However, these laws are based on different definitions of political advertising, which do not always explicitly mention digital or online advertising. For instance, in the State of Washington, political advertising «includes any advertising displays, newspaper ads, billboards, signs, brochures, articles, tabloids, flyers, letters, radio or television presentations, *digital communication*, or other means of mass communication, used for the purpose of appealing, directly or indirectly, for votes or for financial or other support or opposition in any election campaign»[79]; in New Hampshire, instead, political advertising is considered to be «any communication, including buttons or printed material attached to motor vehicles, which expressly or implicitly advocates the success or defeat of any party, measure or person at any election».[80] Also the legislative choices differ from one State to another, but they can be ascribed to two main types: disclaimer and reporting requirements.[81] Disclaimer requirements for online political ads generally require that the ad states the name and, sometimes, address of the ad purchaser.[82] The State of Vermont, for instance, opted for introducing disclaimer requirements, thus electioneering communications disseminated online must clearly state the name and, for all non-audio ads, the address of the candidate, person, or group that paid for it or the candidate, person, or group on whose behalf it was purchased.[83] As for the reporting requirements, they may include the establishment of a database of digital political ads (similar to the EU repository that has been introduced according to the TTPAR), containing information about who paid for the ad, when the ad ran, a copy of the ad and more. These requirements, however, may differ in where they place the responsibility for maintaining the records: the online platforms that host the advertisements or the government. The State of New York, for example, has

---

[77] S. 1356-116th Congress (2019–2020), to enhance transparency and accountability for online political advertisements by requiring those who purchase and publish such ads to disclose information about the advertisements to the public, and for other purposes.

[78] For an overview on these States laws, see Fox and Ekstrand (2020).

[79] Washington State Legislature, RCW 42.17A.005, para. 40.

[80] New Hampshire Revised Statutes, RSA 664:2, para VI.

[81] For an in-depth analysis of the requirements introduces in the various US States, see Fox and Ekstrand (2020, pp. 15–27).

[82] For a comment on this type of requirements, see Trusk (2022, pp. 53–60), who argues that that advertising disclosure regulations fall into two categories: a candidate-based model (which demands disclosures from advertising purchasers) or commercial-advertiser-based model (which requires disclosures from advertising sellers).

[83] 2023 Vermont Statutes, Title 17 Elections, Chapter 61 Campaign Finance, para 2972 Identification in electioneering communications.

implemented a public database under governmental responsibility.[84] In some States, disclaimer and reporting requirements are cumulated. In California, for instance, the California's Social Media Disclose Act (2018) provides for disclaimer requirements under which ads must include the text "Who funded this ad?" with a link to a separate webpage that provides the answer.[85] Moreover, according to the 2024 California Code, under certain circumstances, online platforms shall maintain publicly accessible records about ads, which must include copies of the ad, the number of impressions the ad received, the date and time the ad was first and last displayed, the cost of the ad, the candidate or ballot measure that is the subject of the ad, and the name and ID number of the purchasing committee.[86] Maryland, instead, passed an Act that requires online newspapers and media outlets to publicly disclose the names and contact information of anyone who purchases online campaign or issue ads.[87] The same Act also imposes record-keeping requirements on platforms who disseminate qualifying paid digital communications: the latter are required to maintain publicly accessible, online databases containing different information about the ads depending on who purchased them.[88] Moreover, these platforms are also required to provide the State Board of Elections with information about the candidate or ballot issue discussed in the ad, whether the ad «support[ed] or oppos[ed] that candidate or ballot issue», the first and last date and time the ad was distributed, a copy of the ad, the geographic location and audience targeted, and the number of times the ad was viewed.[89] With regard to these Maryland's record-keeping requirements, it should be noted that in December 2019 the US Court of Appeals for the Fourth Circuit ruled that the responsibilities the law imposed on online platforms were unconstitutional as applied to a group of media plaintiffs, including The Washington Post and the Baltimore Sun, among others.[90] In fact, although the Fourth Circuit determined that Maryland had significant interests preventing foreign election interference, encouraging an informed public and discouraging corruption, the legal requirements for online platforms were not sufficiently tailored to pass constitutional scrutiny under

[84] New York State, Assembly, Bill n. A09930 (2018).

[85] California, Assembly Bill n. 2188 (2018), chapter 754, SEC. 2. This Bill was updated by Bill n. 1798 (2022), according to which electronic advertisements may provide disclosures directly on an ad instead of linking to a website with the disclosures.

[86] 2024 California Code—Government Code, Title 9 Political Reform, chapter 4 Campaign Disclosure, Article 5 Disclosure in Advertisements, section 84504.6, (d)(1).

[87] Maryland, House Bill 981 (2018), Online Electioneering Transparency and Accountability Act, 13-401(a)(1)(i).

[88] *Ivi*, 13-405(b)(6). In sum, for ads bought by a political committee, platforms must record the purchaser's name and contact information, the committee's treasurer, and the amount paid. For ads bought by an ad network, platforms must record the network's contact information and include a hyperlink to the contact page of the network's website. For ads bought by someone other than a political committee or an ad network, platforms must record the purchaser's name and contact information, the amount paid, and the name of anyone that controls the purchaser, like a CEO.

[89] *Ivi*, 13-405(c)(3).

[90] United States Court of Appeals for the Fourth Circuit, *The Washington Post Co. v. McManus*, No. 19-1132 (4th Cir. 2019).

the First Amendment. More in detail, according to the Fourth Circuit, both the aforementioned record-keeping requirements compelled political speech. In essence, by requiring the plaintiffs to make certain information available to the public and to state regulators, the provisions «forc[ed] elements of civil society to speak when they otherwise would have refrained», thereby contradicting the long-standing First Amendment tradition that «freedom of speech 'included both the right to speak freely and the right to refrain from speaking at all».[91] Even though the Court was clear in limiting its holding to the specific facts and plaintiffs of this case, its decision has raised numerous questions regarding how States should draw and justify legislation seeking to regulate online political advertising.[92] On the one hand, it is true that burdening platforms with such record-keeping requirements raises valid First Amendment issues regarding compelled speech, but, on the other hand, a lack of transparency burdens equally important values regarding informed decision-making by the electorate. According to some scholars, this clash of values can be overcome by establishing an independent record-keeping body (like the one implemented by the State of New York) to which the advertisers should report their ad purchases.[93]

Finally, legislating digital political ads may also occur at the city level, but no city has established significant rules on online political advertising so far.

The measures adopted in the US are evidently aimed solely at increasing the level of transparency of online political advertising, but they do not address the issue of the use of targeting and ad-delivery techniques, as the TTPAR instead does. This regulatory gap is partially filled by the self-regulatory measures sometimes adopted by the various digital platforms,[94] but this solution clearly lacks effectiveness because of a high level of inconsistency. Indeed, the vast majority of social media companies have developed their own political advertising policies in the US that include the regulation of targeting, but those policies not only are based on different definitions of "political advertising" but also deeply differ from one platform to another: the criteria upon which the restrictions on the use of targeting techniques rely vary from company to company.[95]

All in all, from this brief overview of the different types of the US rules on political advertising it can be inferred that even though the US and EU frameworks are very different (firstly in relation to the degree of regulatory intensity), their approaches are quite similar, as both have opted for legislative measures, setting aside the arguments claiming that regulation curbs free speech and limits access to the low-cost space of online advertising, or the arguments in favour of self-regulatory approaches only, according to which industry players, rather than legislators, are in a better position to manage digital political ads because they understand the complexity of online advertising. However, as will be seen more clearly below, this approach may soon

---

[91] *Ivi*, 514-15.

[92] For a comment on the judgment, see Trusk (2022), Fox and Ekstrand (2020, pp. 27–31), and Sternstein (2020).

[93] Fox and Ekstrand (2020, p. 39).

[94] For an overview of these measures, see Kurek et al. (2024).

[95] *Ivi*, p. 4.

change, especially for the US, where, quite surprisingly, the First Amendment has not been used as a total shield against regulation in the field of online political advertising so far. For the time being, there is no doubt that the EU rules, adopted in a peculiar legal context tending towards the harmonisation of national laws, are less fragmented and more comprehensive than the US ones, and facilitate the cross-border provision of political advertising services within the European territory.

6 Conclusion

Legal scholarship has long studied the criteria that make elections "free and fair". As the political scientist Robert Dahl puts it, elections are free and fair when «elected officials are chosen in frequent and fairly conducted elections in which coercion is comparatively uncommon».[96] This definition has been extended in other studies by Dahl himself and others, which show that other preconditions of democracy must be met in order to hold free and fair elections. The pre-election period is especially important: it is at this stage that observers must assess whether the election law and the constitution guarantee the freedom of the voters and verify that relevant resources are not too unequally distributed among competing parties and candidates.[97] In order to do so, a number of criteria must be taken into account: the legal framework, the electoral management, the media access, the campaign process and others. Nowadays, a further, partially new, criterion should be added, namely the fair use of media, both offline and online. This criterion would be distinguished from that of media access aimed at verifying whether the freedom of speech is protected and would consist in controlling two aspects: whether a correct information has been guaranteed (since, as it is well known, according to the ECtHR, the notion of "free elections" includes the right to be correctly informed[98]) and whether disinformation methods have been put in place. Today, in fact, the spread of disinformation through political advertising, especially online, adversely affects the freedom of information and opinion and thus the right to vote, undermining the proper course of the electoral processes. Therefore, it constitutes one of the most severe threats to the protection of fundamental rights, democracy and the rule of law.[99]

The legal parameters useful to verify whether the aforementioned additional criterion is satisfied are gradually taking shape. As observed, the EU has recently adopted the TTPAR. This regulation, recognising the relevance of online political communication, thanks to which the barriers and costs for political actors to interact with citizens are reduced, aims at ensuring that citizens have the opportunity to participate in open debates and can exercise their right to vote having fully understood their political choices. Moreover, it also seeks to assure that parties and candidates have

[96] Dahl (1989, p. 221).

[97] Elklit and Svensson (1997, p. 36).

[98] See *supra*, note 16. In doctrine, see Mastroianni (2019, pp. 44–47).

[99] On the current state of health of EU values, see Lenaerts (2025, pp. 278–281).

a fair run in the elections and a fair outcome. In sum, the TTPAR has the objective of restoring the democratic nature of the electoral processes. In doing so, it imposes technical rules on politicians (sponsors), providers, editors of political advertising services and on digital platforms. These rules contribute to ensuring respect for the value of democracy, which according to art. 2 TEU, together with the rule of law and fundamental rights, is part of the identity of the EU.

Compliance with the rules laid down by the TTPAR does not appear particularly problematic not only because the technical requirements imposed seem to be easy to implement by the actors involved, but also because they are well coordinated with the other acts of EU law aimed at establishing, more in general, a comprehensive transparency and accountability regime for online platforms regarding the content they host, namely the DSA. Moreover, as shown by the analysis of the Romanian judgment, also from the point of view of the involvement required to the EU Member States, an efficient legal framework seems to have been created: it brings together international sources such as the Code of Good Conduct in Electoral Matters, more in general focused on the role of the State in ensuring fair and free elections, and the EU law source of the TTPAR, dealing with the enforcement of more technical rules and the corresponding sanctioning powers.

The apparently coherent European picture on the regulation of online political advertising is opposed to a more fragmented and complex US one, composed of a few and varied rules belonging to different levels of regulation. Indeed, the mere existence of such rules in the overseas context already constitutes a step forward: as it is well known, the American regulatory model is market-driven, which means that it «is shaped by discernible techno-optimism, relentless pursuit of innovation, and uncompromised faith in markets as opposed to government regulation».[100] This translates into weakly enforced antitrust laws, a lack of a federal data privacy law, and permissive content moderation rules that shield tech companies from liability, leaving them free to decide whether or not to remove certain harmful content from their platforms.[101] This approach appears highly questionable when it comes to societal aspects and not merely economic ones. In the case of the online political advertising, it is exceedingly difficult to rely on the belief that as long as the marketplace of ideas remains free, truth will ultimately emerge and prevail. There are external influences, social media communication strategies and targeting techniques that can easily hide the truth, as seen during the 2016 US presidential election and the Brexit referendum. Therefore, it is submitted that any regulation adopted by the government to combat disinformation and ensure the freedom of information and opinion and the right to vote should be welcomed.

Overall, in order to answer the research question of the present chapter, which relates to how to regulate online political advertising to ensure democratic electoral processes, it can be stated that the correct approach is the one that balances the aim to prevent disinformation with the freedom of expression. The fact that even in the US, where a market-driven approach is typically followed, a few rules on the

[100] Bradford (2023, p. 33).

[101] Ibidem.

provision of online political advertising services have been adopted (although still far from the regulatory intensity achieved in the EU) suggests that political advertising on digital platforms has nowadays become a too sensitive societal issue, with too relevant practical implications on self-determination and on electoral and legislative outcomes, to be left in the hands of self-regulation only.

However, it cannot be excluded that this US approach may soon change: despite the increasing global consensus regarding the risks in the field of digital technologies, the new Trump administration is adopting a deregulatory stance concerning digital issues, which could also possibly involve online political advertising. For instance, Trump signed several executive orders related to "Removing barriers to American leadership in artificial intelligence",[102] which focus exclusively on economic and competitiveness arguments.[103] Moreover, he issued a Memorandum[104] signaling that his administration intends to take action with respect to tax and regulatory measures affecting US digital service providers, within which an investigation into the EU's Digital Markets Act ("DMA")[105] and DSA has been launched.[106] In essence, the Trump administration is breaking away from the approach adopted under the Biden presidency, which was more aligned with the well-established EU regulatory policy, rooted in the balancing between market objectives and social protection. This shif may be concerning from a user's perspective, insofar as exposure to unregulated digital platforms—especially social media—and artificial intelligence systems may result in insufficient protection against serious individual and collective risks (such as the spread of disinformation). From a researcher's perspective, however, it is of interest with regard to the influence it may have on the application of EU rules on digital matters that, instead, are becoming increasingly detailed.

References

Allen BE et al (2025) Trump revives and expands the battle over digital services taxes. https://www.skadden.com/insights/publications/2025/02/trump-revives-and-expands-the-battle-over-digital-services-taxes

Baade B (2026) Possibilities and limits of regulating disinformation and propaganda in hybrid warfare. In: Mastroianni R, Massa C (eds) Disinformation in new and old media in the XXI century. Springer Nature Switzerland, Cham.

Bradford A (2023) Digital empires. The global battle to regulate technology. Oxford University Press.

[102] Presidential action "Removing barriers to American leadership in artificial intelligence" (2025).

[103] For an in-depth look at the topic of US deregulation in the Artificial Intelligence field, see Pollicino and Gentile (2025).

[104] Memorandum "Defending American Companies and Innovators From Overseas Extortion and Unfair Fines and Penalties" (2025).

[105] Regulation (EU) 2022/1925 of the European Parliament and of the Council of 14 September 2022 on contestable and fair markets in the digital sector and amending Directives (EU) 2019/1937 and (EU) 2020/1828 (Digital Markets Act), PE/17/2022/REV/1, OJ L 265, 12.10.2022, pp. 1–66.

[106] Allen et al. (2025).

Brkan M (2022) The regulation of data-driven political campaigns in the EU: from data protection to specialized regulation. Yearb Eur Law 41:348–373

Caggiano G (2021) Il contrasto alla disinformazione tra nuovi obblighi delle piattaforme online e tutela dei diritti fondamentali nel quadro del Digital Service Act e della co-regolamentazione. Papers di diritto europeo 1:45–71

Confessore N (2018, April) Cambridge Analytica and Facebook: the scandal and the fallout so far. The New York Times. https://www.nytimes.com/2018/04/04/us/politics/cambridge-analytica-scandal-fallout.html

Dahl RA (1989) Democracy and its critics. Yale University Press

De Gregorio G, Goanta C (2022) The influencer republic: monetizing political speech on social media. German Law J 23:204–225. https://doi.org/10.1017/glj.2022.15

D'Ippolito G (2020) Comunicazione politica online: dal messaggio politico commercializzato alle sponsorizzazioni sui social network. MediaLaws 1/2020

Elklit J, Svensson P (1997) What makes elections free and fair? J Democr 8(3):32–46. https://doi.org/10.1353/jod.1997.0041

Eskens S (2024) The role of the Political Advertising Regulation and European Media Freedom Act in the EU's anti-disinformation approach. https://ssrn.com/abstract=4942648

Fowler EF, Franz MM, Ridout TN (2020) Online political advertising in the United States. In: Persily N, Tucker JA (eds) Social media and democracy. SSRC Anxieties of Democracy. Cambridge University Press, Cambridge, pp 111–138

Fox A, Ekstrand V (2020) Regulating the political Wild West: state efforts to disclose sources of online political advertising. https://ssrn.com/abstract=3661978

Hern A (2018) Cambridge Analytica: how did it turn clicks into votes? The Guardian. https://www.theguardian.com/news/2018/may/06/cambridge-analytica-how-turn-clicks-into-votes-christopher-wylie

Holznagel D (2023) Political advertising and disinformation: the EU draft Regulation on Political Advertising might de-amplify political everyday-user tweets - and become a blueprint for stronger online platform regulation. Verfassungsblog. https://verfassungsblog.de/political-advertising-and-disinformation/

Koltay A (2026) A critique of European attempts to regulate online disinformation. In: Mastroianni R, Massa C (eds) Disinformation in new and old media in the XXI century. Springer Nature Switzerland, Cham

Kurek L et al (2024) Rules of the road. Political advertising on social media in the 2024 U.S. Election. https://cdt.org/wp-content/uploads/2024/09/2024-09-19-CDT-Elections-Political-Advertising-on-Social-Media-in-2024-US-Election-brief-final.pdf

Kuti C (2024, Dec 10) On means and ends: the annulment of the Romanian presidential elections. VerfBlog. https://doi.org/10.59704/c9c08659ed569160

Lenaerts K (2025) Democrazia, Stato di diritto e solidarietà: sostenere i valori europei. Eurojus 1(2025):278–284

Massa C (2022) Quando l'UE decide di regolare la pubblicità politica online: luci e ombre della proposta di regolamento. In: Mastroianni R, Ferraro F (eds) Libertà di informazione e diritto dell'Unione europea. Le nuove sfide a tutela della democrazia e del pluralismo, pp 61–72

Massa C (2024) L'European Media Freedom Act e il suo impatto sul Testo unico per la fornitura di servizi di media audiovisivi. In: Mastroianni R, Pollicino O, Bassini M (eds) Il T.U. dei servizi di media audiovisivi. Giuffrè, pp 295–327

Mastroianni R (2019) Fake news, free speech and democracy: a (bad) lesson from Italy? South J Int Law XXV(1):42–74

Mastroianni R (2022) Freedom of pluralism of the media: an European value waiting to be discovered? MediaLaws 1/2022

Memorandum "Defending American Companies and Innovators From Overseas Extortion and Unfair Fines and Penalties" (2025, Feb 21). https://www.whitehouse.gov/presidential-actions/2025/02/defending-american-companies-and-innovators-from-overseas-extortion-and-unfair-fines-and-penalties/

Monti M (2025) La Corte costituzionale romena di fronte alla "disinformazione" e alle nuove frontiere della pubblicità politica online: fra micro-influencer e ingerenze estere. Giustizia insieme. https://www.giustiziainsieme.it/it/news/74-main/138-diritti-stranieri/3395-la-corte-costituzionale-romena-di-fronte-alla-disinformazione-e-alle-nuove-frontiere-della-pubblicita-politica-matteo-monti
Morgese G (2025) Il contrasto alla disinformazione originata da ingerenze straniere nell'Unione europea. In: Messina M (ed) Strengthening the European Union through the European Citizenship and the Rule of Law. Cittadinanza e Stato di diritto per un'Unione europea più forte, pp 89–130
Pollicino O (2022) Migrazioni di idee costituzionali e implicazioni per le opzioni rilevanti di politica del diritto: il caso della strategia europea contro la disinformazione online. In: Mastroianni R, Ferraro F (eds) Libertà di informazione e diritto dell'Unione europea. Le nuove sfide a tutela della democrazia e del pluralismo, pp 89–104
Pollicino O (2026) How seriously should be taken disinformation? Constitutional and policy dilemmas in a comparative perspective. In: Mastroianni R, Massa C (eds) Disinformation in new and old media in the XXI century. Springer Nature Switzerland, Cham.
Pollicino O, Gentile G (2025) How the US threw out any concerns about AI safety within days of Donald Trump coming to office. https://theconversation.com/how-the-us-threw-out-any-concerns-about-ai-safety-within-days-of-donald-trump-coming-to-office-251659
Presidential action "Removing barriers to American leadership in artificial intelligence" (2025, Jan 23). https://www.whitehouse.gov/presidential-actions/2025/01/removing-barriers-to-american-leadership-in-artificial-intelligence/
Richter A (2023) For propaganda without disinformation: draft EU regulation on political advertising. EJIL: Talk! https://www.ejiltalk.org/21919-2/
Sassi S, Sterpa A (2025) La Corte costituzionale della Romania difende la democrazia liberale dalla disinformazione. Prime note sulla sentenza n. 32 del 6 dicembre 2024. Federalismi.it 4/2025, pp 162–181
Sternstein A (2020) Breaking news: the sky is falling, and, according to Washington Post v. McManus, so was first amendment protection under Maryland's online electioneering transparency and accountability act. Maryland Appellate Blog. https://mdappblog.com/2020/01/13/breaking-news-the-sky-is-falling-and-according-to-washington-post-v-mcmanus-so-was-first-amendment-protection-under-marylands-online-electioneering-transparency-and-accountability-act/
Trusk T (2022) Digital advertising and state-level political advertising disclosure schemes after McManus. Wash J Law Technol Arts 17(1):48–87
van Drunen MZ, Helberger N, Ó Fathaigh R (2022) The beginning of EU political advertising law: unifying democratic visions through the internal market. Int J Law Inf Technol 30:181–199
Venice Commission, Council of Europe (2002) Code of good practice in electoral matters: guidelines and explanatory report. CDL-AD(2002)023rev2-cor-e
Venice Commission, Council of Europe (2024) Interpretative declaration of the Code of good practice in electoral matters as concerns digital technologies and artificial intelligence. CDL-AD(2024)044-e
Venice Commission, Council of Europe (2025) Urgent report on the cancellation of election results by constitutional courts. CDL-PI(2025)001
Zuiderveen Borgesius FJ et al (2018) Online political microtargeting: promises and threats for democracy. Utrecht Law Rev 8. https://doi.org/10.18352/ulr.420

Fighting Disinformation and Balancing Free Speech: A Comparative and Supranational Outlook

Barbara Guastaferro

Abstract This chapter explores the challenges of regulating disinformation, particularly during elections. The chapter is divided into two main sections: a comparative analysis and an examination of supranational institutional responses. The first section argues that tackling disinformation is complex because restrictions on propaganda risk are perceived as limitations on free speech, a cornerstone of democratic societies. It follows that the balance between free speech and other fundamental values, such as personal data protection and national security, differs significantly across jurisdictions like the US, the EU, and the ECHR framework. The second section highlights the European Parliament's role in combating disinformation in democratic processes. Starting with the EP's decision of 18 June 2020 to establish a special committee on foreign interference, including disinformation (INGE), the analysis follows subsequent legislative efforts, culminating in the Resolutions of 9 March 2022 and 1 June 2023. These measures aim to safeguard EU fundamental rights, prevent foreign interference that incites hatred against minorities and vulnerable groups, and ensure free and fair elections. By addressing disinformation, the European Parliament seeks to protect the democratic principle and uphold core EU values.

1 Introduction

The use of biased and deceptive information as a strategic communication tool is gaining increasing concern, especially because manipulation of information can often affect essential values at stake such as the protection of national security.[1] Just to give an example, in the case of the EU, the COVID-19 pandemic provided foreign actors with fertile grounds to plant their own narrative about the crisis, as showed by the attempts by Russia and China to present themselves as succeeding and the EU

[1] Guess and Lyons (2020).

B. Guastaferro (✉)
Department of Political Sciences, University of Naples Federico II, Naples, Italy
e-mail: barbara.guastaferro@unina.it

R. Mastroianni and C. Massa (eds.), *Disinformation in New and Old Media in the XXI Century*, Ius Gentium: Comparative Perspectives on Law and Justice 136,
https://doi.org/10.1007/978-3-032-18830-4_6

as failing in managing the crisis.[2] More recently, disinformation, construed as the dissemination of deliberately false information,[3] has been often used during several electoral processes to undermine the soundness of the democratic process.[4]

This chapter argues that preventing and sanctioning disinformation is a difficult task because any kind of limitation to propaganda might be construed as a limitation on freedom of speech, one of the cornerstones of democratic societies. In this respect, all the political efforts and the legal instruments envisaged to fight disinformation—which can be considered a *global* and transnational phenomenon—require an accurate balancing exercise embedded in the *local* and peculiar constitutional traditions which usually set the judicial frame inspiring the courts.[5]

Indeed, against this backdrop, the comparative landscape analysed in the chapter shows how the balance between free speech, on the one hand, and the protection of basic liberal constitutional values such as the protection of personal data or the preservation of peace and national security, on the other hand, can vary significantly in different legal orders such as the US, the EU, and the ECHR one. Notwithstanding these difficulties, the chapter will also analyse the efforts of the EP to counter disinformation, especially when related to the well-functioning of the democratic process.

---

[2] The COVID-19 pandemic period, characterized by the proliferation of numerous widespread—mostly false—theories, was also extremely illustrative of how the proliferation of fake news can easily undermine public trust in democratic institutions (Reglitz 2022).

[3] Disinformation has been widely discussed in academic literature and is now considered one of the most pressing challenges of today's online communication environment (Torok 2024). While the dissemination of false and misleading information is not a new phenomenon (Kapantai et al. 2021), the past decade has seen a significant increase in the prevalence of misinformation and disinformation (Benkler et al. 2018; HLEG 2018; Lewandowsky et al. 2017; O'Connor and Weatherall 2019). Notably, the 2016 U.S. Presidential election and the Brexit referendum were both marked by extensive disinformation campaigns, leading to widespread discussions among scholars from several disciplines about the role of fake news in shaping public opinion. Consequently, some scholars argue that we are now living in a "post-truth" era (Lewandowsky et al. 2017) or an "age of misinformation" (O'Connor and Weatherall 2019). The definition of terms such as disinformation, misinformation, and fake news remains highly debated. In this article, references to fake news generally align with the wider phenomenon of disinformation, as they are seen as «a species of disinformation» (Gelfert 2018, p. 86). The term disinformation is intended to include «all forms of false, inaccurate, or misleading information designed, presented and promoted to intentionally cause public harm or for profit» (HLEG 2018, p. 3).

[4] In this regard, Gergely Gosztonyi (2024, p. 102) goes so far as to claim that: «Since roughly the 2016 US election, there have been few elections in the world where the issue of influencing voters by fake news has not been raised». For a comparative survey on, specifically, Russian interference in electoral processes, Brattberg and Murer (2018) Five European experiences with Russian election interference. In *Europe's counter to fake news and cyber attacks* (Report). Carnegie Endowment for International Peace.

[5] For a comparative survey on the different judicial frames characterizing the US and the European legal traditions, Morelli and Pollicino (2020), Pollicino and Bassini (2014).

2 Fighting Disinformation and Balancing Free Speech: The Case of the US

Digital tools can both enhance and potentially hinder human rights, including freedom of speech. The Internet serves as «a powerful tool in the exercise of freedom of expression»,[6] offering an unprecedented platform for exercising free speech. However, it also poses significant risks due to the rapid spread of false, defamatory, and misleading information, which can erode public trust and disrupt democratic processes.[7] Consequently, various regulatory responses have been developed in recent decades, all aiming to uphold established constitutional principles while addressing the challenges posed by disinformation. A comparative analysis of these approaches provides valuable insights to understand how difficult and sensitive is the balance beween, on one hand, the imperatives of free speech and, on the other hand, the protection of basic liberal constitutional values, such as protection of personal data, the correct functioning of democratic societies, or the preservation of peace and of national security.

In the United States, for example, the First Amendment, according to which *«Congress shall make no law abridging the freedom of speech, or of the press»*, is of such pivotal importance in the constitutional framework that in the earlier case law of the Supreme Court Internet—as an instrument able to expand freedom of speech—was defined *the new free market place of ideas*.[8] In that case, the federal Communications Decency Act (CDA), passed in 1996, made it a crime for anyone to engage in online speech that is *indecent* or *patently offensive*, if the speech could be viewed by a minor. However, the Supreme Court deemed the Act an unconstitutional restriction on free speech, highlighting the dangers of censoring what one judge called «the most participatory form of mass speech yet developed».[9]

More recently, and along similar lines, the Supreme Court of the United States found to be in violation of the First Amendment a law in North Carolina making it a felony for a registered sex offender to access a commercial social networking Web site—knowing that the site permits minor children to create or maintain personal Web pages. The law was considered overly broad and not narrowly tailored to further the government's legitimate interest in preventing child abuse, and, consequently, too restrictive on free speech. Also in this case, "cyberspace", the vast democratic

---

[6] The European Court of Human Rights (ECtHR) expressed itself in these terms, in several sentences, among which *Times Newspapers Ltd v. the United Kingdom* (2009).

[7] See *ex multis* Califano (2021), Caravita (2019), Pitruzzella et al. (2017), Pollicino and Dunn (2024), Revenga Sánchez (2023).

[8] United States Supreme Court, *Reno v. ACLU*, 521 U.S. 844 (1997).

[9] The expression «the most participatory form of mass speech yet developed» originates from the opinion of Judge Stewart Dalzell in *Reno v. American Civil Liberties Union* (1997), who emphasized the unique nature of the Internet as a medium for free expression and argued it was entitled to «the highest protection from governmental intrusion». The ACLU also argued that the censorship provisions were unconstitutional because they would criminalize expression protected by the First Amendment and because the terms "indecency" and "patently offensive" are unconstitutionally overbroad and vague.

forums of the Internet, was defined as the most important place (in a spatial sense) for the exchange of views.[10] Most importantly, also in this case, the constitutional strength of the freedom of expression protected by the First Amendment trumped even important values such as the protection of minors, reinforcing the long-standing principle that government intervention in speech must be narrowly tailored to avoid unconstitutional censorship.[11] In sum, in the US there seems to be a celebration of Internet as a sort of a *Digital agora,* allowing not only the Greek ideal of *parrhesia* (freedom of speech enjoyed by Athenians), but also of *isegoria*, i.e., the possibility to enjoy *equal right of speech* independently from your social status or educational background—as long as you have internet access.[12]

By way of contrast, shifting the attention from the US to Europe, «it should be recalled that if, in Lee Bollinger's words, free speech is '*the paramount right within the American constellation of constitutional rights*', the same cannot be said with regard to European law [...] The extent to which constitutional protection is afforded to freedom of expression is more limited in Europe, where there is no provision carving out a sphere of protection as broad as that provided by the First Amendment».[13] Notoriously, indeed, in Europe, freedom of speech is not supreme or absolute but can be balanced against other values and fundamental rights. Indeed, quite tellingly, the text of the ECHR after stating, in Art. 10, par. 1, that «Everyone has the right to freedom of expression», specifies in par. 2 that «The exercise of these freedoms, since it carries with it duties and responsibilities, may be subject to such formalities, conditions, restrictions or penalties as are prescribed by law and are necessary in a democratic society, in the interests of national security, territorial

[10] United States Supreme Court, *Packingham v. North Carolina*, 137 S. Ct. 1730 (2017).

[11] Since its adoption, scholarly interpretations of the First Amendment have varied. Some academics have adopted an absolutist perspective, asserting that the First Amendment provides unconditional protection to free speech, especially within the realm of democratic self-governance (Meiklejohn 1961). Conversely, others have contended that interpreting the First Amendment necessitates balancing free speech with other societal interests, as unrestrained freedom can conflict with essential democratic values (Mendelson 1962). In recent times, scholars such as Toni M. Massaro and Helen Norton (2018) have argued that the traditional First Amendment framework is inadequate for addressing contemporary challenges, including the rapid spread of misinformation and the manipulation of public discourse by both governmental and private entities. They advocate for a re-evaluation of First Amendment doctrine to better safeguard democratic values in the digital age.

[12] The idea of the internet as a Digital agora aligns with discussions in U.S. jurisprudence and political theory, where it is often seen as an extension of the First Amendment's commitment to an open marketplace of ideas. Scholars like Yochai Benkler (2006) and Cass R. Sunstein (2017), for instance, view the internet as a space for open and democratic discourse that allows individuals to exercise their right to free speech and equal participation. Similarly, the U.S. Supreme Court, in *Packingham v. North Carolina* (2017), referred to social media as the 'modern public square,' emphasizing its role in democratic discourse. It should be noted, however, that in this framework there are also scholars like Zeynep Tufekci (2018) who challenge the theoretical ideal of the internet as an instrument enabling *isegoria*. She argues that algorithmic amplification and platform policies create speech inequalities, where voices with more resources or sensationalist content gain disproportionate influence. This dynamic ultimately undermines the principles of *parrhesia* and *isegoria*, shifting power away from a truly open and egalitarian public sphere.

[13] Morelli and Pollicino (2020), 13 citing also Bollinger (1988).

integrity or public safety, for the prevention of disorder or crime, for the protection of health or morals, for the protection of the reputation or rights of others, for preventing the disclosure of information received in confidence, or for maintaining the authority and impartiality of the judiciary».[14] And even if this accurate list of limitations to free speech—either finalized to protect other fundamental rights or to protect democratic society—is not explicitly found in Article 11 of the EU Charter of fundamental rights,[15] we know from the final provisions of the latter that, pursuant to Article 52(3) of the Charter, the meaning and scope of this right—as well as of all the rights that have equivalent protection in the ECHR—is the same as those guaranteed by the ECHR.

3 The Balancing Exercise of the European Court of Justice on Article 11 of the Charter of Fundamental Rights of the European Union

The ECJ very recently faced some cases where it was necessary to strike a balance between freedom of speech and information—on the one hand—and the protection of other important values, on the other.

In a 2024 case related to Netherlands, the Court of Justice of the EU stated that Article 15 of Regulation (EU) No 376/2014 of the European Parliament and of the Council of 3 April 2014, on the reporting, analysis and follow-up of occurrences in civil aviation, read in the light of the right to freedom of expression and information enshrined in Article 11 of the Charter of Fundamental Rights of the European Union, must be interpreted as meaning that information held by the national competent authorities regarding an "occurrence" relating to aviation safety, is subject to a confidentiality regime the consequence of which is that neither the public nor even a media undertaking has the right to have access to that information in any form. In sum, in view of the limitations surrounding the freedom of speech contemplated by Art. 11 of the Charter and by its equivalent in the ECHR, secrecy related to national security trumped the freedom of information—which is the other side of the coin of the freedom of expression—in the balancing exercise.[16]

There is also another recent case which deserves attention.[17] In December 2006, the newspaper *Le Monde* published an article in which a journalist claimed that

---

[14] For and in-depth analysis on the case law of the ECHR, Torok (2024).

[15] According to Art. 11 CFREU «Everyone has the right to freedom of expression. This right shall include freedom to hold opinions and to receive and impart information and ideas without interference by public authority and regardless of frontiers. The freedom and pluralism of the media shall be repsected».

[16] CJEU, Case C-451/22, *RTL Nederland BV and RTL Nieuws BV v Minister van Infrastructuur en Waterstaat*, Judgment of 18 January 2024, ECLI:EU:C:2024:54.

[17] CJEU, Case C-633/22, *Real Madrid Club de Fútbol and AE v. EE and Société Éditrice du Monde SA*, Judgment of 18 January 2024, ECLI:EU:C:2024:843.

Real Madrid and Fútbol Club Barcelona had retained the services of the head of a doping ring in the cycling world, and such an article was shared by many media outlets, Spanish ones in particular. For this reason, both the French newspaper and the journalist were condemned by a Spanish Court to pay compensation for the non-material damage suffered by a sports club and one of the members of its medical team, due to harm caused to their reputation. Nevertheless, public policy was used as a ground for refusal of the enforcement of the judgment in France—as allowed by Article 34(1) of the Brussels I Regulation—declaring that the judgement gave rise to an infringement of the freedom of the press, as enshrined in Article 11 of the Charter.

Following a reference for a preliminary ruling from the French Court of Cassation, the Grand Chamber of the Court of Justice, while accepting public policy as a ground of refusal, states that it is for the referring court to determine, taking account of all of the circumstances of the case, whether the damages awarded in the judgments are manifestly disproportionate to the reputational harm in question and thus risk having a deterrent effect on future media coverage of similar matters in the Member State in which enforcement is sought or, more generally, on the exercise of the freedom of the press, as enshrined in Article 11 of the Charter. More specifically, in the context of that verification, the Court even suggested to take account of the amounts awarded for similar harm in the Member State in which enforcement is sought, concluding that any discrepancy between those amounts and the amount of damages awarded in the judgments at issue in the main proceedings is not in itself sufficient for a finding that those damages are, automatically and without subsequent verification, manifestly disproportionate to the reputational harm in question. Lastly, should that court find that there is a manifest infringement of the freedom of the press, it should limit the refusal to enforce those judgments to the manifestly disproportionate portion of the damages awarded.

Such an accurate conclusion of the Court in what could be defined as a "guidance" case,[18] underscores the Court's commitment to balancing fundamental rights, ensuring that the conflicting rights do not unjustifiably override the essential role of freedom of speech in a democratic society, but also emphasizing the necessity that all fundamental rights—including freedom of speech—should be limited and not intrude into other rights disproportionately. This is why in the latter case, even if the Court wants to protect freedom of speech and of the press—by allowing a Member State to refuse a judgement of a foreign Court and possibly infringing upon it—it does not consider freedom of speech as a paramount or superior right. By way of contrast, in order to protect other important values such as the protection of personal reputation, the Court seems to require a stringent proportionality test able to show that public policy—coupled with Art. 11 of the Charter—is not abused as a possible ground of refusal of a judgement that restricted freedom of the press.[19]

[18] The expression "guidance judgment" is originated by Tridimas (2011).

[19] In a European perspective, there is also a vast and interesting jurisprudence of the European Court of Human Rights on the matter that, however, is deliberately not debated or referred to here, where I preferred to crucially analyse the most recent cases of the Court of Justice, in comparison with

Even if such an approach is completely at odds with the case law of the US Supreme Court, where the protection of the freedom of speech even trumped the protection of minors on the web, the comparative landscape is much more nuanced if we consider that the European legal framework outlined so far is not always the same for all the Member States belonging to the EU and the ECHR, that might have their peculiarity. For example, in the Italian Constitution the article devoted to freedom of expression is extremely far from the formulation of the list of limitation of the ECHR. As per Article 21 of the Italian Constitution, indeed, «Anyone has the right to freely express their thoughts in speech, writing, or any other form of communication. The press may not be subjected to any authorisation or censorship […]». Needless to say, this formulation must be read in light (and in contrast to) the massive use of press censorship during the totalitarian Fascist regime preceding the approval of the Italian Constitution in 1948.[20] Moreover, even if Art. 21 of the Italian Constitution specifies that «Publications, performances, and other exhibits offensive to public morality shall be prohibited», the Italian Constituent Assembly expressly refused to introduce the "public order" limitation, since this was an abused concept by Fascist regimes.[21] Against this backdrop, the balancing exercise of the Italian Constitutional Court[22] was slightly different from the abovementioned one of the ECJ, in a very similar case where freedom of the press was at stake. Indeed, in a recent judgement, the Court invalidated a provision of the Italian criminal code that, in order to sanction defamation in the press, provided both prison sentences and fines as cumulative rather than alternative, and this was considered too detrimental to the journalist's freedom of expression.[23] The legal reasoning of the Court was that—even when there is a fundamental right to protect such as private life, honour and reputation of the victim—you need to avoid a disproportionate restriction on the right to inform that could trigger a chilling effect on freedom of the press.

4 The Role of the EP in Fighting Disinformation in Democratic Process

Notwithstanding the analysed difficulties in fighting disinformation, supranational actors are introducing some measures to counter it. With the fast development and the rise of geopolitical tensions, the EU is facing the attempt of foreign actors (in particular Russian ones) to disrupt elections and democratic processes across the

---

the US Supreme Court. For analyses of this jurisprudence, see: Sardo (2020), Torok (2024), Vese (2022).

[20] On the importance of constitutional culture Cartabia and Guastaferro (2022).

[21] Valastro (2006), Pace and Manetti (2006).

[22] For a survey on the less recent case law https://www.cortecostituzionale.it/documenti/convegni_seminari/stu_284.pdf.

[23] Corte costituzionale, Sentenza n. 150/2021, 22 giugno 2021.

EU, basically through information manipulation.[24] Even if it has been noted that the Russian foreign interference was more interested in national elections than in European ones, Parliament President Roberta Metsola—addressing the EU heads of state and government in March 2024, just before the last European elections—declared to be well aware of «how far other actors will go to try to disrupt our democratic processes. We are seeing attempts in many states to push disinformation, misinformation and propaganda, which come from actors hostile to the European project. We cannot allow this destructive narrative, propaganda and disinformation to spread without countering it».[25]

Indeed, and not only in view of the 2024 elections, the European Parliament played a pivotal role in fighting disinformation in democratic processes, taking concrete measures, adopting new laws and seeking other ways to safeguard democracy.[26]

---

[24] Numerous reports have documented Russian interference in various elections through disinformation campaigns. The National Endowment for Democracy (NED) noted that Russian-produced or supported disinformation has been evident in the French, German, and American elections in 2016 and 2017; the 2018 Czech presidential election; and the 2017 Catalonian secession vote (NED 2018). In the United States, for instance, the Office of the Director of National Intelligence published a detailed report on Russia's meddling in the 2016 presidential election, concluding that Russian President Vladimir Putin ordered an influence campaign aimed at undermining public faith in the U.S. democratic process and harming Hillary Clinton's electability. Special Counsel Robert Mueller's investigation led to indictments of 32 individuals, 26 of whom were Russian, and three Russian companies over election interference. The disinformation actions in this extensive campaign included Russian operatives commenting on news stories and maintaining numerous fake Facebook and Twitter accounts, with the strategic goal of sowing discord in the U.S. political system, finally polarizing the US society during and after the 2016 presidential campaign. Similarly, researchers identified over 150,000 Twitter accounts that listed Russian as their language and which tweeted about Brexit. In the final days of the campaign, on the referendum day and the day after, they posted over 45,000 tweets about Brexit, mostly to promote the Leave vote [see Gorodnichenko et al. (2018, May)].

[25] Metsola (2024, March 21). Remarks at the European Council meeting. European Parliament. Available at: the-president.europarl.europa.eu.

[26] Beyond the European Parliament, the European Commission has developed policies to strengthen European democracies, making it more challenging for disinformation actors to exploit online platforms and protecting journalists and media pluralism. The Commission's response to disinformation is centered around developing policies to strengthen European democracies, making it more difficult for disinformation actors to misuse online platforms, and protecting journalists and media pluralism (see commission.europa.eu). Additionally, the Council of the European Union has prioritized the protection of democratic processes against the detrimental effects of disinformation, focusing on the need for a coordinated EU strategy against foreign interference (see consilium.europa.eu). These initiatives demonstrate the commitment of all the European institutions to counter disinformation and protect democratic processes within the European Union. Among the other pivotal policies by the EU in combating disinformation, the Digital Services Act (DSA) aims to prevent illegal and harmful activities online, including the spread of disinformation (for a specific analysis on the DSA see, among others, Gosztonyi 2024); the Code of Practice on Disinformation brings together a wide range of players to commit to a broad set of voluntary commitments to counter disinformation. Broadly, on all the measures implemented on the matter by the EU and its Member States, see Bayer et al. (2020).

One of the most important measures is the European Parliament decision of 18 June 2020 on setting up a special committee on foreign interference in all democratic processes in the European Union, including disinformation, and defining its responsibilities, numerical strength and term of office (INGE), and the following European Parliament decision of 10 March 2022 on the very same topic (ING 2),[27] further calling for permanent institutional solutions to fight disinformation and for an accurate selection on the appropriate legal basis of the Treaties entitling the EU to act in this field.

The work of the two special committees ended up in two important resolutions adopted by the European Parliament, such as the Resolutions of 9 March 2022 and of 1 June 2023 «on foreign interference in all democratic processes in the European Union, including disinformation».[28]

The 2023 Resolution addresses, among other issues, the challenge of disinformation and foreign interference in electoral process.[29] In this respect, it stresses the necessity of a coordinated EU strategy against foreign interference, able to consider both the complexity and the multi-dimensional nature of the threats (which, for example, can stem from cyberattacks, as well as from elite capture and cultural events). The Resolution also calls for the national parliaments of the EU Member States to consider establishing their own parliamentary bodies tasked with overseeing actions related to the protection of their democracy against foreign interference and information manipulation, and to set up regular exchanges on these topics. It tries to prevent and counter prohibited financial payments from non-EU countries into the EU's political system welcoming the work of the Authority for European Political Parties and European Political Foundations,[30] and it proposes to strengthen cybersecurity in order to avoid cyberattacks related to democratic processes that have been growing so far. In the first half of 2021 alone, indeed, there were as many recorded cyberattacks on EU institutions as in the whole of 2020 and, notoriously, the European Parliament itself, during the November 2022 plenary session, was the victim of

[27] INGE, which stands for the "Special Committee on Foreign Interference in all Democratic Processes in the European Union, including Disinformation," was established with the decision of 18 June 2020, published in the Official Journal on 21 March 2021 (2021/C 79/01). ING 2, the second special committee following the work of the initial INGE committee, was established with the decision of 10 March 2022, published in the Official Journal on 9 September 2022 (2022/C 347/28).

[28] The text of the Resolution is available at: https://www.europarl.europa.eu/doceo/document/TA-9-2023-0219_EN.pdf.

[29] European Parliament Resolution of 1 June 2023 on foreign interference in all democratic processes in the European Union, including disinformation (2022/2075(INI)) [2023] OJ C/2023/1226, 69–72.

[30] The Authority for European Political Parties and European Political Foundations has been established for the purpose of registering, controlling and imposing sanctions on European Political Parties and European Political Foundations pursuant to Regulation (EU, Euratom) No 1141/2014 of the European Parliament and of the Council of 22 October 2014 on the statute and funding of European political parties and European political foundations.

a cyberattack shutting down the EP's website after a vote on a resolution declaring Russia as a state sponsor of terrorism.[31]

The 2023 Resolution also deals with covert funding of political activities by foreign actors and donors, reiterating its concerns about the regular revelations of massive Russian funding of political parties and politicians and officials in many democratic countries in an attempt to interfere and gain leverage in their domestic processes. It also warns against Russia's wide-ranging interference with secessionist movements in European territories and in the EU, such as in Catalonia.[32] The Resolution also takes note of the legislative work on the transparency and targeting of political advertising,[33] highlighting the importance of curbing opaque political advertising techniques.

In sum, the activity of the European Parliament in this field is of pivotal importance for avoiding democratic regression in the EU. Indeed, fighting disinformation is: first, a way to protect basic fundamental rights of the EU such as the freedom of expression and freedom of opinion; second, a way to prevent a kind of foreign interference which—in fomenting hatred towards minorities, migrants, and vulnerable people—is contrary to the EU democratic values; third, a way to safeguard free and fair elections, as well as transparent electoral process, which represent the cornerstone of democracy.

5 Democracy Against Democracy

Independently from legal traditions, freedom of expression and information is so important because, besides being relevant as such, it is functional to the well-functioning of democracy; it is a sort of instrumental right.[34] This means that in the cases of disinformation, subversive propaganda, defamatory or discriminatory propaganda against minorities, or foreign interference, we have a case in which *democracy* is used against *democracy*, or, if we want to be more precise, one of the *substantive aspect of democracy,* i.e. a fundamental right such as freedom of speech,

[31] To learn more about the cyberattack against the European Parliament's website, see euronews.com. Additionally, the incident was documented in CERT-EU's Cyber Security Brief published on November 23, 2022 at: https://cert.europa.eu/publications/threat-intelligence/cb23-11/?.

[32] European Parliament Resolution of 1 June 2023 on foreign interference in all democratic processes in the European Union, including disinformation (2022/2075(INI)) [2023] OJ C/2023/1226, 73.

[33] *Ibidem*, 77. On political advertising measures, see in this volume Massa (2025), How to regulate online political advertising to ensure democratic electoral processes? Effectiveness, differences and influences of the EU and US measures.

[34] As noted by Barile (1974, p. 425) «La libertà di pensiero…ha dunque un valore centrale in un ordinamento democratico, *al cui corretto funzionamento concorre come presupposto e condizione di ogni altro istituto*» citing also Lavagna (1970, p. 464). See Amato (1981, pp. 285–286); Esposito (1958), 49 ss.

is used to impinge upon a basic *procedural aspect of democracy,* namely free and fair elections.

It goes without saying, indeed, that disinformation, foreign interference etc., affect what John Stuart Mill and Walter Bagheot would define "*government by discussion*". Indeed, especially in preceding elections, it is particularly important that opinions and a variety of information circulate freely, and that the information on candidates is accurate, in order to enable voters to make informed choices.[35] And we know that the progress in artificial intelligence might significantly hamper the right to free elections, and manipulate public opinion. The U.S. 2024 political campaign has clearly exhibited the proliferation of AI-generated content, leading to the creation and dissemination of deceptive images and videos within the U.S. political sphere.[36]

Nevertheless, as this chapter has showed, fighting disinformation is very difficult not only in those cases, such as the US, where freedom of expression is the paramount constitutional rights, but also in those cases, such as the European one, where freedom of expression is subject to several limitation and where also the *passive* dimension of such a freedom (namely the right to be well informed) is constitutionally protected. As interestingly noted, indeed, «whilst the First Amendment addresses mainly the active dimension to the right to express freely one's own thoughts, Article 10 of the European Convention (but also Article 11 of the Charter of Fundamental Rights of the European Union) emphasises the passive dimension to the right to be pluralistically informed. In this respect, it could be argued that fake news is not constitutionally covered by the European vision of free speech. Or to put it differently, the European courts would find it very difficult to accept the view of the US Supreme Court according to which, as alluded to above, 'Under the First Amendment there is no such thing as a false idea. However pernicious an opinion may seem, we depend for its correction not on the conscience of judges and juries but on the competition of other ideas' (US Supreme Court, Gertz v. Welch, 418 U.S. 323 (1974)».[37]

Despite Europe seems to be provided with a constitutional settlement more favourable to limit freedom of speech against its abuses, and, as we have seen, the EU and in particular the European Parliament is countering disinformation and propaganda, a recent study committed by the Special Committee of the European Parliament, devoted to "*Disinformation and Propaganda: impact on the functioning of the rule of law and democratic processes in the EU and its Member States*", highlights at least two other problems in fighting and regulating disinformation, apart from the discrepancies in constitutional cultures analyzed in the previous paragraphs of this chapter.

---

[35] Pitruzzella (2018). On the European "passive" aspect of freedom of speech, and therefore the right to be informed through media pluralism, see also Mastroianni (2022).

[36] In March 2023, AI-generated images surfaced online depicting former President Trump being arrested by New York City police officers; in August 2024, for example, former President Donald Trump shared AI-generated images on his social media platform, Truth Social, implying that singer Taylor Swift endorsed his presidential campaign (ansa.it).

[37] Pollicino (2017, p. 3). See also Morelli and Pollicino (2020), Pollicino and Bassini (2014), Sajó and Ryan (2016).

The first is related to the very same notion of disinformation, described in 2017 by Wardle and Derakshan as «information that is deliberately *false*, with the *intention* to harm people as a social group or society».[38] As it has been noted, those *definitional elements* are inappropriate anchors for regulation, because «the emblematic element, falsity of the allegation alone, is an insufficient basis for prohibition, as verification of truth is not a pre-condition of exercising the right to freedom of expression. [...] The second element of disinformation, the intention to strategic manipulation, is an elusive criterion as well as it requires one to inquire into the state of mind of the perpetrator».[39] It follows that, when disinformation is used for intentionally forged or distorted allegation, some of these actions exhaust the conditions for other traditionally existing speech restrictions, such as defamation, incitement to hatred, or holocaust denial or denial of genocide. While, if this is the case, the disinformation action can be countered on the basis of existing legal rules, it is very difficult to sanction those types of disinformation which fall outside these traditional restrictions on speech.[40]

The second problem in countering disinformation is that technology runs faster than legislators. In this respect, the findings of the study committed by the EP show that the two cases that are mentioned as the best examples of best practices in fighting disinformation, Taiwan and Finland, have nothing to do with the legal or regulatory framework. The most effective countermeasures often stem from strategic initiatives rather than strict regulation. In particular, Taiwan's response to disinformation was very successful in countering fake news with a strategy that has been defined as *humour over rumour*,[41] and without any legal measures restricting free speech. Just to give an example, as reported by the study committed by the EP, in the first days of the pandemic, people were panic-buying toilet paper because of a rumour that it was being used to manufacture face masks. In response, Taiwanese premier, Su Tseng-chang, released a cartoon of him wiggling his bum, with a caption saying: «We only have one pair of buttocks», which went viral in the media and turned out to be very effective in countering the disinformation on the possible running out of toilet paper.[42] Similarly, Finland was targeted as promoting one of the best practices against disinformation, basically through media literacy education that has strengthened public resilience by incorporating critical thinking into school curricula, as shown by a study measuring critical thinking skills in which Finnish secondary school students outperformed American students.[43]

---

[38] Wardle and Derakhshan (2017, p. 20). (while misinformation is considered as "organically-created and unintentionally-spread false information"). More specifically on the definitional element of propaganda, De Brabandere (2023).

[39] Bayer et al. (2021, p. 36).

[40] On the difficulty in envisaging repressive regulation for distorted news, Baade (2019).

[41] Mahdawi (2021, February 17) Humour over rumour? The world can learn a lot from Taiwan's approach to fake news. *The Guardian*.

[42] Bayer et al. (2021, pp. 54–55).

[43] Bayer et al. (2021, p. 57).

Ultimately, protecting democracy against disinformation requires a holistic strategy—one that combines legal instruments, institutional oversight, technological advancements, and public engagement. By integrating these approaches, democratic societies can build resilience against the threats posed by manipulated narratives while ensuring that fundamental freedoms remain intact.

References

Amato G (1981) Libertà (diritto costituzionale). In: Enciclopedia del diritto. Giuffrè, Milano, pp 272–286

Baade B (2019) Fake news and international law. Eur J Int Law 29(4)

Barile P (1974) Libertà di manifestazione del pensiero. In: Enciclopedia del diritto, vol XXIV. Giuffrè, Milano, pp 424–486

Bayer J, Holznagel B, Lubianiec K, Pintea A, Szakács J, Alemanno A, Uszkiewicz E (2020) Disinformation and propaganda—impact on the functioning of the rule of law in the EU and its Member States. European Parliament

Bayer J, Holznagel B, Lubianiec K, Pintea A, Schmitt JB, Szakács J, Uszkiewicz E (2021) Disinformation and propaganda—impact on the functioning of the rule of law in the EU and its Member States-2021 update. European Parliament

Benkler Y (2006) The wealth of networks: how social production transforms markets and freedom. Yale University Press, New Haven

Benkler Y, Faris R, Roberts H (2018) Network propaganda: manipulation, disinformation, and radicalization in American politics. Oxford University Press, Oxford

Califano L (2021) La libertà di manifestazione del pensiero… in rete; nuove frontiere di esercizio di un diritto antico. Fake news, hate speech e profili di responsabilità dei social network. Federalismi.it 26

Caravita B (2019) Social network, formazione del consenso, istituzioni politiche: quale regolamentazione possibile?. Federalismi.it 2

Cartabia M, Guastaferro B (2022) Italy. In: Griller S, Papadopoulou L, Puff R (eds) Member states' constitutions and EU integration. Hart, Oxford

De Brabandere E (2023) Propaganda. In: Max planck encyclopedias of international law. Oxford University Press, Oxford

Esposito C (1958) La libertà di manifestazione del pensiero nell'ordinamento italiano. Rivista italiana per le scienze giuridiche 49–103

Gelfert A (2018) Fake news: a definition. Philos Q 68(271):93–112. https://doi.org/10.1093/pq/pqx070

Gorodnichenko Y, Pham T, Talavera O (2018, May) Social media, sentiment and public opinions: evidence from #Brexit and #USElection. Working Paper No. 24631. National Bureau of Economic Research

Gosztonyi G (2024) How the European Union had tried to tackle fake news and disinformation with soft law and what changed with the Digital Services Act? Front Law 3:102–113. https://doi.org/10.3389/flaw.2024.00012

Guess AM, Lyons BA (2020) Misinformation, disinformation, and online propaganda. In: Persily N, Tucker JA (eds) Social media and democracy. Cambridge University Press, Cambridge

High Level Expert Group (2018) A multi-dimensional approach to disinformation: report of the independent high-level expert group on fake news and online disinformation. European Commission

Kapantai K, Pashalidis N, Papadopoulos C (2021) Digital misinformation: understanding the evolution and impact of disinformation campaigns. J Med Commun Stud 13(1):45–58. https://doi.org/10.1016/j.jmcs.2020.12.003

Lavagna (1970) Istituzioni di diritto pubblico. UTET, Torino
Lewandowsky S, Ecker UKH, Cook J (2017) The psychology of fake news: accepting, sharing, and correcting misinformation. Psychol Sci Public Interest 18(3):1–33. https://doi.org/10.1177/1529100617743546
Massa C (2025) How to regulate online political advertising to ensure democratic electoral processes? Effectiveness, differences and influences of the EU and US measures. In this volume
Massaro TM, Norton H (2018) Free speech in the age of digital platforms. Harv Law Rev 131(4):1234–1259
Mastroianni R (2022), Freedom and pluralism of the media: an European value waiting to be discovered? MediaLaws 1/2021
Meiklejohn A (1961) Political freedom: the constitutional powers of the people. Harper & Row
Mendelson M (1962) The first amendment and the search for truth. Columbia Law Rev 62(1):53–85
Morelli A, Pollicino O (2020) Metaphors, judicial frames, and fundamental rights in cyberspace. Am J Comp Law 68(4):757–791. https://doi.org/10.1093/ajcl/avaa030
National Endowment for Democracy (2018, May 29) Issue in brief: how disinformation impacts politics and publics
O'Connor C, Weatherall JO (2019) The misinformation age: how false beliefs spread. Yale University Press, New Haven
Pace A, Manetti M (2006) Art. 21. Rapporti civili. La libertà di manifestazione del proprio pensiero. In: Branca G, Pizzorusso A (eds) Commentario della Costituzione. Zanichelli, Roma-Bologna
Pitruzzella G (2018) La libertà di informazione nell'era di Internet. MediaLaws 1/2018
Pitruzzella G, Pollicino O, Quintarelli S (2017) Parole e potere. Libertà di espressione, hate speech e fake news. Milano
Pollicino O (2017) Editorial. Fake news, Internet and Metaphors (to be handled carefully). Italian J Public Law 9(1)
Pollicino O, Bassini M (2014) Free speech, defamation and the limits to freedom of expression in the EU: a comparative analysis. In: Savin A, Trzaskowski J (eds) Research handbook on internet law. Edward Elgar Publishing, Cheltenham, pp 508–530
Pollicino O, Dunn P (2024) Intelligenza artificiale e democrazia. Opportunità e rischi di disinformazione e discriminazione. Bocconi University Press, Milan
Reglitz M (2022) Fake news and democracy. J Ethics Soc Philos 22(2):162–187. https://doi.org/10.3817/jeps.2022.22102
Revenga Sánchez M (2023) Dicotomías de la libertad de expresión en la era de la comunicación digital. In: Ferrer Mac Gregor E (ed) La garantía jurisdiccional de la constitución. A cien años del Verfassungsgerichtshof Österreich, a cuarenta años del Tribunal Constitucional de España. XII Encuentro Iberoamericano de Derecho Procesal Constitucional. CEPC, Madrid, pp 1171–1181
Sajó A, Ryan C (2016) Judicial reasoning and new technologies: framing, newness, fundamental rights and the internet. In: Pollicino O, Romeo G (Eds) The internet and constitutional law: the protection of fundamental rights and constitutional education in Europe. Routledge, London
Sardo D (2020) Categories, balancing, and fake news: the jurisprudence of the European court of human rights. Can J Law Jurisprud 33(2):435–460
Sunstein CR (2017) #Republic: divided democracy in the age of social media. Princeton University Press, Princeton
Torok B (2024) Free speech principles to consider when restricting disinformation. Információs Társadalom 24(2):115–128
Tridimas T (2011) Constitutional review of member state action: the virtues and vices of an incomplete jurisdiction. Int J Const Law 9(3–4):737–756

Tufekci Z (2018) Twitter and tear gas: the power and fragility of networked protest. Yale University Press, New Haven

Valastro A (2006) Sub art. 21 cost. In: Bifulco R, Celotto A, Olivetti M (eds) Commentario alla Costituzione, vol I. Giappichelli, Torino, pp 451–473

Vese A (2022) Governing fake news: the regulation of social media and the right to freedom of expression in the era of emergency. Eur J Risk Regul 13:477–513

Wardle C, Derakhshan H (2017) Information disorder: toward an interdisciplinary framework for research and policy making. Council of Europe, report DGI(2017)09

A Cautionary Tale for the European Union: The Stigmatization of Dissenting Voices Through Foreign Agent Laws

Sarah Madsen and Fernanda G. Nicola

Abstract Since 2019, the proposed European Union (EU) directive on Interest Representation and Activities carried out on behalf of Third Countries has sought to harmonize legislation across its 27 Member States, some of which already enforce foreign agent laws. While the EU lacks direct authority over national security, it relies on its internal market competence to address legal discrepancies that could hinder cross-border trade. Several Member States have enacted or are considering such laws, inspired by the U.S. Foreign Agents Registration Act (FARA) of 1938. Similar legislation exists in Australia, Israel, Canada the UK, Russia, and more recently in Hungary, Georgia, and Kyrgyzstan, with Slovakia, Bulgaria and Turkey contemplating similar measures. Hungary's Protection of National Sovereignty Act (PNSA), in effect since February 1, 2024, exemplifies the dangers of such laws that had been set aside and now reappear like zombie-laws. Initially aimed at transparency, in its new version PNSA serves to protect the 'will of the people' by discrediting critics of Hungary's illiberal democracy, reinforcing the government's narrative that foreign-funded groups undermine national sovereignty. This follows a broader trend of governments using foreign agent laws to delegitimize independent watchdogs and civil society organizations. The rise of such legislation in the EU highlights that regulating foreign influence is no longer merely about market integrity but a critical democratic concern throughout the Union. However these measures must strike a careful balance, mitigating risks of abuse, stigmatization, and suppression of dissent while upholding fundamental rights—including privacy, freedom of association, and free speech.

S. Madsen · F. G. Nicola (✉)
American University Washington College of Law, Washington, DC, USA
e-mail: fnicola@wcl.american.edu

S. Madsen
e-mail: sm7854a@american.edu

R. Mastroianni and C. Massa (eds.), *Disinformation in New and Old Media in the XXI Century*, Ius Gentium: Comparative Perspectives on Law and Justice 136,
https://doi.org/10.1007/978-3-032-18830-4_7

1 Introduction: Comparing Foreign Agent Laws in Europe and the United States

The demand for legislation regulating foreign influence has grown in recent years as nations seek to limit foreign influence over domestic political processes such as elections or referenda. Also referred to as foreign agent laws, foreign influence legislation can be defined as "creating *ex post facto* registration requirements for receiving foreign funding or acting on behalf of a foreign actor."[1] Such legislation generally aims to "promote transparency, both on activities and funding (especially of NGOs); to safeguard the democratic processes; and to respond to political activities by actors on behalf of foreign states."[2] However, foreign influence legislation has also become a popular instrument of authoritarian regimes seeking to strengthen their hold on power by extinguishing voices of opposition.

By stigmatizing independent civil society actors, foreign agent laws delegitimize and isolate nongovernmental organizations (NGOs).[3] The archetypal foreign agent law is Russia's 2012 legislation regulating the activities of noncommercial organizations acting as foreign agents.[4] The law amended Russia's Law of Noncommercial Organizations and provides that any nongovernmental organization involved in political activities, media outlet, or individual receiving financing from abroad is considered a foreign agent and may be placed on a list of foreign agents by the Russian Ministry of Justice. Such organizations are also subject to special registration and monitoring rules.[5] The law was adopted in the wake of large-scale protests against Vladimir Putin's rule, mere months after his return as president of Russia. A precursor to the Kremlin's wide-scale repression, it was foundational in entrenching the regime's authoritarianism.[6]

In the last decade, similar laws have proliferated in Eastern Europe in countries with close ties to the Kremlin.[7] Hungary, Slovakia, Georgia, Bosnia and Herzegovina, Kyrgyzstan, and Bulgaria each have attempted to adopt some form of foreign influence legislation with varying levels of success.[8] These laws raise questions of to what extent it is "legally feasible and constitutionally sound... to design effective but democratically safe [foreign influence legislation]."[9] This chapter provides a background on foreign influence legislation generally and critically examines the aims and outcomes of such legislation. More specifically, it will delve into the foreign agent laws adopted in the United States, Russia, Georgia and Hungary, as well as

[1] Robinson (2024, p. 3).

[2] Alemanno and Sames (2023, p. 7).

[3] Commission on Security and Cooperation in Europe (2024).

[4] Kirova (2024).

[5] Roudik (2021).

[6] Kirova (2024).

[7] Frankenberg and Nicola (2025).

[8] RadioFreeEurope (2024).

[9] Alemanno and Sames (2023, p. 3).

those being considered by Slovakia, Bulgaria and the European Union. A comparative analysis of foreign agent laws in Europe and the United States reveals how they have sought to balance competing interests, resulting in wide disparities in the degree of restrictiveness and enforcement of such legislation.

2 Narratives and Goals in the Adoption of Foreign Agent Laws

Foreign agent laws are frequently enacted with the stated goal of promoting transparency about foreign influence. In recent years, an increasing number of governments have adopted legislation that creates foreign influence registries, often attached to additional labeling or compliance requirements for those who register.[10] Insofar as these laws are used to protect transparency and safeguard national political processes, their declared aims appear legitimate.[11] When appropriately tailored, foreign agent laws can both assist governments in defending against malign foreign influence and promote open and democratic governance. However, these legitimate aims tend to be formulated using overbroad and vague provisions and contain "excessive regulatory requirements, that have been used by governments to burden, stigmatize, and criminalize civil society organizations."[12]

Authoritarian regimes often make misleading claims "that their laws are similar to transparency or lobbying laws in the United States and other democratic countries, which have been put in place to make hidden foreign influence more transparent and address propaganda and malign foreign influence."[13] Instead, the foreign agent designation is used to stigmatize and discredit civil society organizations. Such laws also frequently give the government broad authority to involve itself in an organization's finances and activities. Failure to comply can result in fines, closure of an organization, or imprisonment.[14]

2.1 *United States: The Foreign Agents Registration Act (FARA)*

The United States' own foreign influence legislation was adopted in 1938 to monitor and expose Nazi propaganda with the view that such propaganda would be deterred through a regime of forced transparency.[15] It marked the first adoption of foreign

[10] Robinson (2024, p. 2).

[11] Frankenberg and Nicola (2025).

[12] Robinson (2024, p. 2).

[13] Commission on Security and Cooperation in Europe (2024).

[14] Ibid.

[15] Rebo (2022, pp. 277–293).

influence legislation in modern history.[16] The Foreign Agents Registration Act (FARA) "requires certain agents of foreign principals who are engaged in political activities or other activities specified under the statute to make periodic public disclosure of their relationship with the foreign principal, as well as activities, receipts and disbursements in support of those activities."[17]

FARA contains eight exemptions that allow an agent of a foreign principle to avoid registering with the DOJ. They include "(1) diplomatic or consular officers; (2) officials of foreign governments; (3) staff members of diplomatic or consular officers; (4) private and nonpolitical activities, including the solicitation of funds; (5) religious, scholastic, or scientific pursuits; (6) defense of a foreign government vital to U.S. defense; (7) certain persons qualified to practice law and who are engaged in certain legal representation; and (8) persons engaged in lobbying activities and registered under the Lobbying Disclosure Act."[18]

Foreign agents whose activities do not fall within one of the specified exemptions must file a Registration Statement with the DOJ disclosing "information related to their business; the nature of their relationship with the foreign principal, including a copy of their written contract or the conditions of an oral arguments; and statements on activities and money spent and received in connection with foreign agent activities."[19] Registrants must also file supplemental statements at six-month intervals.[20] Violators face both civil and criminal liability punishable by a fine of not more than $250,000 or five years imprisonment.[21]

Congress transferred enforcement of FARA from the Department of State to the Department of Justice (DOJ) in 1942 and clarified FARA's goal as protecting "the national defense, internal security, and foreign relations of the United States by requiring public disclosure... [of] activities for or on behalf of foreign governments."[22] Following World War II, FARA's enforcement focus switched from fascists to communists.[23] By the 1960s, it was being used to target lobbyists and public relations firms acting on behalf of foreign governments. Despite its sweeping nature, FARA has historically been underenforced.[24] The DOJ brought only seven cases under FARA between 1966 and 2015.[25] However, following Russia's interference in the 2016 presidential election, FARA has "gained favor among policymakers and prosecutors as a central tool to respond to a range of foreign influence in U.S. politics, including foreign lobbying, electioneering, and disinformation."[26] The DOJ

[16] Alemanno and Sames (2023, p. 8).

[17] U.S. Department of Justice (2025a, b, c, d).

[18] Straus (2024, p. 2).

[19] Straus (2024, p. 1).

[20] U.S. Department of Justice (2025b) FARA: Frequently Asked Questions.

[21] U.S. Department of Justice (2025a) FARA Enforcement.

[22] Act of Apr 29, 1942, ch 253, Pub L No 77-532 Stat 248.

[23] Rebo (2022, pp. 277–293).

[24] Robinson (2020, p. 1075).

[25] Rebo (2022, pp. 277–295).

[26] Robinson (2020, p. 1075).

prosecuted more FARA cases between 2016 and 2019 than in previous 50 years combined.[27] The recent resurgence in FARA's use has prompted criticism from those who warn that the law's provisions are broad and unclear. These statutory flaws raise the potential for FARA to be used to target nonprofits, the media, and other civil society organizations.[28] FARA's reliance on the DOJ's enforcement discretion has raised additional questions of whether FARA sufficiently protects the civil liberties at stake and whether FARA should be amended to narrow its breadth and scope.[29]

Recent cases brought pursuant to FARA indicate that the DOJ has limited enforcement to high-profile violations.[30] Special Counsel Robert Mueller, charged with investigating Russian interference in the 2016 presidential election, brought charges including failure to register under FARA, against Paul Manafort, Donald Trump's former campaign Chairman.[31] More recently, former U.S. Senator Robert Menendez was convicted in July 2024 as a result of his participation in a years-long bribery scheme. The indictment charged that both Menendez and his wife conspired to have Menendez act as an agent of a foreign principal and that his failure to register under FARA was in violation of 18 U.S.C. § 219.[32] Nevertheless, the significant increase in the number of FARA prosecutions post-2016 election demonstrates that it is vulnerable to unpredictable enforcement. Although FARA has, until recently, existed in relative obscurity, it offers inspiration to countries seeking to develop their own foreign influence legislation.[33]

2.2 *The Blueprint: Russia's NGO Law on Foreign Agents*

In July 2012, just months after taking office as president for a third term, Vladimir Putin signed into law a series of amendments to existing laws governing nongovernmental organizations. The amendments altered the criminal code and the laws "On Noncommercial Organizations," "On Public Associations," and "On Combating Money Laundering and the Financing of Terrorism." The law's core element was a requirement that any organization engaging in political activity that receives foreign funding must register as a foreign agent, regardless of whether the foreign funding actually pays for political activities. The state has the sole authority to determine whether an organization engages in political activity based on its involvement in political acts "aimed at influencing the decision making of public authorities, changing public policy, or influencing public opinion with respect to government policy."[34]

[27] Rebo (2022, p. 277).

[28] Robinson (2020, p. 1075).

[29] Rebo (2022, p. 277).

[30] U.S. Department of Justice (2025c).

[31] Robinson (2020, pp. 1075–1079).

[32] U.S. Department of Justice (2025d) Recent Cases.

[33] Alemanno and Sames (2023, pp. 8, 25).

[34] Machalek (2025).

Designated foreign agents are obliged to comply with a number of additional monitoring requirements including, (1) producing financial reports about any political activities on a quarterly basis, filing documents disclosing the composition of their management bodies and describing their activities semiannually, and submitting to a state audit annually; (2) submitting to an unlimited number of unscheduled audits; (3) registering political activities with the authorities before the organization participates in them; (4) mandatory monitoring of all foreign donations larger than 200,000 rubles ($6,700); and (5) labeling all materials distributed to the media or online as products of foreign agents. Organizations that fail to register with the state are banned from participating in public demonstrations and access to their bank accounts is limited. The state may also impose a fine of up to 300,000 rubles ($10,000) or up to two years in prison for its personnel for violations of the law, which are enforced by the federal agency that monitors money laundering and the financing of terrorism. The law makes limited exemptions for state corporations, business groups, and recognized religious organizations.[35]

The law was widely criticized in the West as an attempt by Vladimir Putin to destroy political opposition and stymie civil society.[36] Since its passing, many NGOs have been forced to close or have seen their activity decimated, including "prominent human rights organizations; anti-corruption, environmental and polling groups; service providers working on issues such as HIV prevention and diabetes care; media organizations; and others."[37] Many more organization have closed down voluntarily, citing the stigmatizing label of "foreign agent," a lack of resources to adequately comply with burdensome reporting requirements, and insufficient funds to pay fines.[38] Responding to criticism, the Kremlin has argued that it modeled its legislation after FARA and seeks to protect its national interests in a similar manner as the United States.[39]

Successive amendments have only expanded the scope of the law. As of 2022, foreign funding is no longer a prerequisite to labeling an organization as a "foreign agent." The law extends to any individual or organization deemed to be under "foreign influence" and alleged foreign agents are excluded from many aspects of public life, including the civil service, elected office, and teaching children. Violators face hefty fines or to up to five years in prison. In 2022, the European Court of Human Rights (ECtHR) ruled that Russia's law violated the European Convention of Human Rights specifically the right to freedom of assembly and association. However, by that point Russia was no longer a member of the Council of Europe and therefore ignored the ruling altogether.[40]

[35] Ibid.

[36] Rebo (2022, p. 277).

[37] Kirova (2024).

[38] Ibid.

[39] Rebo (2022, p. 277).

[40] Kirova (2024).

In 2024, the European Court of Human Rights (ECtHR) held that the Russian Foreign Agents Act failed to meet foreseeability requirements and provided inadequate safeguards against arbitrary and discriminatory enforcement.[41] The Court emphasized that the law's vague definitions and broad interpretations by the authorities resulted in a negative effect on the activities of NGOs, forcing them to choose between accepting foreign funding with burdensome requirements or limiting their operations due to insufficient domestic funding. The ECtHR concluded that the interference was neither "prescribed by law" nor "necessary in a democratic society," highlighting the disproportionate and unjustified restrictions imposed on NGOs.[42] The court examined whether this government interference was necessary in a democratic society and whether it furthered a legitimate aim. It determined that the new foreign agent status of organizations restricted the organization's ability to participate in public life and to carry out activities as they had prior to the law's enactment. The government has claimed that their legitimate aim for the new law was to increase transparency in respect to foreign funding. However, the court found that the means used by the government surpassed proportional means and thus the interference was not necessary in a democratic society.

2.3 *The Transfer of the Russian Law in Georgia, Kyrgyzstan and Turkey*

The ruling party in Georgia passed legislation in May 2024 that requires noncommercial organization and media outlets that receive foreign funding and that engage in political activity to report their activities to the authorities.[43] Specifically, organizations receiving more than twenty percent of their funding from abroad must register themselves as "pursuing the interests of a foreign power."[44] Failure to register could result in fines of up to $9,300.[45] There are over twenty-five thousand NGO's in Georgia which according to a 2020 Report by the Asian Development Bank, receive more than ninety percent of their funding from foreign sources.[46] The law brings the country closer to Russia and threatens both civil society and Georgia's bid for EU membership. The EU announced in July that Georgia's candidate status would be suspended over concerns about the law.[47]

In April 2024, Kyrgyzstan adopted a law requiring organizations that receive foreign funding and engage in political activities to register as "foreign representatives" and label any publications accordingly. It also mandates that NGOs submit to

41 Ecodefence and others v. Russia, App. Nos. 9988/13 and 60 others (2022).

42 *Id.* at para 113.

43 Ibid and RadioFreeEurope (2024).

44 Goedemans (2024).

45 Ibid.

46 Asian Development Bank (2020, p. 5) and Goedemans (2024).

47 Goedemans (2024).

financial reporting requirements and extensive government oversight. Organizations that are not property entered into the national register risk having their activities suspended and their assets frozen until a court can decide whether the group should be permanently liquidated.[48] Despite significant opposition from local NGOs and international organizations, President Japarov has increasingly targeted independent media outlets since rising to power in 2020.[49] A controversial "false information" law passed in 2021 expanded the government's authority to target journalists and media organizations and the recent foreign agent law has already been used to shutter independent organizations.[50]

In May 2024, Turkey's ruling Justice and Development Party (AKP) proposed an omnibus law aimed at amending the criminal code by creating a new offense related to actions deemed to threaten the state's security or political interests. Under the proposal, individuals accused of offenses "against the security or internal or external political interests of the state in line with the strategic interests or instructions of a foreign state or organization" could face prison terms of three to seven years.

After drawing sharp criticism from opposition groups and civil society organizations, the bill was initially set aside. However, by October 2024, the proposal resurfaced—raising renewed concerns among human rights defenders, opposition figures, journalists, and various civic groups.[51] Designed to fit within the chapter on "Crimes against state secrets and espionage," the new Article 339A was intended to expand the scope of traditional espionage-related offenses. It would potentially encompass a wide range of interests, including economic, financial, military, national defense, public health, public security, technological, cultural, transport, communications, cyber, critical infrastructure, and energy matters.[52]

Critics have highlighted that the law's ambiguous wording—using terms such as "strategic interests" and "political interests of the state"—lacks clear definitions, thereby granting authorities excessive discretion in enforcement.[53] Many have drawn parallels with Russia's foreign agent law, arguing that such measures use national security as a pretext to suppress dissent and erode democratic freedoms.[54] When considered alongside the 2022 disinformation law, there are serious concerns that this legislation could lead to further crackdowns on journalists and activists.[55]

[48] Reporters Without Borders (2024).

[49] Committee to Protect Journalists (2024) Kyrgyzstan President Signs Russian-Style 'Foreign Agents' Law.

[50] Ibid and Committee to Protect Journalists (2021).

[51] Committee to Protect Journalists (2024) Turkey's Parliament Expected to Vote on 'Foreign Agent' Law this Week.

[52] Human Rights Watch (2024).

[53] Amnesty International (2024c) Türkiye: Proposed 'Agents of Influence' Law Is Attack on Civil Society and Must be Rejected.

[54] Rowland (2024).

[55] International Press Institute (2024).

Facing widespread opposition both domestically and internationally—with more than 80 organizations urging its rejection,[56] the Turkish government withdrew the proposed amendment in November 2024. Although many in civil society celebrated the withdrawal as a victory, concerns remain that similar legislation could be reintroduced in the future, underscoring the need for continued vigilance and advocacy to safeguard civil liberties in Turkey.[57]

3 Russian-Style Foreign Agent Laws in the European Union

In the past decade, foreign influence transparency laws have increasingly been weaponized to target dissenting voices with the stigma and burden associated with registering as a "foreign agent."[58] These laws are "implemented in a climate of increasing repression of civil society, including NGOs, human rights activists, independent media, and election observers."[59] Although such laws are frequently justified by reference to FARA, they often target U.S. and European supported organizations.[60] The push to adopt Russian-style foreign agent laws has been particularly notable in Eastern Europe in countries with close ties to the Kremlin.[61]

Politicians in Hungary, Slovakia, Georgia, Bosnia and Herzegovina, Kyrgyzstan, and Bulgaria have all introduced some measure of foreign agent legislation modeled on the Russian example.[62] Though each of these countries warrants further study to gain a fuller understanding of this trend, this paper will focus specifically on Hungary, Slovakia and Bulgaria because they are member states of the European Union (EU). As a result, they are subject to EU law—including the EU Charter of Fundamental Rights and they are obligated to the respect the values of the Union under Article 2 of the Treaty of the European Union (TEU)[63]—and must submit to the jurisdiction of the Court of Justice of the EU (CJEU) that is increasingly using these provisions to prevent non-democratic regression[64] and guarantee the rule of law in each Member State.[65]

---

[56] Ozgur Sivil Toplum (2024).

[57] Amnesty International (2024d) Türkiye: Withdrawal of So-Called 'Agents of Influence' Law Is Important Victory for Civil Society.

[58] Robinson (2020, p. 1075).

[59] Commission on Security and Cooperation in Europe (2024).

[60] Ibid.

[61] RadioFreeEurope (2024).

[62] Kirova (2024).

[63] Article 2 TEU.

[64] Case C-896/19 *Repubblika* ECLI:EU:C:2021:311, paras 59–63, 72.

[65] European Commission v. Hungary (Case C-769/22) (2023/C 54/19) and Lenaerts (2023, p. 54).

3.1 The Hungarian Act as a Zombie Foreign Agent Law

The Protection of National Security Act (PNSA) approved in December 2023 is not Hungary's first attempt to stifle independent groups and silence opposition. In 2017, Hungary approved the Law on the Transparency of Organizations Funded from Abroad, which required nongovernmental organizations that receive more than €23,000 in funding from abroad to register as "foreign funded organizations." Such organizations were required to "identify themselves in all published and online material as 'foreign funded organizations;' as well as to provide a detailed account annually on the specific amount and donor, including private donors, for each foreign transaction."[66] Organizations that failed to register could be fined or legally dissolved.[67] The law was ultimately repealed in 2021 after the Court of Justice of the EU (CJEU) ruled that it violates EU law, including the EU Charter of Fundamental Rights protecting freedom of speech, privacy and association. In particular, the CJEU "identified the right to access funding as a substantive element of freedom of association and recognized the chilling effect of such laws, which can foster a climate of distrust in the work of associations."[68]

Despite this first failed attempt, the government of Viktor Orbán approved the Protection of National Security Act as a zombie law aiming to resuscitate its foreign agent law. This time PNSA granted the government even broader authority to target civil society and independent media organizations. The new law has two main elements: (1) the creation of the Sovereignty Protection Office (SPO) which will be responsible for enforcing the law; and (2) an amendment to the criminal code prescribing a prison sentence for groups or individuals using funding from abroad to influence political campaigns. The newly created SPO's mandate includes the power to collect information on groups or individuals that receive foreign funding and influence public debate.[69] The law's vague definitions of "national sovereignty" and "foreign interests" combined with the SPO's sweeping authority to access government and intelligence data has already resulted in a climate of fear and self-censorship in Hungary. There is evidence that the government has already used it to target anti-corruption watchdog organizations including Transparency International Hungary and a local media group.[70]

Anticipating conflicts with EU law, in February 2024 the European Commission initiated the first step of an infringement procedure by sending Hungary a formal notice of incompatibility between PNSA and EU law. The Commission provided Hungary with two months to respond to the formal notice seeking to expedite the infringement procedure once it has received a response. The Commission has also

---

66 Human Rights Watch (2017).

67 Ibid.

68 Kirova (2024).

69 Euro News (2023).

70 Kirova (2024).

requested that the implementation of PNSA be suspended as an *interim measure* as the Commission turns to the CJEU for an infringement proceeding.[71]

In response to Hungary's latest attempt to stymie civil society, the Commission has acted in launching an infringement proceeding against Hungary's zombie law following another infringement against the Hungarian law prohibiting children from accessing LGBTQ + content. However in this case the Commission has added the violation of article 2 TEU protecting as European values "respect for human dignity, freedom, democracy, equality, the rule of law and respect for human rights, including the rights of persons belonging to minorities."[72] Recent examples indicate that these infringement actions,[73] together with preliminary references or annulments cases before the CJEU in which large coalitions of civil society actors are involved has proven to be effective when used as a "stick" against the Orbán government or "carrots" to allow judges to refer the cases to the Court.[74]

In the *interim* however, the PNSA continues to threaten European values such as democracy and rule of law and other fundamental rights, including the right to privacy, freedom of expression, and freedom of association.[75] With the halting of USAID from President Donald Trump in February 2025, this has emboldened Orbán to continue his crackdown of NGOs and independent media by attacking transnational networks and sanctioning civil society organizations that received any financial assistance from the United States.[76]

3.2 Slovakia and Bulgaria's Bills on Foreign Agents Laws

In April 2024 the Slovak Parliament approved a first reading of a bill amending and supplementing Act No. 301/2005 of the Criminal Procedure Code that would label organizations that receive funding from abroad as "organizations with foreign support."[77] The bill now awaits a second reading in National Council.[78] The law is a series of draft amendment that would apply to any organization that receives more than €5,000 a year from foreign sources, including funding from other organizations that receive foreign support. NGOs must also file an annual report disclosing the identity and nationality of any donors or creditors whose contributions or loans

---

[71] Amnesty International (2024a) Hungary's Act on the Protection of National Sovereignty in Breach of EU Law, p. 1.

[72] Associated Press (2024).

[73] European Commission v. Hungary (Case C-769/22) (2023/C 54/19) in which the Hungarian law violates freedom to provide services (Article 56 TFEU); the rights to human dignity; the respect for private and family life; freedom of expression and information; and non-discrimination as protected by the Charter of Fundamental Rights of the European Union and Article 2 of the Treaty of the EU.

[74] Nicola and Cameron (2024a, b).

[75] Associated Press (2024).

[76] Spike (2025).

[77] U.S. News (2024).

[78] Council of Europe (2025, p. 3).

exceed €5,000 a year. Organizations with an annual income exceeding €50,000 would be required to submit an annual report to the Ministry of the Interior, which may fine or dissolve organizations that fail to comply with labeling and reporting obligations.[79]

Since taking office last year, Prime Minister Robert Fico has faced criticism for his government's changes to the criminal code, restructuring of the public broadcaster, ending state military aid to Ukraine, and bringing the country closer to Russia.[80] Critics have warned that "[w]hile the stated aim of the proposed law to amend the existing NGO law is to increase transparency of civil society organizations' funding, it will stigmatize those that receive foreign funding... [and] that the law is in conflict with European core values and fundamental rights and freedoms."[81] The right of groups to seek and receive resources from foreign and domestic sources is an essential component of the right to association, which is protected under the International Covenant on Civil and Political Rights and the European Convention on Human Rights.[82]

The law is similar to the NGO Transparency Law passed in Hungary (and subsequently repealed) in 2017. The European Commission has warned Slovakia that if they "[i]f [they] follow the Hungarian example on the NGOs law, [the European Commission] will launch an infringement procedure (for violation of EU law) immediately," citing the EU Court of Justice's 2021 decision declaring that Hungary's NGO Transparency Law violates EU law.[83] However, journalists and anti-corruption organizations have stated that the "chilling effect" the European Commission warned of has already set in.[84] In January 2025, the Council of Europe's Expert Council on NGO Law released a report on the Slovakia framework, concluding that "the lack of proper public consultation denied the public an opportunity to meaningfully participate in the process" and that "the new disclosure and labeling requirements do not comply with the European standards protecting freedom of association and the right to privacy."[85]

The far-right Revival party in Bulgaria introduced draft legislation in September 2024 targeting foreign agents that is largely modeled on Russia's NGO legislation.[86] The push builds on prior unsuccessful attempts to adopt such legislation in 2022 and 2023, citing the need for a foreign agent law that is similar to FARA in the United

[79] Amnesty International (2024b) Slovakia: Anti-NGO Law a 'Full-Frontal Assault on Civil Society'.

[80] U.S. News (2024).

[81] Philea (2024).

[82] Amnesty International (2024b) Slovakia: Anti-NGO Law a 'Full-Frontal Assault on Civil Society'.

[83] U.S. News (2024).

[84] Nicholson (2024).

[85] Council of Europe (2025, p. 14).

[86] Cameron and Nicola (2024). For the most recent draft of the bill see National Assembly of the Republic of Bulgaria 50-454-01-85 (2024).

States.[87] If passed, the law would apply to any organization or individual receiving more than €500 from abroad, labeling them as "foreign agents."[88] In Bulgaria, the term "foreign agent" is usually associated with "foreign spy" or "traitor." As a result, even the proposal of a foreign agent law serves to stigmatize the civic space. Bulgaria recently adopted anti-LGBTQ legislation that bans "propaganda of non-traditional sexual orientation in schools," indicating that far-right populist rhetoric has been intensifying.[89] In recent years, the space for independent activism in Bulgaria has been steadily shrinking. In the 2024 general election, the Revival party came in third, receiving just over 13% of the votes, while GERB, Bulgaria's center-right party coalition, led with 26%.[90] Although the relationship between the Revival party and the GERB coalition "has historically been antagonistic, the consistent support for Revival suggests a potential shift in Bulgaria's political landscape, with nationalist and pro-Russian sentiments gaining traction."[91] The latest push for a Russian-style foreign agent law is the culmination of this shift and further "illustrates increasing attempts to restrict civil liberties and silence dissent, including journalists and independent media."[92]

4 The Proposal of an EU Directive on Interest Representation

The European Commission's stance on the legislation enacted in Hungary and proposed in Slovakia is now further complicated by a December 2023 proposal to adopt a directive that establishes harmonized transparency requirements for interest representation activities carried out on behalf of third countries in the internal market.[93] Proposed as part of the Defense of Democracy Package, the directive aims to enhance transparency and accountability for third country actors, improve electoral processes ahead of the 2024 European elections, foster civic space, and promote the engagement of civil society organizations.[94] To achieve this, the directive would require Member States to establish national registers that record activities such as lobbying, communication campaigns, and related services, thereby preventing covert

---

[87] Bulgarian Center for Not-for-Profit Law (2024).

[88] Cameron and Nicola (2024).

[89] Bulgarian Center for Not-for-Profit Law (2024).

[90] Reuters (2024).

[91] Cameron and Nicola (forthcoming 2025, p. 8).

[92] Cameron and Nicola (2024).

[93] Directive of the European Parliament and of the Council establishing harmonised requirements in the internal market on transparency of interest representation carried out on behalf of third countries and amending Directive (EU) 2019/1937. COM(2023) 637 final. 2023/0463 (COD). see https://eur-lex.europa.eu/legal-content/EN/TXT/HTML/?uri=CELEX:52023PC0637.

[94] European Partnership for Democracy (2024, p. 3).

foreign influence on EU decision-making. By introducing uniform rules, the initiative is intended to reduce regulatory fragmentation, lower compliance costs, and mitigate risks like corruption and regulatory arbitrage. Additionally, it includes safeguards—such as independent supervisory authorities, judicial review, and a harmonized sanction regime—to protect democratic processes and prevent the misuse of transparency measures.

Under the directive, national transparency registers would be established in EU Member States for any activities carried out on behalf of "third-country entities" that aim to influence policymaking or the development and implementation of legislation. The proposal applies to every entity providing interest representation services—including civil service organizations, academic institutions, think tanks, and lobbyists—to enhance transparency and accountability. However, the directive does incorporate "safeguards such as limiting its scope only to interest representation services carried out on behalf of foreign states, rather than simply the receipt of foreign funds from any source like—a provision that distinguishes it from typical 'foreign agent' laws."[95]

The entities representing foreign states would be required to disclose to the registries in each Member State any funding sources originating from foreign governments or their affiliated entities.[96] Moreover, there is a need for complete independence of the national authorities responsible for managing and supervising these transparency registers. Granting extensive powers to these bodies without adequate safeguards could be particularly problematic in Member States facing rule of law challenges. Ensuring the independence of both the supervisory authorities and those managing the registers is essential to prevent the misuse of the directive.[97]

The directive's proposal to create a register in each Member State for foreign-funded organizations sent shockwaves through European civil society, sparking fears that it might be misused to exercise control and stigmatize rather than foster transparency and effective monitoring. A large number of NGOs have expressed concerns about the risk of silencing civil society and limiting academic freedom, highlighting the potential for the directive to resemble the repressive foreign agent laws adopted by Georgia and Hungary.[98] In fact the proposal's broad definition of "interest representation activities" is problematic, as it risks capturing not only covert attempts by third countries to influence EU policy but also legitimate lobbying efforts by NGOs and other civil society actors. This expansive scope, she contends, could unintentionally stifle democratic advocacy by imposing onerous compliance requirements that smaller, less well-funded organizations cannot afford, thereby exacerbating existing inequalities between corporate interests and civil society.[99]

Another criticism is that the Directive's focus on foreign-funded interest representation is overly narrow. By exclusively targeting third-country influence, the

---

[95] Kirova (2024).

[96] Ibid, pp. 3–5.

[97] Transparency International EU (2024).

[98] Ibid.

[99] Veraldi (2024, p. 2).

proposal replicates problematic "Foreign Agent" laws that have historically stigmatized entities and curtailed freedom of association and expression. Furthermore, this limited scope risks creating regulatory fragmentation across the EU, as existing national registers already encompass all forms of interest representation rather than just those funded from abroad. To enhance transparency and accountability, some have proposed broadening the Directive's scope to include all interest representation activities—irrespective of legal status, place of establishment, funding type, or funding source. For some a universal Interest Representatives Register would close loopholes and reduce opportunities for malign actors to evade scrutiny, an approach seen as crucial for achieving harmonization across Member States.[100]

As the European Parliament prepares to amend the directive, several proposals for changes and improvements to the law are already on the table. At least three reforms have been proposed to address the directive's weaknesses. First, narrowing the definition of "interest representation activities" is recommended in order to clearly distinguish between illegitimate foreign influence and legitimate advocacy efforts, thereby ensuring that only the former is subject to stringent regulatory oversight.[101] Second, there is a call for incorporating exemption provisions for civil society actors whose public interest functions might be impaired by the disclosure requirements.[102] Finally, it is proposed that accountability mechanisms be extended beyond mere transparency; effective oversight and enforcement at both domestic and European levels are deemed essential to protecting democratic decision-making within the EU.[103]

5 The Spectrum of Foreign Agent Laws: Competing Interests and Enforcement Regimes

The development of foreign agent laws is relatively common and has different historical and contextual underpinnings in each county, including the United States, Russia, Hungary and Australia.[104] It is undisputed that "[e]very country has a right to adopt legislation and regulation to prevent foreign interference in its internal affairs, protect national sovereignty, and oversee foreign funding to nonprofits and civil society organizations."[105] But it is difficult to craft foreign agent laws that are both effective and democratically safe as they could implicate restrictions of fundamental rights including privacy, freedom of association, and freedom of expression.[106] Critical issues associated with foreign influence legislation "range from the use of ill-defined

[100] Transparency International EU (2024).

[101] Veraldi (2024, pp. 3–4).

[102] Ibid. 5–6.

[103] Ibid. 6–7.

[104] European Partnership for Democracy (2024, pp. 3–4) and Alemanno and Sames (2023, p. 7).

[105] Cameron and Nicola (2024).

[106] Associated Press (2024) and Alemanno and Sames (2023, p. 3).

language [and] limited and unpredictable enforcement, to their negative democratic implications."[107]

Frequently, governments seek to justify and defend overbroad and restrictive foreign influence legislation by referring to similar laws in historic democracies. The most notable among them is FARA in the United States, which has been in place for nearly a century.[108] While on their face, the laws may appear similar, the implementation differs starkly.[109] For instance, Russia and Hungary have actively enforced their foreign agent laws through civil, criminal sanctions and media stigmatization campaigns, whereas the Unites States launched only a single criminal prosecution under FARA between 1990 and 2010.[110] The Russian and Hungarian examples epitomize how "laws that seemingly purport to prohibit the creation or dissemination of foreign interference have in fact a drastic impact on the legitimate activities of civil society actors acting both locally and transnationally."[111] Not only in their enforcement but also the narratives about foreign agent laws range from mere transparency goals to detect foreign influence in domestic political processes to more aggressive protections of "sovereign interests" leading to more pro-government measures geared to control, stigmatize and eventually suppress dissenting voices. Although several of the previously discussed foreign agent laws in the EU have yet to be adopted (Slovakia and Bulgaria), foreign influence legislation generally can be understood as existing on a spectrum of more or less restrictiveness balancing competing interests of transparency *versus* protection of national sovereignty as articulated in the different goals of the foreign agent laws.

By using this critical comparative approach embedded in legal practice,[112] the Fig. 1 below depicts a horizontal axis that represents this continuum of foreign agent laws from mere transparency measures seeking information to greater restrictiveness seeking to control dissenting voices in civil society. On the vertical axis, we address the variations over the enforcement of foreign agent laws. While at the bottom, enforcement is mostly about monitoring and compliance, such as in the case of FARA in the United States, in contrast at the top enforcement is about punitive civil or criminal sanctions such as in Hungary and Russia geared to stigmatizing and eventually suppressing civil society organizations holding critical positions against the current governments.

The Russian example exists at the extreme—it is both overly restrictive and over enforced.[113] On the other hand, FARA may be overly broad but tends to be under enforced.[114] Hungary's latest iteration of foreign influence legislation is perhaps less restrictive than Russia's but still overly restrictive and over enforced when

[107] Alemanno and Sames (2023, p. 3).

[108] Robinson (2024, p. 3).

[109] Rebo (2022, p. 277).

[110] Kirova (2024) and Rebo (2022, p. 277).

[111] Alemanno and Sames (2023, p. 2).

[112] Nicola and Frankenberg (2024).

[113] Kirova (2024).

[114] Robinson (2020, p. 1075).

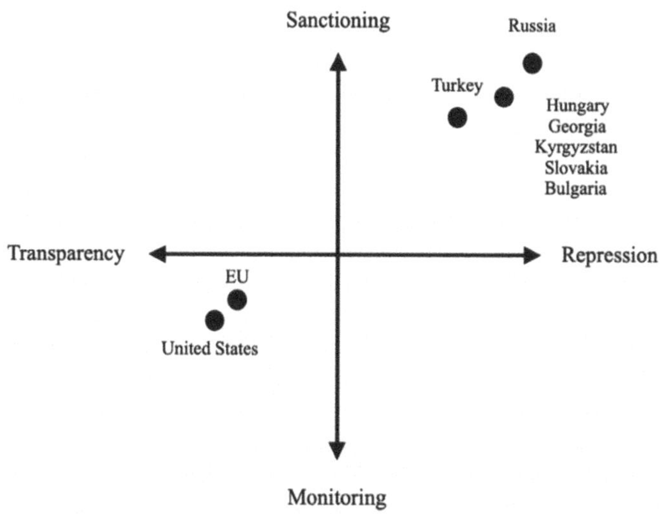

Fig. 1 Comparing goals and enforcement of foreign agent laws

compared to FARA.[115] Slovakia and the EU have not yet implemented their respect foreign agent laws and therefore have not been placed on the enforcement spectrum. However, their draft proposals indicate that their restrictiveness will mirror that of Hungary and the United States, respectively.[116] The matrix provides a visual representation of how countries have balanced (alleged) security and privacy interests, resulting in wide disparities in the degree of restrictiveness and enforcement of their respective foreign agent laws.

6 Conclusion: A Cautionary Tale for the EU Directive

An increasing number of countries have recently introduced legislation that would create a registry of foreign agents.[117] Critics contend that although governments have a legitimate interest in combating malign foreign influence, foreign agent laws significantly restrict the ability of civil society organizations to operate freely.[118] These concerns reinforce the idea that "[b]y fostering resilience, advocating for accountability, and engaging in strategic collaboration, supporters of civil society can enable these domestic organizations to work collectively and share strategies to

[115] Kirova (2024).

[116] U.S. News (2024) and European Partnership for Democracy (2024, p. 3).

[117] Robinson (2024, p. 3).

[118] Cameron and Nicola (2024) and Robinson (2024, p. 3).

safeguard human rights, counter restrictive measures such as foreign agent laws, and reinforce social justice and democratic values across jurisdictions."[119]

This chapter sought to provide an overview of foreign influence legislation generally and critically examine the aims and outcomes of such legislation, including the overarching difficulty of crafting a regulatory regime that is both effective and democratically safe.[120] More specifically, this chapter analyzed the foreign agent laws adopted in the United States, Russia, Kyrgyzstan, Georgia and Hungary, as well those being considered by Slovakia, Bulgaria, Turkey and the European Union.

Comparative analysis of foreign agent laws in democratic and authoritarian regimes reveals striking differences rooted in fundamentally divergent goals, enforcement tools, and distributive outcomes. Today, an increasing number of nations have either recently adopted or are actively considering foreign influence legislation. In some contexts, such measures are designed to enhance transparency in electoral processes and foster robust public dialogue; in others, they serve to suppress and marginalize civil society organizations that challenge the government's views. This divergence underscores the need for further research and advocacy to fully understand both the delicate balance and the spectrum of enforcement and accountability mechanisms that characterize these two opposing applications of foreign agent laws.[121]

References

Act of Apr. 29, 1942, ch. 253, Pub. L. No. 77-532 Stat. 248

Alemanno A, Sames F (2023) How to evaluate a foreign influence legislation? A comparative analysis. The Good Lobby

Amnesty International (2024a) Hungary's Act on the Protection of National Sovereignty in Breach of EU Law

Amnesty International (2024b) Slovakia: anti-NGO law a 'Full-Frontal Assault on Civil Society'. https://www.amnesty.org/en/latest/news/2024/04/slovakia-anti-ngo-law-a-full-frontal-assault-on-civil-society/

Amnesty International (2024c) Türkiye: proposed 'Agents of Influence' law is attack on civil society and must be rejected. https://www.amnesty.org/en/latest/news/2024/11/turkiye-proposed-agents-of-influence-law-is-attack-on-civil-society-and-must-be-rejected/

Amnesty International (2024d) Türkiye: withdrawal of so-called 'Agents of Influence' Law Is Important Victory for Civil Society. https://www.amnesty.org/en/latest/news/2024/11/turkiye-withdrawal-of-so-called-agents-of-influence-law-is-important-victory-for-civil-society/?utm_source=chatgpt.com

Article 2 TEU

Associated Press (2024) The EU launches legal action against Hungary over new law accused of targeting critics. https://apnews.com/article/european-union-hungary-sovereignty-law-democracy-funds-f0024283a6bf6f4bc78b567f59d8e3ee

[119] Cameron and Nicola (2024).

[120] Associated Press (2024) and Robinson (2024, p. 3).

[121] Cameron and Nicola (2024).

Bulgarian Center for Not-for-Profit Law (2024) The law against civil liberties—a new attack on civil rights. https://bcnl.org/en/the-law-against-civil-liberties-a-new-attack-on-civil-rights
Cameron J, Nicola F (2024) The spreading impact of restrictive 'Foreign Agent' laws and how to stop them. Just security. https://www.justsecurity.org/105593/foreign-agent-laws-impact/
Case C-896/19 *Repubblika* ECLI:EU:C:2021:311, paras 59–63, 72
Civil Society Brief: Georgia (2020) Asian Development Bank
Commission on Security and Cooperation in Europe (2024) The proliferation of Russian-style foreign agents laws. https://www.csce.gov/briefings/the-proliferation-of-russian-style-foreign-agents-laws/
Committee to Protect Journalists (2021) Kyrgyzstan parliament approves 'False Information' bill. https://cpj.org/2021/08/kyrgyzstan-parliament-approves-false-information-bill/
Committee to Protect Journalists (2024) Kyrgyzstan president signs Russian-Style 'Foreign Agents' Law. https://cpj.org/2024/04/kyrgyzstan-president-signs-russian-style-foreign-agents-law/
Committee to Protect Journalists (2024) Turkey's parliament expected to vote on 'Foreign Agent' law this week. https://cpj.org/2024/10/turkeys-parliament-expected-to-vote-on-foreign-agent-law-this-week/
Council of Europe (2025) Expert Council on NGO Law: the draft amendments to the Slovakia framework regulation governing non-governmental organizations introducing the concept of "Foreign Supported Organizations." Conf/Exp (2025)
Directive of the European Parliament and of the Council Establishing Harmonised Requirements in the Internal Market on Transparency of Interest Representation Carried out on Behalf of Third Countries and Amending Directive (EU) 2019/1937. COM(2023) 637 final. 2023/0463 (COD). https://eur-lex.europa.eu/legal-content/EN/TXT/HTML/?uri=CELEX:52023PC0637
Ecodefence and others v. Russia, App. Nos. 9988/13 and 60 others (2022) https://hudoc.echr.coe.int/fre?i=001-217751
Euro News (2023) Hungary Passes Controversial Law 'Protecting National Sovereignty'. https://www.euronews.com/2023/12/13/hungary-passes-controversial-law-protecting-national-sovereignty
European Commission v Hungary (Case C-769/22) (2023/C 54/19)
European Partnership for Democracy (2024) A closer look at the defense of democracy directive and the controversy surrounding it
Frankenberg G, Nicola F (2025) Authoritarian transfers. Univ Miami Law Rev 80:1
Goedemans M (2024) What Georgia's foreign agent law means for its democracy. Council on Foreign Relations. https://www.cfr.org/in-brief/what-georgias-foreign-agent-law-means-its-democracy
Human Rights Watch (2017) Hungary: bill seeks to stifle independent groups. https://www.hrw.org/news/2017/06/12/hungary-bill-seeks-stifle-independent-groups
Human Rights Watch (2024) Türkiye: spying bill threatens rights defenders, journalists. https://www.hrw.org/news/2024/11/02/turkiye-spying-bill-threatens-rights-defenders-journalists
International Press Institute (2024) IPI urges turkey to withdraw 'Agents of influence' bill ahead of parliamentary vote. https://freeturkeyjournalists.ipi.media/ipi-urges-turkey-to-withdraw-agents-of-influence-bill-ahead-of-parliamentary-vote/
Kirova I (2024) Foreign agent laws in the authoritarian playbook. Human Rights Watch. https://www.hrw.org/news/2024/09/19/foreign-agent-laws-authoritarian-playbook
Lenaerts K (2023) On checks and balances: the rule of law within the EU. Columbia J Eur L 29:54
Machalek K (2025) Factsheet: Russia's NGO Laws. Freedom House. https://freedomhouse.org/sites/default/files/Fact%20Sheet_0.pdf
National Assembly of the Republic of Bulgaria 50-454-01-85 (2024)
Nicholson T (2024) Slovakia chided for 'Chilling Effect' of changes to NGO, Public Media Laws. Politico. https://www.politico.eu/article/commissioner-upbraids-slovakia-on-changes-to-ngo-public-media-laws-robert-fico/
Nicola F, Cameron J (2024a) First time as tragedy, second time as farce. Verfassungsblog. https://verfassungsblog.de/second-time-as-farce/

Nicola F, Cameron J (2024b) The spreading impact of restrictive 'Foreign Agent' laws and how to stop them. Just Security. https://www.justsecurity.org/105593/foreign-agent-laws-impact/
Nicola F, Cameron J (2025) The chilling effects of foreign agent-style laws. In: Gosztonyi G, Ferenc Lendvai G (eds) Handbook of chilling effects. Springer, New York
Nicola F, Frankenberg G (2024) Comparative law: introduction to a critical practice. Edward Elgar, Cheltenham
Ozgur Sivil Toplum (2024) Joint statement from Civil Society Organizations. https://ozgursiviltoplum.org/
Philea (2024) Philea issues statement of concern about "Foreign Agent Type of Law" in Slovakia. https://philea.eu/philea-issues-statement-of-concern-about-foreign-agent-type-of-law-in-slovakia/
RadioFreeEurope (2024) EU 'Dithers' as foreign agent laws spread across Europe and Central Asia, says rights Watchdog. https://www.rferl.org/a/foreign-agent-law-eu-dithering-russia-georgia-kyrgyzstan-hman-rights-watch/32891284.html
Rebo S (2022) FARA in focus: what can russia's foreign agent law tell us about America's? J Natl Sec L Pol'y 12:277
Reporters Without Borders (2024) "Foreign Agents" law is latest step in Kyrgyz President Japarov's growing authoritarianism. https://rsf.org/en/foreign-agents-law-latest-step-kyrgyz-president-japarov-s-growing-authoritarianism
Reuters (2024) Bulgaria's GERB wins election, coalition talks in sight. https://www.reuters.com/world/europe/bulgarias-gerb-party-wins-parliamentary-vote-preliminary-results-show-2024-10-28
Robinson N (2020) "Foreign Agents" in an interconnected world: FARA and the weaponization of transparency. Duke L J 69:1075
Robinson N (2024) Foreign influence registration laws and civil society: an analysis and responses. International Center for Non-Profit Law
Roudik P (2021) Russian federation: restrictions on media with foreign funding imposed. Library of Congress. https://www.loc.gov/item/global-legal-monitor/2021-05-14/russian-federation-restrictions-on-media-with-foreign-funding-imposed/
Rowland M (2024) Turkiye: "Foreign Agent" Law—a direct assault on Press Freedom and Civil Society. Women Press Freedom. https://www.womeninjournalism.org/opeds/turkiye-foreign-agent-law-a-direct-assault-on-press-freedom-and-civil-society
Spike J (2025) Hungary's Orbán says he will do away with pro-democracy and rights group receiving U.S. Aid. Associated Press. https://apnews.com/article/orban-hungary-eliminate-ngos-usaid-aff22b9f9003f4c6c3115a9798c18af6
Straus J (2024) Foreign Agents Registration Act (FARA): an overview. Cong Rsch Serv IF1049
Transparency International EU (2024) TI EU Policy Position. https://transparency.eu/wp-content/uploads/2024/09/2024.04-TI-EU_DoD_Policy-Position.pdf
U.S. Department of Justice (2025a) FARA Enforcement. https://www.justice.gov/nsd-fara/fara-enforcement
U.S. Department of Justice (2025b) FARA: Frequently Asked Questions. https://www.justice.gov/nsd-fara/frequently-asked-questions
U.S. Department of Justice (2025c) Foreign Agents Registration Act. https://www.justice.gov/nsd-fara
U.S. Department of Justice (2025d) Recent Cases. https://www.justice.gov/nsd-fara/recent-cases
U.S. News (2024) EU Warns Slovakia Against Foreign Agent Law for NGOs. https://www.usnews.com/news/world/articles/2024-07-24/eu-warns-slovakia-against-foreign-agent-law-for-ngos
Veraldi J (2024) On the proposed measures to regulate third country interest representation activities in the European Union. Eur J Risk Reg 1:1

Part II
Disinformation and Propaganda in Times of War

Possibilities and Limits of Regulating Disinformation and Propaganda in Hybrid Warfare

Björnstjern Baade

Abstract In the last decade, almost universally, disinformation and propaganda have come to be recognized as a grave threat. At times, the problem has been exaggerated, but similarly, critiques of proposed solutions like fact-checking have been overstated. This contribution seeks to find a firm middle ground. Legal rules and standards, such as those under the EU's Digital Services Act (DSA), can certainly be part of the solution. But the expectation that regulation will prevent our public discourse from decaying must be tempered. Even if one does not subscribe to the restrictive stance towards regulation often associated with the US, and even if one considers the DSA a bold step in the right direction: On its own, legal regulation cannot suffice. Normatively, International Human Rights Law calls for restraint, and, in armed conflict, International Humanitarian Law even allows for certain types of disinformation. In practice, legal regulation is far from omnipotent. Ultimately, trust in sources of information that deserve this trust is necessary, but citizens cannot be legally ordered to trust.

1 Introduction

Some time ago, disinformation and propaganda—all the more in times of war—were a niche academic interest. This has changed dramatically. Even though the year 2014 saw the occupation of Crimea by unmarked Russian troops,[1] the year 2016 seems to have become the real watershed moment. Attempts at influencing that year's US presidential election via social media rattled politicians, academics, and citizens alike.[2] They have become acutely aware of such information operations. The same year, the European Parliament explicitly denounced a «modern hybrid warfare … deployed to destabilise the political, economic and social situation of a

B. Baade (✉)
Department of Law, Freie Universität, Berlin, Germany
e-mail: b.baade@fu-berlin.de

[1] Reeves and Wallace (2015, p. 361).

[2] See Mueller (2019, pp. 29–32), see also Ohlin (2017, p. 1579).

R. Mastroianni and C. Massa (eds.), *Disinformation in New and Old Media in the XXI Century*, Ius Gentium: Comparative Perspectives on Law and Justice 136,
https://doi.org/10.1007/978-3-032-18830-4_8

country under attack … targeting not only partners of the EU but also the EU itself, its institutions and all Member States and citizens».[3] Relentless Russian efforts at influencing opinions and decisions in other states provided the main motivation for this resolution.[4] They continue to this day.[5]

In the following, I will explore the legal regimes applicable to information operations in times of war. While the issue of disinformation and propaganda among the belligerents of an armed conflict is largely settled under International Humanitarian Law (IHL) (3.), information operations among non-belligerents raise difficult legal issues (4.). The deliberate use of legal gray areas—the blurring of lines between legal regimes, which hybrid warfare can be said to consist of—makes the legal assessment difficult.[6] The very terms «disinformation» and «propaganda» may be part of the problem—which is why I will begin by exploring their meaning and significance as legal concepts (2.).[7] I will end by expressing some thoughts on the different legal and policy approaches to disinformation and propaganda in the United States and the European Union (5.), and finally some concluding observations (6.).

2 Disinformation and Propaganda as Legal Concepts

Even though the terms dis- and misinformation are used in various ways by different actors, a core definition seems to have emerged: Deliberately false or misleading statements of fact are considered *dis*information; inadvertently false or misleading statements of fact, on the other hand, are *mis*information.[8] A *false* statement makes a factual claim that does not conform to reality. A *misleading* statement, on the other hand, is strictly speaking true. Yet, it is selective in a manner that invites factually false conclusions. For example, you could fill an entire newspaper with reports on crimes committed in Europe every single day. There is and has always been enough crime to do that. But doing so would distort the greater picture, give the impression that crime is much more prevalent than it actually is. While media, politics, and academia

[3] European Parliament resolution of 23 November 2016 on EU strategic communication to counteract propaganda against it by third parties (2016/2030(INI)), (2018/C 224/08), Recital E.

[4] Terrorist propaganda by ISIL and Al-Quaeda likewise motivated the resolution.

[5] Institute for Strategic Dialogue, Two Years On: An Analysis of Russian State and Pro-Kremlin Information Warfare in the Context of the Invasion of Ukraine. 2024, https://www.isdglobal.org/wp-content/uploads/2024/02/Two-Years-on_ISD.pdf; Follorou, Une action de déstabilisation pilotée par Moscou a visé des pays de l 'UE, Le Monde 24 February 2024, 4.

[6] See on the ambiguity and other difficulties of the concept Aust (2020, p. 293), Wigell (2019, p. 255).

[7] See for the uncertainty involved in them e.g. Di Turi (2022).

[8] Cf. (with additional requirements) The Strengthened Code of Practice on Disinformation 2022, Fn. 7 and 8, available at https://digital-strategy.ec.europa.eu/en/library/2022-strengthened-code-practice-disinformation.

certainly need to call out and correct both, false and misleading statements, legally speaking various distinctions are in order.[9]

False statements that infringe on the reputation of individuals or undermine trust in the state's institutions and officials can, in principle, be subject to civil or even criminal proceedings. This is well-established in international human rights law.[10] Any such restriction on freedom of expression must pursue a legitimate aim and needs to be proportionate.[11] Most importantly, it must not generate unreasonable chilling effects, e.g. through excessive sanctions or unreasonable due diligence requirements that would discourage proper journalistic work.[12] For example, in *Frisk and Jensen v. Denmark*, the European Court of Human Rights upheld the criminal conviction of journalists who had claimed—without sufficient factual basis—that Copenhagen's university hospital had administered an «experimental drug» to cancer patients, shortening their lives in the process.[13]

Misleading statements are a different matter.[14] Whether the selection and presentation of certain facts is appropriate or misleading is a normative, a value judgment. Such judgments, in particular on political issues, enjoy the highest level of protection under international human rights law. This holds true even for opinions that «offend, shock or disturb the State or any sector of the population», as the European Court of Human Rights has rightly held for almost 50 years.[15]

Misleading statements should be opposed, of course. For example, to criticize the EU for a lack of solidarity during the COVID-19 pandemic without mentioning any of the actions that it did take may rightly be said to be misleading.[16] Nonetheless, that statement remains an opinion. Taking repressive legal action against opinions merely because they seem wrong is incompatible with international human rights law. Independent fact-checkers as well as the EU's East StratCom Task Force, established in 2015 to counter Russian disinformation, should likewise take care to make this distinction. They have at times been too casual in this regard.[17] Such overreach must be avoided at all cost. Otherwise, they lend unnecessary credibility to the misguided

[9] See in more detail for the following Baade (2023a), 403 et seq.; Baade (2020a).

[10] ECtHR, *Janowski v Poland* [GC], 21 January 1999, 25716/94, para. 33; *Taffin et contribuables associés c France*, 42396/04, 18 February 2010, para. 64; *Morice v France* [GC], 29369/1023, April 2015, paras 128–131.

[11] See in detail Milanovic and Webb (2024, pp. 237 et seq.).

[12] See e.g. ECtHR, *Björk Eidsdóttir v Iceland*, 46443/09, 10 July 2012, para. 81.

[13] The journalists were fined about 1,000 Euros each and had to cover the hospital's legal costs of about 20,000 Euros, see ECtHR, *Frisk and Jensen v. Denmark*, 19657/12, 5 December 2017, paras 51–78.

[14] Some statements may be so misleading as to be considered false. For example, reporting that someone was convicted for a crime (in first instance) without mentioning that she was acquitted on appeal (see BGHZ [Reports of the German Federal Court of Justice in Civil Matters] 57, 325). But this will be the exception.

[15] ECtHR, *Handyside v The United Kingdom* [PL], 5493/72, 7 December 1976, para 49; reiterated on various occasions, more recently in *Sanchez v. France* [GC], 45581/15, 15 May 2023, para. 145.

[16] See with further references: Baade (2020a).

[17] For example, qualifying what is clearly an opinion as disinformation: EastStratCom, DISINFO: The EU mission in Armenia is a decoration that will not have any effect, 26 January

proposition that dis- and misinformation are merely «ugly, Soviet-era words» which are intended to hide the fact that those who use them simply cannot stand it when someone holds opinions different from their own.[18]

While the freedom to make false statements is restricted to some degree in probably all democratic states, the use of «propaganda» as a legal concept is mostly confined to authoritarian regimes.[19] One of the reasons for this is that propaganda is notoriously hard to define. It seeks to influence people in their opinions and actions; that much is clear.[20] But so does advertising and election canvassing. Propaganda differs from legitimate strategic communication by its instrumental relationship with the (factual and normative) truth.[21] Not only lies and contradictory value judgments can be employed for propaganda purposes but also true factual statements and very laudable opinions. Propaganda can be rational or emotional; it can be individualistic or harness group identities and their grievances.[22] Anything that helps to convince can be used, but convincing an audience need not even be the aim. Propaganda can seek to produce so much uncertainty, make it so difficult to form an opinion, that ultimately nothing seems to be true anymore.[23] Propaganda is thus a special form of «bullshit» as Harry G. Frankfurt described it: «[T]he bullshitter … is neither on the side of the true nor on the side of the false … except insofar as they may be pertinent to his interest in getting away with what he says.»[24]

Consequently, you cannot distinguish propaganda from legitimate strategic communication by individual statements. You have to assess the conduct over time. Does the actor use anything (true or false, consistent or contradictory) that serves to convince (or disorient) an audience? For political purposes and social science research, this is important. Legally, however, true statements of fact and value judgments generally cannot be restricted just because they form part of a propaganda campaign.

2024, https://euvsdisinfo.eu/report/the-eu-mission-in-armenia-is-a-decoration-that-will-not-have-any-effect/. See also Baade (2020a).

[18] Speech by J.D. Vance on 14 February 2025. For a transcript see: Lu (2025).

[19] See in more detail for the following: Baade (2023b, p. 257).

[20] Whitton (1948, p. 547).

[21] Cf. Orwell (1968, pp. 361, 371): the «primary aim of propaganda is, of course, to influence contemporary opinion … [with an] [i]ndifference to objective truth»; Whitton (1948, pp. 545, 547): «unprincipled», but «… even Goebbels preferred the truth, if possible, for the simple reason that he considered it more effective»; Kearney (2007, p. 3), Gornig (1988, p. 261). See also Baade (2020b, pp. 653, 656–657).

[22] Bontcheva and Posetti (2020, p. 22); Wardle and Derakhshan (2017).

[23] Robinson et al (2018, p. 65), Chifu (2017, p. 119).

[24] Frankfurt (2005, p. 56).

3 Disinformation and Propaganda Among Belligerents

Disinformation and propaganda quite naturally assume an important role in times of war. During armed conflict, belligerents conduct information operations to attain a military advantage, on a strategic, operational, and tactical level. Ruses of war are traditionally distinguished from psychological warfare in this regard, and the law in this area is largely settled and undisputed.[25]

On a tactical and operational level, information operations intend to bring about a more or less immediate military advantage. Disinformation in particular can cause troops to behave in a way that is disadvantageous. The Trojan Horse is the classic example. The US 23rd Headquarters Special Troops, which faked the existence of an entire armored division using false radio messages and inflatable dummies during WWII, are a more modern one.[26]

Despite technological advances like satellite imagery, there is still enough fog of war to be used. In the summer of 2022, Ukraine regained many thousand square kilometers of territory around the eastern city of Kharkiv by misleading Russian troops into thinking that a major attack in southern Kherson was imminent—and thus into redirecting defensive resources accordingly.[27] International Humanitarian Law explicitly allows for such ruses of war, under art. 37(2) of the Additional Protocol to the Geneva Conventions (in the following: AP I)[28] and corresponding customary law.[29]

On a strategic level, troops and the population are addressed in a more general manner. This also tries to induce them to behave in a way that generates a military advantage for the other party to the conflict. Such war propaganda is often referred to as psychological warfare.[30] Virtually all parties to all modern conflicts will have made use of such methods in one form or another. During the 2022 invasion of Ukraine, a Russian-aligned channel spread the false report that President Zelensky had left Kyiv. His response, a Facebook livestream from the center of Kyiv, showed that he and his ministers were indeed staying, and willing to fight. It has become an instant classic of successful counter-propaganda.[31] No one disputes the legality of such psychological warfare.[32]

---

[25] For more detail on the following see Baade (2020c, p. 161).

[26] Beyer and Sayles (2014, p. 10). Similarly in the US civil war, see Sivakumaran (2012, p. 419).

[27] Dylan et al. (2022).

[28] Protocol Additional to the Geneva Conventions of 12 August 1949, and relating to the Protection of Victims of International Armed Conflicts, 1125 UNTS 3.

[29] Rule 57 in Henckaerts and Doswald-Beck (2005a, b, p. 1245).

[30] Chainoglou (2016). In Russia, other terms such as «reflexive control» are used but in essence the concepts are the same, see Rogers and Tyushka (2017, p. 45), Timothy (2004, p. 237).

[31] Hopkins (2022).

[32] Either as a ruse of war: Chainoglou (2016), para. 8; or as an independent legal category: Oeter (2021), 7.40. See also International Committee of the Red Cross (1987, pp. 439–444) (paras 1512–1522). During WWI, this was still contentious, see: Madders (2000), 1394. The fact that international humanitarian law is in this respect *lex specialis* to general international law is shown in particular

Limiting the effect of ruses of war and psychological warfare on the other party to the conflict will often be impossible in today's communication environment. If disinformation and propaganda are directed at a party to an armed conflict but also reach non-belligerent states, such information operations will have to be assessed under International Humanitarian Law in order to ensure the effectiveness of its rules on information warfare. The targeted use of information operations against a non-belligerent state, on the other hand, for example, to persuade it to enter or stay out of the conflict, could violate the prohibition of intervention and the prohibition of propaganda for war.[33]

Ruses of war as well as psychological warfare are, however, limited by other rules of International Humanitarian Law like the prohibition to spread terror among the civilian population by threats of violence in art. 51(2) AP I, and the prohibition of perfidy, i.e. of abusing the adversary's trust in the protection of International Humanitarian Law.[34]

4 Disinformation and Propaganda Among Non-Belligerents

It is a hallmark of hybrid warfare that it employs certain methods of warfare outside the context of an armed conflict that is regulated by International Humanitarian Law. States that are non-belligerents[35] as regards an ongoing armed conflict, or that are merely potential opponents in a future armed conflict, can still be subject to information operations that are aimed at weakening their ability to defend themselves and their allies. In that context, disinformation and propaganda seek to undermine the ability of the target state and its population to cooperate internally, and they seek to strain external relations between allies, to weaken their resolve to support one another.

The use that some states make of the internet, and social media in particular, continues a tradition that was established with the radio in the 1930s. It was the first mass medium that enabled information to be distributed easily and effectively across borders—and was immediately used accordingly. In 1934, the Saar Basin territory, situated between Germany and France, was still under international administration in accordance with art. 49 of the Treaty of Versailles.[36] Its population was about to vote in a referendum on the territory's future affiliation with Germany or France. The German «Minister for Propaganda», Joseph Goebbels, gave a speech that was

by this: Inciting other states' troops to revolt, which in peacetime clearly violates the prohibition of intervention, is undisputedly lawful under the *ius in bello*: Oeter (2021), 7.40.

[33] See below.

[34] Arts 38 and 39 API restrict the use of other states' uniforms, the UN emblem and protective emblems such as the red cross.

[35] For details see Wentker (2024).

[36] Treaty of Peace between the Allied and Associated Powers and Germany, 28 June 1919, printed for example in the United Kingdom Treaty Series (UKTS) 4 (1919).

broadcast to this territory in May 1934. He made various false claims, including that the Commission suppressed German flags in the territory. This continued a radio propaganda campaign that was described as «violent and unjustified» by the League of Nations Governing Commission for the Saar Territory.[37]

While the Soviet Union promoted world revolution with foreign-language radio broadcasts at the time,[38] information operations were not alien to Western democracies either. During the Munich Crisis of 1938, the British government tried to influence public opinion in Germany by broadcasting translations of speeches by the British Prime Minister and the US President on Radio Luxembourg.[39] During the Cold War, Western stations broadcasted in Eastern European languages with the aim of destabilizing socialist countries.[40] These Western information operations, however, hoped to be more effective by broadcasting accurate information.[41] NATO doctrine continues in this tradition.[42]

Between states that are not belligerents in an armed conflict, rules of international law may prohibit certain information operations. Under customary international law, the prohibition of intervention applies. While mere criticism and propaganda writ large are not considered to coercively interfere with states' internal or external affairs,[43] some support has grown in academia[44] and state practice[45] for the proposition that disinformation may constitute such intervention under certain circumstances. For example, covertly planting false information to influence the decision-making process of a state, to my mind, violates this prohibition.[46]

---

[37] See Saar Basin, Speech delivered by Dr. Goebbels at Zweibrücken on May 6th, 1934, 16 May 1934, C.201.1934.VII, at 2, 6. On German propaganda that targeted Austria see Preuss (1934, pp. 664–665), Whitton (1941) War by Radio, Foreign Affairs.

[38] See e.g.: Shultz and Godson (1984).

[39] Pronay and Taylor (1984, pp. 358–360).

[40] Schlosser (2015, pp. 57–58, 73–105).

[41] «Excerpts from the US Information Agency Basic Guidance Paper of 1957», printed in Whitton and Larson (1964, pp. 268–273).

[42] Allied Joint Doctrine for Psychological Operations, AJP-3.10.1. (Edition B Version 1), September 2014, No. 0114, 0116.

[43] Most recently: Czech Republic, Position paper on the application of international law in cyberspace, 27.2.2024, para. 13, https://mzv.gov.cz/file/5376858/_20240226___CZ_Position_paper_on_the_application_of_IL_cyberspace.pdf.

[44] Milanovic (2023, pp. 641, 643), Lahmann (2022, p. 414).

[45] Poland, The Republic of Poland's position on the application of international law in cyberspace, 29 December 2022, 4, https://www.gov.pl/attachment/3203b18b-a83f-4b92-8da2-fa0e3b449131; Germany, On the Application of International Law in Cyberspace, March 2021, 5; https://www.auswaertiges-amt.de/blob/2446304/32e7b2498e10b74fb17204c54665bdf0/on-the-application-of-international-law-in-cyberspace-data.pdf; New Zealand, The Application of International Law to State Activity in Cyberspace, 1 December 2020, para. 10, https://www.dpmc.govt.nz/sites/default/files/2020-12/The%20Application%20of%20International%20Law%20to%20State%20Activity%20in%20Cyberspace.pdf.

[46] See in more detail: Baade (2018).

Treaty law may also come into play. Drafted under the auspices of the League of Nations as an effort at «moral disarmament» after WWI,[47] the 1936 International Convention for Broadcasting in the Cause of Peace (in the following: Broadcasting Convention)[48] was intended to combat a use of modern communication technology that harmed «good international understanding», in particular, as art. 3 held, «by statements the incorrectness of which is or ought to be known to the persons responsible». It is still in force for some 30 states, inter alia the Russian Federation as successor to the Soviet Union.[49] This Broadcasting Convention was also the first to introduce a prohibition of propaganda for war in its art. 2, which was later reiterated in art. 20(1) of the International Covenant on Civil and Political Rights (ICCPR).[50,51] The state itself must refrain from such propaganda, and it must appropriately sanction individuals engaging in it.[52] This prohibition constitutes customary international law, which should be generally accepted, at least since the ICCPR was ratified by almost all states in the world.[53] Only a small number of reservations and interpretative declarations have been entered for art. 20 (1) ICCPR. Reserving states may be able to claim persistent objector status, but likely only insofar as the prohibition relates to individuals.[54]

These legal standards have recently converged in a seminal case.[55] Russian state-sponsored media, such as RT and Sputnik, have long been said to sow doubts about the integrity and functionality of European state institutions, fan grievances in the population, and thereby destabilize these states and their societies.[56] They can rightly be

[47] Preliminary Draft International Agreement for the Use of Broadcasting in the Cause of Peace, 4 January 1934, C.12.1934.XII, Annex 1, 1.

[48] International Convention on the Use of Broadcasting in the Cause of Peace 1936, 186 LNTS 301.

[49] The Soviet Union entered a reservation to the jurisdictional clause in art. 7 Broadcasting Convention.

[50] 999 UNTS 171.

[51] The prohibition can also be found in Art. 13 (5) of the 1969 American Convention on Human Rights (1144 UNTS 123); see on the lack of practice thus far Antkowiak and Gonza (2017, p. 260). See in more detail on the development of the prohibition: Kearney (2007, pp. 21–79).

[52] The obligation, originally considered, to require criminal sanctions was ultimately not reflected in the text of the treaty: Nowak (2005), art. 20 para. 5.

[53] Currently 173 states. See for the significance of a high number of ratifications for the customary law status of a rule: ICJ, *North Sea Continental Shelf Cases* (*Germany v. Denmark/Germany v Netherlands*), Judgment, 20 February 1969, ICJ Reports 1969, 3, paras 27, 73–76. See also: International Law Commission (ILC), Draft Articles on the Identification of Customary Law, 2018, UN-Doc. A/73/10, Conclusion 11 (1)(b), 143–145.

[54] See ILC, *ibid*, Conclusion 15, 152. The Friendly Relations Declaration, generally considered to reflect customary law, recognized the prohibition of state propaganda for war: UNGA, Resolution 2625 (XXV) (Friendly Relations Declaration), 24. October 1974, para. 1: «duty to refrain from Propaganda for wars of aggression»; see also UNGA, Resolution 110 (II), 3 November 1947, para. 1. See on the reservations and interpretative declarations: Nowak (2005), art. 20 paras 3–8, 22.

[55] See for more detail concerning the following: Baade (2023b, p. 257); see also Koltay (2023, p. 27).

[56] The «Lisa case» from 2016, for example, is generally regarded as an obvious example of such fake news: Sarts J, The Impact of Russian Interference on Germany's 2017 Elections, Testimony

considered propaganda channels in the above-mentioned sense. The decisive difference to state-sponsored yet editorially independent Western broadcasters becomes evident when you consider that, unlike their Western counterparts, they would never in any meaningful sense voice criticism about or give a platform to others' criticism of Russian politics. For example, in 2022, the BBC reported on a 7-year-old girl who asked the British Prime Minister to apologize for parties he attended during lockdown while she missed two birthday parties.[57] It is simply impossible to imagine something like this concerning the Russian President on Sputnik or RT. But even if their reporting has not only been misleading but also outright false in many instances, these outlets could not have been banned for that alone in the manner that the European Union did in February 2022. While more stringent standards are traditionally permissible for linear audiovisual media, it would not have been possible to ban RT as completely from conducting journalistic activities as was done. The right to freedom of expression and the special protection that media enjoy would not allow for it—assuming that RT France can rely on these rights, which could well have been denied.[58]

The ban can, however, be based on the prohibition of propaganda for war as established in art. 20 (1) ICCPR. «War» in that sense covers all wars of aggression under public international law, i.e., according to the UN General Assembly's Friendly Relations Declaration, a breach of art. 2 (4) UN Charter that is «of sufficient gravity».[59] It is not only prohibited to make false factual statements to incite or justify a war of aggression but also to express the opinion (even based on entirely true facts) that a war of aggression should be waged.[60] Advocating for Russia's war of aggression, waged to annex another state's territory,[61] is certainly covered by this prohibition of propaganda for war. The General Court of the European Union was right to uphold the ban, pointing to the correct legal basis, even though it could have been even clearer in that regard.[62] Since RT France withdrew its appeal, the Court of Justice will not have the opportunity to pronounce itself on these issues in that case.[63]

---

before the U.S. Senate Select Committee on Intelligence, 28 June 2017, 2, https://www.intelligence.senate.gov/sites/default/files/documents/sfr-jsarts-062817b.pdf. The alleged rape of a 13-year-old girl by men with a migrant background and the alleged inaction of German authorities was picked up by these media and led to protests in Germany by people of Russian descent. Russian Foreign Minister Lavrov stated during the investigation that the girl's disappearance was swept under the carpet for a long time, but that truth and justice must prevail. See in detail: Baade (2018).

[57] Girl who followed party rules asks Boris Johnson for apology, BBC, 5 February 2022, https://www.bbc.com/news/uk-england-south-yorkshire-60271059.

[58] See in detail: Baade (2023b, p. 257).

[59] Which must «be considered in the light of all the circumstances of each particular case»: UNGA, Resolution 3314 of 14 December 1974 (Definition of Aggression), preamble and art. 2. See also Dinstein (2017), paras 381 et seq, para. 865; Cf. also Art. 8 bis (1) ICC Statute, 2187 UNTS 3: «by its character, gravity and scale».

[60] Lonardo (2023, p. 72).

[61] Also emphasizing this: Brunk and Hakimi (2022, pp. 690 et seq.).

[62] GC, *RT France* [GC], T-125/22; see in detail: Baade (2023b, pp. 257, 267 et seq.).

[63] ECJ, *RT France*, Order of 28 July 2023, C-620/22 P.

5 Discursive Trust and the Limits of Legal Regulation

Traditionally, it has been thought that in a public debate that is marked by freedom of expression and freedom of information our cognitive insufficiencies will be compensated for—and truth will ultimately prevail.[64] Since 2016, however, doubts about the functionality of the marketplace of ideas have grown exponentially.[65] Are we asking too much of citizens, media, and their interaction?[66] Cass R. Sunstein is one of the scholars particularly pessimistic in this regard:

> Far from being the best test of truth, the marketplace ensures that many people accept falsehoods or take mere fragments of lives or small events as representative of some alarming or despicable whole.[67]

Indeed, our individual and collective quest for truth is subject to various confounding factors, in particular cognitive biases that are only exacerbated by an ever-faster attention economy. Isn't it evident that our individual and collective defenses against falsehood are vastly insufficient?[68]

> "[O]ur information ecosystem has become polluted and dangerous. We are now facing a monumental and unprecedented crisis of mis- and disinformation." "Every day thousands of propaganda messages are drummed into the heads of readers, listeners, viewers, consumers and producers, and citizens and rulers of the world." "The burden of responsibility to the public carried by The Associated Press and other distributors of news has always been great, yet it has increased enormously in recent years by reason of the rapidly increased efficiency of the distributing mechanism. Advantage has been taken of every device of wit and science to speed up the report until the swift transmission of news is in itself a source of unprecedented danger. The conclusion of Sophocles that 'a lie never lives to be old' was reached before the days of instantaneous communication."

The three preceding quotes intertwine seamlessly. Yet, they stem from times vastly different in terms of information technology. The first remark was made in 2020,

---

64 USSC (1919) 250 U.S. 616, 630, *Abrams v. United States* (Holmes, J., dissenting). Cf. the dissenting vote of Judges Sajó and Tsotsoria, in: ECtHR, *Delfi AS v. Estonia* [GC], 64569/09, 16 June 2015. Even though Justice Holmes' marketplace referred to normative ideas, the concept has since been extended to factual statements. The idea has also been well-received in Europe for a long time, see already Rothenbücher (1928, pp. 6, 11). See also Bontcheva and Posetti (2020, p. 13).

65 See e.g. Kakutani (2018, 21 et seq.).

66 Bambauer (2006, p. 649).

67 Sunstein (2020, p. 393), cf. Franks (2019, p. 119): «[M]arkets do not produce truth or objectively optimal outcomes; they merely reflect consumer preferences. While those preferences might favor the general welfare or truth, they equally might not. The only conclusion one could draw about an idea that has triumphed in the marketplace is that many people like it, or at least the people with the most power in the marketplace like it. Third, even if people had strong preferences for the truth, there is no reason for confidence that the marketplace would help them discover it. As the 'fake news' epidemic has amply demonstrated, Americans are neither necessarily interested in nor particularly gifted at discerning truth from falsity or fact from opinion. Short attention spans, lack of education, and confirmation bias lead many people to believe things that are demonstrably false».

68 Individually: Buchheim (2020), 159, 175 et seq. Collectively: Lahmann (2020, pp. 189–224).

when the importance of social media had become clear;[69] the second in 1972 by a former Czechoslovak disinformation officer.[70] The last is from 1925 when the telegraph had first made the swift transmission of news an unprecedented danger.[71]

During the Cold War, some warned that Western democracies had to use propaganda—in the interest of truth since it would otherwise succumb to socialist propaganda: «It is, in effect, a State that must proclaim an official, general, and explicit truth […] This State-proclaimed truth must be all-embracing.»[72] Even though no democratic citizen or politician would agree with this statement today,[73] stronger regulation of the public debate, particularly online, is considered necessary by many because «given human inadequacies in regard to the search for truth … [c]learly, one's motivation to find 'the truth' is not enough».[74]

Policymakers, academics, and citizens alike have regained an awareness of the dangers involved in disinformation and propaganda. Attempts at influencing elections and the very real effects on public health during the COVID pandemic have shown that the issue needs to be taken seriously. But are we really living through an unprecedented information crisis? Does an «infocalypse»[75] threaten to «pollute» our debates?[76] Will our public discourse become so dysfunctional that our societies fracture socially, making us incapable of making collective decisions?

Despite all the difficulties we do indeed face in this context, this assessment sounds hyperbolic to me. Our convictions and actions are not entirely rational. Our rationality is always bounded. This is well-accepted since the 1950s.[77] Not only *logos* and *ethos* but also *pathos* influence what we believe. This has been known since ancient Greek rhetoric and was never seriously questioned.[78] The once popular idea, however, that «the masses» could be more or less remote-controlled by media exposure[79] has been greatly relativized.[80] A new «surveillance capitalism» is no «puppet master» either «that imposes its will» on us.[81]

We are, of course, influenced by what we read, watch, and listen to. But in what way we perceive and process information, in how far we let ourselves be influenced by certain information, is a complex individual question, which makes it difficult to evaluate the effects of information operations. The Czechoslovak officer quoted

---

[69] Schick (2020, p. 9).

[70] Bittman (1972, pp. ix–x, 16).

[71] McKernon (1925).

[72] Ellul (1968, pp. 250–251, 235).

[73] But see on the resurgence of «Cold War thought»: Aust (2020, pp. 293, 306).

[74] Britt et al. (2019, pp. 94, 99).

[75] Schick (2020, p. 9).

[76] Iglesias Keller and Werneck Arguelhes (2024, p. 188), Benkler et al. (2018, p. 386), Wardle and Derakhshan (2017)

[77] Simon (1957, p. 198).

[78] See, of course: Aristoteles (2020), 1356 a 3, I.2.3.

[79] See only: Bernays (1928, p. 71). More recently: Brkan (2020, pp. 774, 787).

[80] Bonfadelli and Friemel (2017, pp. 30–35).

[81] Zuboff (2019, p. 376).

above admitted that many disinformation and propaganda operations were conducted even though it was entirely unclear to what extent these efforts were successful.[82] Maybe, we really shouldn't be too eager to accept the narrative of how easy we are to manipulate.[83] Hyperbolic problem descriptions can contribute to a disproportionate encroachment on freedom of speech: The greater you consider the threat to be, the more freedom of expression might be restricted.

Technological developments have certainly changed the way we communicate. It is subject to constant research in what way exactly and what difference this makes to our public discourse.[84] The effect of «filter bubbles»,[85] for example, which featured prominently in this debate, has been greatly relativized by more recent research as a «misunderstanding especially about the power of technology ... over human communication».[86] And even though lies were found to spread faster than truth at least on certain social media,[87] other studies indicated that dis- and misinformation only constitute a rather small part of the average user's online experience.[88] Legal academics and practitioners in particular should take care not to rely on intuitively plausible assertions that have been thoroughly questioned if not debunked in later research.[89] The idea that hungry judges pass harsher verdicts is another example in that regard.[90]

Despite all of our cognitive insufficiencies and in spite of all the efforts at manipulating us, there can be no doubt that humans possess the capacity to recognize and accept new facts and act accordingly—even if these facts are detrimental to one's interests and contradict prior convictions. Descriptively, I hope that it is sufficient to appeal to the reader's own experience: Our daily lives are shaped by our capacity to recognize and be led by epistemic reasons.[91] No one lives in a post-factual world. Normatively, an appropriate amount of trust in citizens' capacity for reason and truth is axiomatic for the democratic form of government.[92] It should be noted that this includes the decision of which sources of information to trust. Human deficiencies

[82] Bittman (1972, p. 22).

[83] Bernstein (2021), see also Lahmann (2022, p. 438).

[84] Which remains a very difficult endeavor: Mansell et al. (2025).

[85] Pariser (2011).

[86] Bruns (2019, p. 93); see also with further references Dahlgren (2021, pp. 28–29).

[87] False news was found to spread «significantly farther, faster, deeper and more broadly than the truth» on Twitter (now X), even though those who share falsehoods had less followers, had been active a shorter amount of time, and had been less likely to have a verified account (at a time when this was still considered a marker of credibility). The reason for this seemed to be that falsehoods were novel and emotional. Strategies meant to cope with an oversupply of information, like reading only the headline, exacerbate the problem: Vosoughi et al. (2018, pp. 1147–1150).

[88] With further references: van der Linden (2022, p. 463).

[89] Chatziathanasiou (2022, pp. 462–464).

[90] *Ibid*, 456 et seq.

[91] Nida-Rümelin (2020, p. 32).

[92] Cf. Gärditz (2021, p. 508): «Demokratie als egalitäres Projekt [muss] im Politischen gleiche Urteilskraft unterstellen» [Democracy as an egalitarian project (must) assume equal capacity for political judgment].

in finding the truth and even a purported failure of the marketplace of ideas must generally be tolerated in a free democratic discourse.

Within the limits of international human rights law and national constitutional law,[93] it is for the legislator to determine the restrictions on freedom of speech that are nonetheless necessary. Such restrictions are historically and culturally contingent. The differences between the more permissive US freedom of speech and a European freedom of expression that is susceptible to greater restrictions have often been highlighted.[94] This principled difference seems to continue with regard to social media.[95]

In July 2024, the US Supreme Court held unanimously that content moderation by social media companies, e.g. the deletion or demotion of certain user posts according to community guidelines, enjoys the same protection under the First Amendment as does the editorial choice of a newspaper to publish certain content or not. Applying precedent developed for newspapers, the Court held that the «government may not, in supposed pursuit of better expressive balance, alter a private speaker's own editorial choices about the mix of speech it wants to convey».[96]

The EU's approach is more nuanced. The Digital Services Act (DSA)[97] sets up rules for social media content moderation and institutes a complex net of oversight.[98] Obligations are imposed, in particular, on so-called Very Large Online Platforms to act against illegal content and to assess and mitigate systemic risks.[99] Notably, the European Commission is invested with powers to investigate and enforce these obligations. The precise extent of these obligations and powers still needs to be clarified, and I share the concern that some of these provisions could be handled in a manner that infringes disproportionately on users' freedom of expression and platforms' business operations.[100] Without a doubt, however, these rules *can* be interpreted in accordance with human rights law to reach appropriate solutions. Much will have to be discussed, and likely litigated, in this regard.

A nuanced approach that neither gives the legislator *carte blanche* nor prevents it from regulating the practice of content moderation at all, seems sensible to me. The Supreme Court in *Moody v. Netchoice* did not find sufficient differences between

[93] US constitutional law strikes a stricter balance in favor of freedom of speech when public officials are concerned. Not the person making a defamatory statement must show due diligence but the claimant must prove actual malice (intent or reckless disregard), see USSC (1964) 376 U.S. 254, *N.Y. Times Co. v. Sullivan*.

[94] See e.g. Nolte (1992).

[95] See Koltay (2025), 210 et seq.

[96] USSC (2024) 603 U. S. 707 *Moody v. Netchoice*, 20.

[97] Regulation (EU) 2022/2065 of the European Parliament and of the Council of 19 October 2022 on a Single Market For Digital Services and amending Directive 2000/31/EC (Digital Services Act), OJ L 277, 27.10.2022, pp. 1–102.

[98] See e.g. Husovec and Urban (2024).

[99] See Husovec (2024).

[100] See inter alia, Peukert (2023, p. 278).

social media platforms and newspapers to distinguish them and depart from its precedent in that regard. It certainly could have.[101] Social media platforms are neither common carriers, like telephone companies that in principle have to carry all content, nor do they select their content in a manner identical to newspapers, which rightly enjoy wide-ranging protection from any interference regarding editorial choices.[102] The DSA is based on that assessment.[103] It recognizes platforms' right to establish and enforce community standards, and it limits that right with a view to users' rights. The balance struck can, of course, be criticized. But not every regulation of free speech in general or of platforms' business operations in particular sends us on a freefall toward an Orwellian Ministry of Truth.[104] For example, restricting sufficiently large platforms that open a public forum from arbitrarily disadvantaging certain content surely does not disproportionately affect anyone's rights.[105]

In all this, the ultimate aim of regulating disinformation and propaganda should be considered. Hannah Arendt is often referred to in this context: freedom of opinion, she wrote, is «a farce unless factual information is guaranteed and the facts themselves are not in dispute».[106] «In matters of opinion, but not in matters of truth», she wrote, «our thinking is truly discursive».[107] As much as I admire and agree with Hannah Arendt otherwise, I have to respectfully disagree in this case. There never was, and never will be, a society in which all individuals hold entirely correct factual convictions. Even if factual truth is something that can in principle be discovered (which I think most people would agree on), it is wrong to think of the facts used in our public discourse as something immovable. Any non-trivial factual statement is the product of a process that involves normative and epistemic judgment—and is thus discursive. Arguing about facts is a very normal part of our daily lives, of our scientific and political debates. Those who want to recognize the legitimacy of citizens' factual (or even normative) convictions only if they came about in «the right way», and regulate strongly against any divergent convictions, go astray. Such an overly protective, paternalistic approach to media regulation conflicts with the democratic principle that all adult citizens have the capacity and right to political self-determination.[108] This holds true even if you consider many of your compatriots to be on a pernicious path. It falls on those who disagree to convince others that their views are wrong. This is challenging and it cannot be done by preaching to the choir.

[101] For a detailed argument on the differences see Koltay (2025, p. 214).

[102] These two options were extensively discussed before the US Supreme Court.

[103] Cf. Caruso (2024, pp. 135–136), arguing for an understanding of the freedom of expression that goes beyond a negative right and includes an institutional dimension.

[104] Rightly so Sunstein (2021, p. 46), Buchheim (2020, pp. 159, 168).

[105] Cf. Art. 20(4) DSA which requires providers of online platforms to handle complaints submitted through their internal complaint-handling system in a timely, non-discriminatory, diligent and non-arbitrary manner.

[106] Arendt (1967, p. 554), similarly: Gärditz (2021, pp. 505, 513), Cosentino (2020, p. 2).

[107] Arendt (1967, pp. 556–557).

[108] Mengden (2018, p. 50).

Some provisions, like arts. 26, 27, and 38 DSA that enable users to know why they see the content they see and influence it to some degree, enhance this self-determination. A concept of disinformation and propaganda, however, which is not interpreted and enforced in a sufficiently restrictive and differentiated manner, points in the wrong direction. The weakness and fragmentary character of our instruments against disinformation and propaganda should not only be seen as a deficit. They are also the result of historical struggles against overregulation. Only authoritarian states can seek to comprehensively and effectively enforce «the truth» in the public debate.[109] For decision-making purposes, facts must of course be authoritatively established in some manner that we have agreed on. But that does not mean that citizens may not disagree with that account.

Correlating with their freedom of thought and speech, citizens and politicians have a (mainly moral, sometimes legal) epistemic responsibility regarding the way they form their understanding of the facts.[110] The criticism of the EU's approach to freedom of speech voiced by US Vice President J.D. Vance at the Munich Security Conference in February 2025, fails to live up to that responsibility.[111] As mentioned above, the danger posed by disinformation can be overstated, but criticism of speech regulation can easily be just as hyperbolic. Neither the EU nor its Member States have retreated from the value of freedom of speech. Even if the balance they strike with other interests can be criticized, such criticism must acknowledge that the balance has been very different on both sides of the Atlantic for a very long time. Any criticism must be based on a bona fide understanding of the facts. Cherry-picking and distorting snippets of information because they fit one's argument purposefully violates the epistemic responsibility required of all participants in a public debate. It is profoundly dishonest—and neatly fits the definition of propaganda elaborated above. Contrary to what the Vice President insinuated, the EU cannot, be it under the DSA or any other instrument, annul elections in its Member States. No rule could even potentially be misunderstood in that manner. The EU cannot shut down social media because of «hateful content» during times of civil unrest. Art. 51 (3)(b) DSA merely allows for the competent judicial authority of a Member State to impose temporary restrictions of access under stringent conditions, in particular, the issue must entail a criminal offense involving a threat to the life or safety of persons. Posting «anti-feminist comments» online is *not* prohibited in Germany. However, insulting and defaming persons, threatening someone with and publicly approving of a rape are crimes in Germany.[112]

All these misunderstandings, the first two based on ambiguous statements by the former Commissioner for the Internal Market Thierry Breton, could have been easily cleared up—clarifications were easily available online. But then they would not have fit the Vice President's narrative as neatly. Stating the law of the EU and its

[109] See e.g. regarding Soviet practices Gornig (1988), 737 et seq.; on the Soviet understanding of international law: Mälksoo (2015).

[110] Keil (2024, p. 391).

[111] Speech by J.D. Vance on 14 February 2025. For a transcript see: Lu (2025).

[112] See, in particular, Sections 126, 130, 140, 185–200 of the German Criminal Code.

Member States correctly would have made it seem less outrageous—even if you can, of course, still argue about the need to criminalize certain behavior or the competencies that the European Commission and national authorities should have regarding online platforms. Likewise, you can critically assess the work of fact-checking organizations without rejecting this tool entirely. In many cases, their corrections are an important resource for the interested public to inform themselves efficiently. The Vice President's speech is a case in point.[113]

6 Concluding Observations

All efforts against disinformation and propaganda are to a certain extent paradoxical: They seek to protect the integrity of public discourse by influencing it in one way or another. The law can therefore only ever play a rather small part in the fight against disinformation and propaganda. The opinion of the US Supreme Court that the «remedy for speech that is false is speech that is true», and that this «is the ordinary course in a free society»,[114] still holds true—even if, from a European perspective, more restrictions are permissible. Public discourse simply cannot be regulated as effectively as possible without at some point damaging its freedom. A very effective measure against disinformation and propaganda that is at the same time entirely unproblematic regarding freedom of speech is an oxymoron. Expectations that the law will protect us from disinformation and propaganda should be reduced to a realistic level. There is no silver bullet against disinformation.[115] At the same time, some regulation might indeed help, and not every regulation of free speech is authoritarian.

Way more important than legal regulation is that public discourse remains characterized by a culture of truth in which reasoning and evidence meaningfully limit what we believe, say, and do.[116] Such a culture of truth not only legitimizes the exercise of power but restricts it.[117] Public discourse depends on its participants sharing this and other social standards.[118] In particular, citizens and politicians need to take their epistemic responsibility seriously. If such social standards are lost,[119] the law can only compensate for them to a limited degree.

In the end, it is necessary to generate trust in sources of information that deserve this trust. Such trust, however, cannot be legally ordained.[120] Just like we do with

[113] See e.g. Boffey D, Topping A (2025).

[114] USSC (2012) 567 U.S. 709, 727, *United States v. Alvarez* (plurality opinion).

[115] Cf. Iglesias Keller, Werneck Arguelhes (2024), 206.

[116] Cf. Gärditz (2021, pp. 505, 513).

[117] Benkler et al. (2018, p. 387).

[118] Cf. Ladeur (2018, p. 120).

[119] For example, if people share certain views to «signal political identity», even though they know them to be false: Iglesias Keller and Werneck Arguelhes (2024, pp. 193, 205).

[120] See in more Detail: Baade (2023a), § 5.

the spam in our inboxes, we may have to learn to filter out and ignore disinformation and propaganda which we will never be able to entirely eradicate from a free public discourse.

References

Antkowiak T, Gonza A (2017) The American convention on human rights. OUP, Oxford
Arendt H (1967) Truth and politics, printed In: Baehr P (ed) (2000) The portable Hannah Arendt. Penguin Books, New York, pp 545–575
Aristoteles (2020) Art of rhetoric. Harvard University Press, Cambridge
Aust H (2020) Hybrid warfare and the turn to resilience: back to the cold war? J Int Law Peace Armed Conflict 3:293–310
Baade B (2018) Fake news and international law. Eur J Int Law 29:1357–1376
Baade B (2020a) Don't call a spade a shovel: crucial subtleties in the definition of fake news and disinformation. Verfassungsblog, 14 April 2020, https://verfassungsblog.de/dont-call-a-spade-a-shovel/
Baade B (2020b) Verbot der Kriegspropaganda. EUR 55:653–683
Baade B (2020c) Informationskriegführung und Fake News. In: Kielmansegg S, Krieger H, Sohm S (eds) Die Wiederkehr der Landes- und Bündnisverteidigung: Neue Rechtsfragen eines alten Szenarios. Nomos, Baden-Baden, pp 161–189
Baade B (2023a) Wahrheit und Recht. Mohr Siebeck, Tübingen
Baade B (2023b) EU sanctions against propaganda for war—reflections on the general court's judgment in case T-125/22 (RT France). Heidelberg J Int Law 83:257–281
Bambauer DE (2006) Shopping badly: fallacy of the marketplace of ideas. Univ Colo L Rev 77:649–709
Benkler Y, Faris R, Roberts H (2018) Network propaganda: manipulation, disinformation, and radicalization in American politics. OUP, Oxford
Bernays E (1928) Propaganda. IG, New York
Bernstein J (2021) Selling the story of disinformation, Harper's Magazine, September
Beyer R, Sayles E (2014) The ghost army of World War II. Princeton Architectural Press, Princeton
Bittman L (1972) Deception game. Syracuse University, Syracuse
Bonfadelli H, Friemel T (2017) Medienwirkungsforschung, 6th edn. UVK, Konstanz
Bontcheva K, Posetti J (2020) Introduction. In: Bontcheva K, Posetti J (eds) Balancing act: countering digital disinformation while respecting freedom of expression. ITU/UNESCO, Geneva/Paris, pp 18–35
Boffey D, Topping A (2025) «Thought crime» and cancelled elections: how do JD Vance's claims about Europe stand up? The Guardian, 14 February 2025. https://www.theguardian.com/world/2025/feb/14/thought-and-cancelled-elections-how-do-jd-vances-europe-claims-stand-up. Accessed 25 Feb 2025
Britt MA, Rouet JF, Blaum D, Millis K (2019) A reasoned approach to dealing with fake news. Policy Insights Behav Brain Sci 6:94–101
Brkan M (2020) EU fundamental rights and democracy implications of data-driven political campaigns. Maastricht J Eur Comp Law 27:774–790
Brunk I, Hakimi M (2022) Russia, Ukraine and the future world order. Am J Int Law 116:687–697
Bruns A (2019) Are filter bubbles real? Polity Press, Oxford
Buchheim (2020) Rechtlicher Richtigkeitsschutz: Zugleich ein Beitrag zur Unterscheidung von Meinungen und Nachrichten im Rahmen des Art. 5 Abs. 1 GG. Der Staat 59:159–194
Caruso C (2025) Towards the institutions of freedom: the European public discourse in the digital era. GLJ 26:114–137

Chainoglou K (2016) Psychological warfare. In: Peters A (ed) Max Planck encyclopedia of public international law. https://opil.ouplaw.com/home/mpil
Chatziathanasiou K (2022) Beware the lure of narratives: «Hungry Judges» should not motivate the use of «Artificial Intelligence» in law. GJL 23:452–464
Chifu I (2017) The pattern of Russia's informational war. In: Simons G, Chifu I (eds) The changing face of warfare in the 21st century. Routledge, London, pp 118–168
Cosentino (2020) Social media and the post-truth world order. Palgrave, Cham
Dahlgren PM (2021) A critical review of filter bubbles and a comparison with selective exposure. Nordicom Rev 42:15–33
Di Turi C (2022) Il conflitto in Ucraina e la «propaganda di guerra» della Federazione russa: quali reazioni da parte dell'Unione europea? Eurojus, Fascicolo n. 2. https://rivista.eurojus.it/il-conflitto-in-ucraina-e-la-propaganda-di-guerra-della-federazione-russa-quali-reazioni-da-parte-dellunione-europea/
Dinstein Y (2017) War, aggression and self-defence, 6th edn. CUP, Cambridge
Dylan H, Gioe DV, Littell J (2022) The Kherson ruse: Ukraine and the art of military deception. Modern War Institute. https://mwi.usma.edu/the-kherson-ruse-ukraine-and-the-art-of-military-deception/.
Ellul J (1968) Propaganda: the formation of men's attitudes. Vintage Books, New York
Frankfurt HG (2005) On bullshit. PUP, Princeton
Franks MA (2019) The cult of the constitution. Stanford University Press, Stanford
Gärditz KF (2021) Freie Wissenschaft als Gelingensbedingung der politischen Willensbildung in der Pandemie. JÖR 69:505–534
Gornig GH (1988) Äußerungsfreiheit und Informationsfreiheit als Menschenrechte. Duncker & Humblot, Berlin
Henckaerts JM, Doswald-Beck L (2005a) (eds) Customary international law: rules, vol I. CUP, Cambridge
Henckaerts JM, Doswald-Beck L (2005b) (eds) Customary international law: practice, vol II. CUP, Cambridge
Hopkins V (2022) In video, a defiant zelensky says, «We are here». New York Times, 25 February 2022. https://www.nytimes.com/2022/02/25/world/europe/zelensky-speech-video.html
Husovec M (2024) Principles of the digital services act. OUP, Oxford
Husovec M, Urban J (2024) Will the DSA have the Brussels effect?, Verfassungsblog, https://verfassungsblog.de/will-the-dsa-have-the-brussels-effect/
Iglesias Keller C, Werneck Arguelhes D (2024) Facing disinformation in democratic backsliding: the role of courts in Brazil. WCL 57:187–209
International Committee of the Red Cross (1987) (ed) Commentary on the Additional Protocols of 8 June 1877 to the Geneva Conventions of 12 August 1949. ICRC, Geneva
Kakutani M (2018) Death of truth: notes on falsehood in the age of Trump. Tim Duggan, New York
Kearney MG (2007) The prohibition of propaganda for war in international law. OUP, Oxford
Keil G (2024) Meinungsäußerungen und Tatsachenbehauptungen: Eine kritische Bestandsaufnahme grundrechtsdogmatischer Abgrenzungsversuche. Der Staat 63:367–401
Koltay A (2023) Censorship as a tool against state disinformation: the freedom of Expression implications of the Russian-Ukrainian War. J Intl Med Ent L 10:1–53
Koltay A (2025) Media freedom and the law: the regulation of a common European idea. Routledge, Abingdon
Ladeur KH (2018) Geschichte und Theorie der Medienregulierung. In: von Lewinski K (ed), Immersiver Journalismus: Technik—Wirkung—Regulierung. Transcipt, Bielefeld, pp 101–126
Lahmann H (2020) Information operations and the question of illegitimate interference under international law. Israel Law Rev 53:189–224
Lahmann H (2022) Infecting the mind: establishing responsibility for transboundary disinformation. Eur J Int Law 33:411–440
Lonardo L (2023) Russia's 2022 War against Ukraine and the foreign policy reaction of the EU: context, diplomacy, and law. Palgrave, Cham

Lu C (2025) The speech that stunned Europe, foreign policy, 18 February 2025. https://foreignpolicy.com/2025/02/18/vance-speech-munich-full-text-read-transcript-europe/
Madders KJ (2000) War, use of propaganda. In: Bernhardt R (ed) Max Planck encyclopedia of public international law, vol III. North-Holland, Amsterdam
Mälksoo L (2015) Russian approaches to international law. OUP, Oxford
Mansell R, Durach F, Kettemann M, Lenoir T, Procter R, Tripathi G, Tucker E (2025) Information ecosystems and troubled democracy: a global synthesis of the state of knowledge on News Media, AI and Data Governance. https://observatory.informationdemocracy.org/wp-content/uploads/2024/12/rapport_forum_information_democracy_2025.pdf. Accessed 20 Feb 2025
Mengden M (2018) Zugangsfreiheit und Aufmerksamkeitsregulierung: zur Reichweite des Gebots der Gewährleistung freier Meinungsbildung am Beispiel algorithmengestützter Zugangsdienste im Internet. Mohr Siebeck, Tübingen
McKernon K (1925) Fake news and the public, Harper's Magazine, October, 528–536, 529.
Milanovic M (2023) Revisiting coercion as an element of prohibited intervention in international law. Am J Int Law 117:601–650
Milanovic M, Webb P (2024) False speech. In: Clooney A, Neuberger D (eds) Freedom of speech in international law. OUP, Oxford, pp 220–276
Mueller RS III (2019) Report on the investigation into Russian interference in the 2016 Presidential Election, vol I. https://www.justice.gov/archives/sco/file/1373816/
Nida-Rümelin J (2020) Eine Theorie praktischer Vernunft. De Gruyter, Berlin
Nolte G (1992) Beleidigungsschutz in der freiheitlichen Demokratie : eine vergleichende Untersuchung zur Rechtslage in der Bundesrepublik Deutschland, in den Vereinigten Staaten von Amerika sowie nach der Europäischen Menschenrechtskonvention. Springer, Berlin
Nowak M (2005) U.N. covenant on civil and political rights, 2nd edn. Engel, Kehl
Oeter S (2021) Methods and means of combat. In: Fleck D (ed) The handbook of international humanitarian law, 4th edn. OUP, Oxford, pp 170–248
Ohlin JD (2017) Did Russian cyber interference in the 2016 election violate international law? Tex L Rev 95:1579–1598
Orwell G (1968) Notes on nationalism. In: Orwell S, Angus I (eds) The collected essays, journalism and letters of George Orwell, vol III. Secker & Warburg, London, pp 361–380
Pariser E (2011) The filter bubble: what the Internet is hiding from you. Viking, London
Peukert A (2023) Desinformationsregulierung in der EU–Überblick und offene Fragen. JZ 78:278–296
Preuss L (1934) International responsibility for hostile propaganda against foreign states. Am J Int Law 28:649–668
Pronay N, Taylor P (1984) «An improper use of broadcasting…» The British Government and Clandestine radio propaganda operations against Germany during the Munich crisis and after. J Contemp Hist 19:357–384
Reeves S, Wallace D (2015) The combatant status of the «Little Green Men» and Other participants in the Ukraine conflict. Int'l L Stud 91:361–401
Robinson L, Helmus TC, Cohen R, Nader A, Radin A, Magnuson M, Migacheva, K (2018) Modern political warfare. Rand, Santa Monica
Rogers J, Tyushka A (2017) «Hacking» into the West: Russia's «anti-hegemonic» drive and the strategic narrative offensive. Defence Strat Commun 2:35–60
Rothenbücher K (1928) Das Recht der freien Meinungsäußerung. Verhandlungen der Tagung der Vereinigung der deutschen Staatsrechtslehrer 4:6–43
Schick N (2020) Deep fakes: the coming infocalypse. Twelve, New York
Schlosser N (2015) Cold war on the airwaves: the radio propaganda war against East Germany. University of Illinois Press, Urbana
Shultz R, Godson R (1984) Dezinformatsia: active measures in soviet strategy. Pergamon-Brassey's, Washington
Simon H (1957) Models of man: social and rational; mathematical essays on rational human behavior in a social setting. Wiley, New York

Sivakumaran S (2012) The law of non-international armed conflict. OUP, Oxford
Sunstein C (2020) Falsehoods and the first amendment. Harv JL Tech 33:388–426
Sunstein C (2021) Liars: falsehoods and free speech in an age of deception. OUP, New York
Timothy TL (2004) Russia's reflexive control theory and the military. J Slav Mil Stud 17:237–256
van der Linden S (2022) Misinformation: susceptibility, spread, and interventions to immunize the public. Nat Med 28:460–467
Vosoughi S, Roy D, Aral S (2018) Spread of true and false news online. Science 359:1146–1151
Wardle C, Derakhshan H (2017) Information disorder: toward an interdisciplinary framework for research and policy making. Council of Europe report DGI(2017)09
Wentker A (2024) Party status to armed conflict in international law. OUP, Oxford
Whitton JB (1948) Propaganda and international law. Rdc 72:545–670
Whitton JB, Larson A (1964) Propaganda: towards disarmament in the war of words. Oceana, Dobbs Ferry
Wigell M (2019) Hybrid interference as a wedge strategy: a theory of external interference in liberal democracy. Int Aff 95:255–275
Zuboff S (2019) The age of surveillance capitalism: the fight for a human future at the new frontier of power. Profile Books, Londons

Beyond Propaganda—Hybrid War and Weaponization of Rights

Siniša Rodin

Abstract The aim of this chapter is to identify some contemporary threats to liberal democracy related to disinformation, propaganda, or ideological interference in the broad sense and to suggest a possible line of defense. Such threats do not originate from the nature of contemporary media itself but are facilitated by their impact on political will formation and its susceptibility to external interference. Such interference is capable of not only influencing formation of political ideas but of subverting the very institutional infrastructure within which political process takes place. Moreover, this interference is not limited to propaganda, i.e. one directional spreading of information or ideas, but appears in the form of weaponization. The author takes liberal democracy to mean a model of government where legitimacy is derived from popular consent based on respect for fundamental rights and free and fair elections where majority is restrained by a constitutional system of checks and balances including independent judicial review protecting individual rights against encroachments of State power and, increasingly, powerful private actors. By weaponization, instead, the author understands activities directed at turning the basic building blocks of liberal democratic constitutional order against itself. Weaponization must be distinguished from the concept of abuse of rights. An abuse can be committed by an individual who exercises a given individual right either against its purpose, or with an intention to inflict harm to others. On the other hand, weaponization usually originates from a third party, not the bearer of a right, and is directed towards subversion of the entire institutional system, political and judicial, with an aim of its obliteration. More precisely, the aim of weaponization is de-legitimization of the constitutional order or the system of judicial protection, by using their internal contradictions such as the tension between exercise of individual rights and protection of common good. Weaponization does not have to take place in institutional framework. It may well be directed at civil society, public opinion, or individual preferences. Weaponization may take place equally in the times of peace and in times of war and, to certain extent,

Opinions expressed in this paper are author's personal opinions.

S. Rodin (✉)
Court of Justice of the European Union, Luxembourg, Luxembourg
e-mail: sinisa.rodin@curia.europa.eu

R. Mastroianni and C. Massa (eds.), *Disinformation in New and Old Media in the XXI Century*, Ius Gentium: Comparative Perspectives on Law and Justice 136,
https://doi.org/10.1007/978-3-032-18830-4_9

collapses the distinction between the two. In its different guises it seeks to polarize participants to political process against each other and against the institutions that make political process possible at the first place or to overload the system of judicial protection attempting to make protection of individual rights difficult. Metaphorically, such interference seeks to produce an auto-immune disease by turning pluralistic nature of liberal democracy and its institutions, conflict-resolution mechanisms, and rights against themselves. On the base of those ideas, the author will first try to explain some basic ideas and mechanisms that make weaponization of elements of liberal democracy possible. In the second part of the chapter, the author will focus on free expression and look into the balance between guarantees of freedom of speech and press as a liberal freedom and protection of public interest, such as national security. In the final part the author will suggest a possible defense against weaponization of rights.

1 Introduction

Oxford reference defines a medium as "...[t]he means or agency through which communication takes place; often synonymous with channel" or, most generally, as "any substance or process through which reality is apprehended or constructed".[1]

Means of communication shape not only the political process but also the institutional framework within which the very political process takes place. Neil Postman reports how

> ... [t]he first of the seven famous debates between Abraham Lincoln and Stephen A. Douglas took place on August 21, 1858, in Ottawa, Illinois. Their arrangement provided that Douglas would speak first, for one hour; Lincoln would take an hour and a half to reply; Douglas, a half hour to rebut Lincoln's reply.[2]

Postman concluded that "[t]he Lincoln-Douglas audience apparently had a considerable grasp of the issues being debated, including knowledge of historical events and complex political matters".[3] The debate was not only extensive, but also direct. It required physical presence of the speakers and the audience. In other words, audience was in position to receive and discuss complex political ideas directly, without intermediaries. Articulation of political ideas was taking place without interference of third parties.

The described, direct, form of communication was of fundamental importance for functioning of liberal democracy. Founding fathers of the Constitution of the United States, or of the French Declaration of Rights of Men operated on similar terms. While one could complain that, at the time, political participation was restrictive, excluding large part of the population such as women or enslaved,[4] the fact remains

---

[1] https://www.oxfordreference.com/display/10.1093/oi/authority.20111201123450726.

[2] Postman (2005, p. 44 at place 896).

[3] *Ivi*, p. 46 at place 933.

[4] See e.g. Moyn (2023).

that articulation of political decisions was shaped directly, by participants to the political process who had their skins in the game. Today, more than two hundred years later, electronic media changed everything, far beyond the original form of political debate and far beyond Postman's imagination.[5]

The aim of this paper is to identify some contemporary threats to liberal democracy related to disinformation, propaganda, or ideological interference in a broad sense and to suggest a possible line of defense. Such threats do not originate from the nature of contemporary media itself but are facilitated by their impact on political will formation and its susceptibility to external interference. Such interference is capable of not only influencing formation of political ideas but of subverting the very institutional infrastructure of liberal democracy within which political process takes place. Moreover, this interference is not limited to propaganda, i.e. one-directional spreading of information or ideas, but appears in the form of *weaponization.*

I take **liberal democracy**[6] to mean a model of government where legitimacy is derived from popular consent based on respect for fundamental rights and free and fair elections where the majority is restrained by a constitutional system of checks and balances including civil society, non-majoritarian institutions like central banks, free press and higher education establishments and, not least, independent judicial review protecting individual rights against encroachments of State power and, increasingly, powerful private actors.

By **weaponization** I understand the intentional turning of functional elements of a system against the system itself. In the context of liberal democracy this includes activities directed at antagonizing the basic building blocks of liberal democratic constitutional order against each other by instrumentalization of liberal institutions themselves.

Although weaponization may entail abuse of rights and fraud, it must be distinguished from the two.

An abuse can be committed by an individual who exercises a given individual right either against its purpose, or with an intention to inflict harm on others or public good. Fraud refers to the intentionally inaccurate representation of facts. While weaponization takes advantage of abuse and fraud and often exploits them, it usually originates from a third party, not the bearer of a right, and is aimed not at improper exercise of an individual right but towards subversion of the entire institutional system, political and normative, with objective of its obliteration. More precisely, the aim of weaponization is the de-legitimization of a constitutional order, liberal institutions, or a system of judicial protection, by antagonizing their internal contradictions such as a tension between the exercise of individual rights and the protection of the common good.

Weaponization does not have to take place in an institutional framework of state power, such as the judicial branch of government. It may well be directed at civil society, public opinion, or individual preferences. It may take place equally in times of peace and in times of war and, to a certain extent, collapses the distinction between

---

[5] Postman's main preoccupation was television.

[6] This is not an exhaustive list of constitutive elements of liberal democracy but a general framework within which liberal democratic institutions operate.

the two. In its different guises it seeks to polarize participants in the political process against each other and against the institutions that make the political process possible in the first place or to overload the system of judicial protection attempting to make protection of individual rights difficult. Metaphorically, such interference seeks to produce an auto-immune disease of a society, by turning the pluralistic nature of liberal democracy and its institutions, conflict-resolution mechanisms, and individual rights against themselves.

Following this introductory part, I will first try to explain some basic ideas and mechanisms that make weaponization of elements of liberal democracy possible. Second, I will present examples found in three areas susceptible to weaponization of law, notably, migration, language and freedom of expression. In the final part I will suggest a possible defense against weaponization of rights.

2 Turning Liberal Democracy Against Itself

Disinformation and propaganda are forms of weaponization of freedom of speech, press and media in general. Their objective is to subvert the freedom of speech and press for nefarious purposes. It should also be noted that propaganda strives best on half-truths and contradictions. Therefore, it seeks to create or make use of the existing social reality and to re-interpret it. It little matters whether they are employed in times of war or peace. The distinction between war and peace matters only when it comes to the justification of restrictions on freedom of speech on grounds of public interest where some jurisdictions may look more generously to justification of restrictions of individual rights in times of war then in times of peace.

Disinformation and propaganda can be understood as a part of what is sometimes called a hybrid war. Frank G. Hoffman of Potomac Institute for Policy Studies writes about 4th generation warfare the main objective of which is "…to undermine the will of the existing state, to de-legitimize it, and to stimulate an internal social breakdown".[7] Timothy Snyder talks about "active measures" which in his words "are about inducing the enemy to direct his own strengths against his own weaknesses".[8] He exemplifies the concept by reference to Russian cyberspace project seeking to present Donald Trump as a successful businessman. Activities that Hoffman and Snyder described are not necessarily aimed at governmental institutions such as parliaments, governments, or courts. In fact, they are generally targeting individuals and institutions of civil society such as in the sphere of education, religion, public health or other. In that sense, such activities are aimed to influencing public opinion and destabilization of what Antonio Gramsci called a "cultural hegemony" by means of the "war of position".[9]

[7] Hoffman (2007).

[8] Snyder (2019, pp. 223–224).

[9] Gramsci (1971, place 5783).

By introducing the concept of cultural hegemony Gramsci intended to explain how political power can be won and perpetuated by means of culture.[10] As he clarified, cultural hegemony of the dominant political group is projected to the civil sphere, education, health, culture, to secure consent of the population.[11] Gramsci made a distinction between two aspects of social struggle—war of position and war of maneuver. The former meaning a process of reinforcement of hegemonic positions of the dominant group and the latter comprising activities such as strikes and revolutions.[12] Changing the way in which citizens understand the world and by making them doubt the facts and values they once were taking for granted, would lead to the ultimate victory in what he called a "war of position". Once that war is won the victory is irreversible.[13]

That said, disinformation and propaganda are not only seeking to subvert the functioning of state institutions, such as governments, parliaments, or courts, but also to undermine the construction of social reality and consensus on which institutional legitimacy depends. Disinformation and propaganda are the means of the war of position in Gramsci's sense.

Two remarks at this place. First, what Gramsci calls a "war of position" takes place at, but is not limited to, times of peace, understood as times of absence of military hostilities. Hence, the boundaries between war and peace become blurred. Second, disinformation and propaganda as weapons of war of position are seeking to make social impact in areas of life that, in liberal democracy, are traditionally considered to be within the sphere of personal liberty and thus beyond the proper sphere of government control. Such is the sphere of individual rights, whether we call them fundamental or constitutional. That, intersection of individual liberty and public interest is nowadays largely defined by judicial balancing, i.e. proportionality analysis.

Essentially, weaponization of rights comprises three stages:

1. identification of social and institutional weaknesses and/or inherent contradictions. In a liberal democracy limited by law, the most obvious contradiction is the one between individual rights and rights of others/public interest,
2. creation or amplification of conditions, including by means of disinformation and propaganda, in which such weaknesses and contradictions become obvious, undesirable, or irritating to citizens and, finally,
3. turning one or more elements of the social, institutional or legal order against themselves or one individual right against another.

Such activities typically take place within the context of civil society but increasingly also within a system of legal protection. Being unable to change legislation directly, agents of weaponization direct their activities toward social change and common understanding of facts. Within structure of legal syllogism, their target can be either

---

[10] *Ibidem.*

[11] *Ivi*, p. 103, place 1946.

[12] Rodin (2021, p. 222).

[13] Gramsci (1971, place 5783).

law (major premise) or facts (minor premise). For example, once terrorists are generally understood as freedom fighters, or once the difference between the two becomes blurred and ultimately collapses, law applicable to terrorists does not apply anymore and they become immune in respect of the repressive system of the state. Once right to life is understood not primarily as a prohibition of death penalty but as a right of unborn, the meaning of the right is changed. In that sense weaponization can also be understood as re-contextualization of hitherto stabilized meaning of facts and law.

Abuse of law as a legal concept refers to a situation in which a person attempts to exercise their rights and gain an advantage through an artificial construction, which does not formally run against any specific legal norm but, at the same time, is not in accordance with the aesthetics of the legal system or what is known in French as *l'économie generale.* The judge is therefore confronted with a situation where the person subject to the law is not behaving unlawfully according to the black letter wording of the legal text. This is precisely the difference from fraud, where the subject engages in conduct that is already unlawful according to the wording of a legal text. In other words, fraud involves an element of intent and deception, where facts are misrepresented in such a way as to mislead and gain an advantage. Such deception may for example include providing inaccurate information to, or deliberately concealing relevant matters from, the authorities concerned.

However, in the absence of social consensus as to the facts, fraudulent behavior becomes relative to personal beliefs and convictions. What is more, semantic collapse of legal distinctions may delegitimize the original purpose of applicable legal rules. This is exactly the aim of weaponization. As Hannah Arend has put it in Origins of Totalitarianism,

> In an ever-changing, incomprehensible world the masses had reached the point where they would, at the same time, believe everything and nothing, think that everything was possible and that nothing was true.[14]

And within a legal system that is subject to permanent interpretation by the courts, the meaning of law can change too based on personal (dis)beliefs. In such circumstances a target of weaponization can be anything. Fundamental rights, values, and legitimacy of liberal institutions in general. In such circumstances judges can and sometimes are described as enemies of the people, impeachable if not delivering certain outcomes, places of learning can become undesirable and due process of law irrelevant. This can be facilitated not only by means of disinformation or propaganda, but also by active measures creating a *fait accompli*, such as the artificial creation of a migration crisis.

In the sphere of litigation, weaponization seeks to re-define function and/or meaning of basic legal concepts including fundamental rights. In essence it challenges the fundamental political and legal postulate of liberal democracy according to which individual rights are limited by the rights of others and by public interest.

Some of the situations where fundamental rights and values of the EU have been put to the test include abuse of refugees by Belarus by organizing their crossing of

[14] Arendt (1951, p. 382).

the EU external border, problems of use of the Russian language in higher education and use of government-controlled media outlets such as RT France.

3 Examples of Potential or Actual Weaponization

3.1 Artificial Migration

Consequences of forced migration, notably from Belarus to the European Union[15] have already characterized factual background of some cases before the CJEU. A recent example is the Case C-392/22 of February 29, 2024,[16] where the Court had to find a balance between protection of rights of apparently forced refugees and national border protection measures implemented by Poland at its border with Belarus.

In regulatory arena the phenomenon of weaponization of forced migration was addressed in 2021. The European Council identified the problem and articulated the concept of "instrumentalization".[17] As it reads in point 19 of the Council Conclusions,

> The European Council will not accept any attempt by third countries to instrumentalise migrants for political purposes. It condemns all hybrid attacks at the EU's borders and will respond accordingly.

On December 14, 2021, European Commission introduced a proposal for a Regulation addressing instrumentalization of migrants.[18] However, the original Proposal for a Regulation was never adopted as an autonomous legal act but its elements were incorporated into Regulation (EU) 2024/1359 of the European Parliament and of the Council of 14 May 2024 addressing situations of crisis and force majeure in the field of migration and asylum and amending Regulation (EU) 2021/1147[19] Article 1(4)(b) thereof specifies that:

> a situation of instrumentalisation where a third country or a hostile non-state actor encourages or facilitates the movement of third-country nationals or stateless persons to the external

[15] Ashurkevich (2025).

[16] ECJ, case C-392/22, *X v Staatssecretaris van Justitie en Veiligheid.*

[17] European Council meeting (21 and 22 October 2021), Conclusions, "19. The European Council will not accept any attempt by third countries to instrumentalise migrants for political purposes. It condemns all hybrid attacs at the EU's borders and will respond accordingly".

[18] Proposal for a Regulation of the European Parliament and of the Council addressing situations of instrumentalization in the field of migration and asylum, COM(2021) 890 final. As explained in the Proposal, "...the proposal for the amended Schengen Borders Code defines instrumentalisation of migrants...where such actions are indicative of an intention of a third country to destabilise the Union or a Member States, where the nature of such actions is liable to put at risk essential State functions, including its territorial integrity, the maintenance of law and order or the safeguard of its national security".

[19] Regulation (EU) 2024/1359 of the European Parliament and of the Council of 14 May 2024 addressing situations of crisis and force majeure in the field of migration and asylum and amending Regulation (EU) 2021/1147, PE/19/2024/REV/1, OJ L.

> borders or to a Member State, with the aim of destabilising the Union or a Member State, and where such actions are liable to put at risk essential functions of a Member State, including the maintenance of law and order or the safeguard of its national security.

Both the original proposal of the Regulation and the adopted Regulation 2024/1359 define instrumentalization as being subject to an intention or aim rather than its effect opening questions of evidentiary nature.

The core of the problem in cases of this kind is that forced migration caused by a non-friendly third state or non-state actor challenges the capacity of an EU Member State to properly accept refugees in accordance with law and human dignity. In the circumstances of an uncontrollable influx of forced refugees there is an increased danger of the erosion of EU values in face of national security concerns. In this way hostile third actors may seek to weaponize the system and credibility of EU legal protection.

3.2 Language

In Case C-391/20 of September 7, 2022, *Boriss Cilevičs*, the CJEU was confronted with a question of whether the Russian language can be officially used in tertiary education in Latvia. The litigation was placed in the context of freedom of establishment and the Latvian Constitutional Court addressed a reference to the CJEU asking the two questions:

1. Does legislation such as that at issue in the main proceedings constitute a restriction on the freedom of establishment enshrined in Article 49 [TFEU] or, in the alternative, on the freedom to provide services guaranteed in Article 56 [TFEU], and on the freedom to conduct a business recognised in Article 16 of the [Charter]?
2. What considerations should be taken into account when assessing whether the legislation in question is justified, suitable and proportionate with regard to its legitimate purpose of protecting the official language as a manifestation of national identity?'

The social and legal contradiction that was present in the context of the case was right of education in one's own minority language (Russian) against protection of national language as a part of national identity. Amplification of this contradiction is facilitated by confrontation of Russian national minority and its possibly split loyalty and susceptibility to imperialistic narratives through education (civil society in Gramscian sense). Finally, this contradiction found its articulation in a legal dispute confronting one of the freedoms of the internal market, notably, freedom of establishment against protection of national identity, both being guaranteed by the Founding Treaties. In such a context giving priority to freedom of establishment and official use of Russian language as a minority language in higher education would arguably adversely affect official use of national language as an element of Latvian national identity and open Latvian educational institutions to potentially corrosive foreign influence and interference.[20]

On its face, this case involves finding a balance between two interests protected by EU law and the CJEU expressed this tension in para. 68 of the judgment.[21] However, what was not discussed in the judgment, also raises concerns about possible weaponization of language for purposes of Russian foreign policy all under the guise of legitimate legal interests of a linguistic and ethnic minority.

The CJEU approached the problem in the orthodox way by applying the usual syntax of proportionality analysis: right-restriction-justification. Concretely, after having found a restriction of freedom of establishment continued with proportionality test, found, in para. 70 of the judgment, that promoting and encouraging the use of one of the official languages of a Member State constitutes a legitimate aim that can justify restrictions to the freedom of establishment,[22] and stated, in para. 74, that the Latvian restriction is suitable for defending and promoting the national language.[23]

4 Freedom of Expression

Possibly the most prominent example of an attempt to weaponize freedom of expression was addressed by General Court in judgment of July 27, 2022, *RT France*[24] where the applicant, was seeking, under Article 263 TFEU, the annulment of a

[20] See e.g. EURACTIV (2024), stating "President Vladimir Putin on Monday (5 September) approved a new foreign policy doctrine based around the concept of a "Russian World", a notion that conservative ideologues have used to justify intervention abroad in support of Russian-speakers. The 31-page "humanitarian policy", published more than six months into the war in Ukraine, says Russia should "protect, safeguard and advance the traditions and ideals of the Russian World". The Russian Federation provides support to its compatriots living abroad in the fulfilment of their rights, to ensure the protection of their interests and the preservation of their Russian cultural identity".

[21] ECJ, case C-391/20, *Boriss Cilevičs*, para. 68: "It has thus held that according to the fourth subparagraph of Article 3(3) TEU and Article 22 of the Charter, the European Union must respect its rich cultural and linguistic diversity. In accordance with Article 4(2) TEU, the European Union must also respect the national identity of its Member States, which includes protection of the official language of the Member State concerned (judgments of 12 May 2011, Runevič-Vardyn and Wardyn, C-391/09, EU:C:2011:291, paragraph 86, and of 16 April 2013, Las, C-202/11, EU:C:2013:239, paragraph 26)".

[22] *Ivi*, para 70: "... the objective of promoting and encouraging the use of one of the official languages of a Member State must be regarded as being a legitimate objective which, in principle, justifies a restriction on the obligations imposed by the freedom of establishment enshrined in Article 49 TFEU (see, to that effect, judgments of 16 April 2013, Las, C-202/11, EU:C:2013:239, paragraph 27, and of 21 June 2016, New Valmar, C-15/15, EU:C:2016:464, paragraph 50)".

[23] *Ivi*, para 74: "In the present case, a Member State's legislation which provides for an obligation on higher education institutions to use, in principle, the official language of that Member State appears to be suitable for attaining the objective of defending and promoting that language. That legislation encourages the use of the language in question by the whole of the population concerned and ensures that the same language is also used in education at university level".

[24] GC, case T-125/22, *RT France v. Council*.

Council Decision concerning restrictive measures in view of Russia's actions destabilizing the situation in Ukraine by which the Council suspended the broadcasting license of the mentioned Russia-controlled media outlet.

By it second plea, the RT France claimed that the contested acts disregard the freedom of expression and information guaranteed by Article 11 of the Charter, which corresponds to Article 10 of the Convention for the Protection of Human Rights and Fundamental Freedoms, signed at Rome on 4 November 1950 ('the ECHR'). Among other arguments, the applicants pleaded that:

> ...whatever the editorial policy of a media outlet, or its audience, ultimately a general and absolute prohibition on broadcasting constitutes a genuine act of censorship and cannot be regarded as either necessary or proportionate in order to achieve effectively the objectives on which the Council relies.[25]

The General Court, after having established, in para. 142, a restriction of the freedom of expression, went to examine in para. 148 "... whether the restrictive measures at issue are provided for by law, comply with the essence of freedom of expression, pursue an objective of general interest and are not disproportionate ...". However, for purposes of the present discussion the relevant part of the judgment states in para. 162:

> ... since the propaganda and disinformation campaigns are capable of undermining the foundations of democratic societies and are an integral part of the arsenal of modern warfare, the restrictive measures at issue also form part of the pursuit by the European Union of the objectives, including the peaceful objectives, assigned to it in Article 3(1) and (5) TEU.

Assessing the proportionality of the measures the General Court concluded in para. 201 that:

> As regards the strictly proportionate nature of the restrictive measures at issue, the weighing up of the competing interests shows that the disadvantages entailed in the temporary prohibition on the broadcasting of content are not disproportionate to the objectives pursued, which in turn correspond to objectives of general interest.

While disinformation and propaganda can be described as manipulation of facts which I characterize as fraud, the General Court accepted the reasoning of the Council according to which such activities can undermine the foundations of democratic societies and, in essence, as I would put it, represents a weaponization of freedom of expression. Namely, the action for annulment seeks to abuse a fundamental right by perverting the purpose of freedom of expression and turning one of the basic values of democratic society against its objective. In this light a question can be asked whether such a form of abuse can be justified at all. *Dolus omnia corrumpit.*

---

[25] *Ivi*, para. 128.

5 How to Defend Liberal Democracy Against Weaponization

The starting point in fight against weaponization of liberal rights is to recognize that weaponization is taking place. This is not an easy task having in mind that abuse of rights takes guise as a quest for legitimate legal protection of well-established rights such as international protection, protection of minorities, freedom of expression or, potentially, any legal right or interest. Furthermore, while weaponization typically begins in the real world, as creating the facts on the ground, misrepresentation of facts or re-purposing of law, the ultimate outcome will be often decided by courts.

Today, courts not only decide legal disputes but also define the narrative within which legal disputes are decided and within which legal concepts make sense. In the European Union that narrative is defined by interpretative role of the values specified in Art. 2 TEU and, as I have explained elsewhere,[26] by teleology of European integration.

This said, manipulation of facts, e.g. propaganda, and manipulation of law by re-calibration of its purpose need to be recognized and interpreted in light of values of liberal democracy which is inherent in the legal and political architecture of the EU. This process will typically take form of proportionality test where alleged rights will be balanced against rights of others and public interest. The question to be decided in each particular case is not only whether facts are valid, and law invoked applied in accordance with its purpose, but also what intensity of public interest will justify restriction of legitimately invoked rights.

Two remarks at this point. First, restrictions of legal rights invoked in abusive manner do not require a justification. Finding that a legal right is invoked against its purpose or on grounds of fraudulently manufactured facts would suffice. Conversely, it is not sufficient to simply invoke a legal right in its textual form. Reliance on a right must be embedded in values of liberal democratic society, in the European Union, in Article 2 TEU. Second, in absence of abuse or fraud, justification of restrictions of legitimately invoked rights may vary depending on a variety of circumstances. Some individual rights may require enhanced intensity of judicial scrutiny. In the United States since US S. Ct. judgment in Carolene Products case[27] such higher level of protection is granted to "discrete and insular minorities". In European Union law a higher level of judicial scrutiny is sometimes characterized by expression "strictly necessary". However, in this respect, case law of the CJEU that defines intensity of scrutiny within framework of proportionality analysis is still developing.

---

[26] Rodin (2019, p. 602).

[27] US Supreme Court, 25 April 1938, *United States v. Carolene Products Co.*, 304 U.S. 144, footnote 4.

References

Arendt H (1951) The origins of totalitarianism, Kindle edn

Ashurkevich T (2025) Inside Belarus' secret program to undermine the EU. https://www.politico.eu/article/alexander-lukashenko-belarus-secret-program-to-undermine-the-eu/?utm_source=email&utm_medium=alert&utm_campaign=Inside%20Belarus'%20secret%20program%20to%20undermine%20the%20EU

EURACTIV (2024) https://www.euractiv.com/section/global-europe/news/putin-approves-new-foreign-policy-doctrine-based-on-russian-world/

Gramsci A (1971) Selections from the prison notebooks, Kindle edn

Hoffman F G (2007) Conflict in the 21st century: The Rise of hybrid wars. Potomac Institute for Policy Studies, Arlington VA

Moyn S (2023) Liberalism against itself, Cold War Intellectuals and the Making of our Times. Yale University Press, New Haven and London

Postman N (2005) Amusing ourselves to death, Kindle edn

Rodin S (2019) Interpretation in the Court of Justice of the European Union: Originalism, purposivism, and L'Economie Générale. Am Univ Int Law Rev 34(3).

Rodin S (2021) Liberal constitutionalism, rule of law and revolution by other means. Il Diritto dell'Unione europea, no. 2/2021

Snyder T (2019) The road to unfreedom: Russia, Europe, America. Kindle edn

The Role of the European Court of Justice in Shaping the Boundaries of Free Speech: The Legality of EU Restrictive Measures from Kiselev to RT France

Francesca Finelli

Abstract This chapter examines the role of the Court of Justice in assessing the legality of restrictive measures (sanctions) that interfere with free speech. It focuses on two key rulings, *Kiselev* (2017) and *RT France* (2022), decided by the General Court *before* and *after* the outbreak of the Russia's war of aggression against Ukraine. The *Kiselev* case concerns restrictions imposed on a Russian journalist, whereas *RT France* addresses the legality of an exceptional broadcasting ban targeting Russian media oultes. By comparing the Court's reasoning in the two rulings, this Chapter illustrates the evolving boundaries of free speech in the EU. This comparative analysis highlights how the Court's approach to free speech restrictions has evolved in response to exceptional geopolitical circumstances. While both rulings upheld the legality of the contested measures, *RT France* demonstrates a more comprehensive review and an unprecedented engagement with factual evidence. Notwithstanding the context of an ongoing war at borders of the Union, and the high security interests at stake, the reasoning presented in *RT France* appears to be well-founded, well-structured and ultimately convincing. In contrast to *Kiselev*, where the Court applied a three-step test, *RT France* introduced a four-step methodology, incorporating a more rigorous assessment of fundamental rights interferences. It illustrates the Court's paramount role in scrutinizing restrictive measures while acknowledging the broader implications of propaganda in times of war.

F. Finelli (✉)
Luxembourg School of Business, Luxembourg, Luxembourg
e-mail: francesca.finelli95@gmail.com

R. Mastroianni and C. Massa (eds.), *Disinformation in New and Old Media in the XXI Century*, Ius Gentium: Comparative Perspectives on Law and Justice 136,
https://doi.org/10.1007/978-3-032-18830-4_10

1 Introduction

Free speech is one of the cornerstones of democratic societies. It is one of the fundamental rights guaranteed by the European Union. More precisely, Art. 11 CFREU enshrines that "everyone has the right to freedom of expression", including the freedom to receive information and ideas *without public interference.*[1]

The Union protects free speech as an essential feature of a properly functioning democracy and a free society. However, it also recognises that free speech is not an absolute right, and can be subject to (justified) restrictions. The key question then becomes whether an inference with the right to free speech can constitute a legitimate and proportionate restriction on that right.

This Chapter intends to analyse the role of the CJEU in assessing the *fragile balance* between protecting free speech and pursuing foreign policy objectives, such as preventing security crises or preserving peace.[2] Focusing on two judgements, the *Kiselev* ruling of 2017, followed by the *RT France* ruling in 2022, this Chapter aims to shed light on the legality of restrictive measures (sanctions) when they interfere with free speech.[3] The first case concerns a Russian journalist targeted by EU sanctions since 2014, while the second case regards a media company established in France (but owned by a Moscow-based association which is almost entirely funded by the budget of the Russian Federation) subject to an unprecedent broadcasting since 2022.

By comparing the reasoning in the *Kiselev* and *RT France* rulings, this analysis illustrates how the Court strikes a balance between fundamental rights and CFSP objectives—shaping the boundaries of free speech in the European Union *before* and *after* Russia's aggression in Ukraine.

2 Unprecedented Restrictive Measures in Times of War

The ongoing Russia's war of aggression against Ukraine has triggered a series of tough restrictive measures by the European Union, which has adopted successive "packages" of sanctions against the aggressor state since February 2022. These sanctions have been described as "massive and unprecedented" given the wide scope of their application.[4]

The Union adopted the first set of Russia sanctions back in 2014, but, after 2022, the restrictions imposed by the Council present significant elements of novelty when compared to the initial regime. One of the most unprecedented restrictions adopted post-aggression concerns the so called "media ban". More precisely, on 1 March

---

[1] Art. 11 CFREU corresponds to art. 10 ECHR.

[2] On the concept of "fragile balance" see Szép and Wessel (2023, 1383).

[3] The terms restrictive measures and sanctions will be used interchangeably in this chapter.

[4] See European Council, 'The EU Sanctions Against Russia Explained', https://www.consilium.europa.eu/en/policies/sanctions-against-russia-explained/#sanctions. See also Hofer (2023) and Meissner and Graziani (2023).

2022,[5] the Council introduced a comprehensive prohibition "to broadcast, or to enable, facilitate or otherwise contribute to broadcast, any content" by certain Russian media outlets.[6] Although the Council had targeted Russian journalists before (adding them to the EU "blacklist"),[7] the media ban represents a brand-new sectorial measure against Russian media outlets which the Council identifies to be under the permanent direct or indirect control of the leadership of the Russian Federation.

The first to be targeted by the ban were RT (Russia Today) and Sputnik, while the Council has today identified over 20 additional entities.[8]

It is the first time the Council prohibits the dissemination of certain audiovisual content in the EU.[9] Indeed, the media ban in a highly unusual measure in the context of restrictive measures, never introduced in other regimes.[10] It represents an unprecedented development in the field of EU sanctions.

The exceptional context of the war in Ukraine plays a key role in justifying the adoption of this ban. In the words of the Council, "the gravity of the situation" calls for the adoption of unprecedented measures.[11] More precisely, the Council illustrates that "the Russian Federation has engaged in continuous and concerted propaganda actions" to justify and support its aggression against Ukraine.[12] Those propaganda actions "have been channelled through a number of media outlets under the permanent direct or indirect control of the leadership of the Russian Federation"—targeting the civil society in the Union and neighbouring countries. Such actions are considered "a significant and direct threat to the Union's public order and security".[13]

It is noteworthy that, when introducing the media ban, the Council did not mention the concept of "propaganda of war"—as regulated by art. 20 of the International Covenant on Civil and Political Rights (ICCPR). On the contrary, in the Preamble of its Decision, it only made explicit reference to "hybrid threats", "media manipulation", "distortion of facts", "continuous and concerted propaganda actions". The language use by the Council suggests that the focus is not propaganda *of war* (as

[5] Council Decision (CFSP) 2022/351 of 1 March 2022 amending Decision 2014/512/CFSP concerning restrictive measures in view of Russia's actions destabilising the situation in Ukraine; complemented by Council Regulation (EU) 2022/350 amending Regulation (EU) No 833/2014.

[6] Art. 4g Council Decision 2014/512/CFSP of 31 July 2014 concerning restrictive measures in view of Russia's actions destabilising the situation in Ukraine; complemented by art. 2f Council Regulation (EU) No 833/2014.

[7] Council Decision 2014/145/CFSP of 17 March 2014 concerning restrictive measures in respect of actions undermining or threatening the territorial integrity, sovereignty and independence of Ukraine; complemented by Council Regulation (EU) No 269/2014.

[8] See Annex IX Decision 2014/512/CFSP, as amended.

[9] Despite the fact that, in the past, the Council have already imposed some restrictive measures (in the form of designations) against certain journalists.

[10] There are over 35 sanctions regimes currently in force, see https://www.sanctionsmap.eu and https://data.europa.eu/apps/eusanctionstracker/

[11] Council Decision (CFSP) 2022/351, cit., recital (10).

[12] *Ivi*, recital (7).

[13] *Ivi*, recital (8).

prohibited under international law), but propaganda actions that gravely distort and manipulate facts *in the context of a war.*

The approach of the Council mirrors the statements of other European officials. For instance, the Commission President Ursula von der Leyen said "*In this time of war*, words matter".[14] The former HR/VP Josep Borrell expressed concerns about the "systematic information manipulation and disinformation by the Kremlin".[15] The European Parliament also condemned the "use of information warfare".[16]

The EU institutions appear aligned on the use of words. They do not qualify the Russian disinformation as a "propaganda of war", but as a significant and direct threat to the EU's public order and security. They highlight that the Union is witnessing extraordinary times, and facing unprecedented geopolitical challenges, which call for extraordinary action—including restrictions on free speech.

Given the exceptional introduction of a media ban under EU sanctions, and the vague definition of its objectives (i.e., countering Russia disinformation),[17] it is unsurprising that the restrictions imposed by the Council triggered complex and novel legal questions.[18] The following analysis intends to address one of them, perhaps the key question, which concerns the legality of the media ban as assessed by the CJEU.

3 The "Full Review" of Restrictive Measures Before the CJEU

Before moving to the role of the CJEU in shaping the boundaries of free speech, it is essential to give some preliminary observations about the judicial scrutiny on restrictive measures.

The CJEU is protagonist in ensuring the correct interpretation, application, and review of EU sanctions. Despite Common Foreign and Security Policy (CFSP) matters are generally immune from judicial review, restrictive measures represent an exception. More precisely, they are *the exception to the exception*, which restores the judicial scrutiny of the CJEU as a general rule in a specific area of CFSP.[19] In

[14] See European Commission, Press release 'Ukraine: Sanctions on Kremlin-backed outlets Russia Today and Sputnik', 2 March 2022, at https://ec.europa.eu/commission/presscorner/detail/en/ip_22_1490 (emphasis added).

[15] Ibid.

[16] European Parliament resolution of 1 March 2022 on the Russian aggression against Ukraine (2022/2564(RSP)) (emphasis added).

[17] On the blur relation between propaganda and disinformation see Lendvai (2024).

[18] Numerous legal scholars have commented the legality of media ban shortly after his adoption. See, inter alia, Baade (2022), Popović (2022), and Lonardo (2023).

[19] On the "rule-exception dilemma" see Van Elsuwege and Gremmelprez (2020). See also Butler (2017). Despite the judicial activism on the matter (as well as the ongoing scholar debate), the delineation of the Court's jurisdiction on CFSP remains an open question. The CJEU has usually avoided to provide guidelines on the 'rule- exception dilemma'. In *Opinion 2/13*, it merely noted that 'the Court has not yet had the opportunity to [exhaustively] define the extent to which its

this respect, the Court's oversight is the same as the one it exercises generally, over other EU acts, in line with its mandate established in art. 19 TEU and the principle of effective judicial remedies enshrined in art. 47 of the EU Charter of Fundamental Rights.

It is art. 275(2) TFEU that regulates the judicial scrutiny of CFSP decisions providing for restrictive measures. It offers the possibility to activate the judicial scrutiny of the CJEU and directly contest the legality of the restrictions imposed by the Councill.

Given the 'direct rights-relevance' of sanctions, these legal acts are highly contested in Luxembourg.[20] Hundreds of applicants have initiated proceeding before the Luxembourg court over the years,[21] primarily through direct actions for annulment before the General Court,[22] in which they have challenged the legality of restrictive measures (manly in the form of individual designations).

In this context, the Court plays a key role in monitoring the foreign policy agenda of the Council. In particular, when applicants invoke interferences with fundamental rights, the CJEU recognises that it must perform a rigorous scrutiny.

Since the landmark case *Kadi*, the Court of Justice has affirmed that it "must ensure the review, in principle the full review", of the lawfulness of all EU acts in the light of fundamental rights.[23] This "full review" is an essential component of the European Union as a community based on the rule of law, which shall guarantee a complete system of legal remedies to review the legality of acts carried out by the EU institutions.[24] Since *Kadi*, the Court has recognised its central role in assessing the legality of targeted sanctions. It has acknowledged its pivotal role in striking a fair balance between the pursuit of CFSP objectives through restrictive measures and the protection of fundamental rights of those targeted.

Over the years, the CJEU has recognised that restrictive measures are *detrimental* to the targets' fundamental rights—as well as their reputation and (professional) legal interests.[25] It has ruled that, "by definition", these measures have consequences

jurisdiction is limited in CFSP matters' (para. 250). This area still remains *lex imperfecta*, where only limited judicial remedies are available.

[20] Eckes (2018, 207).

[21] See annual reports ('*Judicial activity*' and '*The year in review*') and statistics of the CJEU, available at https://curia.europa.eu/jcms/jcms/Jo2_11035/rapports-annuels

[22] Pursuant to art. 263(4) TFEU. The legality of restrictive measures is typically contested through *direct actions for annulment* before the GC in Luxembourg, while the validity and interpretation of other provisions contained in EU sanctions acts may be questioned via *requests for preliminary rulings* which enable a judicial dialogue between national courts and the Court of Justice, as firstly established in case ECJ, case C-72/15, *Rosneft*.

[23] ECJ, joined cases C-402/05 P and C-415/05 P, *Kadi I*, para. 326; and ECJ, joined cases C-584/10 P, C-593/10 P and C-595/10 P, *Kadi II*, para. 97 (emphasis added).

[24] See *Kadi I*, cit., para. 281. See also the *Les Vert* jurisprudence, which provides that the European Union is a community based on the rule of law, inasmuch as neither its Member States nor its institutions can avoid a review of the question whether the measures adopted by them are in conformity with the Treaties.

[25] See, for instance, ECJ, case C-266/15 P, *Central Bank of Iran v Council*, para. 53; GC, case T-14/14, *Islamic Republic of Iran Shipping Lines and Others v Council*, para. 206.

which affect fundamental rights, thereby causing harm to their targets (and even to persons who are in no way responsible for the situation which led to the adoption of the sanctions).[26]

Nevertheless, the Court's caselaw underscores that fundamental rights affected by sanctions es are "not absolute" rights, and their exercise can be subject to (justified) restrictions.[27]

Given the "primordial importance" of the preservation of international peace and security, which are the underlying ultimate objectives of EU sanctions, the Court tends to justify the negative consequences of these measures—as not disproportionate to the ends sought.[28] Hence, the Luxembourg judges usually hold that, given the primary importance of pursuing CFSP objectives, "the disadvantages caused [by sanctions] are not inordinate in relation to the ends sought".[29] In this way, the Luxembourg judges generally favour the importance of the sanctions objectives (and the Council's political agenda)—while individual rights and freedoms are often eclipsed by CFSP objectives.

To the author's knowledge, there is only one exception, namely only one applicant who successfully challenged the legality of his designation on the grounds that EU restrictive measures were *disproportionate* interferences with his fundamental rights. This exception concerns Mr. Yassin Abdullah Kadi and his judicial saga in Luxembourg.[30]

Except for the Kadi ruling, the Luxembourg judges have traditionally refrained from welcoming pleas of proportionality with regard to sanctions interferences with fundamental rights. This demonstrates that the assessment of proportionality tends to tip towards the importance of the foreign policy objectives pursued by the Union.

The *Kiselev* and *RT France* rulings confirm this deferential approach. However, they also represent exceptional instances in which the CJEU had the opportunity to showcase its "full review" of EU sanctions in light of a fundamental right that is not usually invoked to contest the legality (or proportionality) of these CFSP decisions: freedom of expression. In fact, the vast majority of sanctions litigation

---

[26] ECJ, case C-72/15, *Rosneft*, para. 149. The Court further clarifies that the importance of the objectives pursued by restrictive measures 'is such as to justify the possibility that, for certain operators, the consequences may be negative, even significantly so', para. 150.

[27] *Kadi I*, para. 355 (emphasis added). See also, ECJ, case C-348/12 P, *Council v Manufacturing Support & Procurement Kala Naft*, para. 121.

[28] Such as the objective of combating terrorism, see, for instance, GC, case T-327/03, *Al-Aqsa v Council*, para. 130. Or the objective of preventing nuclear proliferation in Iran, see GC, case T-564/12, *Ministry of Energy of Iran v Council*, para. 118; GC, case T-68/14, *Post Bank Iran v Council*, para. 100; GC, case T-63/14, *Iran Insurance v Council*, para. 99.

[29] GC, case T-390/08, *Bank Melli Iran v Council*, para. 71. More recently confirmed by GC, case T-742/22, *Mazepin v Council*, para. 209.

[30] In the landmark *Kadi I* ruling, the Court of Justice ruled that, '*in the circumstances of the case*', the imposition of the restrictive measures in respect of the applicant constitutes an unjustified restriction of his fundamental rights (i.e., his right to property, right of the defence, in particular his right to be heard, and his right to effective judicial review), *Kadi I*, cit., para. 370 (see also para. 353).

concerns the legality of economic restrictions on targeted persons,[31] while, only in a limited number of cases, the CJEU has been required to address the proportionality of restrictive measures in relation to free speech.

Hence, *Kiselev* and *RT France* represent rare examples of how the Luxembourg judges assess the legality of EU sanctions vis-à-vis freedom of expression.

4 Shaping the Boundaries of Free Speech Before the War: The *Kiselev* Case

Over the years, journalists operating in third countries have been added on the EU "blacklist", and subjected to asset freezing measures. However, the outbreak of the war in Ukraine has led to an escalating focus on Russian journalists, as well as publishers, directors of news agencies, hosts of TV shows, due to their propagandists efforts.

Mr. Kiselev is one of these propagandists. He represents one of the first individuals targeted by Russia sanctions, listed by the Council on 21 March 2014 because of his position as Head of the Russian Federal State news agency Rossiya Segodnya (RS). The Council considered him a "central figure of the government propaganda supporting the deployment of Russian forces in Ukraine".[32]

Mr. Kiselev is not an ordinary journalist, as he was appointed by a Presidential Decree to direct a news agency controlled by the Russian Government. Unlike other journalists, his work cannot be separated from his role as Head of RS, which actively support the actions and policies of the Russian Government.

In 2015, Mr. Kiselev initiated proceedings before the GC, bringing an action for annulment against the Council's decision to keep him on the list.[33] He raised several complaints, and invoked an infringement of his right to freedom of expression. On 15 June 2017, the GC rejected all claims and dismisses the action.[34]

Despite the unsuccessful outcome for the applicant, this analysis intends to focus on the proportionality test applied by the GC when assessing the interferences of EU sanctions with Mr. Kiselev's right to freedom of expression.

As starting point, the GC holds that "the right to freedom of expression d*oes not constitute an unfettered prerogative* and may, therefore, be limited, under the conditions laid down in Article 52(1) of the Charter".[35] It further clarifies that a

[31] In this context, applicants usually contest interferes with their rights to property and freedom to conduct business, in relation to asset freezing measures.

[32] Entry n. 26, Annex I, Council Decision 2014/145/CFSP of 17 March 2014 concerning restrictive measures in respect of actions undermining or threatening the territorial integrity, sovereignty and independence of Ukraine, as amended; complemented by Annex I, Council Regulation (EU) No 269/2014 of 17 March 2014.

[33] Action brought on 22 May 2015, GC, case T-262/15, *Kiselev v Council.*

[34] GC, case T-262/15, *Kiselev v Council.*

[35] *Ivi*, para. 69 (emphasis added).

limitation to free speech "must satisfy three conditions".[36] *First*, the limitation must be 'provided for by law'. In other words, the Council must have a legal basis for imposing that limitation. *Secondly*, the limitation in question must be intended to achieve an objective of general interest, recognised as such by the European Union. *Thirdly*, the limitation in question must not be excessive.

Following this *three-step* assessment,[37] the Court acknowledges that the limitation imposed on the applicant's right to free speech was proportionate, and therefore lawful.

As to whether the restrictive measures at issue are *provided for by law* (i.e., "Step 1"), the GC finds that they have clear legal bases in EU law, namely art. 29 TEU and art. 215 TFEU. Moreover, the Court holds that the Council presented sufficient reasons justifying the designation of the applicant. Although Mr. Kiselev contested the Council's allegation that he was actively supporting the Russian Government, the GC clarifies that the concept of "active support" concerns various "forms of support which, by their quantitative or qualitative significance, contribute to the continuance of its actions and policies destabilising Ukraine".[38]

As to whether the restrictive measures at issue pursue *an objective of general interest* (i.e., "Step 2"), recognise as such by the European Union, the GC illustrates that "the Council seeks to exert pressure on the Russian authorities to put an end to their actions and policies destabilising Ukraine", which corresponds to one of the CFSP objectives defined in the Treaties.[39] In particular, the Court finds that targeting individuals who support the actions of the Russian Government meets the objective, referred to in art. 21(2)(c) TEU, of preserving peace, preventing conflicts and strengthening international security.[40] Targeting Mr. Kiselev meets this objective, as codified in the Treaties.

As to whether the restrictive measures at issue are *non-excessive* (i.e., "Step 3"), the GC decided to split the analysis in two (sub)steps.[41]

In the first place, it evaluates whether the limitations in question were *necessary and proportionate* to the aim sought (i.e., "Step 3i"). As regards the *necessity* of the restrictions on the applicant, the Court notes that there are no alternative and less restrictive measures that can be used to achieve the objectives pursued, namely exerting pressure on the Russian decision-makers. As regards the *proportionality*, the Court recognises that the Council "must be allowed a broad discretion" in areas which involve political, economic and social choices, and in which it is called upon to undertake complex assessments.[42] The GC then assesses the factual evidence, and concludes that the Council was entitled to consider that the applicant had engaged in

[36] Ibid.

[37] Those three conditions correspond, in essence, to those laid down by the case-law of the ECtHR.

[38] *Kiselev v Council*, para. 74.

[39] *Ivi*, para. 80.

[40] *Ivi*, para. 81.

[41] *Ivi*, para. 84.

[42] *Ivi*, para. 88. See also ECJ, case C-348/12 P, *Kala Naft v Council*.

propaganda. Interestingly, the Court does not provide a definition of propaganda,[43] and does not address the question of whether the applicant was engaged in propaganda of war. Instead, the GC focuses on his involvement in "*propaganda in support of* the actions and policies of the Russian government [..] by using the means and power available to him as Head of RS, a position which he obtained by virtue of a decree of President Putin himself".[44] The Court further clarifies that other journalists (and other propagandists) are not in a comparable situation to that of the applicant.[45]

In the second place, the GC evaluates whether the limitation at stake impair the essence of free speech (i.e., "Step 3ii"). The Court finds that the restrictive measures imposed on Mr. Kiselev do not impair the substance of his free speech. In particular, being a third country national, restrictive measures do not affect his daily life as a journalist in Russia. The applicant remains free to carry out his professional activity in the Russian media sector, in the country in which he resides and works.[46] Moreover, the Court recalls that restrictive measures are "by nature temporary and reversible".[47] They are kept under constant and regular review (at least every 12 months), therefore, they are not intended to be permanent restrictions on the applicant's rights.

Hence, the GC concludes that the interferences to Mr. Kiselev's free speech were legitimate, as necessary and proportionate restrictions that pursue an objective of general interest, namely exerting pressure on Russia.

The key takeaway from the *Kiselev* case concerns the concept of "active support". In fact, the GC sets an important precedent regarding the Council's authority to target certain journalists for their active contribution to the actions and policies of the Russian Government destabilising Ukraine. The concept of "support" is not limited to material support, but it also covers the support that a journalist (appointed by Presidential Decree) provides to his government.

Today, Mr. Kiselev's name remains on the EU list, after more than 10 years after his initial designation. Numerous other journalists have been (more recently) added to the list for spreading Russian propaganda and promoting the war of aggression against Ukraine (e.g., Margarita Simonyan as editor of the television network RT (Russia Today), Vladimir Solovyev as presenter in the Russia-1 channel and Rossia 24, Alexey Nikolov as director of TV-Novosti, as well as other journalists of the state-owned TV stations, such as Tigran Keosayan, Olga Skabeyeva, Roman Babayan, Anton Krasovsky, etc.).[48] Similarly, propagandists have also been targeted under the EU Global Human Rights Sanction Regime in relation to pro-Wagner Group

---

[43] Miadzvetskaya (2018).

[44] *Kiselev v Council*, para. 117 (emphasis added).

[45] *Ivi*, para. 118.

[46] *Ivi*, para. 123.

[47] *Ivi*, para. 124.

[48] Annex I, Council Decision 2014/145/CFSP; complemented by Annex I, Council Regulation (EU) No 269/2014.

propaganda and disinformation campaigns (e.g., the Foundation for the Defence of National Values (FDNV) and Maxim Shugaley).[49]

However, following the *Kiselev* ruling, no further actions have been brought before the General Court by Russian journalists challenging the legality of their designations. The only exception concerns the challenge to the Council's decision to restrict free speech brought by a media outlet, as discussed in the next section.

5 Shaping the Boundaries of Free Speech During the War: The *RT France* Case

Already on 8 March 2022, seven days after the adoption the media ban, RT France lodged an action for annulment before the General Court.[50] In its action, RT France essentially argued that the Council had no competence to impose such a ban, and violated several provisions of the CFREU, including the applicant's right to free speech.

On 27 July 2022, the GC, sitting in a Grand Chamber formation, delivered its judgement.[51]

The timeline of the case is extremely impressive. It was addressed with an expedited procedure,[52] and the Court delivered a final decision little more than 4 months after the application was filed in Luxembourg.

In the judgement, many questions have been addressed,[53] but this analysis is limited to the balancing test provided by the GC in assessing the legality of the broadcasting ban and the proportionality of the restriction imposed by the Council to free speech.[54]

The Court begins its analysis by holding that the media ban (as a temporary prohibition on broadcasting in the EU) constitutes an "interference" with the applicant's exercise of its right to freedom of expression.[55] Then, the GC recalls that the affected right is not an absolute right and may be subject to limitations, under the conditions laid down in art. 52(1) CFREU.

Differently from *Kiselev*, in this case, the Court finds that "in order to comply with EU law, an interference with freedom of expression must satisfy *four conditions*".[56]

[49] See Annex I, Council Decision (CFSP) 2020/1999 of 7 December 2020 concerning restrictive measures against serious human rights violations and abuses; complemented by Council Regulation (EU) 2020/1998).

[50] By separate document lodged at the Court Registry on the same day, the applicant also submitted an application for interim measures. That application was dismissed by order of 30 March 2022.

[51] GC, case T-125/22, *RT France v Council*.

[52] Pursuant to art. 151(2) of the Rules of Procedure of the General Court.

[53] For a comprehensive commentary on the case see Szép and Wessel (2023) and Lonardo (2023).

[54] *RT France v Council*, paras 116–215.

[55] *Ivi*, para. 143.

[56] *Ivi*, para. 145.

In this way, the GC presents a different methodology in assessing the interference of sanctions to free speech, by introducing a new test (with does not align with the 3-step test established in previous sanctions cases).

First, the limitation must be 'provided for by law'. *Second*, the limitation in question must respect the essence of freedom of expression. *Third*, it must effectively meet an objective of general interest, recognised as such by the European Union. *Fourth*, the limitation in question must be proportionate.

The first step (i.e., "Step 1") does not deviate from a settle caselaw, including the *Kiselev* case.

However, the second step (i.e., "Step 2") constitutes a new development in the field of restrictive measures. Unlike previous caselaw, the essence of the applicant's right (in this case, free speech) becomes an autonomous and preliminary step in the review of fundamental rights interferences.[57] It anticipates any assessment of necessity or proportionality, as well as any balancing of competing interests.

As suggested by legal scholars, 'the concept of the essence of a fundamental right implies that every fundamental right has a "hard nucleus" that guarantees to each and every individual a sphere of liberty that *must always remain free from interference*'.[58] The "hard nucleus" should remain absolute and not be subject to any interferences—or any balancing exercise.[59]

If it is established that the essence of a fundamental right has been compromised, the restriction in question would automatically be incompatible with EU law—without the need for any further assessment. Accordingly, the GC decides to evaluate the essence the applicant's rights as a *preliminary* question. This approach indicates that the Court was mindful of the fact that adopting a different interpretation (or a different test) would have had an impact on the relevance and independence of this condition—as set out in art. 52(1) of the EU Charter. Consequently, the GC prioritises the 'essence requirement' as a second step in its analysis—before any balancing exercise.

The Court finds that the sanction imposed on RT France respect the essence of free speech, as the media ban is intended and designed to be a "temporary and reversible" restriction.[60] More specifically, the GC points out that the maintenance of a media ban on RT France is "conditional on two cumulative criteria" (i.e., first, until the aggression against Ukraine is put to an end and, second, until the Russian Federation, and its associated media outlets, cease to conduct propaganda actions against the Union and its Member States) as set forth in the Preamble of the Council Decision.[61] In the event that one of the cumulative criteria is no longer satisfied, there

[57] In previous cases, such as in *Kiselev*, it represented a sub-condition of the last step (i.e., "Step 3ii") concerning the non-excessive nature of the restriction at stake.

[58] Lenaerts (2019, 781) (emphasis added). See also Brkan (2018) and Tridimas and Gentile (2019).

[59] See Tridimas (2023). The author argues that drawing a distinction between *the essence* and *the periphery* of rights is 'highly elusive'. 'Whilst the distinction is logical, in practice it is extremely difficult to draw. This, in turn, limits the functionality of 'essence' as a judicial tool', p. 200. See also the critical views of Dawson et al. (2019).

[60] *RT France v Council*, para. 154.

[61] *Ivi*, para. 155. See also Recital (10) of Council Decision (CFSP) 2022/351, cit.

would be no further need to maintain the measures at issue. In this way, the Court interprets the Recitals of the contested act as fundamental requirements to limit the interference with the applicant's fundamental rights.

By referring to the explicit criteria for lifting sanctions (also known as de-listing criteria) set forth in the Decision, the Court holds that RT France cannot claim that the restrictive measures are intended to apply "without *a time limit defined in advance* by the Council".[62]

Although, the Luxembourg judges have previously highlighted that EU sanctions are intended to be temporary interferences with fundamental rights,[63] in *RT France*, the GC points out, for the first time, that the contested Decision contains an explicit guarantee to ensure that the media ban is *de jure* a temporary restriction.[64] In the Preamble of that Decision, the Council has inserted explicit lifting criteria. In this way, *RT France* presents a new dynamic relationship between the essence of rights and the temporariness of targeted sanctions, whereby the Courts considers the former to be respected only if the latter is guaranteed by law.[65]

In addition to the element of (*de jure*) temporariness, the media ban is considered to respect the essence of free speech because it does not prevent RT France from conducting every activity inherent in freedom of information and expression. In fact, the applicant is still able to carry out its activities outside the European Union, as well as other broadcasting activities within the Union (such as research and interviews).[66]

Hence, in the second step, the GC highlights the limited scope of the ban both *ratione temporis* and *ratione loci.*

Moving to the third step (i.e., "Step 3"), the Court evaluates whether the restrictions at stake pursue an objective of general interest, recognised as such by the European Union. Interestingly, the GC illustrates the existence of an *internal* as well as an *external* dimension of the general interest pursued by the Union when imposing sanctions against certain Russian media outlets.

On the one hand, it acknowledges that the Council can invoke the protection of "the Union's public order and [internal] security" from the threat of systematic propaganda campaign put in place by the Russian Federation, channelled through media outlets under the permanent direct or indirect control of its leadership.[67] In this way, Russian propaganda and disinformation campaigns are perceived as a threat *inside* the Union, since they aim to destabilize its Member States and neighbouring countries. The GC finds that the adoption of the media ban "satisfies the objective set out in Article 21(2)(a) TEU, namely, to safeguard the Union's values, fundamental

---

[62] *Ibid.* (emphasis added).

[63] Since the *Kadi I* case, cit., para. 358. For instance, asset freezing measures 'are not supposed to deprive the persons concerned of their property', see GC, joined cases T-307/12 and T-408/13, *Mayaleh v Council*, para. 175.

[64] Council Decisions usually do not contain de-listing grounds.

[65] Nonetheless, it is noteworthy that the lifting criteria are contained in the (non-legally binding) Preamble of the Council Decision.

[66] *RT France v Council*, para. 156.

[67] *Ivi*, para. 161.

interests, security and integrity". It has been argued that the Court read the protection of the Union's public order as one of the CFSP objectives set out in art. 21 TEU, "anchoring the justification of the restriction to an EU *constitutional objective*".[68] In fact, the GC illustrates that the restrictive measures at issue "form part of the pursuit by the European Union of the objectives [..] assigned to it in Article 3(1) and (5) TEU",[69] in addition to the more specific CFSP objectives, assigned to the Union in art. 21 TEU. Consequently, the Court seems to emphasise the strong connection between the Union's constitutional values and its global actorness.

On the other hand, the GC highlights that the *external* dimension of the general interest pursued by the Council.

In this context, the Court points to the fact that the media ban forms parts of a broader Union's strategy to respond to the war in Ukraine, with the ultimate aim of exerting maximum pressure on the Russian authorities. From this perspective, the contested ban is consistent with the objectives, referred to in art. 21(2)(c) TEU, of preserving peace, preventing conflicts and strengthening international security. The GC also illustrates that putting an end to the war meets an objective of fundamental general interest for the international community as a whole,[70] as Russia is an aggressor state, violating *erga omnes* obligations.[71]

Lastly, the fourth step (i.e., "Step 4") of the analysis is dedicated to "the proportionate nature of the restrictive measures at issue". This last step presents a peculiar structure, as the GC reviews the legality of the media ban according to *four sub-conditions*: (i) the relevance and the sufficiency of the evidence adduced by the Council; (ii) the appropriate nature of the limitations; (iii) the necessity of the limitations; (iv) the weighing-up of the interests.[72]

As for the evidence adduced by the Council (i.e., "Step 4i"), the GC recalls that restrictive measures must be taken on "a sufficiently solid factual basis". In other words, the Council must adduce sufficient factual evidence and avoid any error of assessment.

The GC begins with emphasising that the applicant is entirely funded by the budget of the Russian Federation. In this way, RT France does not constitute an independent media outlet, but an *emanation of (the Russian) state*.[73] Then, the GC addresses the question on whether the applicant had engaged in propaganda actions targeted at civil society in the European Union and neighbouring countries, supporting the Russia's aggression against Ukraine.

Differently from *Kiselev*, here the Court provides a long list of concrete examples of propaganda as broadcasted by RT France in February 2022.[74] The GC undertakes

---

[68] Lonardo (2023, p. 716).

[69] *RT France v Council*, para. 162.

[70] *Ivi*, para. 166.

[71] Nonetheless, the GC did not address the issue of whether EU sanctions could amount to lawful countermeasures against the Russian Federation.

[72] *RT France v Council*, para. 169.

[73] On the concept of sanction against "emanation of states" see Poli (2024).

[74] *RT France v Council*, paras 172–185.

a meticulous examination of multiple videoclips selected from the applicant's television channel. It demonstrates an unprecedented attention to the narrative and the vocabulary used by RT France.

In the judgement, there are plenty of references to the exact words used by the applicant in relation to the war in Ukraine, such as "This is clearly not an invasion" or "Ukraine [was] a creation of Russia". This narrative and vocabulary, appears similar to, in not identical with, that used by the Russian Government, which refers to a 'special military operation', a 'police operation' or a 'defensive and preventive action of the Russian Federation', rather than to 'a war'.[75] On this point, the GC concludes that the Council had presented "a sufficiently concrete, precise and consistent body of evidence" capable of demonstrating that RT France "actively supported" the destabilising and aggressive policy conducted by the Russian Federation towards Ukraine.[76]

As for the appropriateness of the media ban (i.e., "Step 4ii"), the GC holds that the Council enjoyed broad discretion in determining how to achieve the objectives of general interest pursued by the European Union. In this framework, the Council "could validly take the view that" the media ban was capable of "protecting the Union's public order and security and preserving the integrity of democratic debate within European society, peace and international security".[77]

Next, on the necessity of the media ban (i.e., "Step 4iii"), and whether there were other "less onerous restrictive measures", the GC finds that no alternative measure would have been equally effective in achieving the same result.[78]

Finally, as regards the proportionality *stricto sensu* of the media ban (i.e., "Step 4iv"), the GC rules that "the weighing up of the competing interests shows that the disadvantages entailed in the temporary prohibition on the broadcasting of content are not disproportionate to the objectives pursued, which in turn correspond to objectives of general interest".[79] The importance of the objectives pursued by the Union, in accordance with art. 21(2)(a) and (c) TEU, is deemed to prevail over the possibility that certain operators may suffer negative consequences.

The Court also mentions that what is of the utmost importance for the European Union is of the utmost importance for whole international community. In fact, it points to the fact that other international bodies, since February 2022, have adopted various declarations, decisions, positions and measures having the same objectives as those pursued by the Union (in particular the UN General Assembly and the International Court of Justice).

---

[75] *Ivi*, para. 186.

[76] *Ivi*, para. 188.

[77] *Ivi*, para. 193.

[78] *Ivi*, para. 197. For instance, banning certain content would have been "practically impossible" to implement. While other measures, such as an obligation to "display a banner" or warning, would have been of limited effectiveness.

[79] *Ivi*, para. 201.

In the very last part of the *four-step* test, the GC refers the concept of propaganda in "*the context* of an ongoing war". The Court does not explicitly qualify the propaganda conducted by RT France as a "propaganda of war". However, recalling to the prohibition imposed by Article 20(1) ICCPR, it emphasises that the Covenant refers to *'any' propaganda for war*, as to include "not only incitement to a future war, but also continuous, repeated and concerted statements in support of an ongoing war, contrary to international law, especially where those statements come from a media outlet under the direct or indirect control of the aggressor State".[80]

The GC ultimately does not qualify the applicant's broadcasting activities as "propaganda of war". Nonetheless, it holds that RT France was engaged in "a systematic action of broadcasting selected information" with the specific aim of justifying and supporting the Russia's aggression.[81] The Court seems to create a new parallel between (explicit) "propaganda of war" and "propaganda *in a context of war*". It suggests that disinformation *in times of war* is not tolerated. And ultimately, *the misrepresentation of war* can become propaganda of war—if it entails continuous, repeated and concerted statements in support of an ongoing war.

6 Conclusions

The CJEU plays a key role in shaping the boundaries to free speech in the EU. The *Kiselev* and *RT France* rulings illustrate this.

Although the General Court ultimately reaches the same outcome in 2017 and 2022, rejecting the applicants' claims in both rulings, it presents different methodologies in addressing the legality of sanctions. In *Kiselev*, the Court follows a three-step test and stresses the importance of targeting a Russian journalist who actively supported the destabilising and aggressive policy conducted by his country towards Ukraine. In *RT France*, the Court instead introduces a four-step test, and provides a detailed analysis of the media ban, assessing the validity of the imposed restrictions against a range of legal and factual considerations. It appears that art. 52(1) CFREU inspires a rigorous rights-based analysis and a high standard of review. Notwithstanding the context of an ongoing war, and the high security interests at stake, the reasoning presented in *RT France* appears to be well-founded, (perhaps redundant in some parts, but ultimately) convincing.

Differently from *Kiselev*, the GC in 2022 emphasises the twofold objective pursued by the Council in targeting certain Russian media outlets. It illustrates an *internal* as well as an *external* dimension of the general interest pursued by the Council. It recognises that the Council is entitled to pursue, first, the objective of countering *a hybrid threat* from the Russian Federation (spreading *inside* the Union), and second, the objective of preserving peace and strengthening international security

[80] *Ivi*, para. 210.

[81] *Ivi*, para. 211.

(*outside* the Union).[82] The combination of these two objectives strongly legitimises the imposition of the media ban. In fact, the Court acknowledges that the Council's objective of preventing securities crises (in light of art. 21(2)(c) TEU) can be complemented by an internal (constitutional) objective of protecting the Union's public order and security (in light of art. 21(2)(a) TEU).

When assessing the engagement in propaganda actions, the GC refuses to provide precise definitions or legal guidelines.[83] Both Mr. Kiselev and RT France are considered to be Russia-sponsored and ultimately controlled by the Kremlin. However, only in the 2022 ruling, the Court undertakes a detailed assessment of the factual evidence adduced by the Council, which present concrete examples of disinformation. In this way, the reasoning of the GC appears more convincing and the allegation of "continuous and concerted propaganda" are better substantiated by facts.

Unlike *Kiselev*, the GC in 2022 often relies on the "emergency context", namely that of the outbreak of a war at the borders of the Union,[84] to justify the restrictions imposed on Russian media outlets. In *RT France*, the Court recognises that an exceptional context can justify the adoption of exceptional (restrictive) measures.

Some scholars have expressed critical views on the deferential approach followed by the GC. They argued that upholding the legality media ban may result in the legitimisation of a "paternalistic censorship" in Europe.[85] However, the comparative analysis conducted above intends to indirectly respond to these concerns and shed light on the rigorous "full review" conducted by the GC in *RT France*.

Lastly, one might wonder whether *RT France* marks a turning point in the broader discourse on the legality of targeted sanctions. At the moment, it remains to be seen how far this precedent will be followed and consolidated in the future, but it is certainly one to reflect upon.[86] This author believes that broadcasting ban is a highly unusual restriction—unlikely to be adopted in other contexts or sanctions regimes.[87] Similarly, *RT France* represents a potentially isolated decision which aimed at justifying the legality of an extraordinary interference with free speech in an exceptional context. Consequently, the unique nature of the restriction in question is likely to make *RT France* a *sui generis* decision in times of war.

---

[82] *Ivi*, para. 118.

[83] For instance, in both rulings the GC does not address the question of whether propaganda is covered by art. 11 CFREU.

[84] *RT France v Council*, para. 92.

[85] See Lonardo (2022, 51–52).

[86] Numerous sanctions rulings delivered post *RT France* have adopted the *four-step* test, nonetheless, they do not usually perform the same detailed reasoning as the Gran Chamber. Furthermore, they often refer to caselaw that precedes (and contrasts) with the *RT France* test, such as the *Kiselev* or *Rotenberg* rulings. See, for instance, GC, case T-270/22, *Pumpyanskiy v Council*; GC, case T-272/22, *Pumpyanskaya v Council*; GC, case T-305/22, *Rashnikov v Council*; GC, case T-282/22, *Mazepin v Council*; GC, case T-283/22, *Moshkovich v Council*; GC, case T-289/22, *Shuvalov v Council*. Other rulings still refer to a *three-step* test, such as GC, case T-526/21, *Gutseriev v Council*, para. 158; GC, case T-258/22, *BSW holding v Council*, para. 114.

[87] Poli and Finelli (2023, 33).

References

Baade B (2022) The EU's "Ban" of RT and Sputnik: A lawful measure against propaganda for war. Verfassungsblog

Brkan M (2018) The concept of essence of fundamental rights in the EU legal order: Peeling the onion to its core. Eur Const Law Rev 14:332

Butler G (2017) The coming of age of the court's jurisdiction in the common foreign and security policy. Eur Const Law Rev 13:673

Dawson M, Lynskey O, Muir E (2019) What is the added value of the concept of the "essence" of EU fundamental rights? Ger Law J 20:763

Eckes C (2018) The law and practice of EU sanctions. In: Blockmans S, Koutrakos P (eds) Research handbook on the EU's common foreign and security policy. Edward Elgar Publishing.

Hofer A (2023) The EU's "Massive and Targeted" sanctions in response to Russian aggression, a contradiction in terms. Camb YB Eur Leg Stud 25:19

Lenaerts K (2019) Limits on limitations: The essence of fundamental rights in the EU. Ger Law J 20(779):781

Lendvai GF (2024) Media in war: An overview of the European restrictions on Russian media. European Papers—A J Law Integr 8:1235–1245

Lonardo L (2022), Russia's 2022 War Against Ukraine and the Foreign Policy Reaction of the EU Context, Diplomacy and Law (Springer), at pp. 51–52.

Lonardo L (2023) Censorship in the EU as a result of the war in Ukraine. Case T-125/22 RT France v Council. Eur Law Rev 48:707

Meissner K, Graziani C (2023) The transformation and design of EU restrictive measures against Russia. J Eur Integr 45:377

Poli S, Finelli F (2023) Context specific and structural changes in EU restrictive measures adopted in reaction to Russia's aggression on Ukraine. Eurojus 3:19

Poli S (2024) Judicial challenges to EU restrictive measures by individual state organs, 'emanations of non-EU member states' and third countries: The limits to the Council's discretion. In: Adinolfi G, Lang A, Ragni C (eds) Sanctions by and against international organizations. Interentia

Popović I (2022) The EU Ban of RT and Sputnik: Concerns regarding freedom of expression. EJIL, Talk!

Szép V, Wessel R (2023) Balancing restrictive measures and media freedom: RT France v. Council. Common Mark Law Rev 60

Tridimas T (2023) Wreaking the wrongs: Balancing rights and the public interest the EU way. Colum J Eur L 29(185):400

Tridimas T, Gentile G (2019) The essence of rights: An unreliable boundary? Ger Law J 20:794

Van Elsuwege P, Gremmelprez F (2020) Protecting the rule of law in the EU legal order: A constitutional role for the court of justice. Eur Const Law Rev 16:8

Media Sanctions as a New Regulations Instrument in Europe

Andrei Richter

Abstract Traditionally the basic objective of national or international economic sanctions has been applying political and financial pressure upon the governing élite of the country to persuade it to conform to international law. The nature of the current sanctions or "restrictive measures" introduced by the EU and a number of Western countries towards Russian media companies seems to be far from economic or political pressure on the establishment. They rather aim to protect the population of the state(-s) responsible for their imposition from Kremlin propaganda's distortion of facts and foreign audience manipulation in order to enhance its strategy of destabilisation of the so-called "unfriendly States" and governments. Sanctions are considered as "possible new tools", "preventive measures", as "possible responses" to hybrid threats and "foreign interference". The chapter goes into the issue of whether the media sanctions can serve as a model for the rights-based regulatory and policy solutions to overcome challenges of Russian disinformation and propaganda in the region, and fit the democratic principles of free speech. Following the 2024 European Media Freedom Act, with its focus on quality journalism, the chapter looks into a possibility to qualify the media, designated by the sanctions, as "alien" to the very concept of the politically promoted "quality media".

1 Introduction

This chapter aims to look at the popular new instrument of national and regional media regulation, known as "media sanctions". Despite its popularity, the instrument seems to be quite controversial and under-researched from the freedom of the media stand and not as effective as expected. The controversy from the human rights lies in the similarity of the sanctions with censorship, in the conflict between the imposed restrictions and the standards of media freedom and pluralism, which remain the core elements of the fundamental right to freedom of expression.

A. Richter (✉)
Journalism Department, Comenius University, Bratislava, Slovakia
e-mail: andrey.rikhter@uniba.sk

R. Mastroianni and C. Massa (eds.), *Disinformation in New and Old Media in the XXI Century*, Ius Gentium: Comparative Perspectives on Law and Justice 136,
https://doi.org/10.1007/978-3-032-18830-4_11

In most cases, the media sanctions today present a response to the war that Russia wages in Ukraine. The leading intergovernmental driver to implement this new tool is the European Union, with its numerous policy documents adopted since 2014 in this regard. The national policy leader here is Ukraine which started massively using sanctions against Russian and pro-Russian media since 2015.

The analysis presented in the chapter attempts to clarify the nature, appropriateness and effectiveness of what is called "media sanctions" and suggest alternative ways to protect the public from harmful propaganda disseminated by the Kremlin, while respecting freedom of expression.

2 Opening the Toolbox

For several decades the European Union (EU) standard-setting was generally trailing the Council of Europe in the matters of human rights, including the commitments on freedom of expression. Its own regulation, generally based on the principles of free movement of goods and services across internal borders, focused on the rules for the production and dissemination, through broadcasting (and later: online), of audiovisual programmes.

Things have started to change with the adoption of the Charter of Fundamental Rights of the European Union, solemnly proclaimed on 7 December 2000 by the EU institutions. However, its legal status remained uncertain until the entry into force of the Treaty of Lisbon on 1 December 2009. The Charter stipulates the right of everyone to freedom of expression. The scope of this right is largely copied from the Council of Europe's European Convention on Human Rights (ECHR): "shall include freedom to hold opinions and to receive and impart information and ideas without interference by public authority and regardless of frontiers."[1]

Since 2015, the EU policies on freedom of expression are mostly discussed through the prism of disinformation and propaganda for war. It consistently adopted—and implemented— a number of resolutions, strategic communications, and action plans directed, in particular, to set perimeter barriers for war propaganda and hybrid threats. Taken together, they comprised perhaps the most comprehensive political response among all intergovernmental entities.[2] These documents underline, in particular, that incitement of war "cannot 'hide' behind freedom of expression."[3] To put resistance to disinformation on a firmer foundation the EU Digital Services Act was approved in 2022. It created a "crisis mechanism," which enables the governments, in times of crisis involving threats to national security, to impose "a state of

[1] Compare Article 11 ("Freedom of expression and information") CFREU and Article 10 ECHR.

[2] Richter (2024b, p. 69).

[3] Resolution (EU) of the European Parliament of 23 November 2016 on EU Strategic Communication to Counteract Propaganda Against it by Third Parties, 2016/2030(INI), OJ C 224, paragraph 35.

emergency on social media sites, search engines, and online marketplaces" and "to intervene in platforms" policies."[4]

Modern media sanctions in Europe actually started with an action by the Council of the European Union, following the human rights violations in Belarus after 2010 presidential elections, to restrict entry and assets in the EU of several Belarusian top journalists and functionaries in the state media entities then involved in the state propaganda against the opposition. One of the sanctioned journalists, who worked for a state TV channel, successfully appealed his listing in the General Court of the EU (GCEU), a constituent court of the Court of Justice of the EU which hears actions taken against the EU institutions. In his individual case,[5] the Court annulled the sanction on the basis of an error of assessment, as the Council of the EU had failed to present reliable evidence of the applicant's purported responsibility or influence on the breach of international standards and human rights violations in his professional activity.[6]

Following annexation of Crimea in 2014, broad economic restrictions were introduced towards Russian actors, while just one of the "designated persons" turned out to be a media professional: a popular host on a Kremlin's TV channel and DG of "Rossiya Segodnya" news agency (RS) by name Dmitry Kiselev. Like his Belarusian colleague, he also challenged his status in the GCEU, but lost his case. The Court pointed out that the applicant was not a regular Russian journalist. On the contrary, he engaged in aggressive propaganda "by using the means and power available to him as Head of RS, a position which he obtained by virtue of a decree of President Putin himself", thus explaining proportionality of the restriction *vis-à-vis* the journalists' right to "freely expressing their views on political issues of public interest".[7] In a way, the judgment admitted an exceptional incident of a journalist falling under the sanctions.[8]

In the next few years, though, the EU sanctions against the director of RS were wittily employed by the authorities of Estonia, Latvia and Lithuania as a reason to additionally sanction "non-designated entities" under his command. They targeted the national affiliates of RS in those countries as economic resources controlled by the sanctioned person. Moreover, at that time the national officials were claiming that once Kiselev leaves his powerful position, they would immediately lift the related sanctions.

This expansion of the scope to the RS media outlets was approved by the European Commission.[9] Local journalists working for the RS affiliates were officially warned

---

[4] Meaker (2022).

[5] GC, Case T-693/13, *Mikhalchanka v. Council* (10 May 2016).

[6] See Poli (2016, fn 20).

[7] GC, Case T-262/15, *Kiselev v. Council* (15 June 2017), paras 116–117.

[8] For details, see in this volume Finelli F, "The Role of the European Court of Justice in Shaping the Boundaries of Free Speech: The Legality of EU Restrictive Measures from Kiselev to RT France".

[9] See EU sanctions: Commission adopts opinion to clarify the application of financial sanctions,19 June 2020; Consolidated FAQs on the implementation of Council Regulation No 833/2014 and Council Regulation No 269/2014, 22 June 2022, para G1.10.

against violating the EU sanctions through keeping contractual relations with the end beneficiary of their activity. In a similar manner, the EU sanctions against the "designated" Rossiya Bank, its chair and key shareholders were also applied to the bank's media assets then available in the Baltics.[10]

Still, at that time (2014–2021) restrictions of the Russian media were generally introduced as temporary suspensions of retransmissions in a manner that involved decisions of the national media regulatory authorities (NRAs) or courts based on the instances of harmful "hate speech" or propaganda for war to be banned under the clauses of the national law. Such suspensions followed a process with the gradually increased punishments and broad consultations with the EU institutions and even Russian media entities as appropriate.[11]

Then, following the full-scale invasion of Ukraine by the armed forces of the Russian Federation in February 2022, the EU hugely expanded the general sanctions with the aim to cripple Russia's ability to finance the war and to impose painful costs on the country's political elite responsible or instrumental for this military attack. The sanctions also targeted the state-owned media outlets RT and Sputnik (parts of the same RS holding), and their subsidiaries. Since then, the ban has been further expanded to include a number of other media outlets under state control, as well as media actors found to be responsible for supporting and promoting the military aggression.[12] The sanctions are to be maintained "until the aggression against Ukraine is put to an end, and until the Russian Federation, and its associated media outlets, cease to conduct propaganda actions against the Union and its Member States".[13]

Both the European Commission and the Council of the EU noted then that the sanctions are compatible with the European freedom of expression standards, apparently meaning that the restrictions meet the three-part test. Such a test was first introduced in 1950 by the European Convention on Human Rights. According to it, restrictions on freedom of expression are legitimate only if they, (1) are provided by law; (2) pursue a legitimate aim; and (3) are necessary in a democratic society.[14]

The current European policies on media sanctions can be traced back to the law and policies in one non-EU country, Ukraine. It was Ukraine which has recognized that the path of lawsuits and deliberations at the NRA was time-consuming and ineffective in stopping propaganda and introduced, through the national law "On Sanctions"

[10] Richter (2022, pp. 24–26).

[11] Opinion (ERGA) of the European Regulators Group for Audiovisual Media Services on decision No. 68/1–2 of the Latvian National Electronic Mass Media Council restricting the retransmission of the channel Rossija RTR in the territory of Latvia for twelve months (2021), para 51.

[12] See Pingen (2022); Council Regulation (EU) 2022/350 amending Regulation (EU) No 833/2014 concerning restrictive measures in view of Russia's actions destabilising the situation in Ukraine, OJ 2022 No. L65/1 of 1 March 2022, Annex; and Council Decision (CFSP) 2022/582 of 8 April 2022 amending Decision 2014/145/CFSP concerning restrictive measures in respect of actions undermining or threatening the territorial integrity, sovereignty and independence of Ukraine, Annex.

[13] Council Regulation (2022), cit., para. 10.

[14] ECHR 1950, art.10.

(2014), targeted restrictions of Russian media outlets, popular social media and media actors, beginning from 2015. Once challenged as a violation of freedom of expression, media sanctions were upheld, in 2020, by the national Supreme Court – in view of the "facts of aggression against Ukraine". In 2021, sanctions were introduced against *domestic* TV companies and then again approved by the Supreme Court – as they did not "mean a violation of the right to information" (Richter 2025).[15]

3 Nature and Purposes of Media Sanctions

International law says that the basic objective of any national or international economic sanction has traditionally been "applying political and economic pressure upon the governing elite of the country to persuade them to conform to international law".[16] The imposition of sanctions is therefore supposed to substantially affect the interests of state(s) under the elite. Their essence is in freezing assets, suspension of exports and imports of vital products, an increase of trade tariffs or even in economic blockade.

The essence of media sanctions under this review is rather in suspension of broadcasting activities and banning dissemination online of the content of the foreign audiovisual media. The nature of these international and national sanctions, or "restrictive economic measures", as they are often formally labelled, seems to be far from the goal of "economic or political pressure on the elite". To begin with, stability of the Kremlin does not, to any significant degree, depend on the economic or even political benefits from spreading its word through the media channels among the Western audiences. The restrictions, although possessing economic features (such as freezing bank accounts, ban on economic activities), do not actually affect financial sustainability of the media actors under them (or of their sponsor State), even despite a resulting cut-off from the now protected Western audiences.[17] Neither the sanctions undermine political will and stability of those actors, as demonstrated by their ongoing rhetoric of manipulative nature.

The nature of media sanctions is definitely political in nature, as they have been introduced in response to the political stand of the designated media actors, their support of Russia's annexation of Crimea, the military aggression in Ukraine, and/or, or more generally, the Kremlin policies. Generally, the purpose of the restrictions is to protect the population of the state(s) responsible for their imposition and implementation from "manipulation and distortion of facts in order to enhance [foreign state's] strategy of destabilization".[18] They fit the framework of preventive

[15] Richter (2026).

[16] UN Economic and Social Council, Committee on Economic, Social and Cultural Rights, General Comment No. 8 (1997) The relationship between economic sanctions and respect for economic, social and cultural rights, para 4.

[17] Richter (2024a, 234).

[18] Council Regulation (2022), cit., para. 6.

measures, as they follow the general policy to strengthen public's "ability to counter hybrid threats, including disinformation, ensuring the coordinated and integrated use of existing and possible new tools".[19]

When RT France, one of the sanctioned Russian media outlets, appealed sanctions in the General Court of the EU (GCEU), the judges dismissed the claims by saying that the purpose of the restrictions fell under the objective of a wider objective which outweighs "the negative consequences, however considerable, of these measures for certain [media]" (GCEU 2022, para 202).[20] Unlike the earlier *Kiselev* case, this judgment does not directly apply the three-part test, apparently an appropriate mechanism in all media freedom cases.[21] The judges provided and explained in detail the numerous purposes of the media sanctions, generally falling under the objectives of safeguarding the European values, fundamental interests, security, integrity and public order, as well as maintaining peace and international security.[22]

Protection of peace which depends on the integrity and stability of "the foundations of democratic societies", said the GCEU, was under the threat from propaganda and disinformation of the media channels under the Kremlin's control as part of the ongoing "modern warfare".[23] Protection of peace was also explained, in court, by the fact that media sanctions were indeed an element of a larger set of "restrictive measures", designed to exert "maximum pressure on the Russian authorities so that they bring an end to their actions and policies destabilising Ukraine and to the military aggression against Ukraine".[24]

Another objective is security and public order to be protected "from the systematic international propaganda campaign put in place by the Russian Federation… to destabilise neighbouring countries, the Union and its Member States".[25]

Additionally, the media sanctions were to be understood as being the peaceful response by the EU to a violation of the *erga omnes* obligations imposed by international law, as confirmed by a UN General Assembly resolution on the Russian aggression.[26]

Also, these sanctions are often substantiated by the "hybrid threats" or "hybrid warfare" coming from Russia, or other foreign states. As they are introduced through legal means, it is worth reminding that warfare, in a legal sense, may be labelled as such only if it actually amounts to an armed conflict. Sari warns against the use of these words in a metaphorical way: "being a mighty information warrior on social media is not the same as defending a trench against an advancing enemy formation. The dividing line between participants and bystanders in modern warfare may be

---

[19] *Ivi*, para. 5.

[20] GC, Case T-125/22, *RT France v. Council* (27 July 2022), para. 202.

[21] For details, see in this volume Finelli, The Role of the European Court of Justice in Shaping the Boundaries of Free Speech: The Legality of EU Restrictive Measures from *Kiselev* to *RT France*.

[22] *RT France v. Council*, cit., para. 202.

[23] *Ivi*, para 162.

[24] *Ivi*, para 163.

[25] *Ivi*, para 161.

[26] *Ivi*, para 164.

under pressure, but it has not dissolved into thin air."[27] Thus, at least from the legal point, the warfare in Europe is launched against Ukraine only.

As to the purposes of national sanctions, the main reason of the Russian broadcast licenses' revocation in UK, in 2022, was consideration of non-compliance of the media entities with the due impartiality rules required by broadcasting law. In US, several state-controlled television stations from Russia were first sanctioned as their foreign revenue fed back into the Russian state, and then for covert funding a local company to publish videos on social media platforms with pro-Kremlin messages.

In their turn, the Russian national "countersanctions" towards the Western media outlets, first introduced in 2018 and then reinforced in 2022, target assets and content from "unfriendly countries" (meaning almost all democracies) and/or run by "unwanted organizations" as designated by the Kremlin.

The scope of media sanctions is not limited to the developments in Eastern Europe. In 2024, Israeli parliament passed a law that granted the government the power to temporarily ban the broadcasting of international news outlets in Israel, if they were deemed threatening to national security. This law was used to halt Qatari Al Jazeera's media operations in the country.[28] Al Jazeera broadcasts were also recently suspended in the Democratic Republic of Congo over its coverage of the military conflict in the East of the country.[29]

4 Criticism of the Sanctions

EU and national media sanctions have been criticized by a number of human right organizations, professional associations and academics,[30] as damaging the recognized interpretation of freedom of expression and freedom of the media.[31] The leader of the European Federation of Journalists directly called the media sanctions "an act of censorship". He highlighted that the interference is based on a wrong interpretation of fundamental rights in the EU, noting that "[f]or the first time in modern history, Western European governments are banning media".[32]

Some of the allies of the countries, that had introduced them openly refused to follow such practice. The arguments included constitutional protection of political content, a ban on prior restraint, or other preventive measures, ineffectiveness of sanctions in countering propaganda, and fear of reciprocal measures.

[27] Sari (2025).

[28] Federman (2024).

[29] Ilunga (2025).

[30] Such as Popović (2022), Fathaigh and Voorhoof (2022), and Baade (2022).

[31] See more in Richter (2024b, pp. 75–76).

[32] European Federation of Journalists (2022). Fighting disinformation with censorship is a mistake. March 1.

In response, the use of media sanctions as an instrument of regulation was defended by the GCEU,[33] which determined them as a practically appropriate step: "other measures would not have achieved the same outcome, since some of them—such as the prohibition on the broadcasting of certain content, in the case of a rolling news channel—would have been practically impossible to implement, while others—such as the obligation to display a banner or indeed a warning—would have been of limited effectiveness." The effectiveness of sanctions in relation to their aims have been proven in several research projects that witnessed to the decrease of the audiences of the targeted media.[34] On the other hand, a study done by Oleinik and Paniotto admits the effectiveness of Russian TV as a propaganda tool, at least during the first year of Russia's full-scale invasion.[35] Another study speaks of successful circumvention of the EU media sanctions by the Kremlin propagandists.[36]

Eventually, probably also to avoid criticism from the standpoint of free speech, the European institutions have detached the restrictive media policies from the human rights agenda. That is done with the use of a technical term FIMI, or "foreign interference and manipulation of information", explaining it as "a mostly non-illegal pattern of behavior that threatens or has the potential to negatively impact values, procedures and political processes. Such activity is manipulative in character, conducted in an intentional and coordinated manner, by state or non-state actors, including their proxies inside and outside of their own territory."[37]

5 Exceptions for "Alien" Voices

The sanctioned media easily fall under the category of "alien media". Adjective "alien" is used here to describe a broad category of "alien voices" as it allows to bring together several meanings. As provided by the Merriam-Webster Dictionary, alien voices can be "foreign" voices ("relating, belonging, or owing allegiance to another country or government") or "non-human" voices ("coming from another world", extra-terrestrial), as well as "transplanted", "immaterial" voices ("differing in nature or character typically to the point of incompatibility").[38]

In the context of the question, as to whether media sanctions contradict the right of *everyone* to free expression in Europe, it is worthwhile to compare two norms of the European Convention on Human Rights. Its well-rehearsed Article 10 provides for freedom of expression in the sense of the right of everyone that includes, in particular,

---

33 *RT France v. Council*, cit., para 197.

34 See DRFLab (2020), InMind (2024), and Minchenko (2018).

35 Oleinik and Paniotto (2024).

36 See Pamment (2023) and Scott (2022).

37 EEAS (European External Action Service) (2024) 2nd EEAS Report on Foreign Information Manipulation and Interference Threats: A Framework for Networked Defence. EEAS: Brussels, p. 4.

38 See "Alien" (adjective). In: Merriam-Webster Dictionary (2025).

"freedom to hold opinions and to receive and impart information and ideas without interference by public authority and regardless of frontiers".[39]

On the other hand, there is little-noticed Article 16 (ECHR 1950), on restrictions on political activity of aliens in the states that have aligned with the ECHR. It says, that nothing in Article 10 "shall be regarded as preventing the High Contracting Parties from imposing restrictions on the political activity of aliens" meaning that the Governments may impose limitations on the speech, especially political speech and speech "regardless of frontiers", of the aliens. Moreover, the way Article 16 is formulated does not allow to claim violation of the right to non-discrimination on any ground, including national origin or political opinion.[40]

True, Ziegler points that over the decades "Article 16 has fallen into disuetude" and is an anachronism today as it was drafted at a time, when it was considered legitimate to restrict political activities of aliens "apt to disrupt a state's external relations" or elections.[41] He also cites *Cox v Turkey*, wherein the ECtHR provided that that the restrictions of Article 16 on freedom of expression should be narrowly construed "as only capable of authorizing restrictions on 'activities' that directly affect the political process".[42] As we can see from the media sanctions, it is exactly interference in the democratic processes in Europe, and undermining international peace by the "alien" Russian voices that brought them about.

On the other hand, some argue that if the media entities "are affiliated with a foreign state, they cannot invoke fundamental rights under the EU Charter or the European Convention on Human Rights".[43] This might be right, but no one prevents Russian aliens or their proxies from claiming the same right to free expression under the International Covenant on Civil and Political Rights.[44]

What is obvious is that the most recent EU acts on media matters, even though they might look to regulate issues far away from the media sanctions, are in fact designed to curb foreign speech entering the European borders.

The recently adopted European Media Freedom Act (EMFA) naturally speaks of the need to protect media freedom and media pluralism. "At the same time", says the EMFA, it is necessary to keep in mind the need to safeguard "the values that are common to the Union and to its Member States, such as the protection of fundamental rights".[45] One of the three challenges to "the good functioning of the internal market for media services", continues its Preamble, comes from providers from outside the EU, "that systematically engage in disinformation or information manipulation and interference, and use the internal market freedoms for abusive

[39] ECHR (1950).

[40] Ibid.

[41] Ziegler (2021, pp. 174, 178).

[42] ECtHR, *Cox v. Turkey*, 2933/03, 20 May 2010, para 31.

[43] Helberger and Schulz (2022).

[44] International Covenant on Civil and Political Rights (ICCPR) (1966), art. 19.

[45] Regulation (EU) 2024/1083 of the European Parliament and of the Council of 11 April 2024 establishing a common framework for media services in the internal market and amending Directive 2010/13/EU. (European Media Freedom Act, EMFA), PE/4/2024/REV/1, OJ L., Preamble.

purposes, thus thwarting the proper functioning of market dynamics." The EMFA additionally points to the threat of the global online platforms (from outside the control by the EU), which are acting as gateways to media content, with business models that tend to "amplify polarising content and disinformation." Thus, threats of harmful propaganda through the media, with its instruments of disinformation and manipulation of the public, even though "propaganda" is not mentioned in the Regulation, become one of the key purposes of the EMFA. Its relevancy as one of the tools to counter "foreign interference and manipulation of information" was confirmed by the EU External Action, which directly placed the EMFA as part of the EU counter-FIMI toolbox under the rubric of "disruption and regulation of propaganda" (EEAS 2024, 13).[46]

Another recent EU regulation, on transparency and targeting of political advertising (TTPA), applied from October 2025, clearly has in its focus *foreign* actors, when deliberating on its *raison d'être*. The threats include a possible failure of EU citizens to recognise political advertisements and to exercise their democratic rights in an informed manner:

> An increase in the sophistication of disinformation, diversification of actors, the fast evolution of new technologies and intensified spread of information manipulation and interference in our democratic electoral and regulatory processes are important challenges for the Union and for the Member States. Political advertising can be a vector of disinformation, in particular where the advertising does not disclose its political nature, comes from sponsors outside of the Union or is subject to targeting techniques or ad-delivery techniques.[47]

If this is not about FIMI, then what would be FIMI?

In the times of deep fakes, AI and other mechanisms that generate and automatically disseminate disinformation and propaganda online, e.g. through social networks,[48] it is also worth to re-examine whether freedom of expression also belongs to the machine-generated speech. Theoretical justifications for this *human* right are aplenty, making researchers agree that all of them, with their strengths and weaknesses, need to be cumulatively taken into account.[49] The principal justifications for free speech, though, have always been that it is "necessary for the existence of a genuine democracy", crucial for human self-fulfilment, and important for the discovery or confirmation of "truth".[50]

Are algorithmic machine voices protected under the freedom of expression and freedom of the media realm? It seems to be clear that freedom of expression is linked with and is an offspring of freedom of opinion, or freedom of thought. It is clear that the machines, despite the fact that they can produce speech, have no capacity to think or possess an independent opinion.

---

46 EEAS (European External Action Service) (2024), cit., p. 13.

47 Regulation (EU) 2024/900 of the European Parliament and of the Council of 13 March 2024 on the transparency and targeting of political advertising (Transparency and targeting of political advertising, TTPA), PE/90/2023/REV/1, OJ L., Recital 4.

48 EUvsDisinfo (2025).

49 McGonagle (2015, pp. 3–4).

50 Callamard and Parmar (2021, p. 257).

Whether fakes are necessary for the democracy may be a controversial issue, but if we look at the democracy as the "rule by the people", then democracy depends on the free "speech by the people" (as opposite to speech generated by the machines). Human self-fulfilment is also inappropriate argument to protect freedom of non-human expression. And finally, machine-facilitated speech which aims to manipulate the facts and algorithmic dissemination of lies are not justifiable from the *human* rights perspective. Thus, it is legitimate to label machine-generated speech, such as speech produced with ChatGPT and/or disseminated through algorithms as "alien speech", which may be subject of restrictions by the people.

Austin and Levy approached this question through discussing the "speech certainty principle", described by them as "the simple idea that if you don't know what you're saying when you say it, then whatever you said isn't your 'speech' within the meaning of the First Amendment [of the US Constitution]".[51] In any medium, the speaker always knew what she said when she said it. Over centuries, they say, this elemental feature of speech therefore revealed itself as a cornerstone of the US jurisprudence on freedom of the press protection.

6 The EMFA as an Instrument to Restrict Foreign Propaganda

The European Media Freedom Act, that became directly enforced in the EU in 2025, has already brought a lot of excitement among the professionals, experts and the general public. Those engaged in the issues of safety of the media workers note that it obliges national governments to respect the protection of confidential journalistic sources and to limit the use of spyware against journalists. Civil society welcomes its measures to enforce independent and sustainable functioning of the public service media and to safeguard media against unjustified content removal by "very large online platforms" (VLOPs). Access to information activists note the general transparency requirements as to the media outlets ownership and funding, as well as in state advertising for the media service providers and online platforms. Economists positively assess its potential impact on media market concentrations and transparency in audience measurement.

The EMFA professes the future of media freedom in the provision of "quality media services", "quality and plurality of information", "quality impartial information" and the like.[52] Moreover, the key to the new information policy of the EU, that it symbolizes, lies in enabling "recipients of media services" access quality media services.[53]

Thus, the virtue of the EMFA is that, first and foremost, it is a logical next step to counter disinformation and propaganda in the region, making it a major

---

[51] Austin and Levy (2025, p. 85).

[52] EMFA (2024).

[53] EMFA (2024), para 14.

media freedom policy direction for the European institutions. It finetunes the recently introduced policy instruments and procedures, and puts a firmer legal basis for the sanctions on alien propaganda media in the future.

6.1 *Rogue v Quality Media*

The EMFA draws two poles in the media regulation landscape. The negative pole presents the "rogue media", which apparently includes media service providers that are state-controlled, be it financially or editorially, by "certain third countries" and create tensions in the application of the free media rules within the EU.[54]

The positive pole is the "quality media" or "trustworthy media content". Quality media services are presented in the EMFA Preamble as an antidote against disinformation and foreign information manipulation and interference. An effective guarantee of the quality and professionalism of media services is the robust, inclusive and widely accepted media self-regulation. Access to quality services, says the Regulation, should be ensured, such as by preventing attempts to silence journalists, through threats and harassment, censorship and cancelling of dissenting opinions. An opposite could limit the free flow of information into the public sphere by reducing the quality and plurality of information.[55]

The logic of the EMFA is that it simply facilitates a well-functioning market, where

> recipients of media services should be able to access quality media services which have been produced by journalists in an independent manner and in line with ethical and journalistic standards and which, therefore, provide information which is trustworthy and respectful of fundamental rights. That is particularly relevant for news and current affairs content, which comprises a wide category of content of political, societal or cultural interest at local, national or international level.[56]

Thus, media freedom is seemingly guaranteed to the public once the media count as quality ones. Such "quality services", irrespective of whether provided by journalists or other media actors, apparently should seek to supply the public with accurate and reliable information that complies with the principles of fairness, independence and transparency, public accountability and humanity.

The very notion of "quality media services" apparently derives from the concept of "quality journalism" as developed and put forward as a policy priority by the Council of Europe, days after the start of the Russian aggression in Ukraine.[57]

---

[54] EMFA (2024).

[55] Ibid.

[56] EMFA (2024), para 14.

[57] Recommendation CM/Rec(2022)4 of the Committee of Ministers to member States on promoting a favourable environment for quality journalism in the digital age. (Adopted by the Committee of Ministers on 17 March 2022 at the 1429th meeting of the Ministers' Deputies).

6.2 New Role of the NRAs

The national regulatory media authorities or bodies (NRAs) are clearly tasked by the EMFA to stand on guard in view of the risk of prejudice to public security that comes from the media "in the third countries", as the latter can be involved in "systematic international campaigns of foreign information manipulation and interference with a view to destabilising the Union as a whole or particular Member States."[58] The fault of "destabilising the Union or particular Member States" in the EMFA is similar with that of "propaganda actions against the Union and its Member States" which was brought up by the EU as a reason for its broad media sanctions.[59] In this regard, cooperation of the NRAs across Europe is to be strengthened beyond the current framework of the Audiovisual Media Services Directive (AVMSD) and shall be primarily based on the EMFA to ensure the effectiveness and coordination of the national measures to be adopted in accordance with the European law.

The Preamble clearly points out that the AVMSD currently fails to "provide for a structured cooperation framework for national regulatory authorities or bodies", in particular to resolve cross-border cases. The new challenges in the media environment demand entrusting NRAs with "new tasks". Hence comes the need to overcome "the divergence and lack of coordination between Member States' national measures and procedures". Again, it is cooperation between NRAs, says the EMFA, that shall be "key to ensuring that media market players…, that systematically engage in polarisation or information manipulation and interference, do not benefit from the scale of the internal market for media services." By EMFA, the NRAs will now obtain powers that go beyond the scope of the AVMSD, that used to be the main media regulatory instrument in the EU.[60]

6.3 From ERGA to the Board

Some of the criticism of the EU 2022 media sanctions put into doubt the appropriateness of the European Council to regulate the media sector, as it is "usually left to the Member States".[61] Therefore, the European Media Freedom Act included provisions tasking the forthcoming European Board for Media Services with a number of duties, such as to draft and implement uniform rules and opinions in relation to the restrictions on the content of "rogue" media services from outside of the EU "that target or reach audiences in the Union, where such media services prejudice or present a serious and grave risk of prejudice to public security".[62]

---

[58] EMFA (2024), para 47.

[59] Council Regulation (2022), cit.

[60] EMFA (2024).

[61] Helberger and Schulz (2022).

[62] EMFA (2024), art. 13.

This independent European Board for Media Services (note that it is on "media services", not on "media freedom") is established in Brussels in February 2025 and composed of official representatives from the NRAs of the Member States and assisted by the European Commission staff. It replaces the European Regulators Group for Audiovisual Media Services (ERGA), another institution, also composed of such representatives and established, in 2014, by a Decision of the European Commission. In 2021, ERGA was asked (but not tasked) by the Commission to monitor the effectiveness of the Code of Practice in the context of online disinformation about COVID-19. Since then, ERGA's work on disinformation focused, in particular on monitoring political advertising and other issues relating to the European Democracy Action Plan, such as compliance by the signatories of the EU Code of Practice on Disinformation. ERGA also monitors the evolution of NRAs' competencies in countering disinformation.

The new board will have a mandate, much broader than that of ERGA, to include, among other things, the task to promote an effective and consistent framework for countering non-EU speech online and in broadcasting by coordinating national measures to check foreign media that pose risks.[63]

To counter public security threats from propaganda originating from or established outside of the Union and targeting audiences in the EU, the board is tasked to:

- Develop the criteria regarding media service providers established or originating from outside of the EU. Elements to be covered in such a list of criteria could concern, *inter alia,* ownership, management, financing structures, editorial independence from third countries or adherence to co-regulatory or self-regulatory mechanisms governing editorial standards in one or more Member States. Those criteria will be considered by the Commission when drafting the guidelines that should contribute to minimising the risk of the media service providers declaring that they meet certain requirements while engaging in FIMI. "Recognised civil society organisations", fact-checkers and/or co-regulatory or self-regulatory bodies will participate in their drafting.
- Issue opinions with respect to national measures concerning media services from outside the EU, in consultation with the Commission. The objective should be to improve coordination of the NRAs on restrictions of such media services, so that the NRAs take into account the opinions of the Board when considering relevant restrictions.
- Coordinate restrictions by the NRAs of the FIMI content when it presents a serious and grave risk of prejudice to public security.
- Organise a structured dialogue between providers of VLOPS, representatives of media service providers and representatives of civil society to foster access to quality media on VLOPs, discuss experience and best practices related to the application of the relevant provisions of the EMFA, and to monitor adherence to self-regulatory initiatives which aim at protecting users from harmful content.

[63] *Ivi*, art. 17.

This activity will be based on the experience of ERGA in monitoring compliance with the Code of Practice on Disinformation.

7 Conclusion

Media sanctions have become a popular instrument to restrict the media that carry harmful propaganda. Just recently, the European Parliament adopted a resolution where it called for the EU to expand even further its sanctions against Russian media outlets conducting disinformation and information manipulation campaigns supporting and justifying Russia's war of aggression against Ukraine and calls on the Member States to swiftly and thoroughly implement these sanctions and to dedicate sufficient resources to effectively addressing this hybrid warfare.[64]

Such sanctions are designed to protect audiences from continuous and concerted manipulation, which poses significant and direct threat to the public order and security. Having tested a variety of less intrusive instruments, it was Ukraine that provided a workable model of counteracting alien propaganda and disinformation through sanctions. This model has been adopted, with modifications, by other Eastern European countries, as well as by the EU at large.

Without much ado, a new legal framework is being placed in Europe to address the current challenges of alien propaganda online and in broadcasting. Although the EMFA supposedly "does not affect the freedom of expression and information guaranteed to individuals",[65] in fact it can be viewed as narrowing the spectrum of guaranteed freedom of expression and freedom of information primarily to the "quality information".

Taken together, sanctions in their current form, present a dangerous freedom of expression precedent. Yes, they were rationally adopted in the EU with the start of the full-scale military aggression in Europe, but some countries adopted them even ahead of 2022, while others follow the example, independent of existence of an emergency in the region. Yes, they are presented as temporary measures, but after four years of the bloodbath, neither the end of the war is in sight, nor change of the nature of the sanctioned media thus turning the sanctions into a "perpetual measure".[66] Yes, they are so far adopted against the foreign media originating in Russia (well, with some echo voices from Belarus), but there are examples in Europe (such as in Moldova or Ukraine), when sanctioned are domestic media with apparently similar rhetoric as the Russian one. Yes, the sanctions are explained by the ongoing "hybrid warfare", but this war (with its obligatory element of armed attacks) is waged so far in Ukraine only, thus making this argument obsolete elsewhere. Yes, the sanctions are directed against the Kremlin "rogue media", but other subjects, such as those in Europe wishing to learn on events in Russia from Moscow voices, are also affected. Yes, we talk about

---

[64] Resolution (EU) of the European Parliament of 23 January 2025 on Russia's disinformation and historical falsification to justify its war of aggression against Ukraine, para 9.

[65] EMFA (2024), para 15.

[66] Helberger and Schulz (2022).

mostly (but not only) propaganda voices, but the sanctions collaterally include various content, not just conflict-related propaganda. Moreover, the "reciprocal" sanctions introduced by the Kremlin have effectively blocked access of Russian population to the voices from the Western media.

The nature of the current media sanctions is a reflection of another media regulation instrument which is a prior restraint, or censorship. Any existing definition of censorship, if analysed, finds many similarities with the current media sanctions. Such a ban is extra-judicial, introduced directly by the executive (even the European Council is a body of governmental ministers from the EU member states). It prevents future communication entirely without advance approval of the governmental body. The enforcement of the ban to publish (communicate, disseminate, retransmit, make available online) comes, in particular, through a refusal by the service providers to avail communication channels (such as satellites) or online services, under the threat of being found guilty of contempt of the executive decision and punished by taking away their licenses, permits, or other penalty. The ban involves administrative (or sometimes criminal) legislative restraints which make unlawful communication unless there has been previous compliance with specific conditions imposed by the legislative act, including change of political views by the media actor. Media sanctions are bold and broad, which in practice means that there is no need for an apparatus of censors reviewing each piece of content prior to its communication—they all are banned until the executive decides that the situation changes. Even punishment for the violations comes without a review of the content published.[67]

Shifting the burden of imposing sanctions from the European Council to the realm of the European Board for Media Services might be a smart move away from the curse of being accused of censorship. It will happen once the Board becomes an independent expert body that will not only organise relevant cooperation of the NRAs, but will develop the exact and reasonable grounds for necessary restrictions. That will happen if the NRAs, which are now required by the EMFA to be truly independent and transparent, are able to delegate respected experts (and not bureaucrats) to the Board.

The key criteria for the vetted "good" media services now seems to be compliance with the professional standards and national self-regulatory mechanisms, a feature apparently totally missing with the "rogue" propaganda media. Another important element that will be systematically considered is media outlets' distance from the government, the further the better. This is especially important, when their country of origin is an internationally-recognised aggressor, where the media are state-controlled, lack independent self-regulation and recognized journalistic standards.[68]

The EMFA envisions the European Board for Media Services to also serve as a watchdog against an use of the restrictions by the national authorities against opposition media services under the pretext of disinformation, or "fake news." That

---

[67] See Emerson (1955).

[68] See in detail, Richter and Smulders (2025).

will definitely be a service in demand in some Central European countries, but also to understand the differences between the pretext and the reason for the sanctions.

Regulation of disinformation is appropriate if performed according to the general principles established for the regulation of information, such as the three-part test. The EMFA lays some grounds for re-evaluation of the current often knee-jerk practice with a view of clearer principles to be interpreted by the independent Board. Time will show, if the new European institution will be up to its task.

References

Austin M, Levy M (2025) Speech certainty: algorithmic speech and the limits of the first amendment. Stanf Law Rev 77:11–85

Baade B (2022) The EU's "Ban" of RT and Sputnik: a lawful measure against propaganda for war. Verfassungsblog: On Matters Constitutional, Mar 8. https://doi.org/10.17176/20220308-121232-0

Cabrera Blázquez FJ (2022) The implementation of EU sanctions against RT and Sputnik. European Audiovisual Observatory, Strasbourg

Callamard A, Parmar S (2021) Norms in conflict: The restraints on the emergence of a global free speech norm. In: Bollinger LC, Callamard A (eds) Regardless of frontiers: Global Freedom of Expression in a Troubled World, Columbia University Press, New York, pp 255–274

DRFLab (2020) Baltnews Latvia's audience size decreased after domain suspension. Medium Policy. Jan 22

Emerson TI (1955) The doctrine of prior restraint. Law & Contemp Probs 20:648–671

EUvsDisinfo (2025) How Russia uses AI to dehumanize Ukrainians. Feb 7

Fathaigh RÓ, Voorhoof D (2022) Freedom of expression and the EU's Ban of Russia today: A dangerous Rubicon crossed. Communications Law 27(4):186–193

Federman J (2024) Israel clears way to expel Al Jazeera. Channel says Netanyahu's incitement claim is a dangerous lie. AP, Apr 2

Finelli F, The Role of the European Court of Justice in Shaping the Boundaries of Free Speech: The Legality of EU Restrictive Measures from *Kiselev* to *RT France*. In this volume.

Helberger N, Schulz W (2022) Understandable, but still wrong: How freedom of communication suffers in the zeal for sanctions. LSE blog, June 10

Ilunga P (2025) DRC suspends Al Jazeera for broadcasting interview with M23 leader. The East African, Jan 14

InMind (2024) Ukrainian media, use and trust in 2024. Internews Ukraine, Kyiv, Nov

McGonagle T (2015) The development of freedom of expression and information within the UN: leaps and bounds or fits and starts? In: McGonagle T, Donders Y (eds.) The United Nations and freedom of expression and information: critical perspectives. Cambridge University Press, pp. 1–51. https://doi.org/10.1017/CBO9781316018552.002

Meaker M (2022) Ukraine war prompts Europe's New emergency rules for the Internet. Wired, Apr 26

Minchenko O (2018) Vzhe 12 milyoniv ukrayintsiv korystuyutsya Facebook (As many as 12 million Ukrainians use Facebook). Watch, Aug 8

Oleinik A, Paniotto V (2024) Propaganda channels and their comparative effectiveness: The case of Russia's war in Ukraine. Int Sociol 39(3):217–240. https://doi.org/10.1177/02685809241232637

Pamment J (2023) How the Kremlin circumvented EU sanctions on Russian state media in the first weeks of the illegal invasion of Ukraine. Place Brand Public Diplomacy. 19:200–205. https://doi.org/10.1057/s41254-022-00275-1

Pingen A (2022) Council sanctions against Russia and Belarus. Eucrim, Aug 11
Poli S (2016) Protecting Human Rights in the European Union's External Relations: Setting the Scene. CLEER Papers 5
Popović I (2022) The EU Ban of RT and Sputnik: Concerns regarding freedom of expression. EJIL:Talk! Blog of the Eur J Int Law, Mar 30
Richter A (2022) Sanction law against Russian and Belarusian audiovisual media. European Audiovisual Observatory, Strasbourg
Richter A (2023) For Propaganda Without Disinformation: Draft EU Regulation on Political Advertising. EJIL:Talk! Blog of the Eur J Int Law, Feb 24
Richter A (2024a) Russia. In: Trail L (ed) Vibrant information barometer. IREX, Washington, pp 228–244
Richter A (2024b) International legal responses to "propaganda for war" in modern warfare. J Int'l Media & Ent Law 10(1):54–80
Richter A (2025) "Ukraine". In: Charron A, Portela C, Sossai M (eds) Elgar Encyclopedia on international sanctions, pp 47–49. https://doi.org/10.4337/9781035339532.00021
Richter A, Smulders A (2026) Legitimacy of sanctions against media as a counteraction to alien propaganda. In: Senftleben M, Irion K, McGonagle T, Poort J (eds) The Cambridge handbook of European media law and policy. Cambridge University Press, Cambridge, pp 102–120 (in press)
Sari A (2025) Metaphors, rules and war: Making sense of Hybrid Threats and grey zone conflict. EJIL:Talk! Blog of the Eur J Int Law, Jan 31
Scott M (2022) Russian state media flouts European sanctions. Politico, July 20
Ziegler R (2021) Political rights of aliens: Articles 10, 11 and 16 of the ECHR and Article 3 of Additional Protocol I. In: Moya D & Milios G (eds) Aliens before the European Court of human rights: Ensuring minimum standards of human rights protection. Brill, Leiden, pp 172–190

The International Regulation of the Propaganda for War: Some Implications Concerning the Armed Conflict Between the Russian Federation and Ukraine

Claudio Di Turi

Abstract In this paper, I propose to investigate some issues regarding the propaganda for war which has contributed decisively to the aggression of the Russian Federation against Ukraine. In order to demonstrate this thesis, an analysis of the most important international rules prohibiting propaganda for war will be introduced. Thus, a distinction will be made between conventional and soft law rules. The analysis will not neglect the most recent jurisprudence (see the EU General Court judgment *RT France v. Council of the European Union*, 2022), and the work of some monitoring body of the United Nations, such as the United Nations Committee of the Human Rights (the HR Committee) and the United Nations Special Rapporteur on the promotion and protection of freedom of opinion and expression. Once the definition of propaganda for war provided for, the case for the applicability of the relevant international rules to the ongoing international armed conflict between Russia and Ukraine will be discussed. Some final remarks on the possible international criminal responsibility of President Putin will also be presented.

This chapter extensively modifies and updates the essay 'La propaganda in favore della guerra nel diritto internazionale e la sua rilevanza alla luce del conflitto armato russo-ucraino' published on Diritto pubblico comparato ed europeo, 2, 2024.

C. Di Turi (✉)
Department of Business and Legal Sciences, University of Calabria, Rende, Italy
e-mail: claudio.dituri@unical.it

R. Mastroianni and C. Massa (eds.), *Disinformation in New and Old Media in the XXI Century*, Ius Gentium: Comparative Perspectives on Law and Justice 136,
https://doi.org/10.1007/978-3-032-18830-4_12

1 Introduction

The analysis purports to develop some arguments concerning the legal definition, the use and the consequences of the propaganda for war, which has been resorted to before and during the international armed conflict between Russia and Ukraine following the aggression of its territory on February 2022.[1]

As mentioned before, it seems firstly necessary to provide a detailed description of the legal international regulation of the propaganda for war, as it emerges from the most important rules aimed at its discipline. From a methodological point of view, I will dwell upon some conventional rules only, laid down in a multilateral Convention and in a universal treaty. The conventional rules which I will recall here are the Convention on the Use of Broadcasting in Cause of Peace concluded in 1936 under the auspices of the League of the Nations (hereinafter: the 1936 Convention),[2] and the 1966 International Covenant on Civil and Political rights (the ICCPR). As for the rules contained in the so-called soft law, I will focus on some of the most important resolutions adopted by United Nations General Assembly.

The presentation of these rules is also intended to scrutinize whether and to what extent they may be applicable to the ongoing international conflict between Russia and Ukraine, in order to ascertain whether some form of responsibility for international wrongful act can be attributed to the State author of the wrong. This argument will stand on the assumption of the Russia's international responsibility for international wrongful act, and references will then be made to the Draft Articles on the International Responsibility of the State for wrongful acts drawn up by the International Law Commission (the ILC Project),[3] in order to verify whether this legal tool is fit to be applicable. While non-binding, the ILC Project is largely reproductive of customary law, and it may also pave the way to a model which allows third States not directly injured by the wrong to invoke the international responsibility of Russia. The presentation of the international rules concerning propaganda for war, as well as the consequences of their infringement does not exhaust the discussion on the topic. On the one hand, we will wonder what are the differences between propaganda for war and the so-called "hate speech"; and, on the other hand, if international rules as it stands today leaves room for President Putin international criminal responsibility for the commission of acts of propaganda for war committed prior or during the conflict.

---

[1] In its Resolution A/RES/ES-11/1 (2022), United Nations General Assembly uses the word "aggression" to ask Russia to immediately cease its use of force against Ukraine and to refrain from any further unlawful threat or use of it. General Assembly intervened following a call for an emergency special session (S/RES/2623, 2022) under a "Uniting for Peace" resolution. Due to its procedural nature, the resolution could be adopted, thus avoiding Russian veto at the UN Security Council.

[2] *UNTS*, CLXXXVI, 1938, n. 4301–4327, 301.

[3] Yearbook of the International Law Commission, 2001, vol. II (Part Two).

2 The International Convention Concerning the Use of Broadcasting in the Cause of Peace and Its Applicability to the Ongoing Armed Conflict Between Russian Federation and Ukraine: What Implications?

The 1936 Convention is a multilateral treaty signed under the auspices of the League of Nations in a period of strong international tensions immediately before the outbreak of the Second World War, even if the then most important totalitarians countries (Germany, Japan, Italy, Soviet Union) did not adhere to it.[4] Soviet Union became a party to it in 1983 only.

Despite the scarce representativeness in numerical terms of its membership, the provisions of this instrument might be useful for assessing the international lawfulness of certain conducts carried out by organs of the Russian information system, and possibly attributable to the Russian Federation pursuant to the rules contained in the ILC Project.

In particular, the 1936 Convention sets up a list of obligations for contracting Parties, the most important of which enjoin them to prohibit and to stop any transmission which is of such a character as to incite the population of any territory to acts incompatible with the internal order or the security of a territory of a High Contracting Party (art. 1), which incite to war or to acts likely to lead thereto (art. 2), or to harm good international understanding (art. 3). In addition, the Convention commits the parties to insert, in contracts for the concession of transmission services to private companies, clauses inspired by the principles laid down articles 1–3 aimed at inspiring the conduct of these entities (art. 6).

Should a dispute arise regarding the interpretation or application of the 1936 Convention, Parties may have recourse to diplomatic channels, arbitration or judicial settlement. Failing agreement concerning the choice of the tribunal, they shall submit the dispute, at the request of one of them, to the Permanent Court of International Justice (art. 7). Russia has entered a reservation on art. 7 of the 1936 Convention. Accordingly, Russia declares that for the submission of a dispute regarding the interpretation or the application of the Convention, the agreement of all Parties to the dispute shall be essential in every separate case.

The 1936 Convention, still in force, raises some questions: is it applicable to the armed conflict between Russia and Ukraine? If so, do some Russian conducts fall into its scope of application in order to establish Russia's international responsibility for breaching it? Should Russia be held responsible for its breach, can Ukraine claim for reparation? What is the role of other States parties to the Convention with regard to Russian conduct?

---

[4] In addition, the United States, which was not a member of the League of Nations, did not participate in the Intergovernmental Conference; and several states such as France, the United Kingdom, Australia and the Netherlands denounced the Convention in the post-war period in a climate of cold war between western liberal-democratic countries and eastern people democratic countries. On the subject, see Potter (2023, 843 ff) and De Souza Dias (2022).

As for the application of the 1936 Convention it should be said that Russia, as a successor State of the former USSR, is party to it, while Ukraine is not. But this does not prevent the application of this treaty, both in relations between Russia and Ukraine and in those between Russia and other contracting Parties. As it will be shown in detail later, the applicability of the 1936 Convention to States which are not Parties to it is based on the assumption of *erga omnes* nature of the obligations enshrined thereto.[5] This means that this treaty does not lay down purely bilateral obligations. This statement allows us to assess whether certain acts of political propaganda carried out by the Russian Federation can give rise to the international responsibility of that State for violation of the 1936 Convention, and with what consequences. For there to be an international responsibility of Russia for breaching the Convention, there should be evidence of acts carried out by state organs which are attributable to the State. In particular, international responsibility of Russia may arise when one considers some information spread by Russian Federation prior to the launching of the so called "special military operation" of the 22 February 2022. As it emerges from the pending legal dispute between the two countries, Kiev claimed that the recognition of the Popular Democratic Republics of Donetzk and Luhansk in Donbass and the ensuing "special military operation" were justified by Russia on grounds of elements such as false information and the spreading of propaganda regarding the alleged commission of genocide in Donbass, the asserted nazi-like character of the Ukraine political regime, and the non-existence of Ukraine as an independent State.[6] In its order indicating provisional measures, the ICJ found Ukraine argument regarding the non-commission of genocide plausible,[7] and in its judgment on preliminary exceptions raised by Russia ICJ said that art. IX of the Genocide Convention does not prevent UKR from seeking a declaration where ICJ says that Ukraine never committed genocide.[8] But, at the same time, ICJ upheld Russia's preliminary objection that false allegations of genocide, and uses of force based on them, fall outside the scope of the Genocide Convention.

That being said, there exist three alternative models to assert Russia's international responsibility for breaching this treaty.

According to a *first model*, and with regard to the above mentioned "incorrect and false information", since those statements were made by high-ranking Russian

---

[5] In *Barcelona Traction, Light and Power Company*, 5 February 1970 (paras. 33–34) the ICJ made a difference between rules which set obligations *erga omnes* and rules setting synallagmatic obligations: «By their very nature the former are the concern of all States. In view of the importance of the rights involved, all States can be held to have a legal interest in their protection; they are obligations *erga omnes* […]» such obligations derive, for example, in contemporary international law, from the outlawing of acts of aggression».

[6] ICJ, 26 February 2022, *Ukraine v. Russian Federation, Allegations of Genocide under the Convention on the Prevention and Punishment of the Crime of Genocide*, Application instituting proceedings, paras. 1-26 (available at www.icj-cij.org).

[7] ICJ, 16 March 2022, *Ukraine v. Russian Federation, Allegations of Genocide under the Convention on the Prevention and Punishment of the Crime of Genocide*, Provisional Measures (paras. 50–62). See M. Alexianu (2024).

[8] ICJ, 2 February 2024, *Judgment on Preliminary Objections* (paras. 97–99). See M. Milanovic (2024).

State organs (President Putin, Foreign Minister Lavrov and the Ambassador at the United Nations Nebendzja), Russia can be said to have infringed the 1936 Convention through the actions of its organs. Therefore, Russia is internationally responsible under art. 4 of the ILC Project,[9] which is reproductive of international customary law.

According to a *second model*, Russia's international responsibility may arise if one assumes, like the General Court of European Union did in the *RT France v. Council* judgment,[10] that the Russian media system which supported the aggression by spreading propaganda for war is totally depending or controlled by the political power. This equates journalists to Russian State organs again under art. 4 of ILC Project and their propaganda is thus directly attributed to Russian State.[11]

A *third model* for considering Russia internationally responsible for the breach of 1936 Convention, is to assume the Russian media system as partially independent from political power. In this case, propaganda for war made by private subjects or entities would be attributable to Russian State under art. 11 of the ILC Project. This rule states that the responsibility of a State arises when this State explicitly acknowledges and adopts as its own conducts which are made by private subjects, and this happened when Russian journalists were granted prizes and awards by President Putin who unequivocally endorsed their coverage of the war.

Once attributed, directly or indirectly, certain conducts to the Russian Federation one has to wonder whether Ukraine can claim for reparation as a consequence of the violation of the 1936 Convention. In order to answer this question, we must highlight the legal nature of this treaty and the obligations enshrined therein by briefly recalling some considerations expressed *supra*. According to a first interpretation, the Convention is a multilateral treaty of a purely synallagmatic kind, enshrining bilateral obligations: in this case, Ukraine is not entitled to claim for reparation, since it is not a party to it. A different interpretation focuses on the aims of the Convention. Since it aims at safeguarding peace through the prohibition of the war propaganda,

---

[9] Art. 4, labelled *Conduct of organs of a State*, reads as follows: «1. The conduct of any State organ shall be considered an act of that State under international law, whether the organ exercises legislative, executive, judicial or any other functions, whatever position it holds in the organization of the State, and whatever its character as an organ of the central Government or of a territorial unit of the State. 2. An organ includes any person or entity which has that status in accordance with the internal law of the State».

[10] GC, Case T-125/22, *RT France v. Council*, paras. 21, 22, 239.

[11] The equivalence proposed here between the Russian media and the apparatus of the organs of the Russian State seems to be permitted by the Commentary on art. 4 of the ILC Project. Far from limiting the scope of application of the rule only to bodies that have this status according to state law, the Commentary states that «[…] it is not sufficient to refer to internal law for the status of State organs. In some systems the status and functions of various entities are determined not only by law but also by practice, and reference exclusively to internal law would be misleading. The internal law of a State may not classify, exhaustively or at all, which entities have the status of "organs". In such cases, internal law will not itself perform the task of classification. Accordingly, a State cannot avoid responsibility for the conduct of a body which does in truth act as one of its organs merely by denying it that status under its own law. This result is achieved by the use of the word "includes" in paragraph 2». Yearbook of the International Law Commission, 2001, 42 (para. 11).

it enshrines *erga omnes* obligations: so, Ukraine is the injured State under art. 42, para. 1, *b* of the ILC Project[12] and it may invoke all the consequences of the Russian wrong (compensation, assurances of non-repetition, countermeasures, etc.).

Once clarified Ukraine legal position *vis-à-vis* the consequences of the Russian wrongful act, it is useful to ascertain whether the other States parties to the Convention[13] may play a role under the law of international responsibility of a State. This step may elucidate if and to what extent States which are not directly-injured by the Russian wrongful act and, in particular, States parties to the 1936 Convention may ask Russia to end its wrongful act, gives assurances of non-repetition, and provide full reparation to Ukraine under art. 48 para. 1, *b* and para. 2 *a, b* of the ILC Project.[14] Granting those rights enhances the role of third States not directly injured by a breach of an *erga omnes* obligation, and it is consistent with the recent ICJ's case law where not-directly injured States have recently initiate proceedings before the ICJ.[15] In its case-law, ICJ held that any State party to the Genocide Convention, and not only a specially affected State, may invoke the responsibility of another State party with a view to ascertaining the alleged failure to comply with its obligations *erga omnes partes*, and to bring that failure to an end.[16]

May this jurisdictional path have some chances of success with regard the 1936 Convention? Unfortunately, the reservation entered by Russia to art. 7 of the 1936 Convention makes quite unrealistic the acceptation of the ICJ jurisdiction on behalf of Russia: but third States parties can react to the Russian wrong in the spirit of *erga omnes obligations* asking for cessation and reparation.

A final question to be answered is if third States can adopt countermeasures, within the meaning of ILC Project art. 54.[17] Art. 54 of the ILC Project mentions

---

[12] Art. 42 (Invocation of responsibility by an injured State): A State is entitled as an injured State to invoke the responsibility of another State *if the obligation breached is owed* to: *a* (*omissis*) *b* a group of States including that State, *or the international community as a whole and the breach of the obligation: (i) specially affects that State* (*omissis*)". (italics added).

[13] See the list of the Member States in www.treaties.un.org.

[14] Art. 48 (Invocation of responsibility by a State other than an injured State): 1. Any State other than injured State is entitled to invoke the responsibility of another State if: (b) the obligation breached is owed to the international community as a whole. Para. 2 (a) Any State entitled to invoke responsibility under para. 1 may claim from the responsible State: (a) cessation of the internationally wrongful act, and assurances and guarantees of non-repetition; (b) performance of the obligation of reparation in the interest of the injured State or of the beneficiaries of the obligation breached.

[15] See, for instance the applications filed by South Africa against Israel (29 December 2023) and by Gambia against Myanmar (22 July 2022) for alleged violations of the Convention on Genocide (in www.icj-cij.org).

[16] ICJ, 22 July 2022, *Application of the Convention on the Prevention and Punishment of the Crime of Genocide (The Gambia v. Myanmar)*, Preliminary Objections, para. 477; 26 January 2024, Order, *Application of the Convention on the Prevention and Punishment of the Crime of Genocide in the Gaza Strip* (*South Africa v. Israel*), para. 33.

[17] ILC art. 54 reads as follows: «*Measures taken by States other than an injured State»:* «This chapter does not prejudice the right of any State, entitled under art. 48, para. 1, to invoke the responsibility of another State, to take lawful measures against that State to ensure cessation of the breach and reparation in the interest of the injured State or of the beneficiaries of the obligation breached».

the right of any State, entitled under art. 48, para. 1, to invoke the responsibility of another State, to take "*lawful measures*" against that State to ensure cessation of the breach and reparation in the interest of the injured State or of the beneficiaries of the obligation breached. Many States have then imposed economic, financial, trade assets freezing and monetary sanctions on Russia, unilaterally or within international organization, like EU, in the spirit of art. 54.

3 The Legal Discipline of the Propaganda Within the UN System: The International Covenant on Civil and Political Right, the Relevant Resolutions Adopted by the General Assembly and the Ensuing Implications for the Russian-Ukrainian Conflict

The second international treaty dealing with the propaganda for war is the ICCPR whose art. 20, para.1 reads as follows: «Any propaganda for war which shall be prohibited by law».[18] The provision has been scarcely resorted to in international case-law, but in the recent judgment *RT France v. Council of the European Union* the General Court of the European Union, recalling the Covenant, held that the rule «[…] is to be intended to attribute the utmost gravity to propaganda for war».[19] Furthermore, art. 20 poses some conceptual and definitional problems. The first of those problems concerns the existing relationship between war propaganda activities and freedom of opinion and expression, laid down in art. 19 of the ICCPR. As it emerges from the interpretative activity of the HR Committee, both rules complement each other and the acts that are addressed in art. 20 are all subject to restriction pursuant to art. 19, para. 3. But there is also a distinction: in fact, for the acts addressed in art. 20, the Covenant indicates the specific response required from the State: their prohibition by law.[20] However, for the purposes of our analysis, it is of central importance to provide a legal definition of "propaganda for war". Art. 20 (para. 1), however, lacks of a definition of "propaganda for war".[21] So, the "General rule of interpretation" under

[18] The provision prohibits propaganda in favour of war independently of other conventional norms which, on the other hand, sanction the prohibition in the context of the discipline relating to freedom of thought and expression, prohibiting it together «[…] any advocacy of national, racial or religious hatred that constitutes incitement to lawless violence […]»: see the American Convention on Human Rights, 1969 (art. 13).

[19] *RT France v. Council*, cit., para. 209.

[20] Committee of Human Rights, *General Comment No. 34 Article 19: Freedoms of opinion and expression*, UN Doc. CCPR/ C/GC/34, 12 September 2011 (paras 50–51).

[21] As for the notion of "war", in the Charter of the UN, no mention is made of it, with the exception of the Preamble. The terms "use of force" or armed conflicts replace it, depending on the legal context (jus ad bellum, jus in bello).

art. 31 of the Vienna Convention on the Law of Treaties (VCLT)[22] offers little help to interpret this notion. Conversely, the circumstances of the treaty conclusion and its preparatory work as supplementary means of interpretation,[23] reveal that Russia insisted for a prohibition of the propaganda of war to be enshrined in the Covenant, in order to avoid the danger of a return to a nazi-like propaganda, but western capitalist Countries made opposition to this proposition.

According to a legal scholar, the difficulty of defining "war" in international law does not contribute to the emergence of a real definition of "propaganda in favour of war".[24] The lack of a definition of war propaganda is not the only problem raised by the provision. Doubts also persist about the legal value of the ban. In particular, some argue that the prohibition of conduct derives from a rule of customary law,[25] but this argument seems difficult to accept in the light of the reservations and declarations made to Art. 20 (para. 1) by an important group of States.[26]

An important contribution to the interpretation of Art. 20 of the ICCPR has been provided by two United Nations bodies responsible for this purpose: the HR Committee and the Special Rapporteur on the promotion and protection of freedom of opinion and expression. In the 1983 *General Comment no. 11: Prohibition of propaganda for war and inciting national, racial or religious hatred* (art. 20) (the General Comment no. 11), the HR Committee argues that the prohibition enshrined in art. 20 (para.1) is fully compatible with the right of freedom of expression as contained in art. 19, the exercise of which carries with it special duties and responsibilities.[27] Having said that, the HR Committee adds that the prohibition extends

---

[22] The first three paragraphs of the article, entitled *General rule of interpretation*, provide: 1. A treaty shall be interpreted in good faith in accordance with the ordinary meaning to be given to the terms of the treaty in their context and in the light of its object and purpose. 2. The context for the purpose of the interpretation of a treaty shall comprise, in addition to the text, including its preamble and annexes: (a) any agreement relating to the treaty which was made between all the parties in connection with the conclusion of the treaty; (b) any instrument which was made by one or more parties in connection with the conclusion of the treaty and accepted by the other parties as an instrument related to the treaty. 3. There shall be taken into account, together with the context: (a) any subsequent agreement between the parties regarding the interpretation of the treaty or the application of its provisions; (b) any subsequent practice in the application of the treaty which establishes the agreement of the parties regarding its interpretation; (c) any relevant rules of international law applicable in the relations between the parties.

[23] VCLT art. 32: «Recourse may be had to supplementary means of interpretation, including the preparatory work of the treaty and the circumstances of its conclusion, in order to confirm the meaning resulting from the application of art. 31, or to determine the meaning when the interpretation according to art. 31 leaves the meaning ambiguous or obscure; or leads to a result which is manifestly absurd or unreasonable».

[24] Collins (2010), 819, 824. Quoting Whitton (2014), propaganda is a «communication of facts, arguments, suggestions which create or reinforce in the audience the willingness for war not only by directly incite at it, but by setting a favourable environment to the outbreak of war also».

[25] Whitton (1948, 601).

[26] Australia, Belgium, Denmark, Finland, France, Iceland, Ireland, Luxembourg, Malta, Netherlands, New Zealand, Norway, Sweden, Switzerland, Thailand, United Kingdom of Great Britain and Northern Ireland, USA.

[27] See Richter (2015, 496 ff).

to all forms of propaganda threatening or resulting in an act of aggression or breach of the peace contrary to the Charter of the United Nations. This nothwistanding, the provisions do not prohibit advocacy of the sovereign right of self-defence or the right of peoples to self-determination and independence in accordance with the Charter of the United Nations.

The implications of this interpretation for the ongoing conflict between Russia and Ukraine are clear. In fact, the war propaganda carried out in Russia by political power and the press has resulted in armed aggression contrary to the UN Charter, while any activities carried out by Ukraine must be understood as an exercise of the right to self-determination and legitimate defence in the face of the invasion: it ensues that it is not wrongful.

With regard to the Special Rapporteur on the promotion and protection of freedom of opinion and expression, this UN organ has argued that the prohibition of the propaganda for war is understood to be applicable only in relation to aggression or breach of peace contrary to the Charter of the United Nations and limited to incitement of war and not to propaganda *during* war.[28] Differently, the General Court of European Union in *RT France v. Council of the European Union* argued that propaganda for war includes «not only incitement to a future war, but also continuous, repeated and concerted statements in support of an ongoing war, contrary to international law».[29]

Once examined the relevant rule contained in ICCPR, let us conclude the analysis of the other rules regulating the propaganda for war within the UN system. We do this by recalling some acts of *soft law*, i.e. resolutions of the General Assembly (GA) which, although very old because they were adopted during cold war, provide useful elements for interpreting the case.[30] Amongst them, in resolution no. 110/1947 GA condemns «all forms of propaganda either designed or likely to provoke or encourage any threat to the peace or act of aggression», requesting States «to encourage the dissemination of all information designed to give expression to the undoubted desire of all peoples for peace».[31] Two years later, GA called upon Nations «to refrain from any threats or act, direct or indirect, aimed at impairing the freedom, independence or integrity of any State, or at fomenting civil strife and subverting the will of the people in any State, and to remove the barriers which deny to peoples the free exchange of

---

[28] See the Report *Disinformation and freedom of opinion and expression during armed conflicts*, UN Doc. A/77/288, 12 august 2022 (para. 39).

[29] *RT France v. Council*, cit., para. 210.

[30] Regarding the role of *soft law*, for the sake of completeness mention should also be made of the Helsinki Final Act, a document signed at the closing meeting of the third phase of the Conference on Security and Cooperation in Europe held in Helsinki (1975), and out of the UN framework. At Helsinki Conference, participating States declared «to refrain from propaganda for wars of aggression inconsistent with the purposes of the United Nations». *Questions relating to security in Europe*, Part X, *Fulfilment in good faith of obligations under international law, b, i* (www.osc e.org).

[31] *Measures to be taken against propaganda and the inciters of a new war*, A/RES/110 (II), 3 November 1947, para. 1; 2 (b).

information and ideas essential to international understanding and peace».[32] Afterwards, GA declared that propaganda against peace includes measures «tending to isolate the peoples from any contact with the outside world, by preventing the Press, radio and other media of communication from reporting international events, and thus hindering mutual comprehension and understanding between peoples»; and measures «tending to silence or distort the activities of the United Nations in favour of peace or to prevent their peoples from knowing the views of other States members».[33] And, in order to prevent these negative effects of propaganda, GA called upon every nation to remove the barriers which deny to peoples the free exchange of information and ideas essential to international understanding and peace, recognizing that the maintenance of such barriers constitutes a major obstacle to the strengthening of peace and fosters the continuation of false and hostile propaganda against other States and peoples.[34] The explicit provision of a legal obligation to abstain is finally contained in the famous resolution 2625/1970 on the Principles of International Law Concerning Friendly Relations and Cooperation among States,[35] in which the principle of the prohibition of the threat or use of force by States (Article 2, paragraph 4 of the UN Charter), is specified in the sense that States have the duty to refrain from a threat or a use of force, which also includes propaganda for war.

In conclusion, even in the case of international law adopted under the aegis of the UN, it seems to be possible to say that Russian conduct before and during the armed conflict with Ukraine violates these norms.

4 Does the International Responsibility of the Russian Federation for Wrongful Acts Entails Individual Criminal Responsibility of President Putin for the Commission of Acts of War Propaganda Committed Prior or During the Conflict Between Russia and Ukraine?

As we have seen, there are strong arguments for claiming that the Russian Federation has violated two treaties in force and, therefore, is responsible for committing internationally wrongful acts, although there are limits to the concrete possibility that a Court will establish the offence and take action on its consequences. We can now ask ourselves whether the international responsibility of the Russian state can lead to individual criminal responsibility on the part of some supreme individuals-organs

[32] *Essentials of peace*, 290 (IV), 1 December 1949 (paras. 3, 8).

[33] *Condemnation of propaganda against peace*, 381 (V), 17 November 1950 (art. 2, paras. 2–3).

[34] *Strengthening of peace through the removal of barriers to free exchange of information and ideas*, A/RES/819 (IX), 11 December 1954 (preamble).

[35] *Declaration on Principles of International Law concerning Friendly Relations and Co-operation among States in accordance with the Charter of the United Nations*, 1970.

(i.e. President Putin) of the State. In particular, do the speeches with which Russian President Putin accused the Ukrainian government of carrying out acts of genocide in Donbass, creating a climate among the population favourable to the acceptance of armed confrontation, constitute war propaganda? And, if so, do those acts engage President Putin personal liability under domestic or international criminal law[36]?

To answer these questions it is necessary to ascertain the existence of rules—domestic or international—that define conduct aimed at disseminating messages of incitement to war as a crime and excluding, at the same time, that the person responsible (Head of State or Government) can invoke his functional or personal immunity. As for domestic courts, a possibility is offered by those domestic systems informed to the principle of the so-called "universal jurisdiction", both in its "pure" form (characterized by the absence of any connection between the State of the forum, *the locus commissi delicti* and the active or passive nationality of the perpetrator of the crime or his victim); and in its "conditional" form (which requires the presence of the alleged perpetrator on the territory of the proceeding State). In particular, these legal systems could provide for the criminal liability of crimes such as war propaganda, thus configuring a potential legal basis for the opening of proceedings. However, this is a hypothesis doomed to collide with the apparently insurmountable wall of immunity, both personal and functional, that the Russian head of state would invoke to evade any attempt at international or national justice. In other words, although universal jurisdiction offers a powerful and potentially effective legal instrument, its concrete application remains severely limited by political and diplomatic obstacles that are not easy to overcome.

A second possibility, equally difficult to realize, is offered by the legal systems of the Russian Federation and Ukraine, whose jurisdiction is based on the traditional criteria of active or passive nationality or territoriality. In particular, the Russian Criminal Code of 1997, in Chapter XXXIV, Section XII, outlines crimes against peace and security of humanity: in particular, articles 353 which incriminates conducts aimed at planning, preparing, unleashing, conducting a war of aggression, and art. 354 which punishes public calls for the unleashing of a war of aggression are highlighted. In this context, Russian jurisdiction could be exercised according to the criteria of active nationality, but the prospect of putting Vladimir Putin on trial in the absence of a radical change of political regime seems totally unrealistic.

With reference to the Ukrainian Criminal Code of 2001, in the context of "crimes against peace" it punishes in particular propaganda for a war of aggression or armed conflict as well as the production of materials inciting such conduct (art. 436). In the—currently unrealistic—hypothesis of Putin's capture or his handover to the Ukrainian authorities, lacking a political regime change in Russia, the Russian president could not invoke functional or personal immunity by virtue of the analogy application of the customary rule relating to war crimes to all international crimes which, due

[36] This paper is not the proper *sedes materiae* to dwell on a high controversial issue such the personal and functional State immunity of high State official from a Court jurisdiction, be it domestic or international one, when he is accused of committing the most serious crimes (crimes against peace, war crimes, crimes against humanity, genocide, aggression). See: ICC, 6 May 2019, *No.* ICC-02/05-01/09 OA2, *Prosecutor v. Al Bashir,* para. 1; S. Zappalà (2023, 595) and Liu (2023).

to the seriousness of the conduct, are attributed to the individual as such and not only attributed to him as an organ of the State. However, such an argument must be assessed in the light of the international treaties in force, the most significant international case-law and the recent work of the International Law Commission (ILC) on the Immunity of State Officials from Foreign Criminal Jurisdiction.[37] As regards the treaties in force and the case-law, art. 21 of the Convention on Special Missions adopted by the General Assembly in 1969[38] is limited to recognizing to Heads of State the immunities conferred on them by international law, and the ICJ has not had the opportunity to rule on the nature and extent of the immunities of a Head of State accused of having committed *crimina juris gentium*.[39] Conversely, mention is to be made of the well-known sentence issued by the British House of Lords in the case of the former chilean Head of State Pinochet,[40] in which the judge accepted the request to extradite the accused but only on the basis of the Convention against Torture and Other Cruel, Inhuman or Degrading Treatment or Punishment (1984).

Coming now to the above-mentioned ILC codification works on the immunity of supreme State bodies from foreign criminal jurisdiction, an indication of the existence of the afore-mentioned exception to the recognition of immunity is constituted by art. 7 entitled *Crimes under international law* in respect of which immunity *ratione materiae* shall not apply.[41] Given that the ILC denies the existence of a customary rule that allows limits or exceptions to the immunity *ratione personae* of Heads of State, Government and Foreign Ministers in office by virtue of the special representative functions that they exercise, this UN organ also considers that there exist a clear trend precluding such State organs the right to avail themselves of functional immunity from foreign criminal jurisdiction for international crimes committed in their capacity as organs and during the mandate as those crimes are considered extraneous to their official functions.[42]

However, this assumption has been challenged by some members of the ILC: for them, affirming the existence of exceptions to the customary rule on the recognition

[37] Yearbook of the International Law Commission, 2007, vol. II, Part Two, para. 376. The work of the ILC on this matter was affected by the replacement of the first Special Rapporteur Kolodkin, with the next one (Escobar Hernandez) who presented eight reports on the basis of which the Commission adopted eighteen articles at first reading (UN Doc. A/CN.4/L.969, 31 May 2022).

[38] UNTS, vol. 1400, 1985, 231.

[39] However, it has ruled on the alleged commission of international crimes by a Foreign Minister in the case of the Arrest Warrant (Congo v. Belgium), in I.C.J. Reports, 2002, 3 ff.

[40] UKHL, 24 marzo 1999, *Regina v. Bow Street Metropolitan Stipendiary Magistrate, ex parte Pinochet (No. 3)*, UKHL 17 (2000) 1 AC 147. Pinochet was accused of having committed crimes against humanity during his mandate and for this reason he was the subject of criminal proceedings in Spain, which had requested his extradition to the United Kingdom where he was temporarily for medical treatment.

[41] The rule provides that foreign criminal jurisdiction does not apply with respect to the following crimes: genocide, crimes against humanity, war crimes, apartheid, torture, enforced disappearances. Ren and Jin (2021).

[42] Report of the International Law Commission, 10 May–2 June and 3 July-4 August 2017), UN Doc A/72/10, paras. 83, 87, 93, 94, 96, 98, 103, 105, 134.

of the immunity of supreme bodies without these having been accepted through the explicit consent given by States through a treaty, or proven by their broad and consistent practice, undermines mutual trust and weakens the principle of sovereign equality between States.[43] Furthermore, the customary scope of art. 7 of the draft ILC with respect to a possible indictment of President Putin by a Ukrainian court risks being watered down if one considers that the provision does not include among the punishable offences "the crime of crimes", i.e. aggression.[44] Ultimately, according to many legal scholars, before the judges of these two countries no immunity could be invoked by President Putin, but it is unrealistic to believe that he might be tried before a Russian or Ukrainian Court without a strong political change in Russia.

Political considerations aside, the only hypothesis that President Putin does not invoke jurisdictional immunity is given by the possibility of being tried before an international Court, provided that it has jurisdiction both *ratione personae* and *materiae.* Is International Criminal Court (ICC) fit for this purpose? Russian Federation is not a contracting party to the Statute of the ICC, nor does the Statute contemplate the crime of "war propaganda" among those subject to its jurisdiction.[45] Proposals have been made in order to establish a new international criminal tribunal to try Putin,[46] but they do not escape the objection that these would be Courts created *ex post factum*, and with the concurrence of Countries that in condemning the Russian military intervention have supplied important quantities of weapons to Kiev.[47]

De lege ferenda, the only possibility of submitting in the future alleged perpetrators of the crime of "war propaganda" to the jurisdiction of the ICC is to amend art. 8 bis of the Statute pursuant to its art. 121 which provides for the crime of aggression. The amendment will have to include war propaganda as a constitutive element of the case of aggression as a "leadership crime" perpetrated by individuals placed at the top of the State and able to control or direct its political or military action.

---

[43] Meret (2024). On the existence of a customary rule that allows the judge of the forum to trial a foreign Head of State outside of a conventional provision that explicitly establishes his jurisdiction, see Vasiliev (2022) and Lemos (2023).

[44] This is a surprising exclusion, in the light of the Agreement for the prosecution and punishment of the major war criminals of European Axis, signed in London 8 August 1945, instituting the International Military Tribunal (art. 6 *a*), the International Military Tribunal for the Far East (art. 5 a), as well as art. 8 bis of the ICC Statute. The ILC justified this exclusion by wanting to prevent the politicization of the judgment before courts not fully equipped to judge the merits of the crime in question: UN Doc A/72/10, cit., 185, para. 18 of the Commentary. Moreover, even the Institut de Droit international in the resolution *On the Immunity from Jurisdiction of the State and of Persons Who Act on Behalf of the State in case of International Crimes* adopted in the Naples session (2009), considers the exception applicable to all international crimes (art. i, para. 1–2) (www.idi-iil.org/app/uploads/2017/06/2009_naples_01_en.pdf).

[45] It should be noted that war propaganda is not even one of the constituent elements of the "crime of aggression" enshrined in art. 8 bis of the Rome Statute.

[46] Council of Europe, Parliamentary Assembly, *Legal and human rights aspects of the Russian Federation's aggression against Ukraine*, RES. 2482/2023, 26 june 2023.

[47] Mullin and Stanton (2024).

5 Concluding Remarks

On 21th November 2024 ICC Pre-Trial Chamber I issued warrants of arrest for Israel Prime Minister Netanyahu and former defence Minister Gallant, for crimes against humanity and war crimes committed from at least 8 October 2023 until at least 20 may 2024 against civilian population in Gaza. But the situation in Palestine is under examination of the ICJ also, and pending proceedings give the opportunity of make a fundamental distinction between the propaganda for war and «any advocacy of national, racial or religious hatred that constitutes incitement to discrimination, hostility or violence shall be prohibited by law» (art. 20, para. 2).

In the already quoted *General Comment no. 11*, the HR Committee rights argued that the prohibition under art. 20 ICCPR para. 1 extends to all forms of propaganda threatening or resulting in an act of aggression or breach of the peace contrary to the Charter of the United Nations, while para. 2 is directed against any advocacy of national, racial or religious hatred that constitutes incitement to discrimination, hostility or violence, whether such propaganda or advocacy has aims which are domestic or external to the State concerned. For its part, the Special Rapporteur on the promotion and protection of the right to freedom of opinion and expression, in the quoted Report *Disinformation and Freedom of opinion and expression during armed conflicts* has argued that propaganda and advocacy to hatred that constitutes incitement to hostility share some common features, such as detrimental impact on human rights.

These references are important for two reasons. First of all, they allow us to admit that President Putin, although he did not put in place a real propaganda in favour of the war pursuant to art. 20, para. 1 of the ICCPR, together with other Russian Government and high-rank diplomatic officials, has at least prepared the Russian population for the possibility of an armed confrontation with Ukraine through several speeches, interviews and press releases. Secondarily, the line between war propaganda and "hate speech" is often blurred but, fortunately, it is subject to judicial review. An example of this is the dispute pending before the ICJ with which South Africa instituted proceedings against Israel for alleged violations of Convention on the prevention and punishment of the crime of genocide. In its application, South Africa claimed that some high-ranking political and military officials after 7 October 2023, expressed genocidal intent against the Palestinian population through statements, press-conference, interviews[48] and ICC in its order for provisional measures after saying that the facts and circumstances mentioned by South Africa are plausible, ordered that Israel shall take all measures «to prevent and punish the direct and public incitement» to commit genocide in relation to members of the Palestinian group in the Gaza Strip.[49]

---

[48] *Application instituting proceedings and request for indication of provisional measures*, 29 December 2023 (available at www.icj-cij.org) (paras. 101–108).

[49] *Application of the Convention on the Prevention and Punishment of the Crime of Genocide in the Gaza Strip* (South Africa v. Israel), Order, 26 January 2024 (paras. 53 and 79).

Unfortunately, with the advent of Donald Trump as President of United States, some hypothesis on which the present paper rests upon, such as the responsibility of the Russian State for the commission of an international wrongful act, seem fading away. In some of his public speeches, Trump has in fact even denied the Russian aggression against Ukraine, in flagrant contradiction with past President Biden policy and, above all, United Nations General Assembly stand. This distortion of reality cannot delete the blatant violation of one of the most important rules of international legal order, the one prohibiting aggression, and the propaganda for war acts giving rise to it.

References

Alexianu M (2024) Ukraine's ICJ provisional measures: a narrow path to remedies. EjilTalk!

Collins RB (2010) Propaganda for war and transparency. Denver U L Rev 87:819–832

De Souza Dias T (2022) Russia's "genocide disinformation" and war propaganda are breaches of the International Convention concerning the use of broadcasting in the cause of peace and fall within the ICJ's jurisdiction. www.ejiltalk.org

Lemos M (2023) The law of immunity and the prosecution of the head of state of the Russian Federation for international crimes in the war against Ukraine. EJIL:Talk!

Liu Y (2023) Do states party to the International Criminal Court statute have the obligation to arrest Vladimir Putin? EJIL:Talk!

Meret B (2024) Some states' position on draft Article 7 versus the very same states' positions concerning atrocities in Ukraine: an inconsistent stand. EJIL:Talk!

Milanovic M (2024) ICJ delivers preliminary objections judgment in the Ukraine v. Russia genocide case, Ukraine loses on the most important aspects. Ejil Talk!

Mullin E, Stanton G (2024) Prosecuting Putin: creation of a special tribunal for Russian aggression. Opinio Juris

Potter SJ (2023) Broadcasting in the cause of peace: regulating international radio propaganda in Europe, 1921–1939. Int Hist Rev 45(6):843–864

Ren H, Jin Z (2021) The limitations and exceptions to immunity of states officials from foreign criminal jurisdiction: on ILC draft Article 7. Beijing Law Rev 12:287–304

Richter A (2015) The relationship between freedom of expression and the ban on propaganda for war. In: Benedek W, Benoît-Rohmer F, Kettemann M, Kneihs, B, Nowak M (eds) European yearbook on human rights. Intersentia, Graz, pp 489–503

Vasiliev S (2022) Aggression against Ukraine: avenues for accountability for core crimes. EJIL:Talk!

Whitton JB (1948) Propaganda and international law. RCADI 72:542–670

Whitton JB (2014) Aggressive propaganda. In: Bassiouni MC, Nanda VP (eds) International Criminal Law, Charles C Thomas, Springfield, pp 238–272

Zappalà S (2023) Do heads of state in office enjoy immunity from jurisdiction for international crimes? Eur J Int Law 12:595–612

Disinformation in the Age of Generative Artificial Intelligence

Rebecca J. Hamilton

Abstract There is nothing new about the effort to gain a strategic advantage over one's enemy in a conflict setting. As other authors in this volume explain, case law and societal responses for dealing with such disinformation are well-developed. This chapter, however grapples with whether the advent of disinformation in the context of generative artificial intelligence (AI) merits a new set of responses. By working through a futuristic but plausible scenario of a Russian disinformation campaign against Ukraine, this chapter builds the argument that extant responses to disinformation not only risk providing he wrong answers to AI-generated disinformation, but actually risk asking the wrong set of questions. The chapter concludes with a set of reflections on the regulation of generative AI itself.

The effort to gain a strategic advantage through disinformation is as old as war itself.[1] So does that mean, as we enter a world in which generative artificial intelligence becomes widely available to conflict actors, that we can turn to the same responses to disinformation we have used throughout history[2]?

Professor Baade's address reminds us of Justice Kennedy's conclusion in a 2012 US Supreme Court case, that "the remedy for speech that is false, is speech that is true.[3]" Kennedy was of course drawing on a long strand of US Constitutional thinking on the matter—if we just let the marketplace of ideas flourish, truth will

[1] Strauss (2022) and Kuo and Marwick (2021) ("[C]orporations, state actors, and politicians have always spread false and misleading narratives to achieve their ideological goals.").

[2] Marr (2023) (analyzing the differences between "traditional AI" and generative AI).

[3] United States v. Alvarez, 567 U.S. 709, 727 (2012).

R. J. Hamilton (✉)
American University Washington College of Law, Washington, DC, USA
e-mail: hamilton@wcl.american.edu

R. Mastroianni and C. Massa (eds.), *Disinformation in New and Old Media in the XXI Century*, Ius Gentium: Comparative Perspectives on Law and Justice 136,
https://doi.org/10.1007/978-3-032-18830-4_13

eventually win out.[4] And, noting all the problems for a free and democratic society that flow from shutting down false speech rather than just letting true speech flourish over the top of it, Professor Baade aligns himself with this position. I fully agree about the risks of shutting down any speech. Indeed, historically and through to the present, whenever speech has been shut down it has been about the powerful in society silencing the voices of the marginalized.[5]

Nonetheless, it feels important at this juncture to open ourselves to the possibility that what has worked in the past will not in fact be fit for the future. Could it be that asking whether or not we should shut down false speech, is the wrong question for the coming moment?

The other articles in this volume have grappled with responding to the information ecosystem of the past 5–10 years. In this article, by contrast, I seek to look forward to the information ecosystem of the next 5–10 years. First however, I begin where the digital landscape currently lies, with a real world example from just three years ago.

In March 2022, Ukrainian President Volodomyr Zelensky appeared in a video across social media platforms Facebook, YouTube and Telegram, calling on Ukrainian soldiers to lay down their weapons.[6] The video was readily detectable as a fake.[7] Ukrainian intelligence had caught wind of the effort, and so had already put out a warning, and Zelensky had prepared his own video to refute the claim.[8] Facebook and YouTube we readily able to identify the false video as a fake, and removed it from their platforms.[9]

At this point, we are still on terra firma. We can keep our existing wisdom that generally speaking, the remedy for false speech is true speech, and be glad that the US Supreme Court has not (at least, not yet) removed the ability of platforms to exercise editorial judgement to shut down false speech in limited circumstances.[10]

---

[4] Dennis v. United States, 341 U.S. 494, 503 (1951) (finding that because the basis of the First Amendment is predicated on the free debate of ideas, "speech can rebut speech" and "propaganda will answer propaganda"); Whitney v. California, 274 U.S. 357, 377 (1927) (holding that the remedy to false speech is "more speech, not enforced silence"); Abrams v. United States, 250 U.S. 616, 630 (1919) (Holmes, J., dissenting) ("[T]he best test of truth is the power of the thought to get itself accepted in the competition of the market.").

[5] Franks (2024). To this point, at the time of writing, the Trump Administration is pursuing the deportation of a Palestinian man, who recently graduated from Columbia University and is a legal permanent resident of the United States, in an action that whatever its purported legal basis, seems infused with a spirit of retaliation against the man's exercise of his First Amendment rights as one of the leaders of the Columbia University student protests against Israel's war in Gaza. M.K v. William P. Joyce, SDNY 25-CV-1935-JMF (2025).

[6] Ukraine 24 (2022) (confirming that their news station was hacked); Thalen (2022) (displaying the fake video and explaining that it was debunked).

[7] Allyn (2022).

[8] Defense of Ukraine (2022).

[9] Allyn (2022) (noting that while Facebook, YouTube, and Twitter took down posts promoting the video as real, Russian media boosted the video).

[10] In July 2024, the U.S. Supreme Court vacated and remanded two cases on these issues. Moody v. NetChoice, LLC and NetChoice, LLC v. Paxton, 603 U.S. 707 (2024); NetChoice v. Paxton, 49

We might even congratulate ourselves that we have done a decent job with respect to developing critical digital literacy programs, and ensuring journalists have technical tools to detect digital manipulation of audio-visual material.[11] Where I want to take us to next, however, is somewhere far less comfortable.

Let us imagine it is two years from now, assuming no significant changes in the regulatory environment, and there is another video of President Zelensky calling on Ukrainian troops to surrender. In this futuristic scenario however, there is no advance warning, and the video is facially indistinguishable from a real video of Zelensky. Moreover, the video is just one part of much larger Russian propaganda campaign that involves the construction of an entire digital ecosystem.

Our imagined video comes on the heels of synthetic audio leaks of Zelensky discussing the surrender plan with his top advisers, and with falsified U.S. intelligence reports that predict a surrender announcement. It is followed by thousands upon thousands of deep fake videos of Ukrainian soldiers in different parts of the country watching the fake video and laying down their weapons, and of Ukrainian soldiers having tearful reunions with their families back in their villages.

These videos appearing to show the widespread surrender are paired with synthetic videos of Zelensky discussing his decision to surrender with television news anchors. And, importantly, these are not interviews with the anchors of RT, but synthetic videos of well-recognized news anchors from CNN, the BBC, and Al-Jazeera, through to Fox News. In short, the false video appears to be corroborated at every turn, no matter which part of the digital ecosystem you happen to inhabit.

In response, Zelensky again puts out his own video, saying that the surrender video is a fake. But against this barrage of synthetic media, his one true video is not enough. He finds that every interaction he has with a journalist gets bogged down with having to repeat that Ukraine has not surrendered. Meanwhile, one part of the Ukrainian government begins sending film crews out around the country to capture verifiable video footage of Ukrainian soldiers continuing to fight. Another part of the Ukrainian government, frustrated at this diversion of resources, decides instead to start producing synthetic videos of Ukrainian soldiers continuing to fight. Thanks to the OpenAI's Sora, by now widely available and enabling those with no technical expertise to create realistic videos from a prompt of just a few lines of text, the Ukrainian officials can produce these videos in just a fraction of the time, and fraction of the cost, that it takes to create real videos.[12]

And in this morass, of false claims synthetically produced, true claims truthfully produced, and true claims synthetically produced, the entire policy conversation

---

F.4th 439 (5th Cir. 2022), *cert. granted*, 144 S. Ct. 477 (2023) (No. 22–555, 2023 Term); NetChoice v. Attorney General of Florida, 34 F.4th 1196 (11th Cir. 2022), *cert granted* Moody v. NetChoice, 144 S. Ct. 478 (2023) (No. 22–277, 2023 Term).

[11] Knight et al. (2023, 326–228) (discussing the importance of digital literacy for educators and students); Thakur and Rohilla (2020, 11–12) and Weikmann and Lecheler (2023, 8–10) (discussing the challenges to fact-checking disinformation).

[12] Metz (2024) (describing Sora as a tool which could create quick and inexpensive online disinformation with Hollywood-level quality).

among Ukraine's allies is now oriented around the question of whether Ukraine did, might, or should surrender. In short, Russia has achieved its disinformation objective.

Compared to what happened in March 2022, our futuristic scenario involves a radical increase in quality, and decrease in cost of synthetic material. This is not a pie in the sky—by the time this goes to print, we are likely to be there.[13] The result is an exponential increase in the amount of synthetic material being put out, which therefore demands much more from the victim of the propaganda campaign in terms of refuting falsity with truth.

But there is another, more insidious difference in this imaginary scenario I am painting. It is happening after the latest model of OpenAI's Sora has been available to the public. What this means is that both the conflict actors and the general public who are on the receiving end of the propaganda campaign inhabit a world that is flooded with synthetic video in a way that is unimaginable to us, even today.[14] People know, because they have done it themselves, just how easy it is to make anyone appear to say or do something they never did.

In this future world, strategies that have been reasonably effective in recent years in terms of critical digital literacy, begin to break down as we head into an era where the bigger problem than people not effectively questioning false speech, is people starting to question true speech. Or, in the words of Hannah Arendt, an era in which "everything [is] possible and nothing [is] true.[15]"

In a world where we no longer trust our own ability to distinguish fact from fiction, will it still be possible to assume that "the remedy for speech that is false is speech that is true." And will the question of whether we should remove false speech, even still make sense?

So what is the way forward? Let me begin with the spoiler alert: There is no silver bullet answer here. Still, there is one basic fact that should guide us as we try to navigate the coming turbulent years: Conflict actors will exploit any new technology to serve their own strategic goals. So when regulators hear from tech companies about the way generative AI can ensure seamless translation of languages, provide individualized tutoring to middle-schoolers or unlock the cure for cancer (all plausible claims by the way),[16] legislators need to put themselves in the position of a conflict actor, in the possession of a technology powerful enough to do all those things, and regulate accordingly.

We should operate on the assumption that there is a roughly proportionate relationship between the amount of benefit and the amount of harm a given type of technology can deliver. The very same information sharing technology that helped civil society

---

[13] Piper (2024) (comparing the threat of Sora's AI capabilities to the perceived threat by other developments, such as DALL-E); Hadi Mogavi et al. (2024, 1–2) (emphasizing the rapid development of generative AI tools and analyzing the public perception of Sora).

[14] Overton (2023, 3–5, 11) (explaining the rise of synthetic material and the existing societal impacts); Philmlee (2023).

[15] Arendt (1958, 382).

[16] PowerSchool (personal AI assistant for school tutoring); DeepL (AI-powered automatic language translation); Nat'l Inst. Health (2024) (role of AI in cancer research).

protestors to fuel the Arab Spring,[17] was subsequently used by Myanmar's military to incite genocide against the Rohingya.[18] Had legislators regulated for the second scenario instead of being giddy in the face of the first scenario,[19] then we would already have a very different digital ecosystem than the one we currently have.[20]

The past decade of scholarship on content moderation has involved questions about what content should and should not be allowed online, through what process, and under whose authority.[21] Although the specific details differ, these are in broad terms the same questions that have been asked by previous generations in relation to television broadcasting and radio, all the way back to the days of pamphleteering.[22] As we contemplate the world of generative AI, I am less worried about getting the answers to these questions right—after all we have, as evidenced by the other articles of this volume, ample experience from years of case law grappling with these questions that we can draw from. I am more worried, however, that these might be the wrong questions or, at the very least, not the most pressing questions to address at this moment, as we approach this new precipice.

Questions that I would like to see greater attention to include: Who is designing generative AI models? Do they have the global experience and political imagination to design in light of a worst-case use scenario? Are they able to think, at each point in the development process, of the wide variety of ways that creative bad actors could use the model, rather than focus solely on the best-case use outcomes[23]? And, if not, are there regulators with the technical competence who are willing and able to step in?

The narrative generated out of Silicon Valley and amplified by many media outlets, assumes the inevitability of generative AI transforming society at breakneck speed.[24] But there is nothing inevitable about it. The speed at which generative AI enters our societies is the direct result of choices we do—and do not—make about the role of generative AI in the global public square. Long before we become enmeshed in

---

[17] Brown et al. (2012) and Hempel (2016).

[18] Feldstein (ed) (2021, 21) and Amnesty International (2022).

[19] Tufekci (2018) (discussing how positive perceptions of social media vis à vis democracy following its in the Arab Spring and in Barack Obama's successful U.S. Presidential elections led to the vastly unregulated expansion of social media, thereby funneling extremist ideology globally with little oversight).

[20] Communications Decency Act, 47 U.S.C. § 203.

[21] Hamilton (2021, 121–134, 160), Balkin (2018), 2012 (discussing the evolution of free expression throughout the nineteenth, twentieth, and twenty-first centuries); Klonick (2018, 1599, 1603, 1668–69).

[22] Raymond (2003), 8–13 (describing the development in pamphlets and the perception thereof); Pickard (2021) (discussing the "fairness doctrine," a set of government-enforced public interest rules applied to radio and television in the 1940s which later came under First Amendment attack in the U.S.); Allen et al. (2025) (discussing how to regulate television content and who should regulate it in the wake of concerns that violence on the television would translate to increased societal violence).

[23] Hamilton (2022).

[24] Rotman (2023) (discussing anticipated wide-spread economic development from AI); Dhillon (2023) (discussing AI's potential impact on the movie industry).

debates about how to regulate the content that generative AI produces, we need to give ourselves the time to regulate the development of the technology itself. Right now though, it is hard to be hopeful that legislators will act quickly enough to achieve this goal.

Appreciating the difficulty here requires understanding that generative AI is not emerging onto a blank slate. The first-movers in terms of generative AI development draw from the same subset of human and financial BigTech resources that underpin the data surveillance business model that now dominates online life.[25] The core bargain struck between BigTech and its users was that BigTech would offer online platforms at no financial cost to the individual user, in exchange for access to the user's data.[26] BigTech then monetized this data to advertisers. BigTech favored self-regulation and with the public at least initially happy enough with the arrangement, there was little incentive for legislators to push back.

This configuration provided the foundation for the generative AI moment that we now find ourselves in. The data, freely offered up by billions of users around the world, constituted the training data upon which generative AI could be developed. Crucially, the self-regulatory approach, entrenched over the past 20 years, now forms the default starting point for conversations over regulating generative AI.

To take one concrete example: In 2024, the European Union—the most pro-regulatory of actors in the Western hemisphere, adopted the Artificial Intelligence Act.[27] The structure of the legislation involves organizing AI into different risk categories. The higher the risk category, the more stringent the regulatory controls on its use. The catch, however, is the classification of "high risk" systems is done by the companies themselves through what the Act terms a "conformity assessment.[28]" There are, of course, pragmatic arguments about technical expertise that auger in favor of companies being in the best position to assess the risk their products could bring. Yet such concerns are surmountable, or at least they could be, if regulators were committed to reversing the approach taken to BigTech over the past two decades. Instead, regulators continue to be willing to trust that companies will do the right thing for the safety of the online ecosystem, despite little evidence that in a choice between safety and profit, BigTech will risk its bottom line.[29]

If regulators are unable or unwilling to wrest back some modicum of control over the generative AI models that are soon to flood our information ecosystems, then the public will be left to deal with the fallout. At least in terms of the online environment, speech—as it has been understood by courts (and society) until now,

[25] ChatGPT is owned by OpenAI, whose co-founders include Sam Altman and Elon Musk, and which is funded by Microsoft (O'Sullivan 2024). LLaMA is owned by Meta (Guinness 2024). Gemini is owned by Google (Pichai and Hassabis 2023). Amazon provides billions in funding to Anthropic, which owns Claude (Field 2025).

[26] Zuboff (2019).

[27] Resolution (EU) 2024/1689 (2024) and Hansen et al. (2024).

[28] Resolution (EU) 2024/1689 (2024) art 43(b).

[29] Haugen (2021).

will be indistinguishable from content generated by machine learning models that do nothing more than churn out material based on predictive algorithms.

In such a scenario, disinformation—traditionally a tool of adversaries in conflict, will be unleashed against friend and foe alike, across peacetime as readily as in the midst of conflict. Should this become the new normal, existing legal frameworks that prescribe more speech as the remedy to false speech will soon feel painfully antiquated.

References

Abrams v. United States, 250 U.S. 616 (1919)

Allen S, Thompson RJ et al (2025) TV violence and self-regulation. Encyclopedia Britannica. https://www.britannica.com/art/television-in-the-United-States/TV-violence-and-self-regulation

Allyn B (2022) Deepfake video of Zelensky could be 'tip of the iceberg' in info war, experts warn. NPR. https://www.npr.org/2022/03/16/1087062648/deepfake-video-zelenskyy-experts-war-manipulation-ukraine-russia

Amnesty International (2022) Myanmar: Facebook's systems promoted violence against Rohingya; Meta owes reparations—new report. https://www.amnesty.org/en/latest/news/2022/09/myanmar-facebooks-systems-promoted-violence-against-rohingya-meta-owes-reparations-new-report/

Arendt H (1958) The origins of totalitarianism. Harcourt, Brace, Jovanovich, London

Balkin JM (2018) Free speech is a triangle. Columbia Law Rev 118:2011–2055

Brown H, Guskin E, Mitchell A (2012) The role of social media in the Arab uprisings. Pew Research Center. https://www.pewresearch.org/journalism/2012/11/28/role-social-media-arab-uprisings/

Communications Decency Act, 47 U.S.C. § 203

DeepL. https://www.deepl.com/en/translator

Defense of Ukraine (@defenceU) 16 Mar 2022. Twitter. https://x.com/DefenceU/status/1504054999793512449?s=20

Dennis v. United States, 341 U.S. 494 (1951)

Dhillon S (2023) How AI will augment human creativity in film production. Variety. https://variety.com/vip/how-artificial-intelligence-will-augment-human-creatives-in-film-and-video-production-1235672659/

Feldstein S (ed) (2021) Issues on the frontlines of technologies and politics. Available via DIALOG. https://carnegie-production-assets.s3.amazonaws.com/static/files/202110-Feldstein_Frontlines_final3.pdf

Field H (2025) Amazon-backed AI firm Anthropic valued at $61.5 billion after latest round. CNBC. https://www.cnbc.com/2025/03/03/amazon-backed-ai-firm-anthropic-valued-at-61point5-billion-after-latest-round.html

Franks MA (2024) Fearless speech: breaking free from the first amendment. Bold Type Books, New York

Guinness H (2024) Meta AI: what is Llama and why does it matter? Zapier. https://zapier.com/blog/llama-meta/

Hadi Mogavi R, Tu J, Wang D et al (2024) Sora OpenAI's prelude: social media perspectives on Sora OpenAI and the future of AI video generation. ResearchGate. https://doi.org/10.13140/RG.2.2.11199.28320

Hamilton R (2021) Governing the global public square. Harv Int Law J 62:117–174

Hamilton RJ (2022) Platform-enabled crimes: pluralizing accountability when social media companies enable perpetrators to commit atrocities. Boston College Law Rev 63:1349–1420

Hansen M, Peets L, Drake M et al (2024) EU Parliament adopts AI Act. Lexology. https://www.lexology.com/library/detail.aspx?g=952adddc-ce16-4f5a-842e-0c6032ac9f03#:~:text=Implementation%20and%20impact%3A%20The%20AI,will%20apply%20six%20months%20thereafter
Haugen F (2021) Testimony before the United States Senate Committee on commerce, science and transportation sub-committee on consumer protection, product safety, and data security, Oct 4. https://www.commerce.senate.gov/services/files/FC8A558E-824E-4914-BEDB-3A7B1190BD49
Hempel J (2016) Social media made the Arab spring, but couldn't save it. Wired. https://www.wired.com/2016/01/social-media-made-the-arab-spring-but-couldnt-save-it/
Klonick K (2018) The new governors: the people, rules, and processes governing online speech. Harv Law Rev 131:1598–1670
Knight J, Dooly M, Barberà E (2023) Getting smart: towards critical digital literacy pedagogies. Soc Semiotics 33:327–328. https://doi.org/10.1080/10350330.2020.1836815
Kuo R, Marwick A (2021) Critical disinformation studies: history, power, and politics. Harv Kennedy School Misinf Rev 2:3. https://doi.org/10.37016/mr-2020-76
M.K v. William P. Joyce, (SDNY, 2025) 25-CV-1935-JMF.
Marr B (2023) The difference between generative AI and traditional AI: an easy explanation for anyone. Forbes. https://www.forbes.com/sites/bernardmarr/2023/07/24/the-difference-between-generative-ai-and-traditional-ai-an-easy-explanation-for-anyone/?sh=2d35eac8508a
Metz C (2024) OpenAI unveils A.I. that instantly generates eye-popping videos. NYT. https://www.nytimes.com/2024/02/15/technology/openai-sora-videos.html
Moody v. NetChoice, LLC and NetChoice, LLC v. Paxton, 603 U.S. 707 (2024)
National Institute Health (2024) Artificial intelligence (AI) and cancer. National Cancer Institute. https://www.cancer.gov/research/infrastructure/artificial-intelligence
NetChoice v. Attorney General of Florida, 34 F.4th 1196 (11th Cir. 2022), *cert granted* Moody v. NetChoice, 144 S. Ct. 478 (2023) (No. 22–277, 2023 Term)
NetChoice v. Paxton, 49 F.4th 439 (5th Cir. 2022), *cert. granted*, 144 S. Ct. 477 (2023) (No. 22–555, 2023 Term)
O'Sullivan I (2024) Who owns ChatGPT and its creator, OpenAI? all you need to know. Tech Co. https://tech.co/news/who-owns-chatgpt-and-openai
Overton S (2023) Testimony at the hearing on advances in Deepfake technology before the Subcommittee on Cybersecurity, Information Technology, and Government Innovation, 118th Congress, Nov 8. https://www.congress.gov/118/chrg/CHRG-118hhrg54071/CHRG-118hhrg54071.pdf
Philmlee D (2023) Practice innovations: seeing is no longer believing—the rise of deepfakes. Thomson Reuters. https://www.thomsonreuters.com/en-us/posts/technology/practice-innovations-deepfakes/
Pichai S, Hassabis D (2023) Introducing Gemini: our largest and most capable AI model. Google Blogs. https://blog.google/technology/ai/google-gemini-ai/
Pickard V (2021) The fairness doctrine won't solve our problems—But it can foster needed debate. The Washington Post. https://www.washingtonpost.com/outlook/2021/02/04/fairness-doctrine-wont-solve-our-problems-it-can-foster-needed-debate/
Piper K (2024) What two years of AI development can tell us about Sora. Vox. https://www.vox.com/future-perfect/24080195/sora-openai-sam-altman-ai-generated-videos-disinformation-midjourney-dalle
PowerSchool. https://www.powerschool.com/?utm_medium=cpc-g
Raymond J (2003) Pamphlets and pamphleteering in early modern Britain. Cambridge University Press, Cambridge
Resolution (EU) 2024/1689 of the European Parliament of 13 March 2024 on the proposal for a regulation of the European Parliament and of the council on laying down harmonized rules on artificial intelligence (Artificial Intelligence Act) and amending certain union legislative acts (COM(2021)0206 – C9-0146/2021 – 2021/0106(COD)), P9_TA(2024)0138

Rotman D (2023) ChatGPT is about to revolutionize the economy. We need to decide what that looks like. MIT Tech Rev. https://www.technologyreview.com/2023/03/25/1070275/chatgpt-revolutionize-economy-decide-what-looks-like/

Strauss B (2022) The long history of disinformation during war. The Washington Post. https://www.washingtonpost.com/outlook/2022/04/28/long-history-misinformation-during-war/

Thakur R, Rohilla R (2020) Recent advances in digital image manipulation detection techniques: a brief review. Forensic Sci Int 312:11–12. https://doi.org/10.1016/j.forsciint.2020.110311

Thalen M (@MikaelThalen) 16 Mar. 2022. Twitter. https://x.com/MikaelThalen/status/1504123674516885507?s=20

Tufekci Z (2018) How social media took us from Tahir Square to Donald Trump. MIT Tech Rev. https://www.technologyreview.com/2018/08/14/240325/how-social-media-took-us-from-tahrir-square-to-donald-trump

Ukraine 24 (@Україна24) 16 Mar 2022. Facebook. https://www.facebook.com/www.ukraine24.ua/photos/a.702717339921673/1847515118775217/?type=3

Weikmann T, Lecheler S (2023) Cutting through the hype: understanding the implications of deepfakes for the fact-checking actor-network. Digital J 12:8–10. https://doi.org/10.1080/21670811.2023.2194665

Whitney v. California, 274 U.S. 357 (1927)

Zuboff S (2019) The age of surveillance capitalism: the fight for a human future at the new frontier of power. PublicAffairs, New York

Conclusion

Roberto Mastroianni and Claudia Massa

Abstract The present volume shows that while disinformation is an ancient problem exacerbated by modern technology, societies are still grappling with how to effectively combat it without undermining fundamental democratic values like freedom of speech. More than the US, the EU is actively developing a comprehensive legislative framework, which is ambitious and innovative, since it combines both voluntary and legally binding elements, with a growing emphasis on holding large online platforms accountable and fostering a more trustworthy online environment. The EU's proactive stance may serve as a model for other regions grappling with the complex challenges of disinformation in the digital age, especially in times of elections and in times of war. All EU institutions, in fact, paid particular attention to these two contexts, as they represent critical moments where the integrity of information directly impacts core democratic values, public safety, and geopolitical stability.

1. As seen in Russell L. Weaver's chapter, disinformation is a problem that existed throughout the ages, from ancient Rome to the Middle Ages and to today. It has been undoubtedly heightened by the internet and the fact that the internet enables virtually everyone to engage in widespread communication. According to the author, while it is relatively easy to identify the scope of disinformation, it is much more difficult to come up with an appropriate solution to face the problem that is consistent with the premises and values of free and democratic societies.

Nowadays, disinformation can be spread both via "old media" (in particular, newspapers and radio and tv broadcasting) and "new media" (digital platforms, social media and artificial intelligence) and, if disseminated in times of elections and in times of war, it may have an impact on the outcome of the elections as well as in the perception of the general public in situations of armed conflicts. Generative

R. Mastroianni · C. Massa (✉)
Department of Law, University of Naples Federico II, Naples, Italy
e-mail: claudia.massa@unina.it

R. Mastroianni
e-mail: roberto.mastroianni@unina.it

R. Mastroianni and C. Massa (eds.), *Disinformation in New and Old Media in the XXI Century*, Ius Gentium: Comparative Perspectives on Law and Justice 136,
https://doi.org/10.1007/978-3-032-18830-4_14

artificial intelligence, for instance, as seen in Rebecca Hamilton's chapter, can be used to generate realistic disinformation, automate censorship, and influence public opinion at scale during electoral periods or international conflicts.

The spread of disinformation, as also amplified by the expansion of artificial intelligence systems, has captured the attention of policy-makers on a global scale. However, as underlined by Oreste Pollicino, constitutional democracies tend to disagree about the strategies to address disinformation, moving from mostly protecting that type of content as free speech, such as in the USA, to approaching this issue as a risk for democracy as in the EU. In view of the need to avoid the failures of past strategies (including in particular the 2018 Code of Practice on Disinformation) whilst also ensuring a harmonised, unitary approach at supranational level, the EU has recently inaugurated what the author defines as a new phase in the fight against disinformation, characterised by the adoption of more far-reaching and impactful legislation at EU level with a shift from self-regulation towards a more top-down intervention. Among the principal acts adopted, it is necessary to mention the Digital Services Act, the European Media Freedom Act and the Regulation on transparency and targeting of political advertising, as well as a Proposal of an EU Directive on interest representation and the Strengthened Code of Practice of 2022.

The Regulation on transparency and targeting of political advertising, in particular, as seen in Claudia Massa's chapter, has been adopted with a view of combating disinformation through online political advertising, one of the key tools of an electoral campaign. The Regulation imposes the use of digital mechanisms that enable citizens to understand unambiguously, *ictu oculi*, whether they are confronted with paid political content, to know who is behind each political communication and who is paying for it. Moreover, it regulates the use of targeting or ad-delivery techniques, subjecting it to consent and transparency, so that citizens can immediately understand how and why they are reached by a given political advertising message. The relevance of this act had already emerged before the date of its application in Member States' practice, since it was cited in a significant ruling by the Romanian Constitutional Court in December 2024, which annulled the electoral process for the election of the President of Romania of 2024 due to the violations of electoral legislation on social media and the impact of online disinformation campaigns. The act, at the moment, has no equivalent in the US legal order, which only provides for a few, very fragmented disclosure and/or record-keeping requirements for online political advertising at States level. According to the author, the presence of the aforementioned Regulation in the EU legal order is particularly effective, since it constitutes a further and specific legal parameter to verify whether the criterion of the fair use of media, both offline and online, has been met during a given electoral process, thus making it "free and fair".

As far as foreign interferences are concerned, as seen in Barbara Guastaferro's chapter, the European Parliament played a pivotal role in fighting disinformation in democratic processes by adopting a decision on 18 June 2020 to establish a special committee on foreign interference, including disinformation (INGE), and the Resolutions of 9 March 2022 and 1 June 2023. These measures aim to safeguard EU fundamental rights, prevent foreign interference that incites hatred against minorities and vulnerable groups, and ensure free and fair elections. By addressing disinformation through these measures, the European Parliament seeks to protect the democratic principle and uphold core EU values. The European approach and the European constitutional settlement, in fact, by contrast with the US where freedom of expression is the paramount constitutional rights, are more favourable to limit freedom of speech against its abuses. According to the author, in fact, in cases of disinformation or foreing interference, democracy is used against democracy, or, to be more precise, one of the substantive aspect of democracy, i.e. a fundamental right such as freedom of speech, is used to impinge upon a basic procedural aspect of democracy, namely free and fair elections.

Legislation regulating foreign influence has been recently adopted on both sides of the Atlantic, at national, US and EU levels, in order to limit foreign influence over political processes such as elections or referenda. The comparative analysis conducted by Sarah Madsen and Fernanda Nicola on foreign agent laws in Europe and the US reveals how they have sought to balance competing interests, resulting in wide disparities in the degree of restrictiveness and enforcement of such legislation. This situation should be taken into account during the legislative procedure now pending for the adoption of a EU directive that establishes harmonized transparency requirements for interest representation activities carried out on behalf of third countries in the internal market.

The attempts to address the problem of disinformation in the EU, however, could still be improved, as in their current conformation they may pose threats to freedom of expression, as showed by András Koltay in his chapter. The EU current approach, in fact, essentially leaves the decision-making on disinformation up to the platforms, but does not exercise any meaningful control over their decisions, and this could lead to restrictions on otherwise legally and constitutionally permissible expressions.

Also when it comes to disinformation and propaganda of war, public discourse simply cannot be regulated as effectively as possible without at some point damaging its free character. According to Björnstjern Baade, a very effective measure against disinformation and propaganda that is at the same time entirely unproblematic regarding freedom of speech is an oxymoron. Expectations that the law will protect us from disinformation and propaganda should be reduced to a realistic level. Therefore, citizens and politicians need to take their epistemic responsibility seriously and it is necessary to generate trust in sources of information that deserve this trust. Such trust, however, cannot be legally ordained, so we have to learn to filter out and ignore disinformation and propaganda which we will never be able to entirely eradicate from a free public discourse.

In the context of European integration, Siniša Rodin affirms that manipulation of facts such as propaganda and manipulation of law by re-calibration of its purpose need to be recognized and interpreted in light of values of liberal democracy which is inherent in the legal and political architecture of the EU. This process will typically take form of proportionality test where alleged rights will be balanced against rights of others and public interest. The question to be decided in each particular case is not only whether facts are valid, and law invoked applied in accordance with its purpose, but also what intensity of public interest will justify restriction of legitimately invoked rights.

The evolving boundaries of free speech in the EU are commented by Francesca Finelli through an analysis of the role of the Court of Justice in assessing the legality of restrictive measures (sanctions) that interfere with free speech. The author, by focusing on two key rulings, *Kiselev* (2017) and *RT France* (2022), decided by the General Court before and after the outbreak of the Russia's war of aggression against Ukraine, highlights that there is an evolution in the Court's methodology in addressing the legality of sanctions. While in *Kiselev* the Court follows a three-step test and stresses the importance of targeting a Russian journalist who actively supported the destabilising and aggressive policy conducted by his country towards Ukraine, in *RT France,* the Court instead introduces a four-step test, and provides a detailed analysis of the media ban, assessing the validity of the imposed restrictions against a range of legal and factual considerations. It appears that art. 52(1) CFREU inspires a rigorous rights-based analysis and a high standard of review.

Andrei Richter goes into the issue of whether these media sanctions can serve as a model for the rights-based regulatory and policy solutions to overcome challenges of Russian disinformation and propaganda in the region, and fit the democratic principles of free speech. According to the author, these measures put into doubt the appropriateness of the European Council to regulate the media sector, as it is usually left to the Member States. The new European Media Freedom Act, instead, included provisions tasking the forthcoming European Board for Media Services with a number of duties, such as to draft and implement uniform rules and opinions in relation to the restrictions on the content of "rogue" media services from outside of the EU "that target or reach audiences in the Union, where such media services prejudice or present a serious and grave risk of prejudice to public security". The author concludes that shifting the burden of imposing sanctions from the European Council to the realm of the European Board for Media Services might be a smart move away from the curse of being accused of censorship.

The case-law of the Court of Justice in *RT France* also gives the possibility to reflect on the notion of propaganda of war. Thus, Claudio Di Turi, in his chapter, analyses the findings of the Court and the most important international rules prohibiting propaganda. This gives the author the possibility to consider whether, in the context of the conflict between Russia and Ukraine, the international responsibility of the Russian State can lead to individual criminal responsibility on the part of some supreme individuals and/or organs of the State.

2. Overall, the volume shows that while disinformation is an ancient problem exacerbated by modern technology, societies are still grappling with how to effectively combat it without undermining fundamental democratic values like freedom of speech.

More than the US, the EU is actively developing a comprehensive legislative framework, which is ambitious and innovative, since it combines both voluntary and legally binding elements, with a growing emphasis on holding large online platforms accountable and fostering a more trustworthy online environment. Its ultimate success will depend on continuous efforts in implementation, enforcement, adaptation to new threats, and striking a careful balance with fundamental rights. Indeed, the main challenge remains that of balancing regulation with the protection of free expression. However, since disinformation tactics are constantly evolving (e.g., localized campaigns, use of influential individuals, artificial intelligence-generated content like deepfakes), the legislative framework also needs to prove itself to be agile enough to adapt to these new challenges. Another necessary move towards a more effective barrier to disinformation in the dissemination of political messages is a long-awaited regulation of the "conflicts of interest", that take shape when a media owner or controller is also present, directly or indirectly, in the political scene.

The EU's proactive stance may serve as a model for other regions grappling with the complex challenges of disinformation in the digital age, especially in times of elections and in times of war. All EU institutions, in fact, paid particular attention to these two contexts, as they represent critical moments where the integrity of information directly impacts core democratic values, public safety, and geopolitical stability. The EU's heightened attention and robust legislative framework reflect the understanding that disinformation is not a trivial problem but a strategic threat that requires a comprehensive and coordinated response.

The manufacturer's authorised representative in the EU is Springer Nature Customer Service Centre GmbH, Europaplatz 3, 69115 Heidelberg, Germany. If you have any concerns regarding our products, please contact ProductSafety@springernature.com

Printed and bound by CPI Group (UK) Ltd, Croydon, CR0 4YY
21/09/2026
02219989-0009